Fourth Edition

African Americans and the American Political System

Lucius J. Barker, 1928-
Stanford University

Mack H. Jones
Clark Atlanta University

Katherine Tate
University of California, Irvine

Prentice Hall, Upper Saddle River, New Jersey 07458

Library of Congress Cataloging-in-Publication Data

BARKER, LUCIUS JEFFERSON
    African Americans and the American political system/Lucius J. Barker, Mack H. Jones, Katherine Tate.—4th ed.
    p. cm.
    Includes bibliographical references and index.
    ISBN 0-13-779562-9
    1. Afro-Americans—Politics and government.   2. United States—Politics and government—1989– .
I. Jones, Mack H.   II. Tate, Katherine.   III. Title.
E185.615.B33   1998
323.1'196073—dc21
                                         98-25287
                                            CIP

Editorial director: Charlyce Jones Owen
Editor in chief: Nancy Roberts
Acquisitions editor: Beth Gillett
Associate editor: Nicole Conforti
Marketing manager: Christopher DeJohn
Editorial/production supervision: Kari Callaghan Mazzola
Electronic page makeup: Kari Callaghan Mazzola and John P. Mazzola
Interior design and electronic art creation: John P. Mazzola
Director, Image Resource Center: Lori Morris-Nantz
Photo Research Supervisor: Melinda Lee Reo
Image Permission Supervisor: Kay Dellosa
Photo Researcher: Beth Boyd
Cover art director: Jayne Conte
Cover design: Joe Sengotta
Buyer: Bob Anderson

This book was set in 10/12 Meridien by Big Sky Composition
and was printed and bound by Courier Companies, Inc.
The cover was printed by Phoenix Color Corp.

 © 1999, 1994, 1980, 1976 by Prentice-Hall, Inc.
Upper Saddle River, NJ 07458

Printed in the United States of America
10 9 8 7 6

ISBN 0-13-779562-9

Prentice-Hall International (UK) Limited, London
Prentice-Hall of Australia Pty. Limited, Sydney
Prentice-Hall Canada, Inc., Toronto
Prentice-Hall Hispanoamericana, S.A., Mexico
Prentice-Hall of India Private Limited, New Delhi
Pearson Education Asia Pte. Ltd., Singapore
Prentice-Hall of Japan, Inc., Tokyo
Editora Prentice-Hall do Brazil, Ltda., Rio de Janeiro

TO

Maude, Tracey, and Heidi

TO THE MEMORY OF

Clifton and Willie Mae

AND TO

Jean-Michel and Luke

Contents

Preface

President Clinton's 1997 initiative for a National Conversation on Race alerts us once again to the serious vestiges of racial injustices and inequities in American politics and society. Thus, just as in earlier editions, this fourth edition continues to focus on how African Americans fare in the political-social system.

It is painstakingly clear that something more needs to be done about the continuing problem of race. Obviously, much noticeable progress has been made in these matters. But it is also obvious that the symbols and promise of change envisioned in the 1950s and 1960s have simply not been converted into the substance and practice of everyday reality in the 1990s.

And this situation does not bode well as we move toward the new millennium in the year 2000. Sheer constitutional-democratic principles as well as empirical reality suggest that more must be done. Constitutional-democratic principles suggest that more must be done to cope with continuing inequities and disparities that still disadvantage blacks, Latinos, and Asian-Americans. And the dire need to cope with such problems is signaled by the empirical reality of forthcoming demographic changes by which we will soon become a minority-majority country. Even more, lest we seriously jeopardize our own future and that of the entire world, empirical reality suggests that we must show the way to other nations that face similar and even more dire situations of intergroup discord and violence.

The story of how African Americans fare in the political system is both fascinating and frustrating. It continues to provide one of the most penetrating vantage points from which to view the nature and operation of the political system. Indeed, the experience of blacks in American politics allows us to relate the constitutional theory and structure of our political institutions and processes to their everyday operation and practice. We can see most vividly, for example, how and in what ways the structures and functions of the Congress, the Presidency, the bureaucracy, and the Supreme Court affect the aspirations of blacks and other minorities. In a similar vein, we can view the roles that interest groups, political parties, and elections perform in the political system as they relate to blacks. The insights that are unearthed in an analysis of this nature are quite fascinating, revealing the intricate nature and functioning of the political system in ways that might otherwise be obscured.

But we also find the endeavor frustrating. Given the nature and operations of the political system, it is still debatable whether we can bring about the kind of changes necessary for blacks and other minorities to enjoy the full benefits and responsibilities of American society. As we define it in Chapter 2, "the problem" that blacks face in this country has many dimensions. These dimensions include concrete deprivations relating to the socioeconomic status of African Americans. To be sure, certain positive legal actions and some progress have come about in this regard, almost always, however, in response to crisis situations, such as the Civil War of the 1860s and the Civil Rights movement and urban disorders of the 1950s and 1960s. In any case, there have been continuing and growing attitudes that "enough" has been done for blacks. This is exemplified vividly by the passage of California's anti-affirmative action initiative (Proposition 209), and by the agonizing persistence of racial/ethnic hate crimes.

There are other aspects of the problem, however, that are more elusive, intangible, and intractable. We refer here to institutional racism— practices, arrangements, and rules of institutions that act so as to collectively advantage some and disadvantage others. Many institutions (public and private) operate in certain ways so as to seriously disadvantage blacks in contexts where "race" is never mentioned. In their book *Institutional Racism*, for example, Prewitt and Knowles suggest that institutions "reward by providing career opportunities for some people and foreclosing them for others" (p. 8). "They reward," the authors continue, "by the way social goods and services are distributed—by deciding who receives training and skills, medical care, formal education, political influence, moral support and self-respect, productive employment, fair treatment by the law, decent housing, self-confidence, and the promise of a secure future for self and children" (p. 8). As we ponder how African Americans fare today, it is clear that institutional racism remains a continuing and viable obstacle to black progress in both public and private arenas and in all sectors of our politics and society.

Thus, just as in the first edition, our major purpose remains an attempt to describe and analyze America's racial problem in terms of the dynamics and operation of the political system. And we have tried to do more than merely update changes that have occurred over time. We continue to make real efforts to suggest the meaning and implications of these changes for African Americans, for whites and all Americans, and for the political system in general.

For example, we discuss the following in various contexts: (1) The nature and limits of electoral politics in dealing with "the problem"; (2) the opportunities and constraints that shape the role of black elected and appointed officials; (3) the political and social implications of demographic trends; (4) the changing functions and problems facing civil rights groups and their capacity to deal with them; (5) the persistent and changing nature of the problem facing African Americans in general; and (6) factors that influence and shape the response to the problem by institutions in both public and private sectors of our economic order such as Congress, the President, the Supreme Court, interest groups, commerce and business, and the communications and information industry.

Just as in our earlier editions, we continue to provide some special features. For example, at the end of each chapter we provide several topics or questions to stimulate thought and discussion about matters dealt with in the respective chapters. These topics should prove useful in small or large group settings, or as written assignments for papers. We also include at the end of each chapter a selected bibliography for those who might wish to do additional reading. And, as in the third edition, we as authors and black Americans conclude the volume (in Chapter 12) by "speaking out" on certain salient and recurring topics and developments that hold important and long-range implications for our overall politics and society and are designed to stimulate discussion and debate.

In this fourth edition we are pleased to introduce to our readers a new coauthor, Professor Katherine Tate of the University of California, Irvine. Tate, who specializes in voting, mass political behavior, and political psychology, is perhaps most widely known for her pathbreaking volume entitled *From Protest to Politics: The New Black Voters in American Elections*. We trust our readers will agree that Tate's joining us has considerably strengthened and enriched this volume, and bodes well for its future.

Over the years a number of our professional colleagues have contributed to our thinking and to this endeavor in many ways, and we sincerely appreciate them all. Also, the authors wish to thank others who helped in the production of this edition: LaTishie Willridge of Clark-Atlanta University and Belinda Yeomans of Stanford, for their secretarial support, and Jeremy Buchman and Jorge Ruis-De-Velasco of Stanford, for their research assistance. We also wish to express our appreciation to our editors and others affiliated with Prentice Hall who guided this fourth edition through to publication, especially Kari Callaghan Mazzola, who supervised its production. We must also thank those who granted us permission to use materials and photographs to enhance this volume. Specific acknowledgment of them is made elsewhere in the text.

As is usually the case, some of the suggestions that were made to us have been declined at our own peril. And, for the resulting errors of omission and commission, we accept full responsibility. We trust that our readers will call these errors to our attention.

Lucius J. Barker
Mack H. Jones
Katherine Tate

Chapter 1

Black America and the Political System: The Politics of Uncertainty

To avoid conflict with the equal protection clause, a classification that denies a benefit, causes harm, or imposes a burden must not be based on race. In that sense, the Constitution is color blind. But the Constitution is color conscious to prevent discrimination being perpetuated and to undo the effects of past discrimination. The criterion is the relevancy of color to a legitimate government purpose.

—Judge John Minor Wisdom, Fifth Circuit
United States v. *Jefferson*, 1967

While I applaud the judgment of the Court that a University may consider race in its admissions process, it is more than a little ironic that, after several hundred years of class-based discrimination against Negroes, the Court is unwilling to hold that a class-based remedy for that discrimination is permissible. In declining to so hold, today's judgment ignores the fact that for several hundred years Negroes have been discriminated against, not as individuals, but rather solely because of the color of their skins. It is unnecessary in 20th century America to have individual Negroes demonstrate that they have been victims of racial discrimination; the racism of our society has been so pervasive that none, regardless of wealth or position, has managed to escape its impact. The experience of Negroes in America has been different in kind, not just in degree, from that of other ethnic groups; it is not merely the history of slavery alone but also that a whole people were marked as inferior by the law. And that mark has endured. The dream of America as the great melting pot has not been realized for the Negro; because of his skin color he never even made it into the pot.

—Justice Thurgood Marshall, Dissenting Opinion,
University of California Regents v. *Bakke*, 1978

In summary, we hold that the University of Texas School of Law may not use race as a factor in deciding which applicants to admit in order to achieve a diverse student body, to combat the perceived effects of a hostile environment at the law school, to alleviate the law school's poor rep-

1

utation in the minority community, or to eliminate any present effects of
past discrimination by actors other than the law school.

—Judge Jerry Smith, Fifth Circuit
Hopwood v. *Texas,* 1996

The excerpts that appear as epigraphs to this chapter illustrate vividly
the ambivalence of the United States in confronting the race problem
as both a moral and an economic question. In the 1978 *University of
California* v. *Alan Bakke* case, considered by many at the time to be the most
important civil rights case to reach the Supreme Court since the 1954 landmark school desegregation case,[1] the justices—in a 5–4 vote—came to two
major conclusions. First, the court decided that Alan Bakke, a white applicant, must be admitted to the University of California-Davis Medical School
because that institution's special admissions program was so inflexibly structured as to be biased against whites. Second, the Court concluded that it was
not unlawful, under a carefully structured and flexible affirmative action
plan, to consider race as a "plus" in establishing admissions criteria.

Eight years after *Bakke,* in *Wygant* v. *Jackson Board of Education,* the Court
held that although race may be taken into account in hiring to achieve racial
balance, maintaining racial balance cannot be used to apportion layoffs if it
has adverse effects on whites as individuals. And in 1989 the Court went a
step further when it ruled in a Richmond, Virginia, case involving minority
set-aside contracts that race-conscious numerical remedies are suspect and
therefore can be used only to address specifically identified instances of discrimination but not historical patterns of racial discrimination.[2]

Still later, in 1995, the Supreme Court in *Miller* v. *Johnson* declared
that it was unlawful to use race as a dominant factor in drawing electoral
district lines. In 1996 the high court let stand an appeals court decision that
barred the University of Texas Law School from considering race in admissions decisions.

Overall, these cases reflect the continuing efforts of American policy
makers to deal with the race problem without acknowledging that certain
societal elements materially benefit from racial discrimination and, even
more importantly, without accepting the fact that the continuing inequities
cannot be eliminated without material cost to whites, individually and collectively.

We Americans appear to be unable or unwilling to cope with present
realities in order to overcome the sordid legacy of the past. But our "roots"
persist. The problem of race and color will not fade away in clouds of legal
formalities and patriotic symbols. The use of clever slogans such as "dera-
cialization," "children at risk," "diversity" or "the declining significance of
race" diminish neither the racial character nor the urgency of the problem.
It must be faced squarely and forthrightly. The civil rights movement and
subsequent events vividly evidence a determination among African
Americans to share fully and equally in the benefits and responsibilities of

nerican society. And the fact that much observable progress has been does not lessen this continuing determination. If anything, such ,ress increases the impatience with the pains and vestiges of race dis- iination that remain. Of course, the persistence of such problems makes .nat much more difficult to espouse such values as "freedom" and "equal- /" in convincing and meaningful terms.

In addition, it is hard to overlook or ignore the plight of African Americans—the largest minority in the country. African Americans make up about 12.8 percent or 34 million of the approximately 264 million people in the United States. During the 1960s the black population increased by almost 4 million; from 1970 to 1990 the increase was about 5 million and another 4 million from 1990 to 1997. While the population growth rate has thus slowed, the rate of increase among blacks (and among other minorities) continues to be greater than among whites. Between 1980 and 1990 the black population increase was 13 percent compared to 6 percent for whites. The Census Bureau projects that between 1995 and 2025 the black popula- tion will increase by 12 million while the white population will grow by only 16 million.[3]

Our discussion thus far suggests that this problem persists in part because of several factors. First, there is the determination and drive of blacks to share fully and equally in American society. Second, there is the stark realization by many persons, both whites and blacks, that America's evolving and continuing commitment to such values as liberty and equality demands action to overcome such problems. And, finally, there is the plain fact that, in a democracy, the sheer size of the black population makes it not only hypocritical but very impractical to ignore the problem of racial inequality. Consequently, how we deal with the problem of race and color takes on both moral and political importance.

But for many Americans, the matter of race and color is no longer among the nation's "most important problems." To be sure, issues tend to be somewhat cyclical in American politics and seldom command prime atten- tion over a long period. However, regardless of the issue, the matter of race is never far below the surface. For example, a closer look at many of soci- ety's greatest problems as we prepare to enter the twenty-first century, such as deficient primary and secondary schools, growing economic polarization, rampant crime and an overpopulated prison system, and an inadequate and costly health-care system, reveals all too clearly that our inability to deal with these problems can reap untold and disproportionate hardships on blacks and other minorities. And the fact that these problems affect all Americans should not lead us to overlook their extra impact on those who already suffer deprivations because of race and poverty.

In a related vein, however, there is a growing tendency to define what are basically racial problems in nonracial terms.[4] For example, the fact that a disproportionate number of blacks as compared to whites remain unem-

ployed or underemployed is increasingly defined as a class instead of
phenomenon.[5] Put another way, it is often argued that if blacks have th
prerequisites in terms of education and training, then they can compete
cessfully with whites and will not suffer from race discrimination. Thus,
problem is said to be more a matter of class than of race. This, of course, be
the question of why these requisites are so low among one race of people.
also fails to explain why the return on these requisites, education for example, is significantly lower for blacks than for whites. Indeed, in 1996 the
median income for black workers with 4 years or more of college was
$29,105, considerably less than the $35,557 for similarly educated whites.[6]

Another example is the school desegregation controversy, now widely
defined and discussed in terms of "quality education." It is suggested that
"quality education" rather than "racial integration" should be the primary
goal. Obviously, this is a laudable goal, and it is very appealing and attractive
to a great many persons, white and black. But we suggest that blacks should
question this attempt to define the school desegregation controversy in
"nonracial" terms. We need to examine more closely the political and policy
implications of what is involved. The point is that defining the school desegregation controversy in terms of "quality education" could perpetuate inferior, poorly funded schools in predominantly black communities. History has
shown that blacks have invariably not received the kinds of resources (i.e.,
money, professional staff) necessary to achieve and maintain quality public
education. Differential and unequal treatment based solely on race and color
has been so deeply ingrained in the nation's laws and traditions that one
should be wary of mechanisms that permit continued isolation (and differential treatment) of blacks from the American mainstream.

Overall then, it is clever to define the desegregation controversy in
terms of "quality education," since defining the issue in this way stimulates
support from a number of blacks who believe, justifiably in some cases and
wistfully in others, that "our" schools are as good as or better than "theirs."
The banner of "quality education" also stimulates racial pride—for example,
blacks do not need whites to have a "quality" school. And this, too, is
undoubtedly true. But, as Justice Marshall put it so well in his *Bakke* dissent,
we cannot ignore the fact "that for several hundred years Negroes have been
discriminated against, not as individuals, but rather solely because of the
color of their skins." Aside from its other values, public school desegregation
makes it difficult (but not impossible, as the controversy over 'tracking' students shows) to discriminate against blacks "solely because of the color of
their skins." Consequently, while not eschewing the laudable goal of "quality education," blacks should constantly be alert lest this "nonracial" term be
used as a cover to return to a "separate but equal" era where "separate" was
very separate and "equal" was very unequal.

We are aware of the fact that issues may be defined in a particular way
n order to attract maximum support. However, we believe—at least in the

foregoing examples—that the main objective of those advocating "nonracial" explanations of black deprivation is to divert attention from the fact that race remains a real problem. We suggest that such attempts at issue definition (or redefinition) will not, however, permit us to ignore for long that the problem of race is still very evident in American life. As Justice Blackmun put it in his *Bakke* dissent: "In order to get beyond racism, we must first take account of race. There is no other way." It is hoped that we will heed Justice Blackmun's advice and continue to come to grips with the problem of racism.

There are a number of things we need to explore in this chapter as we focus on this continuing problem. In a political system in which population and votes contribute to political power, a sizable minority can have considerable weight. But before we can assess the influence of blacks as such a minority in this political system, we need to know more about African Americans: the distribution of the black population; their socioeconomic status; the political and social characteristics of the black "community"; the kinds and dimensions of problems that blacks continue to face; and the political behavior and participation of the black electorate. We also need to know more about white Americans, particularly their attitudes toward blacks and the race problem. We also must give attention to the values, structures, and dynamics of the U.S. political system and how they relate to the capacity and capability of the United States to deal with problems of race and color. However, we think it is most important to understand the past experience of blacks in the political system. What that experience can suggest to us about the present and future status of blacks, and indeed of the U.S. political system itself, is one of the principal reasons for this volume.

But before addressing any of these questions, it may be useful to explore briefly the frames of reference used in the study of black politics, because the framework employed can determine the meaning or interpretation we give to our experiences. In the remainder of this chapter we (1) discuss several frames of reference used to study African American politics in the United States; (2) review briefly the history of the African American political struggle; and (3) discuss the importance of the size and distribution of the current African American population as a political resource.

FRAMES OF REFERENCE AND AFRICAN AMERICAN POLITICS

African American politics, like all other forms of social activity, can be understood only in the context of a particular approach, or frame of reference. A frame of reference is a set of general assumptions about the nature of the subject or experience being investigated, what concepts or categories of analysis are the most useful for understanding it, what level of analysis should be adopted, and what questions should be answered in order to develop the most useful understanding of that which is being investigated.

Frames of reference serve dual functions in social inquiry: as lenses and as blinders. As lenses they provide the basis for giving a particular meaning to an experience; as blinders they may render the investigator unaware of competing perceptions and interpretations of that same reality. To reinforce the point, a decision to accept certain assumptions as a point of departure is at the same time a decision to reject others. For example, the scholar who begins with the assumption that there is an automatic process through which disadvantaged groups are gradually integrated into the American political, social, and economic systems as equals is at the same time deciding to reject the counterview that the struggle for inclusion should be viewed as a conflict between one group seeking to maintain its dominant position and another seeking to overturn the hierarchy. Similarly, a decision that certain concepts have greater empirical usefulness for understanding reality is a decision that other concepts and the explanations that might be constructed are less helpful. Thus, to accept pluralism, assimilation, accommodation, and related concepts as orienting devices for studying African American politics precludes the use of concepts such as class, class conflict and struggle, and the like. A frame of reference tells us what to look for. In that sense it illuminates our understanding, like a lens. On the other hand, it draws our attention away from other developments and causes us to remain oblivious to other interpretations of reality. In that sense the frame of reference acts as a blinder.

In recent years there has been considerable discussion about the most useful frame of reference for understanding African American political life in the United States.[7] For example, the pluralist, melting-pot model has been challenged on the grounds of both descriptive adequacy and prescriptive usefulness; that is, its adequacy in describing exactly what transpires in the politics of black America and its usefulness in stimulating critical thinking regarding what can or should be done to transform the inequitable conditions under which blacks live. Following, we will discuss the pluralist model since it is the most commonly used, and three alternatives that have challenged its hegemony.

THE PLURALIST, MELTING-POT, RACE RELATIONS CYCLE MODEL

The pluralist model depicts the United States as a society that moves predeterminedly toward a state of equilibrium characterized by countervailing forces that ensure that no one group predominates and all groups get something substantial. The model views the United States as a conglomeration of immigrant ethnic communities that, over time, are melted into an integrated nation. The model assumes that new groups are at first considered outsiders and are relegated to a subordinate status, but that over time they will become more and more Americanized and in the process strengthen their competitive position until they are ultimately accepted as equal ingredients in the American nation. The histories of Irish Catholics and European Jews are often cited as examples that validate this theory. It is only a matter of time, the model implies, before African Americans, like European ethnic groups, become an equal partner in a new equilibrium.

However, inasmuch as African Americans were part of American society long before several of the ethnic groups that have already achieved parity in American society, it was necessary to make special modifications in the pluralist, melting-pot model to make it "fit" the African American experience. The race relations cycle of Robert Park and the citizenship political development cycle of Talcott Parsons offered such modifications.[8]

Park argued that when the cultures of people of different races came into contact, their relations went through four distinct stages: contact, conflict, accommodation, and assimilation. According to this theory, after the initial stage of conflict, the weaker group would accommodate itself to the dictates of the stronger one, and this accommodation would eventually make possible the cultural transformation of the weaker group and, ultimately, its assimilation into the dominant culture.

This process of assimilation was said to be a function of certain laws of human development and therefore irreversible, although the process might be delayed by certain accidents of history. In due course, according to the logic of Park, the "race problem" would be solved through assimilation.

Park's race relations cycle was offered as a general theory to explain the pattern of sociocultural relationships that developed following the contact of racially different cultures. By contrast, Parsons was more concerned with the pattern of political relations that ensued. He hypothesized that, based upon the experiences of European ethnic groups in America, the African American struggle for inclusion would go through three fairly distinct stages before full equality was realized. The first stage would involve a struggle for basic legal rights. It would be followed by agitation for full and effective political participation, which would be won and consolidated. Finally, the subordinate group would shift its efforts toward acquiring the economic and social resources sufficient to permit the group to function on an equal footing with other groups.[9]

Park's race relations and Parsons's citizenship-development cycles are both based upon the assumption that there is a gradual but almost automatic process through which subordinate racial groups gradually achieve equal status. Scholars who employ the race relations or citizenship-development cycle models assume that the African American political experience in the United States is analogous to that of one European immigrant group or another and use the experience of the latter as a benchmark in assessing the presumed position of African Americans along the predetermined path toward assimilation and, eventually, equality. Indeed, much of the public policy discussion and debate about the race problem is couched within the assumptions of the pluralist, melting-pot model. Critics of the civil rights movement who use this model often compare blacks with various immigrant groups and ask why blacks have not made similar progress. Such questions focus disproportionately on the behavior of black people themselves and less upon the historical and contemporary conditions under which they are oblig-ed to live and struggle. Consequently, public policies that evolve from such discussions are more concerned with transforming black people than with transforming the circumstances that structure their lives. Such comments, criticisms, and policy prescriptions flow quite naturally from the model.

Critics of this approach assert that history provides *prima facie* evidence that the African American political struggle for inclusion has been funda-mentally different from that of European and other immigrant groups and that consequently these pluralist models are inappropriate devices for describing the dynamics of black politics. Moreover, critics continue, the cycle models with their teleological focus, assumption of automatic change, and tacit support for gradualism reduce the prospects for analyses that might yield more promising prescriptions for fundamental change.

THE COLONIAL MODEL

During the decades of the 1960s and 1970s when the intensified struggle for African American advancement was met in many quarters with equally intense white resistance, the idea of automatic racial progress and the appro-priateness of political strategies linked to such notions came under attack. Scholars began to search for a frame of reference that, on the one hand would give a more satisfactory description and explanation of the then con-temporary developments and, on the other hand, would lead to more con-vincing prescriptions for effective remedial action. The colonial model as a frame of reference evolved in this context.

Proponents of the colonial model argue that it captures the essence of the economic, cultural, and political dimensions of the African American predicament and that it is therefore especially useful for developing a com-prehensive understanding of black politics. Essentially, the colonial model suggests that the relationship between African Americans and the holders of state power in the United States is similar to that which exists between the colonized and the colonial master. Focusing on the spatially separate African American communities of the urban North and the heavy concentrations of African Americans in the southern Black Belt, the colonial model views African Americans as a unit apart, an internal colony, which is systematical-ly exploited by white society. Blacks are viewed as a separate nation that exports cheap labor and imports finished goods from the broader communi-ty.[10] The sharp and enduring differences between blacks and whites on var-ious indicators of socioeconomic well-being, such as wealth, income, employment, and health care, are depicted as the result of the exploitative colonial relationship.

As powerless colonial subjects, blacks are viewed as being unable to influence positively the decisions that determine the conditions under which they live, even when blacks occupy authoritative positions. This apparent paradox is explained by the idea of neocolonialism. The real holders of power, neocolonialism asserts, are those who control pivotal economic resources, both within and external to the black community. It is they who determine the direction of important political decisions, even when they are made ostensibly by black political authorities.

Just as classic colonizers disrupted and undermined the cultural autonomy of the colonized and imposed upon them the culture of the colonizers, the same is said to be the case with the internal black colony. The black community is pictured as the object of cultural imperialism dating back to slavery and continuing with the appropriation and commodification of black cultural forms during the present epoch. The ability of the black colony to mobilize its resources, and particularly its human resources, for effective political struggle is undermined by the destruction of its cultural base.[11]

THE DOMINANT-SUBORDINATE GROUP MODEL[12]

The dominant-subordinate group model is an extension of "power theory," which conceptualizes politics as an extension of the unending universal struggle for power and black politics in the United States as a local manifestation of the same. What distinguishes the black-white struggle in the United States from other local manifestations of this ubiquitous power struggle, the model infers, is the use of the ideology of white supremacy and the related notion of black inferiority to justify the dominant position of whites and to defend the various institutions and practices that sustain white domination.

Drawing on these assumptions in an earlier work,[13] one of the authors argues that the key to understanding black politics in America is the realization that those in superordinate positions invariably act in such a manner as to preserve their position of dominance and that, therefore, whites in the United States act toward blacks in such a manner as to maintain white hegemony. Thus, rather than conceptualizing black politics as a process through which black people, propelled by some unseen hand, move inexorably to a position of equal status, it is more appropriate to conceptualize it as a power struggle between two groups, one bent on maintaining its position of dominance and the other struggling for liberation.

Historically, dominant groups have used several basic political strategies to maintain their position of dominance. These include (1) assimilation, (2) legal protection of minority rights, (3) pluralism, (4) population transfer, (5) continued subjugation, and (6) extermination. On the other hand, subordinate or oppressed groups have attempted to use the first four strategies along with a fifth—reversal of status through revolutionary activity—to alleviate their oppressed conditions. At any point in time there will be identifiable forces within the dominant community advocating the use of any one or any combination of the six strategies as the optimum method for maintaining control while, conversely, within the subordinate community there will always be groups advocating the use of any one or any combination of the five counterstrategies as the optimum means for alleviating their oppressed condition.

Generally speaking, factions within the respective communities seek, first of all, to solicit intracommunity support for their position and then to influence elements in the formal political structure such that a faction's position becomes national, state, or local policy. For example, the National Association for the Advancement of Colored People (NAACP) seeks, first of all, to convince the black community that integration is the proper strategy for political advancement and then to have its position adopted as national policy. Conversely, more nationalist oriented groups, such as the Nation of Islam or the Republic of New Africa, push for some form of black independence.

Thus, black politics has four distinct dimensions: (1) a struggle within the white community regarding the optimum means for maintaining white control with minimum systemic stress and strain; (2) a struggle within the black community over the optimum strategy for liberation; (3) conflict and collaboration between and among black and white factions; and (4) struggle within formal governmental structures over authoritative policy decisions. These four struggles occur simultaneously and interdependently. Black politics is their sum. It must be noted, however, that these struggles cannot be neatly separated from all other power struggles going on simultaneously in society, and that therefore developments in the realm of black politics are often influenced, disproportionately, by other conflicts.

The dominant-subordinate group model makes several contributions to our efforts to conceptualize black politics. By highlighting the role of the white supremacist ideology in justifying the white position of dominance, it provides a better basis for studying and understanding the intractability and the enduring character of the American race problem than those other approaches that assume a certain preordained evolution toward a predetermined end. It also provides the basis for a more insightful understanding of internal conflicts within both the black and white communities and of the alliances that develop between black and white factions.

For example, the model allows us to understand more clearly why black factions that endorse integrationism as the primary strategy, such as the NAACP, are more compatible with white assimilationist groups than they appear to be with black nationalist organizations, such as the Nation of Islam. It also gives us clearer insights into the historical conflicts between the forces of, say, Booker T. Washington and W. E. B. DuBois or Marcus Garvey and DuBois.

The dominant-subordinate group model, however, is not without its shortcomings. The most glaring one is its failure to provide a basis for identifying and understanding the material basis, the economic elements of the black problem. The assumption that the white community acts in a manner to maintain its position of dominance conveys the impression that white dominance is an unqualified end in and of itself, and in the process the model begs the fundamental question; dominance toward what end and in whose discrete interest.

HARRIS'S ALTERNATIVE FORMULATION[14]

The alternative formulation advanced by Donald Harris, a Stanford economist, was not developed as a frame of reference for black politics per se but rather as a critique of the colonial model as a conceptual scheme for understanding the economic conditions of black America. Nevertheless, it is a useful device for describing and interpreting the material base of black politics and for understanding how the two—economics and politics—converge.

Writing in response to what he perceived to be both the descriptive inadequacy and prescriptive limitations of the colonial model, Harris argues that although there are superficial similarities between the history and conditions of African Americans and conventional colonial subjects, the similarities are more apparent than real. Moreover, the prescription that naturally evolves out of the colonial model—political independence and a separate nation state—is neither a logical nor feasible strategy for African Americans.

Harris's alternate formulation begins with the assumption that the spatial separation of blacks in racially segregated neighborhoods does not mean that blacks exist as a unit apart. Blacks are not a separate economic entity that interacts with a broader and separate American economy of which it is not an integral part, as is the case in a classic colonial relationship. Rather, Harris views African Americans as an integral part of the American political economy and suggests that the persistence of the unequal economic status of blacks is to be explained by examining (1) the basic structure of the American economy, (2) the essential laws of American capitalist development conditioned by the racist ideology of white supremacy, and (3) by understanding how the three—the structure, the laws, and the racist ideology—come together to determine the position of blacks in the economy.

The key to understanding the enduring unequal economic conditions of blacks, according to this model, is to be aware of the fact that the American economy is divided into two distinct sectors, the corporate capitalist and the petty capitalist sectors. The corporate capitalist sector provides a reasonably adequate material life for those workers employed in it. The return to workers in the petty capitalist sector is much less adequate. In addition to the two sectors—and existing in a dialectical relationship to them—is a sizable and fluctuating number of potential workers who are unable to find work in either sector. The existence of these two sectors and the nature of the intersectoral flows between them are said to be functions of the laws of American economic development. The distribution of black workers within these sectors, particularly the disproportionate clustering of blacks in the least rewarding petty capitalist sector of the economy, is said to be the result of the laws of American economic development conditioned by racism. Racism, institutional and personal, ensures that blacks remain in subordinate positions.

The corporate capitalist sector is comprised of large capital intensive enterprises that pay relatively high wages to its largely unionized workers and even higher salaries to its managers. The petty capitalist sector is made up of relatively small, often poorly capitalized, labor-intensive firms with a low paid preponderantly nonunionized work force. The fact that black workers are employed disproportionately in the petty capitalist sector and in the lower job categories of the corporate capitalist sector, according to this model, explains much of the differential in black-white income figures.

Moreover, the extreme deprivation of inner-city blacks both as workers and consumers, which the colonial model explains as the result of super-exploitation, is explained by the alternative formulation as the result of the laws governing the relationship between the corporate and petty capitalist sectors and the dictates of white supremacy. The model assumes that there is always tension between the two sectors because of the dominant corporate capitalist sector's constant drive to expand. When technological breakthroughs and other general economic conditions make it feasible to do so, it expands into areas heretofore exploited by petty capitalists. Thus, the most profitable areas in the petty capitalist sector are constantly being gobbled up by the corporate sector, leaving the petty capitalist to struggle in an increasingly marginal environment. To stay afloat as employers, petty capitalists must get more out of their workers while minimizing labor costs, and similarly, to survive as merchants, they must get maximum return from sales. Thus, according to the model, the low wages and unsafe, repressive working conditions that are increasingly commonplace as one descends the scale in the corporate capitalist sector and that exist in varying degrees throughout the petty capitalist sector are explained at least partially by intersectoral dynamics. The same explanation is said to hold for the shoddy practices of inner-city merchants, landlords, and financial institutions. Racism and the sociocultural structures, institutions, and practices spawned in its ideological wake, the model argues, are important factors in rationing access to the two sectors and in determining the racial composition of the group of workers unable to find places in either sector. But the volume of low paying jobs, repressive working conditions, and endemic unemployment are functions of the nature of the economic system and not merely the consequence of racism.

To the extent that the American culture, like all others, is the product of an evolutionary process, present-day institutions are necessarily and definitionally extensions of their historical antecedents as conditioned by societal values and changing material conditions. Thus, the model assumes that the educational, social, political, and cultural institutions that have evolved are parts of a social whole that routinely recreates and sustains conditions that ensure white access to favored positions and relegates blacks to the least desired ones. The alternative formulation, of course, does not deny that in many instances racism and racist practices may supersede the laws of capitalist development in explaining the inequitable position of blacks in the American economy. Such would be the case when better-qualified blacks are denied job interviews or refused bank loans.

Turning to the implications of Harris's alternative formulation for understanding black politics, it suggests that the struggle against high and enduring black unemployment is a struggle for increasing unemployment among whites. It infers that to the extent that African American politics is first and foremost a struggle to end the general deprivation of African Americans, *it is in part a struggle to equalize the distribution of deprivation throughout the society.* Thus, the reduction of black unemployment, for example, would mean a commensurate increase in white unemployment.

The chief virtue and contribution of Harris's alternative formulation toward understanding black politics is that it brings to the fore the material basis of black politics. It provides a better basis for understanding why certain white interests that enthusiastically supported the general movement for racial integration were less supportive when material considerations, such as affirmative action and minority set-asides, were added to the mix. This approach sensitizes the observer to the need to understand the specific material interests involved and rescues the subject from ethereal discussions of moral dilemmas and psychological domination. It also places it in a more empirically grounded context. While it probably cannot stand alone as a frame of reference for black politics, it is certainly a valuable supplement.

In our view, no single one of the frames of reference discussed can be said to be the correct one. Each of them calls attention to certain important aspects of the black political experience, but some may be more useful than others. Throughout this text we will make use of these and other frames of reference as they may seem appropriate. In the next section we will use the dominant-subordinate group model in our discussion of the historical background of contemporary black politics.

A BIT OF HISTORY: THE POLITICS OF UNCERTAINTY

The black political struggle for inclusion has been at once a struggle to overcome constitutional and statutory barriers to black political participation as well as a campaign to transform the American political culture, which legitimizes and sustains exclusionary institutions and practices. The ultimate objective of black politics, therefore, is to create the conditions under which

African Americans might enjoy material, cultural, and social equality with their white compatriots. In that sense, black politics, like all other politics, is a means toward an end. In the end, it is the end that matters.

Passage of the several civil rights acts of the 1960s, culminating with the adoption of the Voting Rights Act of 1965 and the Housing Act three years later, signal, more or less, the triumph of efforts to overcome legal barriers to black participation and economic access. Three decades later, however, the material, social, and cultural conditions under which African Americans live remain markedly different and *unequal* to those of whites. In fact, there is considerable evidence that suggests that the material inequality between black and white Americans is actually growing. This paradoxical situation provides the setting within which contemporary black politics unfolds. The following brief survey of the history of black politics will help us understand how this paradoxical situation came to be.

THE BEGINNING, 1619–1865[15]

Even though there is some evidence that African Americans may have come to what is now the United States as early as the sixteenth century, the unbroken black presence began when some 20 Africans landed in Jamestown, Virginia, in 1619. Contrary to popular opinion and in spite of the fact that the African slave trade had been going on for more than a century, apparently these first blacks who came to the United States in 1619 did not come as slaves but as indentured servants and for the first two decades their legal status was the same as their fellow white servants. The change of the status of most Africans from indentured servant to slave occurred over several decades in the various colonies and the rise and refinement of the ideology of white supremacy to justify black slavery followed a similar progression.

Indeed, prior to the Civil War, communities of free blacks existed side by side with slavery. When the United States was launched as a republic in 1790, there were 59,000 free blacks—27,000 in the North and 32,000 in the South.[16] Although initially given the right to vote in most states, free blacks were almost completely disfranchised by the 1840s. The various states also imposed other legal restrictions on free blacks, such as limiting their mobility by requiring them to carry passes and by imposing severe limitations on occupations in which they might engage.

Prior to 1857, albeit in piecemeal fashion, the national government signaled its acceptance of the rising ideology of white supremacy.

According to a prominent historian:

> Reflecting the popular concept of the United States as a white man's country, early Congressional legislation excluded Negroes from certain federal rights and privileges and sanctioned a number of territorial and state restrictions. In 1790 Congress limited naturalizations to white aliens; in 1792 it organized militia and restricted enrollment to able bod-

ied white male citizens; in 1810 it excluded Negroes from carrying the United States mail ... on the basis of such legislation, it would appear that Congress had resolved to treat Negroes neither as citizens nor aliens.[17]

But in 1857, the Supreme Court, in the *Dred Scott* decision (quoted at length below), embraced without reservation the dominant ideology of white supremacy and the related view that blacks had no rights that whites were bound to respect. The Court said:[18]

The question is simply this: Can a negro, whose ancestors were imported into this country and sold as slaves, become a member of the political community formed and brought into existence by the Constitution of the United States, and as such become entitled to all the rights, and privileges, and immunities, guaranteed by the instrument to the citizen?

The only matter in issue before the court, therefore, is, whether the descendants of such slaves, when they shall be emancipated, or who are born of parents who had become free before their birth, are citizens of a state in the sense in which the word "citizen" is used in the Constitution of the United States.

We think they are not, and that they are not included, and were not intended to be included, under the word "citizens" in the Constitution and can, therefore, claim none of the rights and privileges which that instrument provides for and secures to citizens of the United States. On the contrary, they were at that time considered as a subordinate and inferior class of beings, who had been subjugated by the dominant race, and whether emancipated or not, yet remained subject to their authority, and had no rights or privileges but such as those who held the power and the government might choose to grant them....

In the opinion of the court, the legislation and histories of the time, and the language used in the Declaration of Independence, show that neither the class of persons who had been imported as slaves, nor their descendants, whether they had become free or not, were then acknowledged as a part of the people, nor intended to be included in the general words used in that memorable instrument.

It is difficult at this day to realize the state of public opinion in relation to that unfortunate race, which prevailed in the civilized and enlightened portions of the world at the time of the Declaration of Independence, and when the Constitution of the United States was framed and adopted. But the public history of every European nation displays it, in a manner too plain to be mistaken.

They had for more than a century before been regarded as being of an inferior order; and altogether unfit to associate with the white race, either in social or political relations; and so far inferior, that they had no rights which the white man was bound to respect; and that the negro might justly and lawfully be reduced to slavery for his benefit. He was bought and sold, and treated as an ordinary article of merchandise and traffic, whenever a profit could be made by it. This opinion was at that time fixed and universal in the civilized portion of the white race. It was regarded as an axiom in morals as well as in politics, which no one thought of disputing, or supposed to be open to dispute; and men in every grade and position in society daily and habitually acted upon it in their private pursuits, as well as in matters of public concern, without doubting for a moment the correctness of this opinion....

The language of the Declaration of Independence is equally conclusive.... The general words ... would seem to embrace the whole human family, and if they were used in a similar instrument at this day, would be so understood. But it is too clear for dispute, that the enslaved African race were not intended to be included, and formed no part of the people.

Chief Justice Taney's opinion in *Dred Scott* was and remains the most clear and candid statement of, and defense for, the ideology of white supremacy to become a part of the American public record.

With such attitudes prevailing it is not surprising that during this period the dominant political strategy among blacks was to secure legal protection for free blacks and emancipation of those held as slaves. As the *Dred Scott* case demonstrated, continued subjugation was the dominant but not exclusive policy in the white community. Strands of legal protection and population transfer were clearly evident. White support for policies other than continued subjugation, however, was essentially a northern phenomenon supported primarily by church-based societies.

Population transfer as a strategy for dealing with the black political presence received support from diverse quarters, including prominent whites such as Thomas Jefferson and President James Monroe. These forces, led by the American Colonization Society, advocated emigration of blacks to Africa. Although many blacks opposed emigration of free blacks because they felt that it would only prolong slavery, there was black support for population transfer schemes by such persons as Paul Cuffie and Bishop Turner. The issue was debated in the black convention movement and in the black press. Several modest population transfer schemes were actually implemented. Some transferred blacks to Africa and others began black settlements in what was then the Western frontier. And it should be noted that there were those committed to the use of violence to bring about revolutionary transformation. Rebellions led by Nat Turner and Denmark Vesey are cases in point.

EMANCIPATION, RECONSTRUCTION, AND NULLIFICATION, 1866–1883

The defeat of the South in the Civil War and the resultant emancipation of those held as slaves ushered in an era in which legal protection and continued subjugation became the primary strategies for maintaining white dominance, while legal protection and assimilation[19] became dominant policy orientations among blacks. Legal protectionists prevailed during the 1860s and 1870s and succeeded in having the Constitution amended and statutes passed that established legal protection against slavery, bestowed citizenship upon blacks, affirmed the right to vote, ensured access to all public accommodations, and guaranteed due process and equal protection of the laws to blacks. Statutes also provided federal guarantees of protection from terror and intimidation from whatever source in the exercise of these rights. Thus by 1875 the legal status of blacks was technically equal to that of whites.

However, as is widely understood, legal victories are merely reflective of the balance of political forces at a given historical moment. Whether such victories can be consolidated, sustained, and become consensual elements of the society's cultural fabric is determined by the evolution of the competing forces. In this case the evolution of forces mitigated against black interests. In effect, the Republicans made a deal with white southern Democrats in order to keep the presidency. Following the compromise of 1877, in which the proponents of legal protection capitulated to the advocates of continued subjugation, the political fortunes of blacks declined precipitously. By 1883 the Supreme Court had nullified the principal sections of the civil rights laws designed to protect black rights and to shield them from intimidation and terror. Consequently, black political participation as voters and officeholders was severely constrained, and blacks were rapidly reduced to a state of penury and powerlessness.

TERROR, LYNCHING, AND REIMPOSITION
OF WHITE SUPREMACY, 1884–1914

From 1884 to the first decades of the twentieth century, continued subjugation through terror remained the major policy among whites, especially in the South. Violence and the threat of violence were used to intimidate and dissuade blacks from political activism. Lynchings, including ritualized burning at the stake, were routine events not only in the South but also as far north and west as Oklahoma, Indiana, Illinois, Ohio, and even Wyoming.[20] Burnings and hangings were spectacles, announced in advance, attended by whites including women and children, and covered on assignment by newspaper reporters in a manner not unlike contemporary coverage of sporting events.[21] The practice was so widespread that in 1881 Tuskegee Institute, a predominantly black university in Alabama, began issuing annual reports on the incidents of lynching. Not until 1952 did it report that there were no lynchings to report in a given year.[22]

Many blacks, quite understandably under the circumstances, withdrew from political activity altogether. Among those who continued to struggle politically, fighting for legal protection remained the dominant tendency, but advocates of assimilation, population transfer, and revolutionary transformation were also active. All-black towns were established in several states, and numerous back-to-Africa movements surfaced. The white use of terror, however, accomplished its purpose. Blacks won no major political victories during this period. By 1901 the last black congressman had left office, and the state and local governing bodies were rapidly reclaiming their lily-white complexion. Nevertheless, black political struggle did go on. Much of the political infrastructure upon which future black political activity would rest

For almost a century, lynching and other acts of terror were used to intimidate and repress African Americans. Congress refused to make lynching a federal crime. This photo is from a 1930 lynching in Marion, Indiana. (*UPI/Corbis-Bettmann*)

was built during these years. The celebrated debate between Booker T. Washington and W. E. B. DuBois over the appropriate strategy for black advancement occurred, and both the NAACP and the National Urban League were founded during this period.

THE STRUGGLE FOR THE VOTE, 1915–1944

This period marked the beginning of the end of legal exclusion of blacks in the South and the end of de facto exclusion in the North. In 1915[23] the courts outlawed the infamous grandfather clause used to "legally" prevent blacks from voting.[24] However, through a series of disingenuous ploys that came to be known as the white primary, the southern states were able to defeat the intent of the 1915 *Guinn* decision and continue to curb black political participation. Following the strategy of legal protection, blacks mounted campaigns to have such practices declared unconstitutional. However, each victory in court was met with enactment of still another exclusionary device—in 1927,[25] 1932,[26] and 1935.[27] Not until 1944 in the *Allwright*[28] decision was the white primary effectively declared unconstitutional.

In the North, the migration of blacks from the South increased the black population such that it became an important political force. Black voters in Chicago were able to send Oscar DePriest to the U.S. Congress in 1921, and elsewhere black voters were able to help defeat several senatorial candidates who seemed hostile to black interests. As a result of growing black electoral strength, the northern wing of the Democratic party, under the leadership of Franklin Roosevelt, began to court black voters by advocating legal protection of black rights. At the same time, protest activities, including picketing, sit-ins, and consumer boycotts, precursors to the civil rights campaigns of the 1960s, were carried out to bring about integration in the urban centers of the North.

THE STRUGGLE FOR RACIAL INTEGRATION, 1945–1965

Following the death of the white primary in 1944, black political activity increased significantly. Assimilation/integration became the dominant policy orientation among both black and white factions. The seminal *Brown v. Board of Education* ruling in 1954, which repudiated the separate but equal doctrine, buoyed the proponents of integration and served as the midwife of the incipient civil rights movement.

Proponents of assimilation/integration, after considerable struggle to overcome those committed to continued subjugation, persuaded Congress to pass several laws, culminating in the Voting Rights Act of 1965, which when taken together, repudiated all forms of segregation and discrimination. These laws also committed the country, at least formally, to the full integration of African Americans in American society.

However, the intense opposition by many white interests to integrationism and the noticeable lag in the pace of material advances in comparison to the legal victories led some to challenge the effectiveness of integration as the major policy orientation. As a result, groups supporting pluralism, nationalism, and revolution as optimum strategies all began to compete for and win adherents within the black community. For example, the Student Nonviolent Coordinating Committee (SNCC), which began as an integrationist organization and played a major role in ending state-sponsored segregation and voting rights discrimination, adopted a nationalist-pluralist orientation. The Congress on Racial Equality (CORE) that had played a leading role in the fight to end segregation in public accommodation soon followed. The Republic of New Africa was also formed during this period. This group vowed to establish an independent black nation in the southern Black Belt.

THE STRUGGLE FOR ECONOMIC EMPOWERMENT, 1966–PRESENT

The century-long struggle for political access was based upon the premise that unfettered political participation would lead to social and economic equality. The significant increase in black political participation, particularly as elected officials, during the 1970s and 1980s, set the stage for testing this premise. Economic empowerment was the focal point of black political activity.

Black politics during this period, which is commonly referred to as the era of Black Power, was conditioned by both nationalist and integrationist sentiments. Nationalist ideas were employed to lobby for public policies designed to help create a black entrepreneurial class and to exhort black consumers to support black businesses. On the other hand, integrationism was used to support the assimilation of black entrepreneurs into the American corporate elite.

Specifically, political pressures were brought to bear upon both government and private corporations to induce them to adopt affirmative action programs for hiring and promoting black workers and to increase their transactions with black-owned firms. Governments were asked to set aside designated percentages of the contracts for goods and services for black enterprises. Private companies were urged to award more franchises to black entrepreneurs.

This quest for economic empowerment through political pressure threatened the self-interest of some whites and was interpreted by many of them as a movement to secure preferential treatment for black Americans. As a consequence, the national consensus that had developed during the latter stages of the civil rights movement began to disintegrate.

Affirmative action and other race-specific programs were characterized by some as reverse discrimination. Consequently (as discussed more fully in Chapter 2), the American electorate began to turn away from issues supported by black leadership. By 1980, the black political agenda had become isolated from the American political mainstream. This was most evident in the presidential elections of 1980, 1984, and 1988 when blacks were the only major constituency that supported the nominee of the Democratic party.

In 1992, however, blacks were on the winning side when the Democratic nominee, Bill Clinton, was elected president with approximately 39 percent of the white vote and 82 percent of the black vote. Perhaps understandably, yet ironically, black political leadership in the 1992 campaign tacitly agreed not to raise race specific issues in order to help the Democratic nominee. When Clinton was reelected in 1996 he received 84 percent of the black vote but only 43 percent of the white vote.

THE IMPORTANCE OF POPULATION SIZE
AND STRATEGIC DISTRIBUTION

Armed with (1) an understanding of how frames of reference condition what we come to know, (2) a cursory understanding of the several frames of reference used to interpret black political life, and (3) the brief discussion of the history of black political activity in the United States, we may complete our introductory discussion with an analysis of the black population as a political resource. But first it may be useful to elaborate on what we mean by power and potential sources of power.

We understand power to be the ability of one individual or group to persuade a second party to do something in its interest that the second party was not already predisposed to do. Thus, power is a relationship between, say, party A and party B. In order for party A to exercise power over party B, party A must have control over resources that it can manipulate to influence the behavior of party B in the desired direction. Manipulation may take the form of rewards or punishment or threats of the same. Various resources, such as money, status, jobs, votes, office holding, and control of instruments of violence, are all potential sources of power. For them to be converted into actual power, party B must be vulnerable to their manipulation by party A. In the case of voting as a potential source of power, for example, if the votes of the majority community are split evenly between two candidates and the minority community controls 10 percent of the vote, the candidates are vulnerable to manipulation of the minority vote even though it may be relatively small. Under these circumstances, the vote may become a source of actual power. In another situation in which the minority may control a greater share of the vote, perhaps 30 percent of the vote, but the majority population is unanimous in its support for one of the candidates, the minority vote even though it is greater than it is in the first example cannot be converted into actual power because the would-be target would not be vulnerable to its manipulation. That is to say that if the majority is unanimous in its support for a given candidate or issue, it is not vulnerable to the manipulation of the minority vote. Thus, in such an instance, the minority vote cannot be converted into actual power.

In the U.S. political system, the wealth controlled by a particular group and the size and distribution of its population are perhaps its two most important sources of potential political power. Since blacks control little wealth, population strength becomes their major source of potential political power. Thus, a brief comment on the social-political profile of the black population is in order.

The special importance of the size of a group's population, of course, lies in the "one person, one vote" principle that undergirds the American electoral process. There are, however, special features in the electoral system that, under certain circumstances, might render a group potentially more politically powerful than its size alone would justify.[29] The process through which the president is elected is one such feature. It is probably the most important one because of the dominant role of the president and the presidency in the American political scheme.

The winner-take-all system through which the president is elected makes it possible for a group to exert disproportionate influence on the process if its population is strategically located. The president is not chosen by popular vote but by the electoral college, in which each state has a number of votes equal to its representation in the House of Representatives and the Senate. The fact that a candidate who gets the most votes in a given state gets all of that state's electoral votes obviously places a premium on winning in those states with large numbers of electoral votes. As a result the potential political power of a group is enhanced if its population is strategically distributed such that it can influence election results in the larger states.

It is also true that from time to time and for various reasons political leaders from certain areas of the country, New England, for example, and especially New York, may exert disproportionate influence on the political direction of the country. In such an eventuality, being able to influence the electoral process in those areas could translate into significant political power. Finally, given the increasing urbanization of the country, the major metropolitan areas within the states are especially important in both state and national politics. Consequently, influence within them may be parlayed into valuable political capital.

Theoretically then, the size and distribution of the black population could give the black community a strategic voice in these areas, and by extension, significant national political influence.

THE BLACK POPULATION: POLITICAL-SOCIAL PROFILE

At the time of the Emancipation Proclamation, the black population was heavily southern and rural. Since that time, responding to the push-pull dynamic of more stringent racial restrictions in the South and growing economic opportunities in the North and West, the black population has become highly urban. It is not only urban but strikingly big-city oriented. Indeed, there are 30 cities with 100,000 or more black residents. Slightly more than 10 million, or 30 percent of the black population, lives in those cities. In 1996 more than 86 percent of the black population lived in metropolitan areas, with 54 percent living in central cities of such areas. As Table 1-1 demonstrates, the urbanization of the black population continued unabated from 1950 to 1996 in spite of the general decline of the cities.

Black political potential, as a result of the continued urbanization, has increased noticeably, although prospects for converting that potential into real power is another matter. In 1970 there were 7 major cities with black population majorities, and 4 of them had black mayors. By 1980 there were 17 such cities, and 13 had black mayors. By 1990 all 17 cities had black mayors.

As of 1997, with the net out-migration having ended in the early 1980s, more than half of the black population, 54.9 percent, remains in the South. The Northeast and the North Central regions have approximately 18 percent each, and the West, 9 percent. The Census Bureau projects that between 1995 and 2025 the black population will increase by 12 million and that 64 percent of the increase will occur in the South.[30] Thus, the greatest potential is in the southern region of the United States, where 6 of the 7 states with a black population of 20 percent or more are located. Only

Table 1-1   Percent Distribution of Population Inside
and Outside Metropolitan Areas by Race, 1950–1997

	1950		1960		1970		1980		1990		1997	
	B	W	B	W	B	W	B	W	B	W	B	W
Metropolitan Areas	59	63	68	67	74	68	82	75	83	75	86	77
Central Cities	44	35	53	32	58	28	60	27	56	24	54	22
Outside Central Cities	15	28	15	35	16	40	22	48	27	51	31	55
Outside Metropolitan Areas	41	37	32	33	26	32	18	26	17	25	13	22

Note: B = Black; W = White
Sources: U.S. Department of Commerce, U.S. Bureau of the Census, various publications.

the border states of Delaware and Maryland, along with Illinois and New York among the non-southern states, have black populations of 15 percent or more.

With population size as a principal resource, the black political potential is also greater in the South at the municipal and congressional district levels. By 1996, five of the nine largest cities with black population majorities were in the South, although only three southern cities were among the ten states with the largest number of black residents.

At the congressional level, 57 of 98 districts with a black voting age population (VAP) of at least 15 percent were in the South, as were 22 of 44 with at least a black VAP of 30 percent. Ten of 25 majority black congressional districts were also in the South.[31]

To round out the picture, we may note there are 70 electoral votes in the 7 states in which the black population is 20 percent or more of the total electoral college, and that there are 238 electoral votes in another 12 states in which blacks comprise between 10 and 19 percent of the population. Thus, it is clear that the size and distribution of the black population make it a significant potential resource.

However, potential power may be converted into actual power only if the means for doing so are also available and utilized. In the case of black population strength, presently several factors and trends work against its conversion into significant power. First of all, black electoral strength in the nation's larger cities is offset by their intractable problems and a diminishing resource base in these jurisdictions. As the out-migration of the affluent continues in tandem with the influx of the poor and dispossessed, control of the cities becomes a hollow prize, as much of a liability as an asset in the larger political equation. In 1970, for example, only about 55 percent of the poor blacks lived in metropolitan areas; by 1990 the figure was up to 83 percent.

Over half, 56 percent, of the nation's poor blacks now live in central cities of metropolitan areas.

Indeed, the growing impoverishment of blacks in the urban centers of the Midwest and Northeast where black political power historically has been highest questions the real impact of electoral participation. It was in the Midwest—Gary, Chicago, Detroit—and in the Northeast—New York, New Jersey—that black congresspersons and the first of a spate of big-city black mayors were elected. Yet by 1990 the poverty rate for blacks was higher in the Midwest, 36 percent, than in any other region of the country, including the South.[32] The black poverty rate in the Northeast has also climbed dramatically and continues to grow. In 1990 it was 29 percent, compared to 33 percent in the South and 24 percent in the West.

Regarding congressional districts, continued intransigence of white authorities along with other factors has mitigated against converting black population strength into real political power. Until 1990, this was especially true in the South, where the black political potential is greater. For example, in 1990 only 5 of the 123 congresspersons from the 10 states of the Old Confederacy were black. No state had more than 1 even though blacks comprised more than 25 percent of the population in 5 of the 10 southern states and more than 15 percent in 8 of them. However, following the 1990 census, blacks were able to use the Voting Rights Act to force southern legislatures to reapportion in a more racially equitable manner. As a result, southern legislatures created a number of black majority districts, and the number of black congresspersons from the region increased from 5 to 17, with every southern state except Arkansas having at least 1 black congressperson and 5 having 2 or more.

However, the effort to convert black population strength into political power was quickly undermined in 1995, when the Supreme Court ruled in *Miller* v. *Johnson* that race could not be a predominant factor in redistricting. Following *Miller*, several groups, including one called the Campaign for Color-blind America Legal Defense and Education Fund, filed suits challenging majority black legislative districts at both the congressional and state levels. The result has been the dismantling of majority black districts in Louisiana, Georgia, and Texas. Indeed, in response to the permissive ruling by the Supreme Court, states with sizable black populations drew redistricting plans that scattered the black population across districts in a manner that ensures white dominance. The pattern is evident in several southern states. For example, in Mississippi, a state that is 35 percent black and has five congressional districts, one district has a black population majority while the black VAP in the other four districts ranges from 17 to 37 percent. The situation is similar in South Carolina and Louisiana. South Carolina, with six districts and a black population of 30 percent, has one majority black district and a black VAP ranging from 17 to 28 percent in the other five. Among Louisiana's seven districts, there is one majority black district and five other districts with the black VAP ranging from 23 to 32 percent. Given the history of racially polarized voting in these states, the potential power inherent in population strength will not be realized.

Nationally, as is the case in majority black cities, black population strength as a political resource is also undermined by the prevailing dire economic conditions. For example, in 1990 six of the nation's ten districts with the highest poverty ratio were represented by a black congressperson.

Finally, the growing conservatism of whites in recent presidential elections has depreciated the strategic importance of black population strength as a political resource. As a minority, black population strength is more readily converted into political power when there is a split among white factions and black voters can combine their numbers with one of the white factions to ensure victory of the candidate more supportive of black interests. This has always been a key element in black political strategies. However, since 1968, even though blacks have given no less than 82 percent of their vote to the presidential candidate perceived by them to be more supportive of black interests, the candidate favored by them has been successful only three times.

The fact of the matter is that there has been a conservative shift in white voting behavior and growing racial polarization in presidential elections dating back to the 1968 presidential campaign of Alabama Governor George Wallace, who, at that time, was known only for his ardent support for racial segregation. Appealing to diverse interests thought to be discontented with what was pictured as the profligate American welfare state, the Wallace movement captured national attention and 13.5 percent of the popular vote, a surprisingly high figure for a third-party candidate. Together, the two more conservative candidates in the 1968 election, Wallace and Nixon, received 62 percent of the white vote. Black voters gave Hubert Humphrey, the liberal Democrat, 85 percent of their vote.

Since 1968, this pattern has intensified. Blacks have given no less than 82 percent of their votes to the candidate thought to be more supportive of their interests, but, as noted earlier, except for 1976, 1992, and 1996 its candidate has been soundly beaten in every election. The 1976 election was something of an anomaly because the successful Jimmy Carter campaign benefited both from the political fallout of the Watergate affair and Carter's ability to appeal to southern whites as a native son. With the exception of the anomalous 1976 election, from 1968 to 1996 there was an unbroken progression of white voters toward the more conservative end of the political spectrum with the increasing isolation of blacks around the center being the result. Under these circumstances, black voters had little chance of identifying whites with whom they might coalesce to form majorities to pursue mutually beneficial ends. Thus, the strategic distribution of the black population has been robbed of its political significance.

Some have argued that this increasing isolation of blacks could and indeed should be ended by blacks following their white compatriots toward political conservatism. However, to date, black voters by and large appear to be unimpressed by this counsel to end their isolation by supporting candidates and programs they believe inimical to black interests.

CONCLUSION

We have seen quite clearly that the status of African Americans in American society has largely been determined, as Chief Justice Taney said in *Dred Scott*, by the "indelible marks" of race and color. For the most part, these are the same "indelible marks" that continue to shape the everyday life of blacks in this country. We have also seen that there is a material base to the race problem. We have observed that certain material inequities are routinely generated by the American political economy and that the indelible marks of race and color and the institutions built around them serve to visit a disproportionately large share of these inequities upon African Americans.

Although the interconnected nature of racism and the material imperatives of American society explain much of the black predicament, we have noted that there is a more "purely" racial dimension as well. This is reflected in the indignities and harassment that blacks, regardless of their material possessions, experience simply because of their race. For example, whites have no worry about whether they can buy a house where they choose or will be identified as a potential shoplifter by a clerk or security guard merely because of their race. Such worries, however, are constantly with African Americans and are important elements in their perceptions of American society.

We have also seen that blacks have been involved in an unending political struggle to transform their unhappy circumstances and that this struggle has borne considerable fruit in spite of sustained efforts of white factions of considerable means to maintain white domination and black subjugation. By the end of the 1960s, all legal barriers to black political participation and access to pivotal economic institutions had been removed. Nevertheless, the overall well-being of the black community remained substantially less satisfying than that of whites.

The history of black political participation is not at all encouraging. There have, of course, been some notable advances. But basically blacks still do not realistically enjoy the same opportunities, rights, and privileges that white Americans do. To be sure, there continue to be attempts in both the public and private sectors to address this general problem. Overall, however, there remains a certainty and an uncertainty about the life chances of blacks in this country. The certainty is that blacks, in widely disproportionate numbers, are at the lower ends of just about every important segment of American life. The uncertainty is whether or not we can generate "the will" to overcome this certainty within the existing political-social order.

TOPICS FOR DISCUSSION

1. The authors state that "how to achieve racial justice with harmony remains our most critical and potentially explosive internal problem." Do you agree with this assessment? Why or why not?

2. The Harris alternative framework suggests that the economic debilities that afflict African Americans, that is, unemployment, low income, poverty, and substandard housing, are systemic and that racism ensures that blacks receive more than their fair share of them. Assuming that Harris is correct, does this mean that the struggle to reduce the level of black unemployment and poverty is at the same time a movement to increase the level of these debilities among whites?

3. Since the early 1970s, African Americans have shifted from "protests to politics" in attempts to achieve their policy objectives. However, even though blacks have made substantial gains in the political arena, the gap in socioeconomic well-being between blacks and whites remains substantial. What inference would you draw from this regarding the efficacy of political participation as a strategy for black advancement?

4. The U.S. Supreme Court has been instrumental in the denial and procurement of rights for African Americans. For instance, during slavery and Reconstruction, the Court sanctioned policies that intensified black subordination. The Warren Court, on the other hand, was instrumental in eliminating racial segregation. The current Rehnquist Court has diluted the impact of policies adopted during the civil rights era of the 1960s and 1970s. How do you assess the overall impact of the Supreme Court on the struggle for racial justice?

SUGGESTED READINGS

Anner, John, ed. *Beyond Identity Politics: Emerging Social Movements in Communities of Color*. Boston, MA: South End Press, 1996. A collection of essays highlighting the need for and possibilities for social movements that transcend race.

Bardolph, Richard. *The Civil Rights Record: Black Americans and the Law, 1849–1970*. New York: Thomas Y. Crowell Company, 1970. An extensive collection of documents with respect to African Americans' changing legal status.

Beard, Charles A. *An Economic Interpretation of the Constitution of the United States*. New York: Macmillan Company, 1954. A work concerning the constitutional history of the nation, with emphasis on the economic basis of the Constitution.

Bell, Derrick A. *Faces at the Bottom of the Well: The Permanence of Racism*. New York: Basic Books, 1992. A forceful analysis of the intransigence of racism in American life.

———. *Race, Racism, and Law*, 3rd ed. Boston, MA: Little, Brown, 1992. A collection of cases and materials that portray the racism in American law.

———. "The Racial Imperative in American Law." In *The Age of Segregation: Race Relations in the South, 1890–1945*, ed. Robert Haws. Jackson, MS: University of Mississippi Press, 1978. A study of the role that the American legal system played in ensuring that the rights of African Americans would be denied in the antebellum South.

Bennett, Lerone. *Black Power U.S.A.: The Human Side of Reconstruction, 1867–1877*. Chicago, IL: Johnson Publisher Co., 1967. A humanistic interpretation of Reconstruction.

————. *The Challenge of Blackness*. Chicago, IL: Johnson Publishing Co., 1972. A collection of essays on and about the struggle by African Americans to attain political and cultural power in the United States.

Berlin, Ira. *Slaves without Masters, The Free Negro in the Antebellum South*. New York: The New Press, 1974. An excellent discussion of social and political status of free blacks in the antebellum South.

Cooper, Anna J. *A Voice from the South*. New York: Oxford University Press, 1988. A philosophical analysis of race and American culture during the late nineteenth and early twentieth century by a black female intellectual.

DuBois, W. E. B. *Black Reconstruction*. New York: Harcourt Brace Jovanovich, 1935. A forceful essay devoted to analyzing the role of blacks in the attempt to reconstruct democracy in America, 1860–1880.

Franklin, John Hope. *From Slavery to Freedom: A History of Negro Americans*, 6th ed. New York: Alfred A. Knopf, 1988. The seminal study on the history of African Americans in the United States, which analyzes slavery, Reconstruction, the New Deal, the civil rights movement, and the present.

————. *Reconstruction after the Civil War*. Chicago, IL: University of Chicago Press, 1961. A penetrating discussion of the plight of blacks immediately following the Civil War.

Frazier, E. Franklin. *The Negro in the United States*. New York: Macmillan Company, 1957. An assessment of the status of blacks in America.

Giddings, Paula. *When and Where I Enter*. New York: Bantam Books, 1984. A comprehensive anthology of commentaries on the impact of black women on the struggle for racial and gender justice in America.

Hamilton, Charles V. *The Black Experience in American Politics*. New York: Capricorn Books, 1973. Readings that analyze the plight of blacks in America.

Harrington, Michael. *The Other America*, rev. ed. Baltimore, MD: Penguin Books, 1970. A seminal work on the problems of being poor in America.

Hartman, Chester, ed. *Double Exposure: Poverty and Race in America*. New York: M.E. Sharpe, 1997. A collection of essays by some of the nation's leading thinkers and activists on the interrelationship between race and poverty in America.

Henderson, Lenneal J., Jr., ed. *Black Political Life in the United States*. San Francisco, CA: Chandler Publishing Co., 1973. Articles that deal with various aspects of black political experiences. Includes a detailed bibliographical essay by editor.

Higginbotham, A. Leon, Jr. *In the Matter of Color: Race and the American Legal Process. The Colonial Period*, vol. 1. New York: Oxford University Press, 1978. An analysis of race and the legal process from 1619 to the Declaration of Independence and the American Revolution (1776).

Jaynes, Gerald, and Robin Williams, eds. *A Common Destiny, Blacks and American Society*. Washington, DC: National Academy Press, 1989. A collection of thoroughly researched articles on the socioeconomic, cultural, and political status of African Americans.

Jennings, James, ed. *Race Politics and Economic Development*. London: Verso Press, 1992. A collection of critical essays on the economic oppression of the black urban population.

Jones, Franklin, and Michael Adams. *Readings in American Political Issues*. Dubuque, IA: Kendall/Hunt, 1987. A wide ranging collection of readings covering political beliefs, political participation, political institutions, and public policy.

Kelley, Robin D. G. *Hammer and Hoe: Alabama Communists during the Great Depression.* Chapel Hill, NC: University of North Carolina Press, 1990. An analysis of the radical tradition in black political movements focusing on Alabama Communists during the Great Depression.

Kilson, Martin. "Political Change in the Negro Ghetto, 1900–1940s." In *Key Issues in the Afro-American Experience*, ed. Natan I. Huggins, Martin Kilson, and Daniel M. Fox. New York: Harcourt Brace Jovanovich, 1971. This work, like those in the entire volume, examines the changing status of African Americans

Logan, Rayford W. *The Betrayal of the Negro.* New York: Collier Books, 1965. A comprehensive analysis of the status of blacks in America between 1877 and 1901.

McPherson, James M., Laurence B. Holland, James M. Banner, Jr., Nancy J. Weiss, and Michael D. Bell. *Blacks in America: Bibliographical Essays.* Garden City, NY: Doubleday & Co., 1972. Detailed bibliographical essays organized around important topics and periods in black history. A useful tool for research.

Meier, August, and Elliot Rudwick, eds. *Along the Color Line: Explorations in the Black Experience.* Urbana, IL: University of Illinois Press, 1976. Essays on black leadership, nationalism, power, and nonviolent protest.

Morrison, Toni, ed. *Race-ing Justice, En-gendering Power.* New York: Pantheon Books, 1992. A collection of essays focusing on the Clarence Thomas-Anita Hill controversy that dramatize the role of race and racism in the construction of social reality.

Myrdal, Gunnar. *An American Dilemma.* New York: Harper & Row, 1964. A classic study analyzing the status of blacks in America.

Oates, Stephen B. *The Fires of Jubilee: Nat Turner's Fierce Rebellion.* New York: Harper & Row, 1990. A gripping account of Turner's rebellion and the terroristic response of the state.

Obadele, Imari. *America, the Nation State: Politics of the United States from a State-Building Perspective.* Baton Rouge, LA: House of Songhay, 1995. Examines the process through which the United States became a nation-state and the nature and role of black oppression in the process.

Perry, Huey, and Wayne Parent. *Blacks and the American Political System.* Gainesville, FL: University of Florida Press, 1995. A collection of essays examining current developments in African American politics.

Rainwater, Lee. *Behind the Ghetto Walls.* Chicago, IL: Aldine Publishing Co., 1970. An examination of the dynamics of the socioeconomic inequality of the American political system with emphasis on the ghetto.

Robinson, Donald. *Slavery in the Structure of American Politics.* New York: Harcourt Brace Jovanovich, 1971. An insightful account of the impact of slavery on deliberations at the Constitutional Convention.

Sloan, Irving, Jr., comp. and ed. *The Blacks in America: 1492–1977*, 4th rev. ed. Dobbs Ferry, NY: Oceana Publications, 1977. Essays on the varied experiences of blacks in America.

Smith, Robert C. *Racism in the Post Civil Rights Era: Now You See It Now You Don't.* Albany, NY: State University of New York Press, 1995. A systematic critique of racism both individual and institutional in the post civil rights period.

Sniderman, Paul, and Michael Hagen. *Race and Inequality: A Study in American Values.* Chatham, NJ: Chatham House Publishers, 1985. A careful analysis of American attitudes toward blacks and racial inequality.

Taeuber, Karl E., and Alma F. Taeuber. *Negroes in Cities: Residential Segregation and Neighborhood Change.* Chicago, IL: Aldine Publishing Co., 1965. A penetrating comparative analysis of the pattern as well as the process of residential segregation over time.

Walters, Ronald W. *Black Presidential Politics in America.* New York: State University of New York Press, 1988. An imaginative discussion of the strategic use of presidential politics in the struggle for racial justice.

NOTES

1. *Brown* v. *Board of Education of Topeka,* 349 U.S. 483 (1954). This affirmative action case is discussed in detail in Chapter 5.
2. *Richmond* v. *Croson,* 448 U.S. 469 (1989).
3. Paul R. Campbell, *Population Projections for States by Age, Sex, Race, and Hispanic Origin: 1995–2025* (U.S. Bureau of the Census, Population Division), pp. 5, 47.
4. See Frank J. Sorauf, *Party Politics in America,* 3rd ed. (Boston, MA: Little, Brown, 1961), Chapter 8.
5. *Ibid.,* p. 54.
6. U.S. Bureau of the Census, *The Black Population in the U.S.: March 1996,* pp. l–70.
7. See, for example, Chandler Davison, *Biracial Politics* (Baton Rouge, LA: Louisiana State University Press, 1972), especially Chapters 1–4. Also, Mack H. Jones, "A Frame of Reference for Black Politics," in *Black Political Life in the United States: A First as the Pendulum,* ed. Lenneal Henderson, Jr. (San Francisco, CA: Chandler, 1972), pp. 7–20.
8. The following discussion of Park and Parsons draws heavily on Stanford M. Lyman, *The Black American in Sociological Thought: A Failure of Perspective* (New York: Capricorn, 1972), especially Chapters 2 and 4.
9. Talcott Parsons, "Full Citizenship for the Negro American," in *The Negro American,* ed. Talcott Parsons and Kenneth Clark (Boston, MA: Houghton Mifflin, 1966), especially pp. 716–744.
10. See William E. Tabb, *The Political Economy of the Black Ghetto* (New York: Norton, 1970); Robert Allen, *Black Awakening in Capitalist America, an Analytic History* (New York: Doubleday, 1969); and Ronald Bailey, "Economics Aspects of the Black Internal Colony," in *Review of Black Political Economy* (Summer 1973).
11. See Harold Cruse, "Revolutionary Nationalism and the Afro-American," in *Rebellion or Revolution* (New York: William Morrow, 1968), pp. 74–96.
12. When first developed, the model was labeled the dominant-submissive group model. Since that time the author has concluded that the term "subordinate" is more appropriate than "submissive." See Jones, *Frame of Reference.*
13. The following discussion is reprinted with slight modification from Mack H. Jones, "Black Politics from Civil Rights to Benign Neglect," in *Negotiating the Mainstream, A Survey of the Afro-American Experience,* ed. Harry A. Johnson (Chicago, IL: American Library Association, 1978), pp. 164–195.
14. See Donald Harris, "Black Ghetto as Internal Colony: A Theoretical Critique and Alternative Formulation," *The Review of Black Political Economy* (Summer 1972), pp. 3–33.
15. This historical overview draws extensively from Jones, "Black Politics," pp. 164–195.

16. Figures computed from Table 1 in Hanes Walton, *Black Politics, a Theoretical and Structural Analysis* (New York: J.B. Lippincott Co., 1972), p. 52.

17. Leon Litwack, *North of Slavery* (Chicago, IL: University of Chicago Press, 1961), p. 31.

18. *Dred Scott* v. *Sandford*, 60 U.S. 393, 19 Howard 393 (1857). Of course, federal courts prior to *Dred Scott* had rendered pro-slavery decisions. See for example, Derrick Bell, "The Racial Interpretation of American Law" in *The Age of Race Relations in the South, 1890–1945*, ed. Robert Haws (Jackson, MS: University of Mississippi Press, 1968).

19. Given the cultural taboo on interracial marriage, no white faction and perhaps no black faction either can be said to have advocated complete assimilation as a strategy for solving the race problem. Perhaps integrationism may be a more appropriate term.

20. See Ralph Ginzberg, *100 Years of Lynching* (New York: Lancer, 1962), especially pp. 253–270.

21. *Ibid.*, p. 46. The author reproduces a newspaper clipping that describes the chagrin of newspaper reporters when those who had scheduled a lynching granted a reprieve to a victim in order to allow him to have a farewell interview with his family. The scheduled change made it difficult for reporters to meet their deadlines.

22. World Almanac, *Words That Set Us Free* (New York: Pharos Books, 1992), p. 88.

23. *Guinn* v. *United States*, 238 U.S. 349 (1915).

24. States adopted constitutional provisions that established stringent property, literacy, or other qualifications as prerequisites for voter registration, but excluded those whose ancestors could have qualified to vote prior to 1865. This allowed the "legal" exclusion of blacks while most whites who could not pass the literacy test retained their eligibility.

25. *Nixon* v. *Herndon*, 273 U.S. 536 (1927).

26. *Nixon* v. *Condon*, 286 U.S. 73 (1932).

27. *Grovey* v. *Townsend*, 295 U.S. 45 (1935).

28. *Smith* v. *Allwright*, 321 U.S. 649 (1944).

29. For elaboration of this point, see Dianne Pinderhughes, "The Black Vote—The Sleeping Giant," in *The State of Black America 1984*, pp. 69–93.

30. Paul Campbell, *Population Projections for States by Age, Sex, Race, and Hispanic Origin*, p. 17.

31. Data on congressional districts computed from tables in David A. Bositis, *Blacks and the 1996 Democratic National Convention* (Washington, DC: Joint Center for Political and Economic Studies, 1996).

32. Figures on regional poverty rates are taken from David Swinton, "The Economic Status of African Americans During the Reagan-Bush Era: Withered Opportunities, Limited Outcomes, and Uncertain Outlook," in *State of Black America 1993* (New York: National Urban League, 1993), pp. 135–200.

Chapter 2

The Nature
of the Problem

Economic realities dominate life within black America, but to many white Americans the struggle of blacks is over, and nothing further needs to be done. They see that blacks vote now with little impediment, they have jobs they never held before, they hold elective offices, they can go to the best schools, and they are free to patronize the hotel or restaurant of their choice.

But what is apparent on the surface fails to reveal what is underneath. Within black America a third of its people are at or below the poverty line and have a fifty percent chance of growing up underprivileged, undereducated and underemployed. A third of its adults who want to work can't find it, and two out of three of its teenagers are in the same boat. Its average income is 58 percent of that of white America.

—John E. Jacobs, *The State of Black America,* 1988[1]

In allocating income, wealth, status, knowledge, occupation, organizational position, popularity, and a variety of other values every society also allocates resources with which an actor can influence the behavior of other actors in at least some circumstances.... Extreme inequalities in the distribution of such key values as income, wealth, status, knowledge and military prowess are equivalent to extreme inequalities in political resources.

—Robert A. Dahl, *Polyarchy*[2]

In this chapter we explore two important dimensions of the black predicament in the United States—the unequal socioeconomic conditions of African Americans and the divergent perceptions that blacks and whites have of this reality. This will sharpen our understanding of the setting within which black politics unfolds.

African Americans, like other disadvantaged groups, have always viewed political participation as a means through which full equality in the social, economic, and cultural life of the country could be obtained.

Accordingly, when the civil rights movement of the 1960s succeeded in eliminating legal restrictions on black political participation, it did not mean that the black political struggle was over. Rather, it meant that the struggle to use political participation to transform the unequal social, economic, and cultural status of blacks had just begun.

Throughout the history of the United States, blacks have lagged behind white Americans on practically every accepted measure of socioeconomic well-being. This has been and continues to be true of all categories of African Americans, male and female, young and old, urban and rural, married and single, and in every geographical region of the country.

To be sure, there has been considerable improvement over the years. Blacks are decidedly better off than they were a few decades ago. They have shared in the overall economic growth and development of the country, but the gap between black and white well-being has remained more or less constant. In fact, recent evidence suggests that the gap may be widening. However, current perceptions of the socioeconomic conditions of African Americans and therefore of the conditions that black politics must address are not necessarily consistent with reality. Indeed the perceptions of this reality by blacks and whites differ markedly.

According to poll results, discussed later in this chapter, many whites apparently believe that conditions supportive of black equality have been realized and that, consequently, further government action to promote black advancement is neither necessary nor constitutionally appropriate. Many blacks, on the other hand, take a diametrically opposed view.

Before discussing further these differing perceptions of reality, we will first attempt to describe reality as it is reflected in socioeconomic statistics compiled primarily by the national government.

UNEQUAL SOCIOECONOMIC CONDITIONS—WEALTH AND INCOME

In market economies such as the United States, wealth and income are reliable indicators of socioeconomic well-being. Wealth holdings and the type and amount of income that one receives indicate one's potential role in the political and economic system. Types of income are listed in Table 2-1.

Property income reflects ownership of wealth in the form of liquid assets, such as real or personal property. Those with significant property income will likely have substantial wealth and, consequently, they will possess the potential for greater political power.

Income from wages and salaries, on the other hand, means that the individual is a supplier of labor. Except for those with especially high salaries, this source of income does not reflect disproportionate political strength.

Self-employment has the potential for generating political power and farm self-employment income represents potential political power because it is directly related to ownership of land.

Table 2-1   Types of Income Received by Families
by Race, 1969–1990 (Percentage Distribution)

Type of Income		1969	1974	1979	1983	1990
Earning						
Wages and Salaries	Black	85.4%	81.7%	80.8%	79.6%	79.6%
	White	79.8	78.0	75.9	74.7	72.3
Non-Farm Self-	Black	3.0	2.0	2.3	1.8	2.5
Employment	White	7.7	6.7	6.6	6.1	6.1
Farm Self-	Black	0.4	0.2	(c)	(c)	(c)
Employment	White	1.5	1.5	1.2	0.6	0.5
Other Than Earnings						
Property Income[a]	Black	0.6	0.6	0.9	1.4	2.0
	White	4.0	4.2	5.5	6.4	7.9
Transfers and All	Black	10.6	15.4	16.2	17.5	15.0
Other[b] Income	White	6.8	9.6	10.5	12.2	13.4
Public Assistance,	Black	4.2	6.0	5.1	4.7	3.3
Welfare	White	0.4	0.7	0.6	0.6	0.5

[a]Includes dividends, interest, net rental income, income from estates or trusts, and net royalties.
[b]Includes social security or railroad retirement income, public assistance or welfare payments, supplemental security income, retirement and annuities, veterans payments, and unemployment.
[c]Base less than $75,000; useful calculations could not be made.
Sources: U.S. Bureau of the Census, *Current Population Series*, P-60, *Money Income of Families and Persons in the United States*, various years. 1990 figures taken from David Swinton, "The Economic Status of African Americans: Limited Ownership and Persistent Inequality," in *The State of Black America 1992* (New York: National Urban League, 1992), p. 92.

Transfer income, which includes among other things social security payments, private retirement pensions, unemployment compensation, and welfare payments, is second only to wages and salaries as a source of income. A considerable proportion of transfer income is distributed by the government to persons experiencing financial difficulty. Thus, it reflects the absence of wealth and the political potential associated with it.

Both black and white families receive the same types of income, but the proportions of their incomes that come from the different sources vary significantly. Those sources of income associated with political power are more prominent among whites than among blacks.

From Table 2-1 we see that the preponderant source of income for both black and white families is wages and salaries, but blacks receive slightly more of their income from this source than whites. Since 1969, however, the proportion of total family income derived from wages and salaries has declined for both groups.

The other two types of earned income—farm and non-farm self-employment—are also declining as a proportion of family income for both black and white families. Among black families, farm self-employment income is virtually nonexistent and non-farm self-employment accounts for less than 2 percent of family income.

Both of the non-earning categories—property and transfer income—have increased as a proportion of family income since 1969. However, the proportion of black income coming from property income remains insignificant. The per capita black property income was $181 in 1990 compared to $1207 for whites.[3] The proportion of white families reporting some property income was more than twice that of blacks and on average white recipients of property income received more than four times the amount received by blacks.

Transfer income, which is often associated with economic deprivation but not exclusively so, provides a high proportion of the income of black families, and the proportion of black families receiving income from this source is slightly higher than that for white families. In 1990, 48 percent of black families and 38 percent of white families received government transfer income.[4] Twelve percent of black family income compared to 9 percent of white family income came from government transfer payments in 1990. Public assistance or welfare, which is only one of several types of transfer income, accounts for 3.3 percent of black family income, but only about one-half of one percent of the income of white families.

Despite the fact that higher proportions of blacks receive transfer income and the fact that a greater proportion of black income derives from

Above, unemployed workers respond to a job announcement. Unemployment is a routine outcome of the economic process, but black unemployment is almost always twice as high as the white rate. (*Charles Bennett/AP/Wide World Photos*)

transfers, blacks in 1990 received smaller mean (i.e., the average amount received per recipient) transfer income, $4,832, than whites, whose mean figure was $6,505.[5] The fact that white families receive a disproportionately large share of non-public assistance transfer payments, such as private pensions, annuities, and so forth, explains this seemingly paradoxical situation.

In summary, those sources of income that reflect potential political power—property and self-employment income—are disproportionately high among white families; and those that reflect limited political potential—welfare and other transfers—are more important sources of black family income.

BLACK WEALTH

As Swinton and others have pointed out, the importance of ownership in capitalist societies is obvious. Yet little attention has been given to the impact that limited wealth holdings have on the perpetuation of black subordination in American life. The gap between blacks and whites on indices such as income and poverty is well known, but the racial disparity in wealth holdings is actually much greater. A 1988 report showed that the mean wealth holding for blacks was $27,230 compared to $116,661 for whites, a ratio of 4:1. Black per capita wealth holding of $9,359 was only 21 percent of the $44,980 figure for whites.[6] Oliver and Shapiro argue that government policies have impaired the ability of many African Americans to accumulate wealth. Specifically, they assert the following:

> What is often not acknowledged is that the same social system that fosters the accumulation of private wealth for many whites denies it to blacks, thus forging an intimate connection between white wealth accumulation and black poverty. Just as blacks have had "cumulative disadvantages," many whites have had "cumulative advantages." Since wealth builds over a lifetime and is then passed along to kin, it is, from our perspective, an essential indicator of black economic well-being.[7]

Thus, they argue, the elimination of the racial disparity in wealth holding must be central to any program for black empowerment.

MEDIAN FAMILY INCOME

The disparity between black and white family income has been both persistent and strikingly consistent since the 1940s. As Figure 2-1 shows, during the four decades since the end of World War II—a period of sustained economic growth punctuated by periods of both expansion and recession—the median income of black families has fluctuated around 50 to 60 percent of the median for white families.

In 1950 the median income for black families was equal to 53 percent of the median for white families. Ten years later it was virtually the same, 53.8 percent of the white median. As Figure 2-2 shows, during the Vietnam War era black family income rose to around 60 percent of the median of

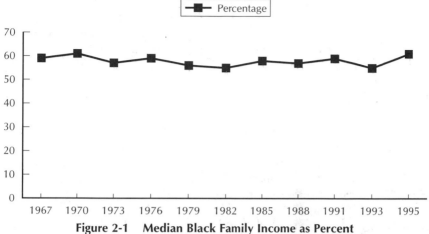

**Figure 2-1 Median Black Family Income as Percent
of Median White Family Income, 1967–1995 (1995 Dollars)**

Source: U.S. Bureau of the Census, *Historical Income Tables—Families,* 1997.

white families, reaching a high of 62 percent in 1975. However, as the war-induced economic boom receded, so did black family income. By 1982 it had fallen to about 55 percent of the median of white families, which was the lowest ratio since 1960. The 1995 median income of black families of $25,970 was only 61 percent of the $42,646 median for white families.

In recent years some analysts have suggested that the disproportionately large number of households headed by single black women explains the sizable gap between black and white median family incomes. However, the issue appears to be much more complex.

It is true, as shown in Table 2-2, that the difference in median income

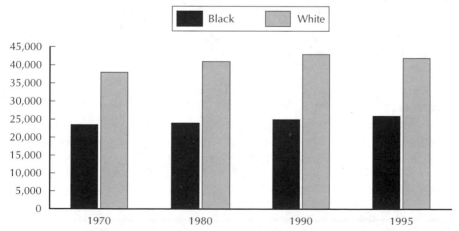

Figure 2-2 Median Income, Family Income by Race, 1970–1995 (1995 Dollars)

Source: U.S. Bureau of the Census, *Historical Income Tables—Families,* 1997.

of black and white married couples is less than that of the overall black and white populations. However, in 1994 black married couples had considerably less income than their white counterparts. The median for black couples was $35,218 compared to $43,675 for whites. Adding to the complexity, families headed by white women had a median income of $20,000 compared to $11,909 for black female-headed households. Moreover, the median income of households headed by white women was slightly more than the $19,476 median of families headed by single black men and a little less than the $22,207 of black couples with the wife not working outside the home.

It should be noted that the disparity between black and white family incomes is not simply a regional problem. As Table 2-3 shows, the out-migration of blacks from impoverished areas of the South over the last 30 years, together with the economic decline of the cities of the Northeast and Midwest, has eliminated the heretofore significant regional differences in the ratio of black to white incomes. The median income for black families in 1993 was virtually the same in the South and the Midwest.

INCOME AND PUBLIC SECTOR EMPLOYMENT

Both blacks and whites who work for government on average have higher earnings than workers in the private sector. This is so at least partially because a higher proportion of the public workforce consists of profession-

Table 2-2   Median Family Income in 1990 and 1994
by Race, Number of Earners, and Type of Family

	1990			*1993*		
	B	*W*	*B/W Ratio*	*B*	*W*	*B/W Ratio*
Type of Family						
Married Couples	$33,784	$40,331	.84	$35,218	$43,675	.81
wife works	40,038	47,247	.85	44,805	51,630	.86
wife not working	20,333	30,781	.66	22,207	30,878	.72
Male Householder	21,848	30,570	.71	19,476	29,269	.66
Female Householder	12,125	19,528	.62	11,909	20,000	.60
Number of Earners						
Total	21,423	36,915	.58	21,541	39,300	.55
No Earners	6,305	17,369	.36	6,858	17,565	.39
One Earner	16,308	27,670	.59	16,571	28,574	.58
Two Earners	34,050	43,036	.79	37,124	48,332	.77
Three Earners	43,813	54,632	.80	49,849	58,561	.84
Four or More	59,983	67,753	.89	59,678	73,269	.81

Note: B = Black; W = White

Sources: U.S. Bureau of the Census, *Current Population Series*, P-60, various years; *Statistical Abstract of the United States, 1996*, Table 721.

Table 2-3   Median Family Income in 1984,
1990, and 1993 by Race and Region of Country

	1984			1990			1993		
	B	W	B/W Ratio	B	W	B/W Ratio	B	W	B/W Ratio
Northeast	$16,326	$29,705	.55	$20,674	$34,387	.60	$25,002	$42,526	.59
North Central	14,367	27,683	.52	17,204	31,054	.55	20,974	40,158	.52
South	14,863	26,054	.57	17,662	29,162	.61	20,372	36,504	.56
West	19,209	28,509	.67	23,984	31,794	.75	26,182	39,614	.66

Note: B = Black; W = White

Source: U.S. Bureau of the Census, *Current Population Series*, P-60, *Money Income and Poverty Status of Families and Persons in the United States*, various years.

als. However, the difference between the earnings of blacks who work for the government and those employed in the private sector is much greater than that which prevails for white workers.

A 1983 study reported that the average earnings of black male government employees was $15,174, compared to $11,794 for those in the private sector, a difference of 29 percent.[8] The margin of difference for the white male public sector worker was only 8 percent. For black women the average public sector earning was $11,819, compared to $8,789 for the private sector.

Within the federal workforce the public to private sector earnings gap was greater than for government workers in general. The average earnings of black males working for the federal government in 1983 was $19,324, a margin of 64 percent above average private sector earnings. Black women employed by the national government earned $13,988, or 59 percent above the private sector average. The margins for white men and women employed by the national government were 31 and 63 percent, respectively. Earning levels have changed, of course, since the 1983 study, but there is no reason to believe that the saliency of public sector employment in the well-being of African Americans has changed.

Not only do blacks receive proportionately higher wages in the public sector, but they also hold a higher proportion of public sector jobs, particularly within the federal workforce. In 1994, blacks comprised only 11 percent of the civilian workforce, but they held 16.7 percent of all federal jobs. Public sector jobs, which include jobs with federal, state, and local governmental units, accounted for 24 percent of all jobs held by blacks but only 15 percent of those held by whites.[9]

Unfortunately for black workers, however, since the early 1990s there has been little or no growth in public sector employment. The federal workforce actually declined from 3.1 million in 1990 to 2.9 million in 1993. State and local employment grew only slightly from 15.2 million in 1990 to 15.8

million in 1993. As a 1997 study on the decline in the public sector work-force of New York City reported, blacks suffer disproportionately as government jobs dwindle.[10]

LABOR FORCE PARTICIPATION

The labor force participation rate is the proportion of the working age population actually working or actively seeking a job. The labor force includes the employed and the unemployed, but it does not include those who are not looking for jobs even if they want one.

Historically, blacks were more likely than whites to be in the labor force.[11] For example, in 1900, 65 percent of blacks aged 14 and over, compared to 52 percent of whites, were in the labor force. During recent times black and white labor force participation rates have been roughly equal with black men having slightly lower rates and black women having higher rates than their white counterparts.

Since 1970 the makeup of the American labor force has changed considerably as women have entered in greater numbers and the proportion of males has declined. During these same years, the position of blacks in the labor force has deteriorated. Black male participation rates have declined more sharply than those of white men while the increase in the rates for black women has lagged behind the increase of white women.

As Figure 2-3 shows, the labor force participation rate for black men dropped from 81 percent in 1962 to 66.5 percent in 1994. The decline for white males was much less dramatic, from 82 percent in 1962 to 74.9 percent in 1994. Black women increased their participation rate from 48 percent in 1962 to 58.7 percent in 1994. The rate for white females, however, went up from 37 to 58.4 percent.

The declining fortunes of blacks in the labor force are the result of fundamental structural changes in the American economy. The decline of heavy industries of the Midwest and Northeast and the closing of lumber mills and other industrial plants of the South have curtailed employment opportunities for all workers, but especially for black males. Many experienced black workers have dropped out of the labor force after losing their jobs because the skills they possessed cannot be used in growth areas of the economy. Increasing numbers of black youth who have really never held a job face a similar problem. Often they too do not have marketable skills. The skill deficiency of those workers is compounded by the fact that the economy is not creating new jobs as fast as the labor force is growing. A disproportionate share of the job shortage is falling on black workers.

EMPLOYMENT AND UNEMPLOYMENT

The unemployment rate is the percentage of those in the labor force who are unable to find work. In the modern era, black unemployment has been consistently and substantially higher than that of whites. In 1955, the black

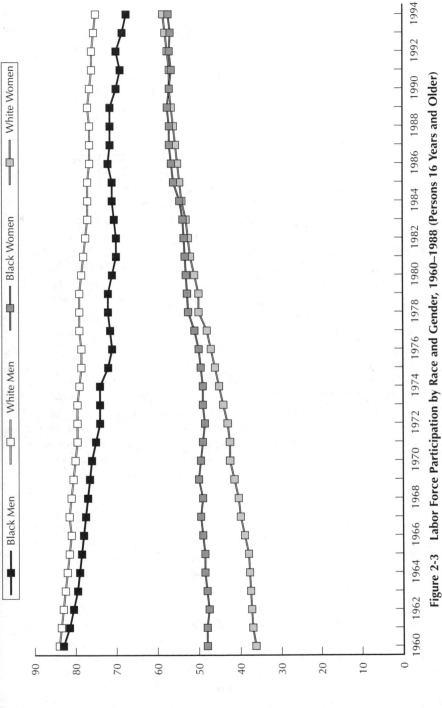

Figure 2-3   Labor Force Participation by Race and Gender, 1960–1988 (Persons 16 Years and Older)

Source: *Handbook of Labor Statistics*, various years.

Black Men   White Men   Black Women   White Women

unemployment rate doubled the white rate for the first time. Since then, as is evident from Figure 2-4, black unemployment has been at least twice that of whites in every year except three—1970, 1971, and 1975. From 1980 to 1990, the average annual unemployment rate for black men was 15.4 percent and 14.8 percent for black women compared to 6.3 percent for white men and 6.2 percent for white women. From 1990 to 1994, the average rate for black men was 10.7 percent and 11.9 percent for black women while the rates were 5.4 percent for white women and 6.2 percent for white men.

As noted earlier, the differential in black and white unemployment rates remains even during the best of economic times. For example, in 1997, with the American economy booming and the overall jobless rate at the lowest level in 24 years, 4.9 percent, the rate for whites was 4.2 percent but the black rate remained at a recession level of 9.8 percent.[12]

The employment ratio, which focuses on those who have jobs rather than those who are unable to find them, is the percentage of the working age population that is employed either part time or full time. Thus, while the unemployment rate is the proportion of the labor force without jobs, the employment ratio is the percentage of the population with jobs. Those who drop out of the labor force, that is, stop looking for jobs, are not included among the unemployed, but since they are still in the population they are considered when calculating the employment ratio. Taken together, the employment ratio and the unemployment rate yield a better understanding of how a group is faring in the work force.

Because black male unemployment has been increasing and their labor force participation has been declining, the employment ratio for black men has been falling faster than the unemployment rate has been increasing. The employment ratio for black men has also been falling faster than the labor force participation rate. Between 1962 and 1977, the employment ratio for black men went down from 72 percent to 66 percent. The employment ratio for white males dropped only half as much from 78 percent to 75 percent.

For black women whose labor force participation rate has increased, the employment ratio went up from 42 percent in 1962 to 57 percent in 1997. The increase for white women was much greater than that of black women, from 36 percent to 57 percent. Thus, by 1997, a significantly higher proportion of the working age population of whites had jobs. Blacks are being pushed from the ranks of the gainfully employed at an alarming rate.

POVERTY

The national government has developed a formula to determine the amount of cash income necessary for families to maintain a certain quality of life. Under the formula, the poverty threshold, which varies according to the family size and location, is an amount equal to three times "an economy food plan." In 1995 the poverty threshold for a family of three was $12,158 and $15,569 for a four-member family.

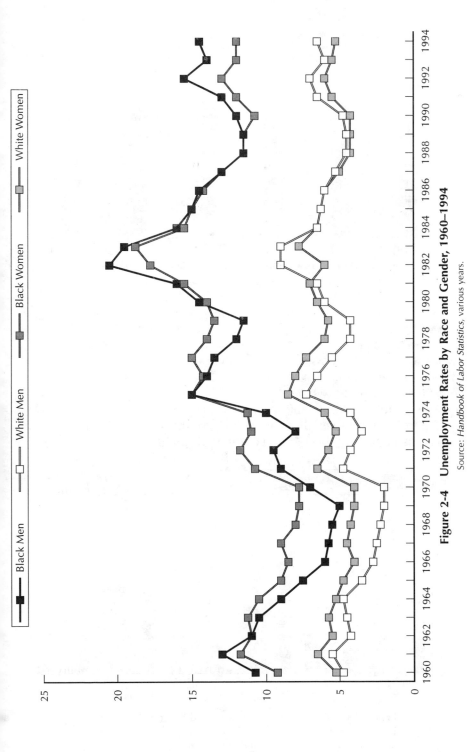

Figure 2-4   Unemployment Rates by Race and Gender, 1960–1994

Source: *Handbook of Labor Statistics*, various years.

Black Men   Black Women   White Men   White Women

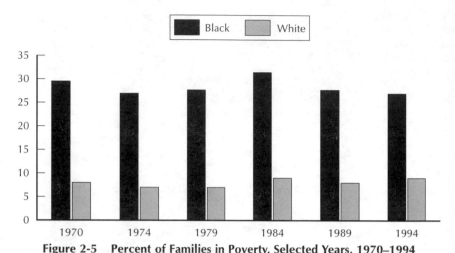

Figure 2-5   Percent of Families in Poverty, Selected Years, 1970–1994

Source: U.S. Bureau of the Census, *Statistical Abstract of the United States, 1996*, Table 738.

Since the government began measuring poverty in 1959, the proportion of black families living in poverty has declined dramatically, from 48 percent to 27.3 percent in 1994. However, the ratio of black-to-white poverty has shown little improvement. Throughout this 35-year period, the proportion of black families classified as poor has fluctuated between three and four times the rate for whites.

As Figure 2-6 and Table 2-4 show, black families are disproportionately poor in every region of the country, and the ratio of black to white poverty is largely unaffected by educational attainment. The poverty rate

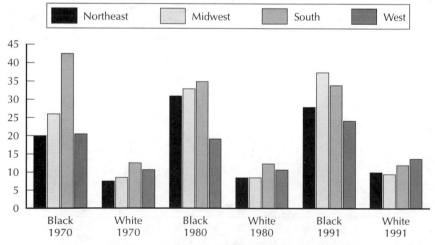

Figure 2-6   Poverty Rates by Race and Region, 1970–1991

Source: U.S. Bureau of the Census, *Poverty in the United States, 1991*, August 1992, Table 9.

Table 2-4 Percent of Families below Poverty Level by Education of Householder, 1994

Education of Householder	Black	White	Black/White Ratio
No High-School Diploma	40.1%	20.6%	1.9
High-School Diploma, No College	26.0	8.5	3.0
Some College, Less than Bachelor's	17.7	6.2	2.9
Bachelor's or More	5.1	2.1	2.4

Source: U.S. Bureau of the Census, *Statistical Abstract of the United States, 1996*, Table 739.

among black college graduates has remained more than twice the rate of their white counterparts.

The constancy and persistence of the ratio of black-to-white poverty suggest that both the factors that cause poverty in general and those that account for the difference in black and white poverty rates are basic features of the American economic system.

BLACK BUSINESS OWNERSHIP

Historically, the low level of black business ownership has been cited as both a cause and an effect of the unequal position of blacks in American life. Consequently, strategies for black advancement have almost always been linked to efforts to increase black business ownership. Such efforts became national policy in the 1960s under the slogan of "black capitalism." Beginning in 1968, the national government inaugurated a series of programs designed to encourage the development of new black-owned firms and to strengthen and sustain existing ones. These programs offered assistance in a variety of ways. Some offered technical and financial assistance to black entrepreneurs. Others specified that certain proportions of federal contracts were to be set aside for minority-owned firms. Many state and local governments adopted similar programs. Governments were joined by many of the nation's large philanthropic foundations and major corporations in their efforts to promote black business development. In spite of such efforts, however, black business ownership remains minuscule. As Table 2-5 shows, although the number of black-owned firms has continued to increase, the significance of black-owned firms in the economy is actually declining.

In 1992, the last year for which data is available, black firms comprised about 2.3 percent of all firms and accounted for slightly less than 1 percent of all business revenues. Between 1987 and 1992, the number of black firms with paid employees actually declined by 8 percent, although the average number of paid employees increased from 3.1 to 5.1.

Gross receipts (not to be confused with profits), that is, the total revenue taken in by a firm and from which all operating costs must be paid, remain exceedingly modest. Average gross receipts for all black-owned firms

Table 2-5   Selected Characteristics of Black-Owned Businesses, 1982–1992

	1982	*1987*	*1992*
Number of Firms	308,260	424,175	620,912
Number w/Paid Employees	37,741	70,815	64,478
Average Number Employees in Firms with Paid Employees	4.0	3.1	5.1
Average Gross Receipts, All Firms	$31,204	$46,592	$51,854
Average Gross Receipts in Firms with Paid Employees	150,750	199,540	350,347
Average Gross Receipts in Firms without Paid Employees	14,475	15,940	17,266

Source: U.S. Bureau of the Census, *Survey of Minority Owned Business Enterprises*, MB 87, 1990, and MB 92-1, 1992.

was approximately $52,000 in 1992, compared to a national average of $350,347.

BLACKS AND WHITES DO NOT SEE THE SAME REALITY

Efforts to use the political process to eliminate black inequality would certainly be enhanced by biracial consensus on the nature and cause of the black predicament and an agreement on the range of appropriate remedial policy choices. Unfortunately for the country, no such consensus exists. Although neither community is monolithic, the perceptions and attitudes of black and white Americans differ markedly on these matters.

Polls show that blacks continue to believe that racial discrimination is the major cause of black inequality, while whites assign greater weight to the behavior of blacks themselves. As Campbell and Schuman put it some time ago:

> While admitting the presence of discrimination, white people show a strong tendency to blame the disadvantaged circumstances of Negro life on Negroes themselves. Although they do not subscribe to genetic theories of racial inferiority they find much to criticize in the attitudes and behavior patterns they see as characteristic of Negroes and apparently feel that it is within the power of Negroes to improve their own situation.[13]

Blacks, on the other hand, see a different reality. As one reporter observed:

> To be a black American in 1985 is to be trapped in a no man's land. The trap is to listen to whites happily tell you that the battle against racism has been won, the world is colorblind, you can compete and make it on your own.
> The reality, to black eyes, however, is to know that while life is better than 20 years ago, you still are treated, seen and identified on the basis of your color.[14]

A longitudinal analysis of polling data presented in Tables 2-6, 2-7, and 2-8 firmly supports the foregoing characterization of black and white perceptions. As is evident from the tables, in 1981 and 1989 more than two-thirds of black respondents believed that racial discrimination was the primary cause of black inequality. Perhaps even more foreboding, more than three-fourths of blacks surveyed agreed with the assertion that whites do not want blacks to get ahead. Conversely, 38 percent of whites, a sizable minority, agreed that black inequality was mainly due to racial discrimination but only 18 percent thought that whites did not want blacks to get ahead.

The sharp perceptual differences between blacks and whites are also reflected in their responses to questions about the presence of discrimina-

Table 2-6   Black and White Explanations of Racial Inequality in 1981 and 1989 (Percentages*)

	1981		1989	
	Black	*White*	*Black*	*White*
Mainly due to discrimination				
Yes	67%	38%	69%	46%
No	27	58	29	52
Because blacks have less inborn ability				
Yes	25	23	24	14
No	69	74	76	84
Because blacks don't have chance for education it takes to rise out of poverty				
Yes	72	53	67	63
No	25	44	31	36
Because blacks don't have sufficient will power or motivation				
Yes	47	58	44	43
No	47	36	54	54
Because whites don't want blacks to get ahead				
Yes	74	46	75	43
No	20	47	20	52
There is discrimination, but many of the problems are brought on blacks by themselves				
Yes	50	73	52	56
No	40	19	42	35

*Percentages do not total 100 because "no response" and "don't know" answers are omitted.

Source: Adapted from Table 5-3 in Lee Sigelman and Susan Welch, *Black Americans' Views of Racial Inequality* (New York: Cambridge University Press, 1991), p. 91.

Table 2-7   Black and White Perceptions of Discrimination
against Blacks, 1981 and 1989 (Percentages[a])

	1981		*1989*	
	Black	*White*	*Black*	*White*
Getting a quality education				
Discriminated	27%	6%	37%	11%
Not discriminated	68	90	61	87
Getting decent housing				
Discriminated	42	16	52	20
Not discriminated	53	78	47	76
Getting unskilled labor jobs[b]				
Discriminated	41	10		
Not discriminated	50	83		
Getting skilled labor jobs				
Discriminated	56	19	53	15
Not discriminated	36	72	44	79
Getting managerial jobs				
Discriminated	57	22	61	23
Not discriminated	31	64	36	71

[a]Do not total 100 because "don't know" and "no response" omitted.
[b]Not asked in 1989.
Sources: Polling data from national surveys. Adapted from Table 3-3 in Lee Sigelman and Susan Welch, *Black Americans' Views of Racial Inequality* (New York: Cambridge University Press, 1991), p. 57.

tion in various aspects of American life. In the five areas listed in Table 2-7, a preponderant majority of whites in 1981 and 1989 believed that there was no discrimination in the three job-related categories nor in education or housing, but a majority of blacks in 1989 believed that there was discrimination in the job market and in housing. In 1997 whites were even more sanguine about the treatment of blacks in education, housing, and the job market. A majority of blacks in 1997 also believed that they had as good a chance as whites in education and housing, and 46 percent believed that matters were equal in the job market.

Differences in the perceptions of blacks and whites also extend to their views of the major issues facing the country and their assessment of existing policies and circumstances. During the 1984 presidential campaign, a Joint Center for Political Studies-Gallup poll[15] found that 48 percent of whites were satisfied and 43 percent were dissatisfied with the "way things were going," but 79 percent of blacks said they were dissatisfied and only 14 percent reported being satisfied. In 1997, 51 percent of whites and 44 percent of blacks reported that they were satisfied with the "way things are going in the United States."

The 1984 survey revealed that 68 percent of whites thought that the situation "had gotten better for blacks" over the past five years and only 4

Table 2-8   Black and White Attitudes
about the Black Predicament, 1997 (Percentages)

	Black	White
Blacks treated same as whites	49%	76%
Blacks treated less fairly		
on the job	45	74
in downtown stores and malls	46	19
by police	60	30
Blacks have as good a chance as whites		
to get any kind of job	46	79
to get quality education	63	79
to get quality housing	58	86
Quality of life for blacks has improved		
over past ten years	33	58
Government should make every effort		
to improve conditions for blacks	59	43
Government should not make any special		
effort; blacks should help themselves	30	59

Source: Adapted from *Gallup Poll Social Audit on Black and White Relations in United States,* June 1997, Gallup Poll Organization.

percent of whites thought the conditions of blacks had gotten worse. Among blacks themselves, 30 percent said that things had gotten worse and 37 percent agreed that things had gotten better. By 1997, 58 percent of whites felt that the quality of life for blacks had improved over the last ten years, but only 33 percent of blacks felt the same.

Perhaps even more indicative of the perceptual gap between the two groups are their responses to the question, "Do you think most white people want to see blacks get a better break, or do they want to keep blacks down?" Forty percent of the black respondents felt that whites wanted to keep blacks down, while 23 percent disagreed. The white response was just the opposite, with 43 percent viewing white intentions in a positive light.

Finally, in 1984, 38 percent of blacks but only 6 percent of white respondents listed "civil rights of minorities" as a major public policy issue. And in 1997, 59 percent of whites and 30 percent of blacks believed that government should not make any special effort to improve conditions for blacks and that, instead, blacks should help themselves.

Given the information discussed here, there can be little doubt that blacks and whites see a different reality. However, as mentioned earlier, neither community is monolithic. In both communities there are opinion groups of varying sizes that agree with the majority opinion of the other community. That is to say, on many issues significant numbers of whites agree with the majority of blacks, and vice versa.

For example, even though a preponderance of blacks cite racial discrimination as the primary cause of black inequality, there is considerable support among black respondents for arguments that the behavior of blacks themselves are major contributing factors to black inequality: Some 45 percent of blacks agreed with whites that blacks do not have sufficient will power and motivation to pull themselves out of poverty; 47 percent believe that blacks would be as well off as whites "if they would try harder," and 80 percent of blacks agreed that blacks who are well off financially do not do as much as they should to help other blacks; 30 percent of black respondents said that government should not make special efforts to assist blacks.

Similarly, although whites are less inclined to perceive discrimination, a sizable minority of white respondents agreed that black inequality was due mainly to discrimination. A majority of whites agreed with the proposition that blacks "don't have a chance" to get the education it takes to rise out of poverty. Finally, 37 percent of whites disagreed with the argument that blacks lacked the motivation and will power to pull themselves out of poverty.

In the long run, the level of agreement and the range of shared perceptions among blacks and whites may be more important than perceptual differences because if a consensus is ever developed it will likely grow out of these areas of initial agreement.

CONCLUSION

The examination of socioeconomic data presented in this chapter demonstrates conclusively that the gap between the well-being of blacks and whites remains a reality. Moreover, since 1959 the gap has remained virtually unchanged. About this there can be no dispute. However, much dispute remains about the meaning of this information. What does it tell us about the nature and causes of black inequality? What does it imply about the most promising public policy options for promoting black equality?

There is no agreement on the answers to these questions in either the scholarly literature or the popular media. In 1997, President Clinton created a national commission to promote interracial dialogue on the question of race and deprivation in America. Perhaps that commission will provide some of the answers. In our view, the data suggest that black inequality is systemic and that its elimination will require fundamental changes in the political and economic systems. Why do we hold this view?

During the quarter century covered in this chapter, the American economic system experienced unprecedented economic growth and expansion. This period also witnessed an intense and largely successful campaign to end all government-sanctioned racial discrimination. Most societally significant, overt racially discriminatory practices by private individuals and groups were also eliminated. Yet in spite of these developments, the gap between black and white well-being persisted. It persisted in every area of the country and for every category of educational attainment. Overall, the size of the gap was more or less constant. Black unemployment was consistently twice that of whites, black median income stagnated between 50 and 60 percent of the white median, and the black poverty rate hovered around three times the white poverty rate.

All of this suggests to us that consistent with the tenets of Harris's alternative framework, continuing black inequality is the result of certain dynamics of the American economic and political systems. That is to say, it appears to us that when the basic institutions of American society—institutions such as our schools, financial institutions, corporations, labor unions, and welfare agencies—are functioning according to legal stipulations and consistent with our cultural expectations, they, willy-nilly, routinely create and reinforce conditions of black inequality. If we are correct, the elimination of black inequality will require fundamental changes in the American political and economic systems.

TOPICS FOR DISCUSSION

1. "The nature of the problem of blacks in the American political system is more than socioeconomic inequality. There is an attitudinal dimension that is of equal importance but it is somewhat more difficult to grasp." Discuss the meaning and significance of this comment, and in doing so give particular attention to data that offer evidence on the "attitudinal dimension" of the problem.

2. How can we explain the fact that over the past 25 years the gap between blacks and whites on most indicators of socioeconomic well-being has remained more or less the same, even though black political participation has increased dramatically? To what extent do the frames of reference discussed in Chapter 1 help us understand this paradox?

3. What resources are needed to overcome these inequities? Who has control of them? How can they be brought to bear on the problem?

4. "The struggle to reduce poverty and deprivation among black Americans is, willy-nilly, a struggle to increase these debilities among whites." Evaluate this assertion. For the purpose of discussion, assume that it is valid and discuss its implications for the prospect of solving the race problem.

5. Polling data presented in this chapter show that blacks and whites do not see the same reality. In your view, what accounts for these differences? How can this perceptual gap be overcome?

SUGGESTED READINGS

Braun, Denny. *The Rich Get Richer: The Rise of Income Inequality in the United States and the World*. Chicago, IL: Nelson-Hall Publishers, 1991. A careful analysis of forces that account for income inequality in modern economies.

Carnoy, Martin. *Faded Dreams: The Politics of Economics and Race in America*. New York:

Cambridge University Press, 1994. An examination of the interplay of economics and politics and their impact on the well-being of African Americans in the 1990s.

Dye, Thomas. *The Politics of Inequality.* Indianapolis, IN: Bobbs-Merrill, 1971. Deals with the social and political inequities of the American political system.

Feagin, Joe R., and Melvin Sikes. *Living with Racism: The Black Middle-Class Experience.* Boston, MA: Beacon Press, 1994. Demonstrates how racism affects even the most privileged African Americans.

Glasgow, Douglas G. *The Black Underclass.* San Francisco, CA: Jossey-Bass, 1980. An empathetic analysis written from the perspective of inner city youth.

Hochschild, Jennifer. *Facing Up to the American Dream.* Princeton, NJ: Princeton University Press, 1995. Examines how blacks and whites view each others' economic opportunities and their faith in the American Dream.

Jones, Barbara A. P., ed. *New Perspectives on Unemployment.* New Brunswick, NJ: Transaction, 1984. Collection of ideologically diverse critiques of alternative explanations of unemployment.

National Urban League. *The State of Black America.* Washington, DC: National Urban League, January 1992. A group of essays focusing on the current status of blacks in various areas, for example, economic, education, health, and political participation.

Newman, Dorothy, et al. *Protest, Politics, and Prosperity: Black Americans and White Institutions, 1940–1975.* New York: Pantheon Books, 1978. A critical analysis of historical developments in social and economic institutions with respect to the status of blacks over time (1940–1975) in various issue areas, for example, employment and equal employment opportunity, housing and fair housing legislation, health-care delivery, and job requirements and education.

Schuman, Howard, Carlotta Steeth, and Lawrence Bobo. *Racial Attitudes in America: Trends and Interpretations.* Cambridge, MA: Harvard University Press, 1985. A comprehensive compilation and analysis of survey data on racial attitudes.

Sigelman, Lee, and Susan Welch. *Black Americans' Views of Racial Inequality.* New York: Cambridge University Press, 1991. A comprehensive analysis of the views of African Americans on racial inequality, with some comparison of black and white attitudes.

Smith, Robert C., and Richard Seltzer. *Race, Class, and Culture: A Study in Afro-American Mass Opinion.* Albany, NY: State University of New York Press, 1992. A thorough analysis of the subject using public opinion survey data.

Sniderman, Paul, and Michael Gray. *Race and Inequality, A Study in American Values.* Chatham, NJ: Chatham House, 1985.

Sowell, Thomas. *Economics of Politics and Race.* New York: Quill, 1983. An ambitious effort to place race and politics in an international perspective.

Stewart, James, and Joyce Allen-Smith. *Blacks in Rural America.* New York: Transaction Publishers, 1995. A collection of articles describing and explaining the continued impoverished state of blacks in rural America.

Thurow, Lester. *Generating Inequality: Mechanisms of Distribution in the U.S. Economy.* New York: Basic Books, 1975.

Wilson, William J. *The Declining Significance of Race: Blacks and Changing American Institutions.* Chicago, IL: University of Chicago Press, 1978. An argument that race is becoming less important in American society.

Yates, Michael. *Longer Hours, Fewer Jobs*. New York: Monthly Review Press, 1994. An analysis that demonstrates the systemic character of unemployment and its impact on American workers.

NOTES

1. John E. Jacobs, *The State of Black America* (New York: National Urban League, 1988), p. iii. Reprinted by permission of the National Urban League.
2. Robert A. Dahl, *Polyarchy* (New Haven, CT: Yale University Press, 1971), p. 82. Reprinted by permission.
3. David Swinton, "The Economic Status of African Americans' Limited Ownership and Persistent Inequality," in *Economic Status of Black America* (New York: National Urban League, 1992), p. 95.
4. U.S. Bureau of the Census, *Current Population Reports*, Series P-60, no. 174, *Money Income of Households, Families, and Persons in the United States, 1990* (Washington DC: Government Printing Office, 1991).
5. Swinton, *Economic Status*, p. 93.
6. U.S. Bureau of the Census, *Household Wealth and Ownership, 1988* (Washington DC: U.S. Government Printing Office, 1990).
7. Melvin Oliver and Thomas Shapiro, *Black Wealth/White Wealth, A New Perspective on Racial Inequality* (New York: Routledge, 1977) pp. 5–6.
8. The figures in this discussion of the role of the public sector in black employment are drawn from Andrew Brimmer, "The Future of Blacks in the Public Sector," *Black Enterprise* (November 1985), p. 39.
9. 1994 public sector employment figures were computed from U.S. Office of Personnel Management, *Demographic Profile of the Federal Workforce* (Washington, DC: 1994); and U.S. Bureau of the Census, *Statistical Abstracts of the United States, 1996*, "Labor Force, Employment, and Earnings," various tables (Washington, DC: U.S. Government Printing Office, 1996).
10. See Kirk Johnson, "Blacks Bear the Burden as Government Jobs Dwindle," *New York Times*, February 2, 1997, p. 1.
11. John Reid, "Black America in the 1980s," *Population Bulletin* 37, no. 4 (December 1982), p. 26.
12. John M. Berry, "Jobless Rate Hits 24-Year Low," *Washington Post*, May 3, 1997, p. A-1.
13. Angus Cambell and Howard Schuman, *Racial Attitudes in Fifteen American Cities* (Ann Arbor, MI: Institution of Social Research, University of Michigan, 1968), p. 25.
14. Jack Williams, "So You Think Blacks are Better Off Today than 20 Years Ago?" *Washington Post National Weekly Edition* (April 15, 1985). Quoted in Thomas Cavanagh, *Inside Black America* (Washington, DC: Joint Research Center for Political Studies, 1985) p. 3.
15. Thomas Cavanagh, *Inside Black America*, pp. 2–6.

Chapter 3

The Nature
of the System

When we talk about black politics we are not talking about ordinary politics. And we are not talking about ordinary politics because the American political system has not created a single social community in which the reciprocal rules of politics would apply. Conventional politics cannot solve this problem, because conventional politics is part of the problem. It is part of the problem because the political system is the major bulwark of racism in America. It is part of the problem in the sense that the political system is structured to repel fundamental social and economic change.

We hear a great deal about the deficiencies, real or imagined, of certain black leaders, but not enough attention, it seems to me, is paid to the framework within which they operate. That framework prevents radical growth and innovation—as it was designed to prevent radical growth and innovation.

—Mervyn M. Dymally, "The Black Outsider
and the American Political System"[1]

W hy do people talk about the "system" or the "establishment"? What are the values of the system, and what are its basic features? What are its biases? How do blacks view the system? How are they affected by the system's values, features, and structures? These and related questions comprise the focus of this chapter. Our immediate purpose here is to get an overall view of the system, the political philosophy that conditions it, its values, its features, and its nature.

POLITICAL PHILOSOPHY AND AMERICAN POLITICS

Understanding the political philosophy of a people is one key to understanding their political system, because every political system originates in the context of a political philosophy and, in turn, the political philosophy shapes the growth and development of the political system.

In the United States as in other Western democracies, liberalism is the dominant political philosophy. The struggle for racial justice in the United States has been, on the one hand, a struggle to force the country to fulfill the political promise of the liberal philosophy and on the other hand a critique of its economic limitations. In this section we discuss the nature and function of political philosophy and demonstrate how the liberal philosophy has conditioned the black struggle in the United States.

Political philosophy is comprised of coherent sets of assumptions about the nature of political reality and the political ideals to be pursued.[2] It includes theories about human nature, the origins of government, the relationship between individuals and government and between government and society. Political philosophies also identify practices, institutions, and historical agencies through which the desired future should be pursued. They include ethical standards for judging both individuals and institutions. Thus, a political philosophy stipulates both means and ends and provides evaluative criteria for assessing programs and policies undertaken in its name.

Political philosophies are not the products of idle theorizing. Rather, they originate within the context of ongoing debates about the nature of political reality and struggles over societal goals and the most efficacious means for achieving them. Ordinarily, political philosophies arise as challenges to the status quo. They provide the basis for a different interpretation of reality and give ideological support for an alternative course of human development.

For example, the liberal philosophy of the Enlightenment provided the ideological justification for replacing the old feudal-mercantile order with the liberal state. And in turn, Marxism as a political philosophy made the case for socialism as the successor to the liberal state.

Political philosophies are also both instrumental and symbolic. The institutions, agencies, and practices stipulated by them are instrumental devices through which proponents of the new order can replace their predecessors and build the new world envisaged by the philosophy. The rights of man, popular suffrage, and representative government, for example, were instrumental devices that allowed the rising property classes of the eighteenth and nineteenth centuries to replace the old dominant classes and build the modern liberal state.

Political philosophies are symbolic because the goals, agencies, and institutions proposed by the philosophy become potent symbols around which the entire political process evolves. Goals such as freedom and equality and agencies such as representative government, universal suffrage, and free enterprise, though instrumental in their origin, become ideological precepts and potent political symbols that can be used to condition political behavior and in turn establish the boundaries of legitimate political discourse and debate.

Once the boundaries of legitimacy are established, all contending factions, both those who wish to conserve and those who wish to transform the present system, are expected to embrace the goals implied in the dominant philosophy. And both are expected to pursue their objectives through agencies and institutions sanctioned by the philosophy. Thus, the agencies and institutions articulated by the dominant philosophy are projected as devices for both conservation and transformation.

The quotation from Congressman Mervyn Dymally that introduced this chapter reflects his awareness of this contradiction. He suggests that the "rules" within which American politics are played are structured to prevent the kind of changes that might eliminate black inequality. Yet blacks are obliged to defer to these rules in their struggle for transformation.

The following discussion of some of the important assumptions of liberalism, the dominant philosophy that guides American political practice, will further clarify this contention.

In the course of our discussion, we will distinguish between the liberal philosophy and liberalism—the "L" word used as a pejorative label in political campaigns. As mentioned earlier, the liberal philosophy arose in Europe as a reaction to the authoritarian and restrictive practices of the feudal and mercantile periods. With emphasis on the rights of property holders, the inviolability of individual rights, and its celebration of the emancipatory character of the market economy, the liberal philosophy provided the ideological justification and the structural outline for the rise of the modern capitalist state.

The liberal philosophy provided the ideas and ideals for transforming the old order into a more just and egalitarian system in which the productive capacities of individuals and society could be maximized. Individualism, freedom, and equality were among its basic values and goals. Popular suffrage, representative government, political parties, free market institutions, and other derivative structures were agencies through which the liberal society was to be realized.

To a considerable extent, the liberal philosophy lived up to its promise. Freed from theocratic domination and mercantilist restrictions, the rising property classes of Europe and subsequently the United States created societies with unmatched political freedom and material plenty for some. By the turn of the twentieth century, the new order—the modern liberal state—had been firmly established in the United States, although its promise of egalitarian development was far from a reality. Moreover, the Great Depression of the 1930s demonstrated that the agencies of transformation originally prescribed by liberal philosophy were incapable of obviating the new problems that arose as the liberal state matured.

The new problems included, among other things, unregulated, rapacious business practices, endemic unemployment, an exploited and unprotected workforce, substandard housing and health care, and continuing racial segregation and exploitation. New agencies, institutions, and practices had to be grafted upon existing ones to address these problems. These new agencies, for the most part, involved some form of government intervention. And, as the problems of the mature liberal state became more and more intractable and government interventionist activities proliferated, the role of government in addressing social and economic problems became the primary cleavage in American political thought. Those less supportive of government intervention are identified as conservatives and more supportive ones retain the liberal label. Both, however, are adherents of the liberal philosophy, and both are committed to the preservation of liberal society. They differ on the best means for doing so. In contemporary American political parlance, the "L" word (liberal) is used to refer to those who support greater government intervention to solve social and economic problems.

This schism among the adherents of liberal philosophy in the United States has special implications for the struggle for racial equality and economic justice, because most black strategists have assumed that government intervention is a necessary though not sufficient prerequisite for black advancement. This assumption has of necessity placed blacks as a more or less permanent fixture on the left side of the dominant societal cleavage. And in turn it has robbed blacks of potential political power that could exist under more favorable circumstances. That is to say, if whites were more or less evenly divided, blacks could tilt the system toward interventionist practices.

There are two other elements in liberal philosophy that have special implications for the struggle that we wish to discuss. One is the principle of inequality and immobility of income and wealth, and the other is the portrayal of economic deprivation as a necessary stimulant for economic growth and development. Both of these have had negative effects on the struggle for black advancement. Liberal philosophy offers equality as both a value and a goal, but inequality and immobility of income are culturally sanctioned features of the American political system. By inequality and immobility of income, we mean that a rather small segment of the population receives a disproportionately large share of the national income and that the pattern of inequality remains more or less constant. Kolko,[3] for example, has shown that when the population is divided into tenths, the top one-tenth receives an amount equal to the share received by the bottom five-tenths and that this pattern has existed throughout the twentieth century. Recent reports suggest that changes in this pattern are unlikely to occur in the foreseeable future.[4]

Regarding the nature and causes of material deprivation, liberal philosophy argues that individual rights and responsibilities are paramount and that government's primary responsibility is to create and safeguard conditions under which individual fulfillment can be pursued. To create such conditions, the philosophy suggests, market forces should be allowed to function unhampered by arbitrary intervention. Such a course of action, it is said, would ensure wise and efficient allocation of resources and, in the process, would provide an adequate standard of living for all who are willing to work.

But, according to some liberal philosophers—both historical and contemporary—the masses must be goaded or cajoled into productive labor. As Townsend argued in the late nineteenth century:

> Hunger will tame the fiercest animals, it will teach decency and civility, obedience and subjection to the most perverse. In general, it is only hunger which can spear and goad them [the poor] on to labor.[5]

Thus, liberal philosophy condones drastic income inequality but depicts poverty and deprivation as the result of individual or group failure. The special significance of these two related aspects of liberal philosophy lies in the way in which they structure perceptions of black deprivation and condition public discussions of appropriate policy responses.

Due to reasons discussed elsewhere in this book, blacks cluster disproportionately in the bottom tenths of the national income pyramid. The systemic forces that account for the inequality and immobility of income in the broader population make it difficult for blacks to advance as a group. An interlocking set of social customs, economic institutions, political practices, and legal conventions—all conditioned by the ideology of white supremacy— produce conditions that sustain the deprived state of African Americans.

However, inasmuch as liberal philosophy portrays deprivation as a largely self-inflicted debility, public policy discussions focus more on reforming black individuals and groups than on reforming the system itself. We see this in the unending stream of welfare and education reform schemes designed to treat the symptoms rather than their systemic causes.

There are other political values that condition our understanding of the problem. They too are conditioned by the liberal philosophy. To them we now turn.

AMERICAN POLITICAL VALUES AND "THE PROBLEM"

Individualism, Equality, and Freedom

Individualism, equality, and freedom are values that are interwoven in the American political fabric. But the definition, scope, and application of these values remain illusive and subject to intense controversy. The Declaration of Independence provides one of the earliest and most vivid expressions of these concepts in the American experience. In it, Thomas Jefferson wrote that "all men are created equal and are endowed by their Creator with certain inalienable rights ... and among these are life, liberty, and the pursuit of happiness." Government, according to Jefferson, was instituted to secure these ends. Whenever any government destroys them—that is life, liberty, or property—it is the right of the people to throw off such governments and to institute others that will secure these ends.

Here, we get the basic thrust for the notions of individualism: the importance and worth of each individual and the view that individuals have certain "rights" with which no state government should interfere. Indeed, it is the very purpose of government to protect these rights. This emphasis upon the importance and worth of the individual is certainly one of the main currents throughout the history of liberal-democratic thought. Similarly, we get the notion of equality, a noble concept but a difficult one to harness. As it has evolved in the American experience, we may view equality as having three parts: political, legal, and social.

Political equality is perhaps best expressed, at least in more recent times, through the "one person, one vote" principle. Each person's vote in public affairs—elections—should count the same as that of any other person. By *legal equality* is meant that no person is above the law; all are subject to the law. Put another way, every individual is equal under the law. All people have the right to life, liberty, and property. This means, in terms of *social equality*, that individuals should not be treated badly because of their station in life or the circumstances of their birth. Each person should enjoy an equal chance to succeed in life and develop to full potential within the limits of the human and material resources available to them.

This, in turn, requires that all individuals should have maximum freedom to do what they choose to chart their lives and to determine their own interest as they see fit without external interference, especially from government. To exercise such self-determination in pursuit of their chosen interests or goals is the essence of *freedom*. This means that the individual has certain rights and freedoms upon which government should not intrude. In short, government has *limits*. It is in our understanding of individual freedom that we begin to see the central features of American politics.

Government, of course, is not the only corporate body that may interfere with the exercise of individual freedom. Large corporations and professional associations, because of their control over material resources and access to channels of impersonal communications, may effectively alter the range of choices available to individuals. Indeed, they may influence the individual's perception of what the possible choices can be.[6] The individual has at least a formal political relationship with government. But with other corporate bodies there may be no formal relationship at all and thus no avenues for redressing grievances. Thus private power may be just as important as government in constraining or facilitating individual freedom.

These basic political values, however, were not originally meant to apply to blacks. This was true of Jefferson's Declaration of Independence as well as other early American documents, including the Constitution. That this was the case was forcefully shown by Chief Justice Taney in the *Dred Scott* decision. However, these values did not begin with Jefferson; nor, of course, did they end with him. Indeed, putting the basic values of liberal-democratic theory into practice is quite another matter. Intense controversy continues over the definition, scope, and application of these values. For one thing, in particular circumstances these values may and do collide and conflict with each other. Individualism, for example, may conflict with what many might think is necessary to safeguard the "public interest" or to promote the "general welfare."

As the history of African Americans in this country clearly shows, the denial of these basic values can diminish both the material and the psychological well-being of a people and lead to persistent frustrations. And such frustrations may lead to disruptive behavior, which can affect the individual as well as society. In part, this is an example of the interrelationship among the three values. Political, social, and legal equality are so closely related that it is difficult, if not impossible, to enjoy one type of equality if denied the other types. Or put another way, to deny equality in one area affects the realization of equality in other areas. Many blacks, because of socioeconomic inequities, do not enjoy political or legal equality, and vice versa.

Of course, some may hold that the American concept of equality is not as all-encompassing as just described. It is plausible to suggest that the central thread running through the development of the idea of equality in America is something that may be called "equality of opportunity." But, as exemplified in *Regents* v. *Bakke*, there is considerable disagreement over the meaning of this phrase. Many view "equality of opportunity" in a very formal, legal manner. They point to the civil rights laws of the 1950s and 1960s to support their position. Past history aside, they argue, the fact is that now (since the passage of these laws) there is "equality of opportunity," and this concept should be accepted and applied equally to *all* persons. Indeed, the differences of interpretation have apparently cost blacks the support of some of their traditional allies. But our view is that, as thus construed, "equality of opportunity" has become a fashionable way by which many white liberals and others, whether they mean to or not, continue the status quo in American society. Sufficient attention must be given to overcoming the "accumulated disadvantages"—incurred in over 200 years of massive deprivation, authorized in law, and actualized in practice—before the *formal* "equality of opportunity" as articulated in recent court decisions and civil rights laws takes on real meaning. The doctrine does indeed ring hollow when it is so often used to rationalize vacuous notions like "reverse discrimination," or as an explanation when blacks and other minorities are denied jobs and other advantages because they are not "qualified." The data presented in Chapter 2 and throughout the volume clearly suggest that the wide disparities between blacks and whites in the socioeconomic realm are due to a combination of racial discrimination and certain basic features of the American economy rather than to "individual differences." They suggest to us that perhaps equal opportunity should be considered a means for achieving the ultimate goal of equal outcomes.

Majority Rule and Minority Rights

In a sense, the concept of minority rights is reflected in our discussion of individualism. But we compare it here with majority rule to indicate how Americans hold to two values that seem to be contradictory. The idea that political decisions should be made by majority rule (or at least by pluralities) is based on the premise that individuals enjoy political equality, that is, that one person's vote should count as much as the next. Thus, there is a strong preference that decisions of the majority (or plurality) should prevail over any minority or smaller group of individuals. Having majority rule work as a way of making decisions rests as much on acquiescence of the minority as it does on the sheer weight of numbers of the majority. But, as we have indicated, Americans hold to both majority rule and minority rights. Therefore, there is a built-in tension between the two values. This tension involves not only the *process* of making decisions but also the *content* of the decision. For majority rule to be accepted as legitimate and for it to prevail without coercion, it must respect and have the respect of minorities.

Majority rule is perhaps an ideal way of making public decisions in a homogeneous political community in which there is a high consensus on values and a widely accepted agreement on what to disagree about. In the absence of fundamental antagonisms, parties to a dispute are willing to accept the outcome of majority decisions because they have no reason to fear that the outcome will severely threaten the survival of their way of life. And equally as important, they can be confident that in other future conflicts their side has a good chance of being part of the prevailing majority.

In the United States, unfortunately, the race question has always been a fundamental antagonism, particularly between blacks and whites. Substantial factions from each community are inclined to view an unfavorable outcome as a threat to its way of life. Under such circumstances, majority rule decisions are often met with defiance by one side or the other. Such tensions are inherent when there is a commitment to both majority rule and minority rights.

Legalism

We have heard many times the expression that America has a "government of laws and not of men." The phrase symbolizes the legalistic mold of the American political system. The chief symbol of this American attachment to legalism is the written Constitution, which is the fundamental law. From the town or city council to the state and national governments, the citizen is overwhelmed with legalism. It flows from laws enacted by legislative bodies, with orders of executives, and with rules and regulations coming from many bureaucratic structures. In this sort of situation, the symbols assume an importance of their own, aside from the actual impact of particular laws on individuals. This strong attachment to the idea of written law is accompanied by the view that it is not only practical but also *desirable* to have such regulations. This idea is so widespread in American thinking that it goes beyond government policies and actions and extends into private life and organizations. Consequently, it is not unusual for a new organization or club to argue about "bylaws" that will govern the group's activities.

To be sure, the attachment to legal forms is important to the function of the political system. The law is used to shape major directions or change in social policy. And it is called into play in distributing benefits, costs, policies, and programs to various groups. But laws, no matter how well written, are neither self-enforcing nor self-interpreting. Moreover, the law is not always what the statute says it is. Frequently, one can find gaps or room to maneuver within the legal boundaries. It is this characteristic of American law that can be as important to individual citizens as that which is written. In any event, this preoccupation with law and legalism gives importance to those who are trained in law. It gives lawyers a dominant role in politics and government far beyond their sheer numbers. It also points up the importance of courts as policy-making arenas in allocating benefits and values in the political system. This subject is explored more fully in Chapter 5.

The excessive attention that Americans often give to the law and legalism sometimes obscures a fundamental point about the law and the American political system—to a great extent, the law is but a reflection of the resolution of conflicts between factions contending for material advantage. When bills are passed or rulings are made by courts and regulatory bodies, there are winners and losers. Invariably the winners attempt to make their victory permanent by incorporating its terms into the permanent law. The losers seek to minimize their loss by influencing the interpretation and implementation of the law as best they can.

When the law is viewed in this fashion, the expression that the United States is a government of laws and not of men takes on a different meaning. It means merely that present conflicts are regulated and moderated by the community-sanctioned resolutions of past conflicts.

Conflict but Compromise

Given their heterogeneous population mix, Americans have come to expect conflict. But we have also come to expect that conflict can be managed. Conflicts cover many issues in American life. They may be drawn along a number of lines: racial, ethnic, social, economic, political, or, more likely, over a combination of these. And as we shall discuss later, some of this conflict is built into the system itself. In any event, the racial conflict (or problem) cuts across all these lines. It promotes sharp divisions and provokes strong emotions from the parties involved. To many Americans, mainly white Americans, it is a conflict that not only has to be managed by the system, but one that can also be managed through restraint and reason.

Essentially, this means that both sides must give a little and compromise their differences. This willingness to compromise is perhaps the most important characteristic of American politics. Neither side can expect the other side to give in completely; the *American* way is the *middle* way. To hold fast to your position, no matter what the cause, is viewed as hostile, unsportsmanlike, uncooperative. All "legitimate" positions must fall within the prevailing consensus on what to disagree about. Positions that do not are considered extremist and therefore illegitimate.

Identification of what constitutes the middle way, however, is contingent upon prior understanding of what are the outermost boundaries of legitimate debate and conflict in American politics. The boundaries were established initially by the Federalists and anti-Federalists when the Republic was founded in 1789. Both accepted the white supremacist ideology. Their major differences centered around the role of the government in the economy. This cleavage, though modified by circumstances of history, remains the primary point of debate in American politics.

When the country was founded, political participation was limited to property-holding white men, and the differences, which became the dominant cleavage in American politics, reflected the interests of and divisions within the propertied classes. These classes, then, established the prevailing boundaries and determined the rules of the political game.

Over the years, of course, the American political process became democratized as non-property-holding white men, black men, and later women were eventually given the franchise. However, as Schattschneider pointed out some time ago,[7] new participants entering the political system were obliged to accept the existing boundaries and to pursue their interests within the constraints and according to the rules imposed by them. These conditions for admission as participants in the American political system undermined the effectiveness of black political participation as a strategy for black advancement because, as mentioned earlier, the existing rules of the game created and reinforced the conditions that are responsible for black inequality.

FEATURES OF THE SYSTEM

The political values we just discussed are so tied to the nature of American politics that it is difficult to say whether such values have more influence on the system or vice versa. What we can say is that both the values and the features of the system reinforce one another. For example, the idea that the people are sovereign, that they are supreme, is firmly implanted in the Constitution and its amendments. This supremacy is voiced by the people through regular and periodic elections in selecting a representative government. The people, however, retain sovereignty. Through a written constitution they limit what the representatives can do. This is the idea of limited government. It finds expression in the Constitution through such provisions as the delegated powers of the Congress and the Bill of Rights. The Bill of Rights, for example, is designed to limit governments from intruding upon the rights of the individual. But, as with many features of American government, when we go below the surface a number of factors emerge. The problem of defining the people (and hence making the concept of popular sovereignty work) has been a continuing one for democratic governments generally and American government in particular. The problem is one of inclusion and exclusion. Blacks, women, 18-year-olds, as well as malapportioned urban residents, readily come to mind. And while all of these groups are now formally included as part of the people, their actual inclusion may be another matter. For, as African Americans well know, constitutional-legal inclusion does not necessarily guarantee inclusion in practice.

Let us explore this idea a bit further. Elections are a main way to translate popular sovereignty into working, *representative* government. But this raises a number of questions. For example, what are the dynamics of American elections? What are the structures of elections? What consequences flow from these structures, such as single-member districts or the frequency of elections? Who is advantaged by these structures? Who is disadvantaged? In the single-member district, for instance, the winner takes all. This means that the majority (even if a coalition of minorities) rules and the minority loses. But elections, as we know, afford a way of managing conflict, quieting issues, and promoting compromises.

In any event, the election winner is pictured as representing all constituents. And the official may indeed try very hard to reflect the views of all constituents up to the point that it tends to jeopardize chances for reelection. But can an official *really* represent a group if the official is not a member of that group? This, of course, raises an age-old question about representation. We pose it here only to emphasize its continuing importance to blacks and others insofar as it pertains to the structure of elections and the nature of representative government.

Of course, other constitutional-legal features, such as federalism and separation of powers, also shape our political landscape. With respect to federalism, the Constitution provides for a division of powers and authority between a central government and the states. This division of powers certainly has consequences for how we deal with problems and how we manage conflict. For one thing, it means that the number of forums to deal with conflict is 51 rather than 1, as would be the case of a single central government. This increase in the number of forums to deal with conflict often brings about an increase in conflict itself. And, of course, some people see benefits in using states as experimental political laboratories. Others see the need for unified action, for a single national policy. The point here is that federalism is not without its advantages and disadvantages in given situations. Federalism, for example, permitted southern states to "handle" the racial problem as they saw fit; this worked to the advantage of whites but to the serious disadvantage of blacks. In any event, federalism, like so much of the political system, often requires negotiations, bargaining, and compromise among various controlling interests in state and national government.

The Constitution also incorporates the doctrine of *separation of powers*. Under this doctrine, the authority of the national government is divided among three branches: legislative, executive, and judicial. The functions are allocated accordingly: The legislature makes laws, the executive enforces laws, and the judiciary interprets laws. But the lines of separation are not this neatly drawn. Indeed, under another arrangement—*checks and balances*—the Constitution also gives each branch some say in how the other branches carry on their functions. For example, Congress can pass legislation, but the president may veto it. However, the legislation can still become law if Congress can muster enough votes (two-thirds of both houses) to re-pass it over the president's veto. And, of course, the Supreme Court can invalidate laws passed by Congress, even those approved by the president. But the Constitution provides the Supreme Court with neither the "sword nor the purse" to enforce rulings. It must depend on the president and others to do so. Thus, while the Constitution provides for three independent branches, at the same time it so intermingles their authority as to make it necessary for the branches to be *interdependent* rather than *independent* of each other. In short, one purpose of the separation of powers and the checks and balances is to keep government officials from becoming too powerful.

These constitutional features are also designed to prevent any group, even a majority, from a complete domination of government at any one time. The Constitution provides that officials of the three branches are to be selected for different terms of office and by different constituencies. For example, all members of the House of Representatives are elected every two years from essentially local constituencies, the congressional districts. Presumably, they represent different interests from the senators who are elected statewide for six-year terms, with one-third elected every two years. The president is elected by the entire nation via the electoral college for a four-year term with the entire nation as his constituency. And members of the federal judiciary, including the Supreme Court, are appointed by the president with the approval of the Senate. They hold office for life and are not subject to popular election. Overall, the manner in which the Constitution provides for the selection and tenure of public officials poses formidable barriers to the complete domination of government by any group or interest at a given time. As Parenti has noted, they also insulate government from mass sentiment.[8]

Just as with federalism, the actual operation of the separation of powers and checks and balances fosters both conflict and cooperation. Different constituencies and overlapping terms of office tend to cause conflict. But the fact that the three branches share in each other's powers—as, for example the president and Congress do in law making—tends to compel cooperation and compromise. In short, federalism, separation of powers, and checks and balances reflect the diversity of interests in American politics. They also institutionalize and preserve the prevailing rather than aspiring interests. They promote incremental and marginal change rather than decisive and fundamental change. And no matter what their virtues, these features of American politics pose built-in disadvantages to the kind of decisive, fundamental change needed to deal with problems facing African Americans and other minorities.

The two-party system also stands out as a striking feature of American politics. Our parties have developed as the political system has developed, and vice versa. Indeed, so interwoven are political parties within the political system that many Americans perhaps assume that such organizations are expressly provided for in the Constitution. They are not. Understandably, then, the two-party system both influences and promotes the dominant political values of the system. Consider, for example, that the role of parties in forming majorities leads to an attempt to get diverse interests and individuals to work together and to the necessity of conflict management through moderation and compromise. As Sorauf put it:

> At the most fundamental level the American parties, and those of the other democracies, serve democracy by reaffirming and promoting its basic values. The very activities of the two gigantic and diversified American parties promote a commitment to the values of compromise, moderation, and the pursuit of limited goals. They also encourage the political activity and participation that a democracy depends on. And they reinforce the basic democratic rules of the game: the methods and procedures of orderly criticism and opposition, change by the regular electoral processes, and deference to the will of the majority.[9]

Political parties certainly reinforce the basic values of American politics. These organizations operate on and promote the assumption that all problems can be settled peacefully within the political system. That parties are large and diversified organizations also means that they handle problems so as to promote the values of "compromise, moderation, and the pursuit of limited goals." As such, our party system serves to reinforce the type of "incremental and marginal change" that is so characteristic of American politics. At the same time, the political parties serve as barriers to fundamental change.

ON ELITES AND POLITICAL PARTICIPATION

African Americans, perhaps more than other citizens, have reason to show more concern over elites and "the tyranny of the majority." They are, despite increased participation and importance in the political process, almost a "permanent minority" in American politics. Many blacks continue to be the

Recognizing the importance of group solidarity in interest group politics, a million African American men marched in Washington, DC, to call attention to continuing inequities in American democracy. *(James Nubile/The Image Works)*

victims of discriminatory practices, as individuals and as a group. The notions of majority rule and agreement on values combine with the elite presence to make up a political system that African Americans view as inevitably hostile to their interests. From the perspective of the black minority, the middle-class, "politically actives," "amateur democrats," as well as the upper class, constitute an establishment. Because the consensus on American values depends heavily on the actions and attitudes of such groups, the black minority tends to regard them as essentially the same with respect to black concerns.

In the late 1950s social scientists such as Floyd Hunter and C. Wright Mills produced books that seemed to show that there existed what has come to be known as the "power elite" in most American communities. These elites were said to exercise much influence on the shaping of public policy. Seldom were the members of these elite groups elected officials. Their activities were frequently out of the public view. The work of these two scholars touched off an academic debate that continues to the present.[10]

In this chapter we do not directly enter the power elite debate. However, we do take the position that at both the national and local levels certain individuals, because of their institutional affiliations and positions, exercise greater political power than others and that blacks are woefully underrepresented in such positions.

Thomas Dye[11] has attempted to identify a "national institutional elite" by identifying what he calls the major national institutions and the positions of authority within each of them. He divides American society into 12 sectors: (1) industrial corporations, (2) utilities, (3) banking, (4) insurance, (5) investments, (6) mass media, (7) law, (8) education, (9) foundations, (10) civic and cultural organizations, (11) government, and (12) the military. Using admittedly subjective criteria, Dye determines which firms or units within each sector are "major institutions" and which positions within these institutions are positions of authority.

Dye's system revealed 7,314 positions of authority occupied by 5,778 different individuals. Only 20 of them were black.[12] He concluded that "no blacks have ever been presidents of a major industrial corporation, bank, utility, insurance company, investment firm, communication network, prestigious university, or top civic cultural organization."[13] Since that time a small number of black men and an even smaller number of black women have ascended to positions in the elite establishment, but their numbers remain minuscule.

Dye's system for identifying the elite is open to question.[14] However, any other system would in all probability yield similar results. No matter what criteria are used, only a few blacks are among the power elite. Moreover, the process of institutional elite recruitment is such that those who ultimately reach such institutional position, be they black or white, will likely share the dominant institutional outlook.

CONCLUSION

The American political system is grounded in the liberal philosophy of the Enlightenment, which offered individualism, equality, and freedom as major values and which championed representative government, popular suffrage, and free market economic institutions as historical agencies through which the goals of a more just and egalitarian society could be realized.

The system that eventually evolved in the United States has been one of unprecedented material advancement and widespread political participation. African Americans, however, have not shared equally in the material development of the country. Nor have they been equal political participants. This is so because certain other values embedded in liberal philosophy and reinforced by the ideology of white supremacy gave rise to an interlocking set of economic, political, and cultural forms that create and sustain conditions of black inequality.

Liberal philosophy accepts income inequality and immobility as part of the natural order of things. For well-known historical reasons, blacks have always been represented disproportionately among the impoverished of America. The institutions and practices that routinely function to sustain income inequality and income immobility in general also sustain black inequality.

TOPICS FOR DISCUSSION

1. The text states that "it is plausible to suggest that the central thread running through the development of the idea of equality in America is something that may be called 'equality of opportunity.'" But the text goes on to state that "there is much disagreement over the meaning of the term, that is, 'equality of opportunity.'" What is the nature of this disagreement? How might it relate to the controversy over the current problems that disproportionately affect blacks? Discuss.

2. Liberal democracy seeks to ensure equal opportunity for all and protection of minority rights while egalitarian democracy is committed to equal outcomes. Can racial inequalities in America be eliminated so long as the United States remains committed to liberal democracy?

3. The political value system in America contains values that appear (at certain times, at least) to be contradictory. For example, some of the connotations of "individualism" (and "minority rights") seem contradictory or in opposition to the value of "majority rule." Discuss how these values—individualism (minority rights) and majority rule—work to the advantage and disadvantage of blacks and other minorities in their struggle for equality.

4. It has been suggested that certain features of the American political system (e.g., separation of powers, two-party system) pose built-in disadvantages to the kind of decisive, fundamental change needed to deal with problems facing blacks and other minorities. Do you agree with this view? Are there situations in which these features might work to the *advantage* of blacks and minorities? Discuss.

5. "Constant unemployment and poverty are enduring systemic features of the U.S. economic system. Institutional racism allocates these debilities disproportionately among black Americans." Evaluate this assertion and discuss its implications for efforts to achieve racial equality.

SUGGESTED READINGS

Ani, Marimba. *Yuguru: An African-Centered Critique of European Cultural Thought and Behavior*. Trenton, NJ: Africa World Press, 1994. A critical analysis of European and American political philosophy and thought.

Bachrach, Peter. *The Theory of Democratic Elitism*. Boston, MA: Little, Brown, 1967. A critique of the democratic creed in America.

Cruse, Harold. *Plural but Equal*. New York: William Morrow, 1987. A critical examination of the position of blacks and the performance of black leadership in America's plural society.

Dahl, Robert A. *Pluralist Democracy in the United States: Conflict and Consent*. Chicago, IL: Rand McNally & Co., 1967. An analysis of the American political system by one of the leading exponents of pluralism.

———. *Who Governs? Democracy and Power in an American City*. New Haven, CT: Yale University Press, 1961. A description of decision making in New Haven, Connecticut, exemplifies how pluralist democracy operates in that city.

Dye, Thomas. *Who's Running America? Institutional Leadership in the United States*. Upper Saddle River, NJ: Prentice Hall, 1996. A theoretical and empirical analysis of the leadership class in the United States.

Feagin, Joe, and Herman Vera. *White Racism*. New York: Routledge, 1995. Probes the

dynamics of white racism through analysis of a number of recent racist incidents in the United States.

Fresia, Jerry. *Toward an American Revolution*. Boston, MA: South End Press, 1988.
Analysis of the nondemocratic forces that influenced the drafting of the U.S.
Constitution.

Hacker, Andrew. *Two Nations*. New York: Ballantine Books, 1995. Demonstrates how
racism continues to divide American society.

Hartz, Louis. *The Liberal Tradition in America: An Interpretation of American Political
Thought since the American Revolution*. New York: Harcourt Brace, 1955.

Holden, Matthew, Jr. *The White Man's Burden*. New York: Chandler Publishing Co.,
1973. An examination of the possibilities of the American republic to reconcile
racial conflict.

Kariel, Henry S. *The Decline of American Pluralism*. Stanford, CA: Stanford University
Press, 1961. A critique of pluralism in the American political system.

Levitan, Sar A., et al. *Still a Dream*. Cambridge, MA: Harvard University Press, 1975.
A thoughtful analysis of the changing status of black Americans from 1960 to
1975.

Marable, Manning. *How Capitalism Underdeveloped Black America*. Boston, MA: South
End Press, 1983. An ambitious effort to show that black inequality is a function of the dynamics of U.S. capitalist development.

Mills, C. Wright. *The Marxists*. New York: Dell, 1962. Provides a conceptual framework for analyzing political philosophies and succinct descriptions of both the
liberal and Marxist political philosophies.

———. *The Power Elite*. New York: Oxford University Press, 1956. A study of the
dominance of "power elite" in the American social system.

Newman, William M. *American Pluralism: A Study of Minority Groups and Social Theory*.
New York: Harper & Row, 1973. Pluralism examined in the context of the
attempts by minority groups to participate effectively in American society.

Oliver, Melvin, and Thomas Shapiro. *Black Wealth/White Wealth*. New York: Routledge,
1997. Advances a new perspective on racial inequality by suggesting that it is
the absence of wealth that sustains black inequality and that the creation of
black wealth is a necessary condition for black advancement as a group.

Parenti, Michael. *Democracy for the Few*, 3rd ed. New York: St. Martin's Press, 1980.
Focuses on the theme that the American political system functions to serve the
interests of corporate wealth at the expense of the majority of the people.

Perry, Huey, and Wayne Parent. *Blacks and the American Political System*. Gainesville,
FL: University of Florida Press, 1995. A collection of original essays on blacks
and the political process by a diverse group of scholars.

Smith, Robert. *Racism in the Post Civil Rights Era: Now You See It Now You Don't*. Albany,
NY: State University of New York Press, 1996. Offers an incisive definition of
racism and institutional racism and discusses the more subtle manifestation of
racism in contemporary America.

NOTES

1. Mervyn M. Dymally, ed., *The Black Politician: His Struggle for Power* (Belmont, CA:
Wadsworth, Inc., 1971), p. 120. Reprinted by permission of the publisher,
Duxbury Press.

2. This discussion of the nature of political philosophy is adapted from C. Wright Mills, *The Marxist* (New York: Dell, 1962), pp. 11–29.

3. Gabriel Kolko, *Wealth and Power in America* (New York: Praeger, 1962), pp. 14–20.

4. See David Swinton, "The Economic State of Black America in the 1980s," in *The State of Black America 1990*, ed. Janet Ewart (New York: National Urban League, 1990), pp. 31–32. See also Martin Carnoy, *Faded Dreams* (New York: Cambridge University Press, 1994), especially Chapters 5 and 6.

5. William Townsend, *Dissertation on the Poor Laws*, cited in Paul Therkildsen, *Public Assistance and American Values* (Albuquerque, NM: University of New Mexico, 1964), p. 9.

6. For further explication, see Michael Parenti, *Inventing Reality, The Politics of the Mass Media* (New York: St. Martin's Press, 1986).

7. E. E. Schattschneider, *The Semisovereign People* (New York: Holt, Rinehart & Winston, 1964).

8. See Michael Parenti, *Democracy for the Few* (New York: St. Martin's Press, 1987). See also Jerry Fresia, *Toward an American Revolution, Exposing the Constitution and Other Illusions* (Boston, MA: South End Press, 1988), especially Chapter 3.

9. See Frank J. Sorauf, *Party Politics in America*, 3rd ed. (Boston, MA: Little, Brown, 1976), Chapter 8.

10. For the original statements of these views, see Floyd Hunter, et al. *Community Power Structure* (Chapel Hill, NC: University of North Carolina Press, 1953); and C. Wright Mills, *The Power Elite* (New York: Oxford University Press, 1956). Perhaps the most notable critiques of the positions set forth in these works are contained in Robert A. Dahl, *Who Governs* (New Haven, CT: Yale University Press, 1960); and Nelson W. Polsby, *Community Power and Political Theory* (New Haven, CT: Yale University Press, 1963). The writings of Peter Bachrach and Morton Baratz provide a contrasting interpretation to those presented by Dahl and Polsby; the reader should carefully examine the arguments put forth in their essay "The Two Faces of Power," *American Political Science Review* (1962), pp. 947–952.

11. Thomas Dye, *Who's Running America*, 5th ed. (Englewood Cliffs, NJ: Prentice Hall, 1990).

12. *Ibid.*, p. 197.

13. *Ibid.*, p. 199.

14. Dye's system defines institutional elites as (1) those occupying positions of authority in companies controlling over half of the nation's total corporate assets; (2) those occupying formal positions of authority in the major civilian and military bureaucracies of the national government; and (3) those occupying positions of authority in the mass media, prestigious law firms, major philanthropic foundations, the leading universities, and the recognized national civic and cultural organizations.

Chapter 4

The Quest
for Political Power

A race of people who are excluded from public office will always be second class.

—Tom McCain, quoted in *Civil Liberties*, an ACLU publication[1]

There was a critical limit to what five black councilmen could do. Getting the power to put up that stop sign meant staying on [the white mayor's] good side, and with rare exceptions, the councilmen wouldn't push anything the mayor was dead against.... When it got down to the real thing, power and equity for black people as a group as opposed to doing something for this black and that black, we were up a damn creek.

And anyway, the white majority on the council could do or block whatever it wanted.

—J. L. Chestnut, Jr., civil rights attorney and Selma native[2]

Those who seek change through politics must have the power to persuade or force other political actors to respond in a manner supportive of the desired change. To bring about such a response, the group must have not only the resources necessary to influence the target group but also the means for converting the resources into actual power by bringing them to bear upon those whose behavior must be influenced.

In democratic societies such as the United States, economic wealth, favorable population distribution, voting, and holding public office are all potential sources of power. Each of these can be used to political advantage by those who possess them providing they have the means for converting them into actual power. The politics of African Americans has been a constant struggle to acquire such resources and convert them into actual power.

In previous chapters we discussed economic wealth and black population distribution as political resources. In this chapter the focus is on group mobilization, voting, and holding office as political resources. The struggle to win political power has not been won; it is ongoing. Blacks are still underrepresented in government. Here, we examine three case studies of efforts of blacks to convert these resources into actual political power. The dynamics of the struggle for empowerment through electoral activity is, to an extent, unique to time and place. Accordingly there can be no general model of the process of empowerment. Rather our general understanding must come through case studies over a variety of situations chosen for their theoretical relevance. One case study will examine efforts of blacks in the rural South to achieve empowerment through electoral participation. The second case study discusses the efforts of blacks to achieve political power in Chicago. The third case study analyzes efforts to create a national black political organization to enhance black political empowerment. This chapter also discusses efforts to achieve black empowerment through presidential politics and the rise of black conservatives and their efforts toward resource mobilization.

As we shall see, the efforts to achieve political power have been thwarted by a number of factors, chief among them electoral systems designed to limit the effectiveness of the black vote, co-optation in their alliances with political machines, and the absence of leadership and internal divisions. Political representation is not power; power can only be realized through its expression in the policy responsiveness of governments. Policy responsiveness, in turn, is the result of participation in the dominant governing coalition. The means through which blacks become members of that governing coalition is still under debate.

VOTING AS A LIMITED RESOURCE

Securing the right to vote dominated the black political agenda from Emancipation until the 1960s. Passage of the Voting Rights Act in 1965[3] pushed the struggle for black political empowerment to a new level, and converting black voting strength into political power became the focal point of the black movement.

In order to convert voting strength into actual political power, a group must be able to maximize voter registration and voter turnout, develop institutional structures for recruiting supportive candidates for public office, and mobilize support for such candidates. Once supportive candidates have been elected, the group must develop a system to hold the candidates accountable to the group.

Thus, neither the election of black officeholders nor being the swing vote that determines which white candidate will be elected is *prima facie* evidence that the black vote has been converted into actual political power. The acid test of political power is the extent to which those who are elected with black support are able to secure passage of public policies supportive of black interests. To date, blacks have made considerable progress in stimulating voter registration and electing blacks to political office, but their impact on policy outcomes, however, has been much less pronounced.

Table 4-1 shows the considerable progress that blacks have made in stimulating voter registration. Although black registration continues to lag behind the national rate, since 1965 the gap has been narrowed significantly. Black registration trailed the rate for the total population by ten percentage points in 1966, but by 1984 the difference was less than three percentage points. Some attribute much of the increase in black voter registration to enthusiasm spawned by Jesse Jackson's candidacy for the presidency in 1984 and 1988. By 1992, however, the gap had begun to widen again, but it is still smaller than it was during the 1960s.

Black voters as a percentage of total voters also increased significantly, from 7 percent in 1966 to 10 percent in 1988. Moreover, black voters as a percentage of all voters compared favorably with their percentage of the total voting age population, which was 10 percent.[4]

The voter registration and voter turnout figures reported in Table 4-1, it should be noted, are national estimates. They do not convey the considerable variations that exist throughout the country and among different age groups. These variations can have serious consequences for efforts to convert the vote into political power. For example, in some jurisdictions in which the black vote may be the potential swing vote, registration may be low, and as a result the potential to determine the outcome of close elections may not be realized. In others where blacks constitute preponderant majorities, black registration may be unusually high. There are other electoral districts in which blacks are a majority of the voting age population but a much smaller fraction of the total registered voters.

The process through which voting is operationalized as political power depends, among other things, upon the nature of the electoral environment. If the group is a majority in the electoral district, it can elect a representative

Table 4-1   Reported Registration and Turnout by Race, Selected Years

	Percent Reported They Registered		Percent Reported They Voted	
Presidential Election Years	*Black*	*White*	*Black*	*White*
1980	60.0%	68.4%	50.5%	60.9%
1984	66.3	69.6	55.8	61.4
1988	64.5	67.9	51.5	59.1
1992	63.9	70.1	54.0	63.6
Congressional Election Years				
1982	59.1	65.6	43.0	49.9
1986	64.0	65.3	43.2	47.0
1990	58.8	63.8	39.2	46.7
1994	58.3	64.2	37.0	46.9

Source: U.S. Bureau of the Census, *Statistical Abstract, 1996*, Table 456.

of its own choosing. If it is not, its members must forge coalitions with others to elect candidates and pursue their interests.

Since 1965 blacks have made measurable progress in electing black candidates to public office, especially from electoral units in which they are in the majority. Relatively few black officeholders, however, have been elected from majority white electoral districts.

There were some 8,015 black elected officials in 1993, compared to 1,469 in 1970.[5] However, blacks still constituted only 1.6 percent of all elected officials. The preponderant majority of them, 92 percent, were elected in county and municipal jurisdictions. In 1993, throughout the United States there were only 21 blacks who held statewide elected positions. Although the number of black officials at county and municipal levels is impressive when compared to those at the state and national levels, black representation is far from being proportionate to black voting strength.

MOBILIZATION AND EMPOWERMENT
IN THE ALABAMA BLACK BELT

Contrary to popular perceptions, the civil rights movement and the Voting Rights Act did not immediately put blacks into political office in the South. In a few counties and localities where blacks became voting majorities through the Voting Rights Act, blacks were able to win political power as early as 1970.

In many other communities, however, several decades would pass before blacks would be able to elect representatives of their choice in the South, largely because of the electoral mechanisms adopted by state legislatures after the Civil War to exclude blacks from political power. Many political science textbooks have highlighted the means used to disfranchise blacks, or to prevent blacks from registering and voting, such as literacy tests, poll taxes, and white primaries. Southern states had also adopted more sophisticated electoral devices to dilute or negate the impact of blacks' votes. *Vote dilution* is defined as "the practice of reducing the potential effectiveness of a group's voting strength by limiting its ability to translate that strength into the control of (or at least influence with) elected public officials."[6] Vote dilutive devices such as at-large elections, racial gerrymandering, and majority-vote run-off requirements ensured that if large numbers of blacks voted, they would be unable to elect candidates of their choice. These electoral systems would have to be changed, oftentimes only through lawsuits that took decades to litigate, before blacks could win political office.

One such area is the "Black Belt" counties of southwest Alabama. The struggle by blacks to gain control in this region has been unrelenting for more than a quarter of the twentieth century. The opposition of the white elites has been equally as spirited. In their efforts to prevail, both sides have sought support from both national and state political actors. Consequently, the struggle in the Alabama Black Belt, though local in scope, has national significance.

The Alabama Black Belt is composed of ten contiguous rural counties

ALABAMA BLACK BELT COUNTIES

in southwest Alabama. Blacks are a majority of the population in eight of the counties, and approximately 42 percent in the other two. Some 58 percent of the region's 200,000 inhabitants and 53 percent of the registered voters are black.[7]

The contemporary struggle for empowerment in the Alabama Black Belt goes back to the voter registration campaigns of the early 1960s, which captured national and international attention. The region was a staging ground for much of the political mobilization and agitation that culminated with the passage of the 1965 Voting Rights Act. The Student Nonviolent Coordinating Committee (SNCC), a civil rights organization that played a major role in overturning the racial caste system of the rural South, was active in Lowndes and surrounding counties. Martin Luther King, Jr., and the Southern Christian Leadership Congress Conference conducted campaigns in Greene County. The infamous murders of Jimmie Lee Jackson, a black voter registration worker, and two white sympathizers, the Reverend James Reeb and Viola Liuzzo, all occurred in the Alabama Black Belt.

The area was also the scene of the infamous bloody confrontation on the Edmund Pettis Bridge. On March 7, 1965, 500 civil rights protesters began a 50-mile march from Selma to Montgomery. Met by state troopers at the bridge, they were clubbed and gassed. The horrific event became known as "Bloody Sunday." Violence and intimidation, along with discriminatory

On March 7, 1965, civil rights protesters marching from Selma to Montgomery were clubbed and gassed by state troopers. A few days later, Martin Luther King, Jr., led marchers down the same route, but King and the marchers were turned back by state troopers. Finally, the third attempt to march from Selma to Montgomery was successful. The photo above shows Martin Luther King, Jr., leading an estimated 10,000 civil rights marchers out on the last leg of their Selma-to-Montgomery march. (*UPI/Corbis-Bettmann*)

application of registration laws, ensured that whites would remain the voting majority in the majority-black counties of Alabama's Black Belt. While Selma's county, Dallas, was 57 percent black in the 1960s, prior to the Voting Rights Act, less than 1 percent of the voting-eligible blacks were registered.[8]

Even after the act was passed, when black voter registration became sufficient to challenge white dominance, elections were structured in ways that prevented black voters from electing candidates of their choice. Selma's ten-member city council was elected at-large, or citywide. The at-large elections guaranteed that as a voting minority, no black would ever win a seat to the city council. In the 1970s, threatened with a lawsuit under the Voting Rights Act, Selma's city government changed its electoral system from an at-large one to a mixed plan, with five double-member districts and an at-large council president. Changing from an at-large to a district or ward-based system resulted in blacks representing a majority in some of the new double-member districts. Blacks were able to win five seats under the new system, but whites still kept the legislative majority through the at-large elected council president that they controlled. According to J. L. Chestnut, Jr., a Selma resident and civil rights attorney, after the elections, more was done for blacks in the city than ever before. He writes, for example, that "Black folk began to be treated more politely at City Hall and ... more black policemen and firemen were hired."[9] Nevertheless, whites still controlled city government and that limited the ability of the black city council members to improve conditions for the city's black majority.

County governments function as the powerful administrative appendages of state governments; they generally maintain and control the county's budget and expenditures; oversee roads, bridges, and toxic waste; and appoint department heads. The Dallas County government would remain all white until the courts, after a decade of litigation, finally ruled that it must adopt a single-member district plan. In 1988, three blacks won seats on the five-member county commission. Similarly, it took a court-ordered redistricting plan for blacks to gain a majority of seats on Selma's city council. Selma's mayor, however, remains the same white segregationist first elected in 1964, who had publicly opposed the civil rights march, Joe Smitherman. As of 1998, he is serving his ninth term in office.

The experience of blacks in Selma and in Dallas County was not an isolated one. Greene County came under black control in 1970, but breakthroughs did not occur in the other counties for more than a decade. Indeed, as of 1998 black representation remained minimal in two of the counties. The county seat, which is usually the financial and commercial center in the rural South, remained under white control in each county.

The dominant white elites used a variety of tactics, both legal and extralegal, to thwart black efforts. Both black and white factions solicited involvement of outside interests in their efforts to prevail. The first concerted push for black empowerment occurred in Greene County in 1966. Blacks ran a full slate of candidates for county offices, but in spite of an over-whelming black voting majority, only one black candidate was elected. Two years later, following a more intense voter registration and voter education campaign, blacks nominated a set of candidates under the banner of a newly formed independent black political party. However, the white county pro-bate judge defied a decision of the U.S. Supreme Court and refused to place the names of the black candidates on the ballot, and the government remained all white. Ultimately, the federal courts voided the results of the 1968 election and ordered the county to hold a special election in 1969. It was in the 1969 election that blacks gained control of the county governing board. The next year blacks were elected as probate judge and tax assessor, giving them control of all county offices.

Following the success in Greene County, black civic leagues in other counties embarked upon similar efforts. However, they faced intense oppo-sition from local whites who engaged in legal subterfuge and economic and political intimidation to discourage black voter registration.[10] Some counties permitted registration only at the county court house during normal work-ing hours. Although state law authorized the use of deputy registrars to make registration more convenient, several counties refused to do so.[11]

When black registration became sufficient to challenge white domi-nance, various strategies were pursued to reduce the power of the black vote. Following the election of two black commissioners in Wilcox County in 1980, the Alabama legislature, under the local courtesy rule,[12] passed bills requiring voters in four Black Belt counties to "reidentify" themselves or be purged from the rolls. In effect, the bills allowed the counties to clear regis-tration rolls because all registered voters had to appear in person to reiden-tify themselves or their names would be dropped from the rolls. Black lead-ers argued that this was a thinly disguised effort to undercut black voter reg-istration. The Justice Department ultimately rejected reidentification bills for two of the counties.

Whites also used racially biased annexation and incorporation schemes to prevent black empowerment. In some counties, heretofore unincorporat-ed areas were incorporated within racially gerrymandered boundaries to ensure white majorities. Other municipalities simply annexed white areas to create white majority towns. These discriminatory changes in electoral pro-cedures were not submitted to the Justice Department for review, in viola-tion of the Voting Rights Act.

Black Belt whites also used their state and national political connec-tions to maintain their dominant position. One example was their campaign to destroy the Federation of Southern Cooperatives, a black-controlled, eco-nomic self-help organization, which was located in Sumter County and was a major independent resource for blacks throughout the Black Belt. The fed-eration provided educational and technical assistance to 130 cooperatives of low-income and mostly black farmers in 14 states. With a well-trained and politically astute staff, a modern training facility with sophisticated publishing capabilities, and a budget of several million dollars funded primarily by federal grants and gifts from foundations, the federation's communication and mobilizing capabilities exceeded those of most other institutions in the region. For blacks in rural Alabama, it was an unprecedented resource. To local whites it was a threat to their privileged position.

The federation was technically a nonprofit and therefore nonpolitical organization, but persons associated with it were active in regional politics. The educational and technical assistance available through the federation reduced the vulnerability of local blacks to economic and political intimidation from whites. This was apparent in 1978 when a former staff member of the federation led a boycott of the Sumter County school system in opposition to policies of white officials who continued to run the public school even after their children were transferred to the white segregated academy.

Persons identified with the federation were also identified with a group of black residents who outmaneuvered a group of local white businessmen, which included the mayor of the county seat, and bought a valuable stretch of riverfront property. The land purchase was especially significant because the land was along the Tombigbee River, which was to become part of the Tennessee-Tombigbee Waterway, a billion-dollar federal public works project that would connect the Midwest to the Gulf of Mexico. For local blacks to compete with the dominant white interests in such a venture was unusual, and for blacks to prevail was almost unthinkable.

In 1979, shortly after the school boycott and a few months before introduction of the reidentification bills, a meeting was called by white leaders to develop a strategy to deal with the threat posed by the federation. At the meeting, which was attended by several county officials, representatives from the offices of both U.S. senators and reportedly the local U.S. congressman, a decision was reached to ask the General Accounting Office, the investigating arm of the U.S. Congress, to investigate charges that the federation had misused federal funds.[13] Local whites said that there was evidence that such funds had been misused. Federation officials saw the request for the audit as political harassment.

The General Accounting Office, after a preliminary audit, reported to the Alabama congressman that it found no evidence of malfeasance.[14] A few months later, however, the federation became the subject of a federal grand jury investigation. The focus of the investigation was never disclosed publicly, but according to those questioned by the FBI agents, the FBI was seeking evidence that the federation had misused federal funds.

The grand jury subpoenaed practically all of the federation's records dealing with federally funded programs and questioned more than 200 people living in five states.[15] After almost two years of investigating, the U.S. attorney ended the investigation without seeking an indictment against any of the officers of the federation.

However, while the federation was being investigated by the federal grand jury, its financial status declined considerably. Contributions from government and philanthropic foundations fell from $2.5 million to $500,000 annually. This resulted in staff layoffs and a general decline in the strength of the federation. Officials of the federation accused federal officials of conspiring with local whites to destroy it.

In a similar situation, though the Justice Department has traditionally been a strong partner in the voting rights struggle in the South, in a surprise turn, it charged several black political activists with voter fraud in Greene County and Perry County in 1985. The government charged that black leaders misused the absentee ballot process to favor their candidate. Traditionally, in rural Alabama significant numbers of people vote absentee.[16] These include workers who commute to jobs outside their voting district and the sick and elderly for whom traveling to the polls may be an ordeal. Maximizing one's share of absentee ballots is an important concern of most political campaigns. Political activists attempt to identify their supporters and arrange for absentee ballots to be sent to them and for the completed ballot to be returned to county election officials. Absentee ballots often provide the winning margin in close elections.[17]

The 1985 cases grew out of federal grand jury investigations in the five Black Belt counties where blacks were making important political strides. Many voting rights activists felt that the prosecutions were racially and politically motivated. The government's indictments aided the efforts of whites to curtail the black vote. Others suspected that the growing strength of the black vote was a threat to the Republican Party's electoral fortunes in the South.

Eight black political leaders and one sympathetic white in Perry and Greene Counties were indicted on a total of 215 criminal charges of altering, falsely witnessing, and mailing absentee ballots. The 3 defendants from Perry County were acquitted on all charges. In Greene County, 1 defendant was convicted on 4 of 37 charges, and 2 other defendants, in a plea bargain, pleaded guilty to 1 misdemeanor each. During the course of the investigations, however, scores of black political activists were subpoenaed to appear before grand juries. Hundreds of elderly blacks who had voted absentee were questioned by FBI agents, and many of them were called upon to travel to distant places and testify as witnesses in various trials.

The struggle for black empowerment and white opposition to it also surfaced in the reapportionment process following the 1980 census. State legislative districts were drawn in a manner that blacks in the Black Belt felt was discriminatory. Ultimately, the federal courts imposed a redistricting plan that made possible the election of black legislators. In 1983 one senator and three state representatives were elected from the region. Following the 1990 census, a majority black congressional district that included Black Belt counties was created.

The election of black legislators represented a significant increase in

the beginning of black empowerment. How political power is used in conjunction with other resources will determine the extent to which empowerment is realized. In the Alabama Black Belt, political control has not brought about empowerment.

KEY FACTORS FOR BLACK EMPOWERMENT IN THE SOUTH

Blacks' struggle for political empowerment in Alabama has proven to be at times bloody, arduous, and much longer than the impression left by political science and history books. Nonetheless, in many ways, Alabama blacks are politically better off than blacks in other southern states where white resistance to the black vote was less organized. First, states with the worst voting rights records were covered under the 1965 Voting Rights Act. As Table 4-2 shows, in states targeted by the original act, blacks have achieved greater representation than in states that were initially exempt.

Alabama, in fact, in spite of its terrible civil rights history, currently has the second greatest proportion of blacks serving in government (16.2 percent) next to Georgia at 18.3 percent. In the old Confederacy, in states that were not covered by the 1965 Voting Rights Act (those not having a test or device as a precondition of registering *nor* having less than 50 percent of the voting-age population registered to vote or voting in the 1964 presidential election),[21] black representation remains proportionately low. Blacks held 2.5 percent and 3.8 percent of all elected positions in Tennessee and Florida, respectively, in 1993. Also shown in Table 4-2 are parity ratios that measure the extent to which blacks are proportionately represented in government. It is calculated by dividing the proportion of the group in government by the proportion of the group in the population. A score of 1.0 is perfect parity, indicating that the group's representation in government matches their relative size in the population.[22] Mississippi's parity ratio is .48, calculated by dividing their percentage of black elected officials in the state (15.2 percent) by the percentage of the state's population that is black (31.6 percent). To achieve proportional representation or a perfect parity score, the percentage of black elected officials in the state of Mississippi would have to double to 31.6 percent.

Covered states and localities were required to submit changes in "any voting qualification or prerequisite to voting, or standard, practice or procedure with respect to voting" to the U.S. Attorney General or the U.S. District Court for the District of Columbia for approval (called pre-clearance).[23] If pre-clearance was not granted, the new voting procedure could not be implemented. Section 5 kept covered states from redesigning their electoral systems in order to discriminate against black voters and keep them out of government. A Supreme Court ruling in 1971, *Connor* v. *Johnson*, however, allowed U.S. district courts to approve state redistricting plans, writing that "A decree of the U.S. district court is not within the reach of Section 5 of

Table 4-2   Annual Change in Number of Black Elected Officials in Federal, State, and Municipal Governments, from 1970 to 1993

Year	*Total* N	*% Change*	*Federal* N	*% Change*	*State* N	*% Change*	*Municipal* N	*% Change*
1970	1,469		10		169		623	
1971	1,860	26.6%	14	40.0%	202	19.5%	785	26.0%
1972	2,264	21.7	14	0	210	4.0	932	18.7
1973	2,521	15.8	16	14.3	240	144.3	1,053	13.0
1974	2,991	14.1	17	6.3	239	−0.4	1,360	29.2
1975	3,503	17.1	18	5.9	281	17.6	1,573	15.7
1976	3,979	13.6	18	0	281	0	1,889	20.1
1977	4,311	8.3	17	−5.6	299	6.4	2,083	10.4
1978	4,503	4.5	17	0	299	0	2,159	3.6
1979	4,607	2.3	17	0	313	4.7	2,224	3.0
1980	4,912	6.6	17	0	323	3.2	2,356	5.9
1981	5,038	2.6	18	5.9	341	5.6	2,384	1.2
1982	5,160	2.4	18	0	336	−1.5	2,477	3.9
1983	5,606	8.6	21	16.7	379	12.8	2,697	10.0
1984	5,700	1.7	21	0	389	2.6	2,735	1.4
1985	6,056	6.2	20	−4.8	396	1.8	2,898	6.0
1986	6,424	6.1	20	0	400	1.0	3,112	7.4
1987	6,681	4.0	23	15.0	417	4.3	3,219	3.4
1988	6,829	2.2	23	0	413	−1.0	3,341	3.8
1989	7,226	5.8	24	4.2	424	2.7	3,595	7.6
1990	7,370	2.0	24	0	423	−0.2	3,671	2.1
1991	7,480	1.5	26	8.3	458	8.3	3,683	0.3
1992	7,552	1.0	26	0	484	5.7	3,697	0.4
1993	8,015	6.1	39	50.0	533	10.1	3,903	5.6

Source: *Black Elected Officials, A National Roster,* 1993

the Voting Rights Act."[24] This created a huge loophole, which the state of Mississippi exploited, by using court-ordered plans that continued to rely on multimember districts to dilute the black vote. Four years later, the Supreme Court closed the loophole by ruling that the U.S. district courts had erred in reviewing the litigation over the redistricting plan prior to Section 5 review. Finally, because many of the southern states' racially discriminatory electoral systems had been enacted well before 1965 (generally at the turn of the century along with the disfranchising devices, such cumulative poll taxes and "good citizen" tests), they had to be challen in court. Many federal courts located in the South were hostile to the ing rights challenges of black plaintiffs. Thus, justice often only through Supreme Court precedents and finally through the amer

Table 4-3   Black Representation in the 11 States of the Former Confederacy, in 1993

	Percentage of Black Voting-Age Population	Total Number of Elected Officials	Total Number of Black Elected Officials	Percentage of Black Elected Officials	Parity Ratio
Alabama*	22.7%	4,315	699	16.2%	.71
Arkansas	13.7	8,331	380	4.6	.34
Florida	11.4	5,256	200	3.8	.33
Georgia*	24.6	6,556	545	18.3	.74
Louisiana*	27.9	4,966	636	12.8	.46
Mississippi*	31.6	4,944	751	15.2	.48
North Carolina*	20.1	5,531	468	8.5	.42
South Carolina*	26.9	3,692	450	12.2	.45
Tennessee	14.4	6,841	168	2.5	.17
Texas	11.2	26,932	472	1.8	.16
Virginia*	17.6	3,112	155	5.0	.28

*One of the seven states covered by the 1965 Voting Rights Act. Note, however, that only part (100 counties) of North Carolina was covered under the original act.

Source: *Black Elected Officials, A National Roster,* 1993, p. xxiii. Parity ratios calculated by authors.

and extension of the Voting Rights Act in 1982. An exception to this was District Judge Frank M. Johnson, Jr., of Alabama, who was a noted liberal on civil and voting rights cases.

Secondly, the massive resistance of whites to black voting rights ironically helped blacks organize and remain politically organized long after the civil rights movement died. In Alabama, a new generation of young attorneys began to represent blacks in the state in voting rights cases. They worked in close collaboration with the Alabama Democratic Conference (ADC), which served as an alternative to the racist white Alabama's state Democratic Party, as had the Mississippi Freedom Democratic Party. ADC still continues to sponsor candidates and organize the black vote, although in 1984, many members divided over whether to support Walter Mondale or Jesse Jackson in the Democratic national primary and broke off to form another black political organization, New South. Thus, in addition to coverage by the Voting Rights Act, black electoral success in the South depended on leadership and political organization.

MACHINE POLITICS AND BLACKS IN CHICAGO

e political experience of blacks in the North was a night-and-day differ-
 from their experience in the South. At the turn of the century, cities in
 orth provided immigrants unprecedented opportunities to use politics
 ans to get ahead. Tens of thousands of southern blacks, escaping the

oppressive and degrading Jim Crow system for jobs in the North, were also brought into politics—from World War I up to the 1960s.

Like the Poles, the Irish, and the Germans, many black southerners would experience their first taste of politics in Chicago. Black political power in Chicago was impressive. Black Chicagoans, in fact, would send the first three blacks to Congress since Reconstruction—Oscar De Priest, Arthur Mitchell, and William Dawson. A native of Alabama, DePriest started out as a house painter but amassed a fortune in real estate. He was elected to the Cook County Board of Commissioners in 1904 and then to the city council in 1915, where he would resign two years later amid charges of accepting bribes. He was acquitted of the charge, and when the first congressional district on Chicago's South Side opened up, the Republican party gave him the nomination. In 1928 he defeated both a white Democrat and a black independent to become the nation's first black elected to Congress in the twentieth century. While serving in the House, DePriest introduced bills providing a monthly pension to ex-slaves and making Abraham Lincoln's birthday a national holiday.[25]

While many blacks retained their identification with the party of Lincoln, many also began voting Democratic as a consequence of the Great Depression and the great appeal of Roosevelt's New Deal programs. DePriest would be defeated after his third term in office by a black Democrat, Arthur W. Mitchell. A native son of Alabama as well, Mitchell had switched parties to become the first black Democrat ever sent to the U.S. House of Representatives in 1934. Mitchell would introduce the numerous anti-lynching bills that President Roosevelt, fearing the wrath of the southern base of his party, refused to support. In 1942, Mitchell retired and was replaced by another party switcher, William "Big Bill" Dawson. Dawson would represent the first district for over one quarter of a century, from 1943 to 1970.

History leaves Dawson as a controversial figure. Dawson's legislative record can hardly be compared to that of the legendary Adam Clayton Powell, Jr., the black Congressman from Harlem who served concurrently with Dawson. Powell was ultimately expelled by majority vote from Congress in 1967, much due to the built-up resentment many members had against him for his propensity to attach civil rights amendments to routine bills making their way out of Congress. Re-elected again, Powell would be vindicated by the Supreme Court, which held that the House lacked constitutional authority to deny Powell a seat. Powell was clearly a "race man," speaking out against racism and discrimination at every opportunity, whereas Dawson kept silent on the subject. Were Dawson and Powell different types of black leaders because they had different personalities—Powell being a flamboyant publicity hound, and Dawson as reticent and quiet—or because they had different political allegiances? A Democrat, Powell nevertheless operated independently of his party, while Dawson was a loyal lieutenant in Chicago's Democratic machine.

The record of machine-controlled black politicians has been poor. Robert Nix, Sr., of Philadelphia was also a machine politician who had the honor of being the third black elected to Congress in 1958. Having served the second district of Philadelphia for 20 years, he had one of the lowest voting participation rates in Congress. Describing his service to black Philadelphians, one political scientist writes that he "rarely campaigned, rarely returned to his district, and rarely participated in Black Caucus functions; his detractors dubbed him 'the Phantom.'"[26] Black Power, Stokely Carmichael and Charles V. Hamilton wrote in 1967, "does not mean merely putting black faces into office." Referring pointedly to the blacks elected with machine support, they added, "Most of the black politicians around the country today are not examples of Black Power. The power must be that of a community, and emanate from there. The black politicians must start from there. The black politicians must stop being representatives of 'downtown' machines, whatever the cost might be in terms of lost patronage and holiday handouts."[27] Further examination of the politics of urban machine organizations revealed that, while machines helped early immigrant groups like the Irish gain citizenship and jobs, entrenched post-war machines did little to help successive groups, including southern and eastern Europeans, blacks, and Hispanics, get ahead.[28] Machine organizations provided blacks with decades of representation, but that representation was "merely symbolic."[29] Black political power in Chicago was illusory.

THE ELECTION OF HAROLD WASHINGTON

By 1970, blacks represented one-third of the city's population. Daley's death in 1976 would provide blacks the opportunity to gain meaningful representation in the city. A ruthless leader, Daley had left no heir apparent, as he had deliberately sowed the seeds of division midst his ranks. However, in contrast to other discontented groups contesting for power in the city, blacks were both leaderless and disorganized at this time. Those who had served the longest in Daley's machine were either too old or had been politically compromised, while the new black elite lacked the experience and social stature of their predecessors. A black had previously challenged Daley for the mayor's post, but he failed to win the support of black council members who feared the all-powerful machine. Moreover, fearing revolt during the tumultuous sixties and early seventies, the Daley machine had long abandoned the practice of getting blacks to register and vote, and black voters, as a means of expressing their dissatisfaction with the machine, stayed home.[30]

A Daley loyalist, Michael Bilandic, would be elected mayor in the 1977 special election. Due to a series of snowstorms that paralyzed the city, Bilandic would be defeated by a newcomer two short years later. A former member of the Daley machine, Jane Byrne campaigned against the "evil cabal," as she called it, and won support from the groups in the city that had become disenchanted with machine rule. Although Byrne's narrow victory over Bilandic mainly came from the black community, she would quickly alienate blacks through a number of her policy actions. Not only did Byrne select a white ethnic to head the city's police department (rejecting the acting black police chief she had previously named), she maintained white ethnic control of the city's Board of Education, even though the public schools had long ago become mostly black. When she finally gave in to the tremendous pressure to appoint a black school superintendent, it was only after the school system's finances were put under the control of a school finance board where whites were in the majority. As one analyst commented, "Byrne's [actions] ... implied that blacks weren't good enough, or properly qualified, for positions of leadership over institutions that were critically important to the black community. Her actions also indicated that she would not listen to the recommendations of black community groups or their leaders."[31] Furthermore, blacks in the Byrne administration were typically outsiders who, lacking their own base of support, were politically weak. Byrne's policies indicated that she intended to continue to provide better city services to white ethnic voters in the city, shortchanging in the process the interests who had been vital to her election.

Byrne had hoped to follow Daley's strategy, one that took for granted that a majority of blacks would support the machine no matter what. In fact, Byrne's actions were even more blatantly hostile and alienating to blacks than Mayor Daley's had been. The political climate had changed in ways that motivated blacks to finally rebel against their poor representatives in government. President Ronald Reagan's policies had hurt blacks economically. Their collective dissatisfaction with Reagan coupled with their rising population in the city motivated blacks to politically mobilize. The registration drive took the form of a political movement, initiated by a boycott of the city's annual summer fair, ChicagoFest. Blacks boycotted ChicagoFest in an effort to demonstrate the significance of their community to the city's economic well-being. Because the boycott gained the participation and sponsorship of a number of grass-roots black organizations, it quickly rolled over into a political movement. Black churches joined the movement, and black business leaders donated money for a three-week campaign to promote the registration drive on black radio stations. Meanwhile, black Congressman Harold Washington, persuaded by the registration drive and organization-building that had taken place in the preceding months, announced his candidacy for mayor.

The registration drive dramatically reversed the racial balance in voting participation in the city. Where prior to 1979 white registration turnout had always exceeded that of blacks, in 1983 black registration passed that of whites by as much as 6 percentage points.[32] Moreover solidly lined up behind Washington with 85 percent of their vote.

as black voting secured his nomination, Washington also benefited from the decision of one of Mayor Daley's sons, Richard M. Daley, to run for mayor. Whites in the city split their votes between Byrne and Daley.

Winning the Democratic primary in a city as heavily Democratic as Chicago is tantamount to winning the election for mayor. Washington, however, barely edged out his Republican opponent, and the prospect of having a black man become mayor caused the city's long-suppressed racial tensions to finally explode. The race issue had been evident in the primary; the city's Democratic party chairman told Jane Byrne supporters at a rally on the city's Northwest Side that a "vote for Daley was a vote for Washington," adding, "It's a racial thing. Don't kid yourself. I am calling on you to save your city, to save your precinct. We are fighting to keep the city the way it is."[33] The level of racial divisiveness enveloping the 1983 general election was astonishing, surpassing, perhaps, that seen in Richard Arrington's 1979 bid to become Birmingham, Alabama's first black mayor. White supporters of the white Republican in the general election began distributing racist campaign literature, including buttons that proclaimed, "Vote Right, Vote White." For his part, Bernard Epton, the Republican, aired a television commercial that concluded with the statement, "Epton for Mayor, Before It's Too Late." The city's major newspapers denounced the racist activities taking place in the Epton camp as well as the commercial, but Chicagoans still voted along racial lines. Washington won 90 percent of the black vote, but took only 12 percent of the white vote.[34] His white support principally came from "lakefront" liberals; white ethnics had mobilized and turned out for the Republican. With well over a million votes cast, Washington won by 48,250 votes.

Racial tensions did not immediately ebb once Washington took office. The machine fought the mayor's reform efforts in city council tooth-and-nail. So deep was the political stand-off between the mayor and the city council during the early 1980s that it was labeled "the Council Wars," in reference to the sci-fi classic film "Star Wars." But by 1986, Washington's allies defeated enough machine politicians to hold a majority of seats on the city council. Shortly after winning reelection in 1987, Washington would die in office of a massive heart attack. Politics in Chicago would once again take an unexpected turn, as Washington's political enemies would hatch a plan that divided blacks and ended their short spell as leaders of the governing coalition. The machine bloc would support a black alderman from the machine tradition, Eugene Sawyer. Black reformers, however, wanted Alderman Timothy Evans, who had served as Washington's floor leader in council, to succeed him. As the news leaked out that Sawyer had the s to become the city's interim mayor, a crowd of angry black demon-s gathered at City Hall, screaming "traitor," "no deals," and "Uncle Sawyer could not overcome the stigma of the backroom dealing d with his election. Blacks predictably divided their votes between

Sawyer and Evans, and Richard M. Daley, whom Washington had defeated in 1983 in the same manner, became the city's next mayor.

POLITICAL LESSONS FROM CHICAGO

Politics in Chicago illustrates the critical difference between political *representation* and *incorporation*, a distinction Browning, Marshall, and Tabb make in the award-winning *Protest Is Not Enough*. Representation is often measured as the proportion of elected seats blacks hold in government. Since 1915, blacks have been represented in Chicago's city government, but blacks were not incorporated. Incorporation "concerns the extent to which group interests are effectively represented in policy making."[36] Having elected representatives in government does not necessarily yield proportionate influence over the decision-making process; the representation of black interests is only achieved through membership in the dominant governing coalition. Blacks either had to hold the majority of legislative seats and control who sat in the mayor's office or are members of the coalition that directed city policy. Political incorporation, in other words, is achieved through participation in the *dominant governing coalition*. Browning, Marshall, and Tabb are able to establish in their empirical study of ten California cities that government was responsive to policy interests of blacks and Hispanics in cities where they were politically incorporated. Minority representation, in contrast, had a much smaller, inconsistent impact on the policy responsiveness of government.

Blacks had many representatives serving on Chicago's city council, and they were also part of the machine's electoral coalition from the 1930s to the 1970s; why, then, was government unresponsive to their interests? Several explanations have been offered. First, political scientist Dianne Pinderhughes argues that the extreme degree of racial discrimination in American society accounts for the inability of blacks to transform their electoral advantages (geographic concentration, size, bloc voting) into real political power.[37] White ethnics in the city were benefiting from the racial discrimination leveled against blacks in housing, jobs, public education, and city services. In practical terms this meant that black politicians who wanted to raise race discrimination as a political issue faced censure and expulsion from the machine. In broader terms, the continued racial conflict between whites and blacks remains a critical barrier to liberal biracial coalitions. In cities such as New York and Los Angeles, blacks would lose their grip on power as liberal whites, their former allies, would turn away from them and vote Republican mayors into office in the aftermath of riots and fiscal problems that compounded the unresolved racial divisions in these cities.

Secondly, internal divisions among blacks can explain why blacks m be represented in government but lack political influence. By co-op black leaders, exploiting divisions among them, and recruiting its own and subservient team, Chicago's political machine could safely ignc

policy interests of blacks. Thus Richard M. Daley would be elected because blacks were divided over Sawyer or Evans as successors to Harold Washington. The failure of blacks to hold on to power in Chicago today, however, is based less on internal division than the absence of viable black leadership. Cities such as Cleveland,[38] Philadelphia,[39] and New Orleans[40] serve as better examples of how political ambition and long-standing rivalries between black leadership have split blacks into two politically impotent camps, leaving more conservative groups in control of city government.

The Chicago case touches on a longstanding and intensely argued debate in black politics, namely how best to win and hold onto political power? In *Black Power*, Stokely Carmichael and Charles V. Hamilton argued that blacks should eschew alliances with other groups, specifically white liberals, to organize on their own. They came to this conclusion for three reasons. First, the interests of blacks are never identical to those of labor groups, white liberals, and other reform groups. Second, all too often black participation in coalitions has been under terms dictated by the more powerful also participating in the coalition. Third, lacking their own base of political power, blacks have tended to rely on moral persuasion and "friendship" to influence their allies with poor results. Until blacks act independently of whites and build their own separate political organizations, their interests will always be subjugated to the interests of the more powerful group. Chicago clearly illustrated Carmichael and Hamilton's point: "As long as the black people of Chicago—and the same can be said of cities through the country—remain politically dependent on the Democratic machine, their interests will be secondary to that machine."[41]

In *Protest Is Not Enough*, Browning, Marshall, and Tabb argue against black political independence, maintaining that the surest path to minority political incorporation occurred in cities where blacks mobilized and formed alliances with white liberals. They point to a biracial coalition formed in Berkeley, California, that put blacks in key leadership posts to influence city policy as early as the late sixties. In Oakland, California, by contrast, the separatist and radical political activists of some black groups caused black incorporation to be delayed by a decade, basically until black population growth gave blacks control of city government. Black demand-protest and electoral mobilization, they conclude from their study of ten Californian cities, are often not enough to propel blacks into political power, but require the political support of liberal whites. And in cities where blacks are less than 20 percent of the population, the support of white liberals has been vital, such as the elections and re-elections of black mayors in Los Angeles, Seattle, and n Francisco.

While Washington needed the 10–15 percent of white support he got rily from "lakefront liberals" in his 1983 election victory, Chicago still supports the argument of Carmichael and Hamilton. It was not until blacks organized on their own and mounted an independent challenge to the machine establishment that they finally won influence and power in city hall. Liberal, reform-minded whites had also become dissatisfied with machine rule, but a biracial coalition failed to form as one might expect from the model that Browning, Marshall, and Tabb espouse. White reformers, instead, ran their own candidates to challenge Daley, while blacks backed their own. Liberal whites would not form an alliance with blacks until after blacks had built up their own independent organizations and had established their political clout in city politics, as Carmichael and Hamilton predicted. New York City serves as another case that contradicts their formula for minority incorporation. As John Mollenkopf points out: "New York City long had the political raw materials that Browning, Marshall, and Tabb say will enable a liberal, biracial coalition to win office and bring about minority political incorporation."[42] First, blacks were politically active, having black representation in the area since the Great Depression. Second, one-third of New York City's white voters are liberals. Thus, one would have expected a liberal, biracial coalition would have won power by the early 1970s; instead, blacks were politically subordinated in New York City until they helped elect the city's first black mayor, David Dinkins, in 1989. Dinkins would only serve one term before his defeat by a white Republican in 1993. Dinkins lost much of his support among white Catholics and Jews in part because of events like the Crown Heights riot and the Korean boycott, but also because of their growing economic conservatism, concern about crime, and rising taxes. Their defection to the Republican party gives support to Carmichael and Hamilton's portrayal of white liberals as "fair-weather friends." The ideological liberalism of whites, whites' "goodwill," as it is labeled in *Black Power*, is simply not enough to sustain a biracial political coalition when the racial or economic interests of whites clash with the policy interests of blacks.

Nevertheless, those who espouse biracial or multiracial coalitions as the best way for blacks to advance politically argue they provide a more durable foundation for holding onto political power. Oftentimes, the independent organizing of blacks has been reactive rather than proactive. In Chicago, the stimulus was the ChicagoFest boycott. In Philadelphia, blacks began to register and vote in reaction to Mayor Frank Rizzo's racially hostile administration. Black political organizations built in response to such events generally disappear once immediate political goals are attained. Pinderhughes put it this way: "This [grassroots protest] structure worked for blacks in pressing forward the civil rights movement and in winning control of the Chicag[o] mayor's office; it also works especially well for managing crises, for meeti[ng] political challenge, for mounting protest, and for mobilizing voters. [This] structure has not, however, been used to develop or maintain gras[sroots] interests in governing and policy making, in contacting and commun[icating] with public officials, or in negotiating with or choosing among polit[ical lead]ers within the community."[43]

Secondly, the election of Washington had a much more circum-scribed impact on city policy than had it come about through the formation of a biracial coalition, some have argued.[44] Looking back, it is doubtful whether Washington could have, in fact, made peace with the white ethnic-dominated machine during his first term, but he could have put blacks in a politically more secure foundation had he worked toward alliances with county and state white Democrats. Certainly, even though the son of Boss Daley was elected without much black support in 1989, he has worked toward securing the support of black elected officials. Daley would win re-election in part because he had won over some black politicians through skillful political exchanges. For example, the country's first black female U.S. Senator, Carol Moseley Braun, endorsed Daley over his black challenger, Roland Burris, former comptroller and secretary of state, in the 1994 mayoral race.[45] Politically vulnerable among whites, Moseley Braun greatly needs the mayor's support to help win re-election to the Senate in 1998. Daley's black support, therefore, has grown. It will be difficult for blacks to unify and contest Daley for the mayor's office in future elections. Blacks might have been able to retain influence and power in Chicago politics had they figured out a way to work within the Democratic establishment. Yet, the hidden pitfalls of biracial coalitions and the dangers of reliance on the Democratic Party still stand.

NATIONAL ORGANIZING AS A POLITICAL RESOURCE

One key instrument through which political potential may be converted into actual power is an ideologically informed, disciplined political organization that can develop an issue agenda, convert the issue positions into policy options, and mobilize support for those options. The need for such a national organizational base has not escaped black political leaders, but efforts to develop such organizations have yielded only limited results.

Such attempts date back to the 1840s when free blacks called conventions to develop strategies to protect their interests. During the contemporary era, the Gary Convention of 1972, named after the Indiana city in which it was held, was the most significant attempt to build such a national black political organization. The Gary Convention was called by a number of prominent black elected officials, civil rights leaders, and others to develop a strategy for mobilizing black political power nationally. The 3,000 delegates, ᵒom 44 states[46] who attended the convention represented a cross section of ᵕck America.

Deliberations at the convention revolved around an "Outline for a Agenda," a document that had been prepared by a task force of black ᵗuals and other designated persons prior to the convention. The pre-serted that "the American system does not work for the masses of ᵊ and it cannot be made to work without radical fundamental change." The agenda enumerated 30 objectives designed to "eliminate racism and exploitation from American life" and stressed the need for blacks to organize to realize them. Delegates authorized the establishment of a continuing national structure (to be called the National Black Assembly) and state assemblies to mobilize resources and maximize black political strength. National black political conventions were to be held quadrennially to coincide with U.S. presidential elections.

In sum, the national organization envisaged by the conventioneers of the Gary Convention would comprise state assemblies, which, in turn, would have regional subdivisions. Participation would be open to elected officials; representatives of religious, civil rights, and other organizations; and private individuals. There would also be a national assembly in which states and major black organizations would be represented. This would be a comprehensive organization through which all elements in the black community could find expression.

The National Black Assembly authorized by the Gary Declaration was formed but almost instantly it was torn asunder by ideological, strategic, and tactical differences, and it soon ceased to function.[47] Perhaps more so than any other event in the recent history of black political struggle, the Gary experiment demonstrated that both black leadership and the rank and file are aware of the need for an independent comprehensive national black political organization. The rapid demise of the National Black Assembly, on the other hand, dramatized that, good intentions notwithstanding, there are systemic factors that make the development of such organizations difficult if not impossible. An examination of the factors that led to the speedy demise of the National Black Assembly will clarify this point.

Driven by the slogan "unity without uniformity," the black agenda adopted at Gary was little more than a transitory compromise between largely incompatible tendencies: between nationalist and integrationist; between those who advocated an independent black political party and those committed to working within the conventional two-party system; and between those committed to revolutionary ideals and those seeking reformist solutions.

These diverse and sometimes contradictory interests were able to unite behind a common declaration. However, as efforts were made to go beyond the declaration and begin building structures through which the objectives were to be pursued, serious schisms surfaced among the different groups. For example, certain elements were unwilling to participate if persons identified with opposing ideologies occupied prominent positions in the assembly.

In addition to ideological differences, the way in which various black groups and their leaders are integrated into the overall American political system made it difficult for them to pursue certain provisions of the agenda without compromising their effectiveness within the system. For example, members of the Congressional Black Caucus, who were prime sponsors of the Gary Convention, felt compelled to disassociate themselves from certain provisions of the foreign policy section of the document that were perceived by some to tilt toward the Arabs in the Arab-Israeli dispute. Had they not done so, they risked losing support among their Jewish constituency, which is an important source of financial support for many black politicians.

The fact that most of the elected officials, particularly the nationally prominent ones, were active members of the Democratic party left them unenthusiastic about the idea of forming an independent black political party. Similarly, the NAACP, a leading organization in the reformist integrationist movement, took exception to the separatist tone of the Gary Declaration and denounced it as being revolutionary rather than reformist.[48] To be associated with separatist revolutionary efforts would have undermined the effectiveness of the NAACP.

On the other hand, the more radical community-based organizations, such as the Congress of African People, were unencumbered by ties with mainstream American institutions and groups. For them the National Black Political Assembly was an instrument to be used in the struggle for revolutionary transformation.

Under such circumstances the demise of the National Black Political Assembly was predictable. The diverse groups that came together at Gary might have found numerous opportunities to work together on an ad hoc basis, but being part of a united front with a common corporate identity was an entirely different matter. Within such structures individual organizational identities give way to the identity of the new collective. Each constituent unit of the collective inherits the enemies of each of the other constituents. The negative assessments that detractors may make of any one of the constituent organizations may be extended to any or all of them.

The leadership of the constituent groups, under such circumstances, may view the cost of membership in such a united front as prohibitive. Membership in the united front, they may reason, does not strengthen their ability to deal with forces external to the black community, at least in the short run, and it undermines their traditional base of support. Seen in this way, the forces and circumstances that give rise to the need for disciplined, independent black political organizations are the same ones that make the survival of such organizations problematical.

In the absence of such a national organization, efforts toward national black political empowerment continued to evolve around the politics of presidential elections. This is the subject of the next section.

PRESIDENTIAL POLITICS AND RESOURCE MOBILIZATION

The presidency is the centerpiece of the American political process, and it has been at this level in the political process that blacks have exercised their greatest political influence. The winner-take-all feature of the presidential election system and the strategic location of black voters in populous eastern and midwestern states give blacks potential power in presidential politics that exceeds their numbers.

During the 1960s black leadership used this potential to enlist the moral authority and the political muscle of the presidency in the struggle for empowerment. As a result, black representation in the federal bureaucracy, the court system, and regulatory agencies increased considerably. Many private corporations and state and local governments followed the lead of the national government in creating new opportunities for African Americans.

However, as noted in Chapter 2, the black vote is becoming increasingly marginalized in presidential politics. From 1968 to 1984 the candidate favored by black voters lost every election except the anomalous 1976 election.[49] In no election since 1968 has the candidate favored by blacks received a majority of the white vote. President Reagan in 1980 and 1984 received 55 percent and 67 percent, respectively, of the white vote while almost 90 percent of the black vote went to his Democratic opponent on both occasions. As mentioned earlier, even though the candidate favored by blacks was elected in 1992 and 1996, on neither occasion did he receive a majority of the white vote.

Thus, there appears to be a realignment of white voters in presidential elections. The shift of white southerners from the Democratic to Republican party is the most dramatic element in this realignment. Should this pattern continue, the ability of blacks to use the presidency as a political resource would be diminished, and that could have a negative multiplier effect on the overall movement.

The growing marginalization of the black vote in presidential politics has given rise to three related and somewhat paradoxical responses that may have long-term consequences for the evolution of black politics in the United States. First of all, black voters view the Republican party as being increasingly hostile. A 1986 national poll revealed that 72 percent of black respondents felt that leaders of the Republican party did not care about their problems; 42 percent felt that Republican leaders were getting worse; and more than half, 56 percent, perceived the President to be a racist.[50] At the same time, the Democratic party, apparently fearful of becoming a minority party composed of minority groups, began to retreat from those programs that made it attractive to black voters. But in the absence of a more attractive alternative, black voters remain as unenthusiastic partners in a relationship gone sour, as was evident in 1984 and 1988 in the wake of Jesse Jackson's unsuccessful presidential campaigns. Even though many black voters were unhappy with the manner in which party leaders reacted to Jackson, they still gave overwhelming support to the Democratic party.

To complete the paradox, a small but growing number of nationally prominent black thinkers in the early 1980s began (and still continue) urging blacks to end their increasing marginalization by joining white voters in their shift to conservatism and the Republican party. Let us examine this argument in more detail.

IDEOLOGY AND RESOURCE
MOBILIZATION—THE NEW BLACK CONSERVATISM[51]

The views of the new black conservatives, like those of other groups, are not monolithic. Nevertheless, we can identify certain positions that constitute the core of their creed. What distinguishes them from the more traditional black leaders and thinkers is their belief that rather than being a positive force, government and government-sponsored social welfare programs are primarily impediments to black progress. Like their white counterparts, black conservatives are generally opposed to the interventionist state. They deride social welfare programs and claim that government and government-created dependence are among the major problems confronting African Americans.

The ideological presuppositions of the black conservatives generate a perception of the black predicament that is radically different from that espoused by the traditional black leadership. For example, economist Walter Williams, a leading black conservative, argues that it is not racial bigotry but the "rules of the game" that account for many of the problems faced by blacks.[52] Another black economist, Thomas Sowell, claims that government has been responsible for suppressing black advancement and that the "great achievement of the civil rights organizations has been getting government off the back of blacks."[53]

Similarly, black economist Glenn Loury received national attention in 1984 when he argued in several prestigious journals that inasmuch as the civil rights movement was virtually complete, it was necessary to look beyond racism to explain the problems of the black poor. The explanation, he argued, is to be found in the values, social norms, and attitudes of the poor blacks themselves.[54] Loury accused conventional black leadership and the black middle class from which it comes of refusing to confront the "enemy within." Instead, the black leadership, he claimed, use the plight of the black poor to justify state interventionist programs that actually benefit the black middle class.

According to Loury, the problem of the black poor is really a moral one, beyond the reach of effective government action. Primary responsibility for uplifting the black poor, in his view, lies with the black middle class. Pleas by the latter for government intervention to ameliorate the problems of the black poor are characterized by Loury as inappropriate appeals to others for deliverance.

When viewed in perspective, however, the argument that the problems of the black poor are the result of government intervention is contradicted by both popular perception and available evidence. No data are available that establish a correlation between state intervention and black deprivation. However, the reverse seems to be the case. The multiplicity of state interventionist transfer payment programs, of which welfare is only one, were all adopted to remedy widely recognized problems in the American political economy. Programs such as Aid to Families with Dependent Children (AFDC), Medicare, Medicaid, and housing assistance were approved by Congress only after the need was demonstrated through extensive public debate. Moreover, the fact that in 1990 such a large proportion of all Americans received some form of federal transfer payments—29 percent of whites and 33 percent of blacks[55]—challenges the notion that such programs are a primary cause of the problems of the black poor.

The claim that government has been a party to the suppression of blacks is true. But it is also true that it was intervention by the national government in response to the militant black protest of the 1960s that outlawed state-sanctioned segregation and discrimination in the South. This set in motion an interdependent and inseparable series of developments that led to the inclusion of African Americans in institutions and positions in both the public and private sectors that had been previously closed to them.

The argument of the black conservatives that the problems of the black poor are essentially functions of the "enemy within," that is, the presumed pathological culture of the black poor, and that the persistence of black poverty is a reflection of the moral failure of black leadership and the black middle class, is perhaps the most popular tenet of the conservative creed. This argument dovetails quite nicely with the longstanding white supremacist notion that the unequal position of blacks is due neither to racism nor to systemic economic conditions but to the inappropriate behavior of blacks themselves. This explanation absolves the broader society of any guilt in causing the problem and excuses them from any responsibility for resolving it.

How the creed of the new black conservatives differs from that of the more conventional black leadership and the implications of these differences for the struggle for racial equality can be clarified further by examining their policy recommendations.

POLICY RECOMMENDATIONS OF THE BLACK CONSERVATIVES

Educational reform and enhanced labor force participation are two major concerns of black conservatives. They argue that substandard schools and the educational deficiencies that result from them account for much of the economic inequality experienced by blacks. Current federal education programs, in their view, are at least part of the problem. As a solution, conservatives advocate the development of free market educational systems stimulated by preferential tax laws and direct assistance to needy students.

Publicly financed vouchers would be given to eligible low-income students to attend schools of their choice. Voucher holders, according to the conservative thesis, would gravitate toward schools of demonstrated quality. As a result, substandard schools would be forced to improve their quality or go out of business.

But there are those who suggest that such free market education might have consequences far beyond those imagined by black conservatives. For example, one possible outcome of such an educational system would be the siphoning off of the better prepared black youngsters into a few prestigious secondary schools while the learning environment of the bulk of black youth remained unchanged. Black graduates of such selective secondary schools would be the most objectively qualified to enter the equally selective major universities. Upon graduation from college, this privileged group would be in line to receive the most prestigious and rewarding positions open to blacks. And, as far as they might be concerned, their privileged position would be the result of merit. Conversely and by inference, the subordinate positions occupied by their compatriots who were left behind in inner-city schools would also be explained by racially neutral meritocratic factors. Consequently, both privilege and deprivation would be seen as the result of individual effort. The view that the poor are responsible for their plight would be reinforced.

Furthermore, black leadership and those who staff and administer the social, economic, cultural, and educational institutions that manage the disadvantaged black communities would be chosen disproportionately from this privileged group. Having spent their crucial formative years in institutions in which they were the only black or one of a few, many might be inclined to accept the interpretation of the black predicament that prevails in such institutions. Consequently, as professionals and leaders they would bring to their work perceptions of the black poor that differed little from those of their white counterparts. Such black professionals would serve more as buffers facilitating the continued domination of the poor than as agents for transformation. This would heighten class contradictions within the black community and further diminish the prospects for black unity and, hence, for black empowerment as well.

A second policy recommendation of the black conservatives is the imposition of a subminimum wage to enhance the position of blacks, particularly black youth, in the labor force. Minimum wage legislation, conservatives argue, overprices labor and as a consequence eliminates many jobs that could be held by black teenagers and other unskilled workers. Experience gained through such jobs, the argument runs, would lead to better paying positions in the future. This new pool of experienced workers with marketable skills would create its own demand and have a long-term beneficial impact by reducing the number of unemployable youth and the chronic social problems that are said to result from their presence.

Critics of the black conservatives charge that there is little evidence that a subminimum wage would have such a positive impact.[56] Under the present law, they point out, 63 percent of all trade and 85 percent of service establishments can already legally pay young people a subminimum wage.[57] A 1970 Labor Department study showed that, of 4,615 firms authorized to hire full-time students at a subminimum wage, "over half used less than their authorization or did not use them at all."[58] Studies of workers who are illegally paid subminimum wages reveal that white workers hired under such conditions are likely to be teenagers but that blacks working for subminimum wages tend to be adults and primary wage earners in the family. All of this suggests to some critics that the introduction of a subminimum wage would reduce the return to labor below the acceptable minimum while doing little to promote black advancement.

Overall, though black conservatives remain a relatively small minority within the black community, their views are increasingly well received by important policy makers at the state and national levels. Several prominent black conservatives have syndicated newspaper columns and others have highly promoted radio talk shows. Some, such as Justice Clarence Thomas of the Supreme Court, speak from forums and positions of authority that tend to overexaggerate the support the conservatives and their politics have in the black community. Another one of their members, Ward Connerly, led the successful move to amend the California state constitution to outlaw all forms of affirmative action in that state. Even so, such perceptions and developments have important implications for the quest for resources and black politics generally.

MEASURING THE IMPACT OF THE BLACK POLITICAL POWER

It would be wrong to conclude our chapter on the efforts of blacks to win political power without discussing the impact of blacks having power today. As in the case of the strategies necessary to win political power, there is a debate over what blacks have achieved through politics and through office holding. On one side, there are those who discount the significance of black representation and incorporation. Because big cities today are in financially poor shape and dependent on economic aid from states and the federal government, political control of the cities is a "hollow prize," in the words of one such analyst.[59] The fiscal problems of local and state governments have limited the abilities of black politicians to implement policies that can help alleviate the multiple and complex set of social and economic problems facing the black poor. Because of their cities' precarious fiscal states, black mayors generally have opted for traditional, business-oriented development policies rather than community-based redistributive programs.[60] These policies have helped revitalize the central business districts in cities like Atlanta, Detroit, and Newark and have benefited the black business elite, even while the conditions of the black poor have deteriorated.

On the other side, there are a number of studies documenting that the elections of black mayors and city council members have lead to large increases in black municipal employment, improvements in city services for blacks, and limited increases in expenditures for social services.[61] Such elections, nevertheless, have not produced the radical and profound changes envisioned by the civil rights activists of the 1960s. Politics has had little effect on the economic inequalities that persist between the races. Some might conclude, as had William Keech, a political scientist writing in the late 1960s, that the black vote "is most useful for the least important gains."[62]

If the impact of the black vote and of black political incorporation is disappointing, it is not because the institutions that they control are lacking in economic resources. Mayors of big cities today manage billion-dollar budgets. Envisioning the budget as a giant pie, they, along with the members of city councils, determine how that pie is going to be sliced; which group is going to get which piece. Control over the city's budgetary process is, therefore, hardly "hollow," but a prize of tremendous importance. As the federal government continues to devolve significant policy powers to the state, the groups that influence state governments have tremendous power over the lives and well-being of every other group in those states.

Black governance is curtailed not by the economic limits of the institution, but by political barriers that are only now becoming fully understood. Black political power in Chicago during the machine era was illusory because the machine co-opted black leaders and ultimately de-mobilized blacks. Black political representation in Selma was limited because, as the quote at the beginning of the chapter makes plain, until very recently, blacks were not in the legislative majority. Lack of cooperation during Chicago's council wars weakened black power under Washington. Washington had to contend with a majority in city council hostile to black interests. In short, black power in American politics is limited by the system. Reform of the political system may be the only way that blacks can realize the full extent of holding the reigns of power in American government.

CONCLUSION

Of the several potential sources of power, favorable population distribution, voting, and holding public office appear to be the most promising ones for black empowerment. Considerable progress has been made in increasing black voter registration and electing blacks to public office. Black voters have determined the outcome of many important elections. Nevertheless, voting and holding office are limited resources, and their limited potential has not been fully realized due to the absence of disciplined independent black political organizations.

However, to say that it is the absence of a disciplined independent organizational base that accounts for the limited payoffs from electoral politics may be engaging in circular reasoning. The same forces that account for the inequitable position of blacks in America also account for the circumstances that mitigate against the development of disciplined, independent black political organizations.

Let us elaborate. Enhancing the economic strength of the black community and thereby lessening its vulnerability to outside forces has always been viewed as a prerequisite for black political empowerment. However, efforts to create a viable black entrepreneurial class, if they are to be successful, almost always require supportive action from government and the mainstream business community. For this reason both the black economic and political elite are reluctant to be identified with independent black organizations perceived by whites to be threatening. Moreover, as the black elite pursues its objectives of economic empowerment, it becomes functionally integrated into the existing system, such that its own well-being is linked to the response of the very mainstream institutions that a disciplined black organization would confront. Of course, other less vulnerable forces in the black community could attempt to develop such organizations. However, such efforts would threaten the hegemony of the existing black leadership and for that reason might be opposed by the latter. Moreover, the established black leadership would likely cite their positive and functional relationship within mainstream institutions to reinforce their claim to be effective leaders and to undermine the appeal of any would-be challengers. The black leadership that emerges under such circumstances is inclined neither to build independent disciplined organizations nor to challenge the fundamental assumptions and practices of the existing order.

TOPICS FOR DISCUSSION

1. Identify what you believe are one or two of the major problems facing African Americans. Now identify the resources required to solve or ameliorate these problems. Who controls the resources, and how likely are they to use them to solve the problems in question? Discuss thoroughly and justify your position.

2. List four or five potential sources of black political power and discuss how each may be converted into real power. What are the prospects for doing so?

3. Think about the extent of black power in your own community. How have black candidates won or failed to win political office? Are blacks incorporated or not, and why? Don't overlook the role that the electoral system may play in your answer.

4. Think about black participation in Chicago's machine as a glass half-full and then half-empty. How did blacks benefit from their alliance with the Democratic machine? In what ways did that alliance cost them politically?

5. Are biracial coalitions possible in the South's rural areas, like Dallas County? What strategies should blacks pursue to win political power in the rural South?

6. Examine critically the arguments of black conservatives such as Glenn Loury, Thomas Sowell, and Walter Williams. What do they see as the causes of black inequality, and what resources are required to end it?

SUGGESTED READINGS

Anderson, Claud. *Black Labor, White Wealth*. Edgewood, MD: Duncan & Duncan, 1994. Demonstrates the role of black labor in creating American wealth and suggests how it can be converted into a vehicle for black economic growth and development.

Bachrach, Peter, and Morton S. Baratz. *Power and Poverty: Theory and Practice*. New York: Oxford University Press, 1970. An analysis of political power, authority, influence, and force in the policy-making process.

Barker, Lucius, ed. "Black Electoral Politics." *National Political Science Review* 2 (1990). Features a symposium on big-city black mayors.

Bates, Timothy. *Banking on Black Enterprise*. Washington, DC: Joint Center for Political and Economic Studies, 1993. An analysis of the prospects and possibilities of black empowerment through urban economic development.

Browning, Rufus P., Dale Rogers Marshall, and David H. Tabb. *Protest Is Not Enough*. Berkeley, CA, and Los Angeles, CA: University of California Press, 1984. An award-winning longitudinal study on the efforts of blacks and Latinos to win political power in ten California cities.

Browning, Rufus P., Dale Rogers Marshall, and David H. Tabb, eds. *Racial Politics in American Cities*, 2nd ed. New York: Longman Publishers, 1997.

Carmichael, Stokely, and Charles V. Hamilton. *Black Power*. New York: Vintage Books, 1967. A classic statement on how African Americans should mobilize and organize independently in order to successfully push for social and economic change.

Crotty, William J. *Political Reform and the American Experiment*. New York: Thomas Y. Crowell Company, 1977. A study of how the reforms in the American electoral system, especially changes in franchisement rules and voter registration, have affected the American political system.

Davidson, Chandler, and Bernard Grofman, eds. *Quiet Revolution in the South: The Impact of the Voting Rights Act, 1965–1990*. Princeton, NJ: Princeton University Press, 1994. Systematic and detailed case examinations of the impact of the Voting Rights Act on eight states in the South.

Davis, Angela. *Women, Culture, and Politics*. New York: Vintage Books, 1990. Essays highlighting gender-specific problems in American politics.

Edelman, Murray. *The Symbolic Uses of Politics*. Chicago, IL: University of Illinois Press, 1967. An examination of the impact of symbolic action on both spectators and players in the political game.

Erie, Steven P. *Rainbow's End*. Berkeley, CA, and Los Angeles, CA: University of California Press, 1988. A post-revisionist account of how machines formed and organized the politics of urban immigrants.

Foster, Lorn, ed. *The Voting Rights Act*. New York: Praeger, 1985. A collection of articles on the implementation of the Voting Rights Act.

Gomes, Robert, and Linda Williams. *From Exclusion to Inclusion: The Long Struggle for*

African American Political Power. Westport, CT: Greenwood Press, 1992. A collection of articles on the topic.

Grimshaw, William J. *Bitter Fruit: Black Politics and the Chicago Machine, 1931–1991*. Chicago, IL: University of Chicago Press, 1992. A theoretically enriched account of black politics in Chicago during the Daley years, up to the election of Daley's son.

Grofman, Bernard, Lisa Handley, and Richard G. Niemi. *Minority Representation and the Quest for Voting Equality*. New York: Cambridge University Press, 1992. Up-to-date coverage of voting rights law and the methods used to determine minority vote dilution.

Guinier, Lani. *The Tyranny of the Majority*. New York: Free Press, 1994. A lucid analysis of electoral schemes to strengthen the representation and power of minorities in American political life.

Howard, John, and Robert Smith, eds. *The Annals of the American Academy of Political and Social Science* 439 (September 1978). A collection of theoretical and empirical articles on black urban politics in the 1960s and 1970s.

Jennings, James, ed. *Blacks, Latinos, and Asians in Urban America*. Westport, CT: Praeger, 1994. A collection of essays describing relationships among the several groups and discussions of prospects for joint action.

Judd, Dennis R., and Todd Swanstrom. *City Politics*. New York: HarperCollins College Publishers, 1994. Excellent textbook on urban governments and their politics.

Karnig, Albert K., and Susan Welch. *Black Representation and Urban Policy*. Chicago, IL: University of Chicago Press, 1980. Empirical examination of how black candidates are elected and their impact on public policy in American cities.

Keiser, Richard A. *Subordination or Empowerment? African-American Leadership and the Struggle for Urban Political Power*. New York: Oxford University Press, 1997.

Kleppner, Paul. *Chicago Divided, The Making of a Black Mayor*. DeKalb, IL: Northern Illinois University Press, 1985. Richly described account of Harold Washington's election as Chicago's first black mayor in 1983.

Kousser, J. Morgan. *The Shaping of Southern Politics: Suffrage Restriction and the Establishment of the One-Party South, 1880–1910*. New Haven, CT: Yale University Press, 1974.

Lawson, Steven F. *Black Ballots: Voting Rights in the South, 1944–1969*. New York: Columbia University Press, 1976. A study of how the legal and political institutions in the United States responded to black efforts to attain the vote in the South in the years following World War II.

Lewinson, Paul. *Race, Class, and Party*. New York: Russell, 1965. A study of black suffrage and white political strategies in the South.

Mitchell, William C. *Why Vote?* Chicago, IL: Markham, 1971. A counter to the argument that voting is merely a symbolic event.

Morrison, Minion K. C. *Black Political Mobilization*. Albany, NY: State University Press of New York, 1987. A study of political empowerment in rural Mississippi.

O'Reilly, Kenneth. *Nixon's Piano: Presidents and Racial Politics from Washington to Clinton*. New York: The Free Press, 1995. An analysis of racial politics of the presidency.

Parker, Frank. *Black Votes Count*. Chapel Hill, NC: University of North Carolina Press, 1991. An excellent study of the struggle for black empowerment in Mississippi from 1965 to 1988.

Pinderhughes, Dianne M. *Race and Ethnicity in Chicago Politics*. Urbana, IL, and Chicago, IL: University of Illinois Press, 1987. Establishes how the pluralist model of American politics is invalidated by the political experience of blacks in Chicago.

Preston, Michael, et al., eds. *The New Black Politics*. New York: Longman, 1982. A collection of articles on black empowerment in local, state, and national settings.

Roberts, Ronald. *Clarence Thomas and the Tough Love Crowd*. New York: New York University Press, 1995. A thoughtful analysis of the political philosophy of the new black conservatives.

Rose, Peter I., et al., eds. *Through Different Eyes: Black and White Perspectives on American Race Relations*. New York: Oxford University Press, 1973. A reader examining the differing perspectives of black and white Americans on race relations.

Simms, Margaret C., and Julianne Malreaux, eds. *Slipping Through the Cracks, The Status of Black Women*. New Brunswick, NJ: Transaction Books, 1986. A collection of descriptive and analytical articles on the socioeconomic status of black women in the United States.

Swain, Carol. *Black Faces, Black Interests: The Representation of African Americans in Congress*. Cambridge, MA: Harvard University Press, 1993. A study challenging the effectiveness of same-race representation in Congress.

Tate, Katherine. *From Protest to Politics: The New Black Voters in American Elections*. Cambridge, MA: Harvard University Press, 1993. A comprehensive analysis of differentiated attitudinal patterns among contemporary black voters.

Walton, Hanes. *African American Power and Politics: The Political Context*. New York: Columbia University Press, 1996. A detailed study of how the Reagan and Bush presidencies restructured the discussion of race in American politics.

Woodward, C. Vann. *The Strange Career of Jim Crow*, 3rd rev. ed. New York: Oxford University Press, 1974. A classic study both of southern segregation under the "Jim Crow" system and of the extension of these ideas into contemporary society.

NOTES

1. Quote appears in Rufus P. Browning, Dale Rogers Marshall, and David H. Tabb, *Protest Is Not Enough* (Berkeley, CA, and Los Angeles, CA: University of California Press, 1984), p. 17. Reprinted by permission.

2. J. L. Chestnut, Jr., and Julia Cass, *Black in Selma* (New York: Farrar, Straus, and Giroux, 1990), pp. 262–263. Reprinted by permission.

3. For an excellent discussion of the struggle for voting rights, see David J. Garrow, *Protest at Selma* (New Haven, CT: Yale University Press, 1978).

4. U.S. Bureau of the Census, *Current Population Reports*, Series P-20, *Voting and Registration in the Election of November 1988* (Washington, DC: U.S. Government Printing Office, 1989).

5. *Black Elected Officials, A National Roster 1993* (Washington, DC: Joint Center for Political Studies), Table 1.

6. Engstrom, Richard L., "Racial Discrimination in the Electoral Process: The Voting Rights Act and the Vote Dilution Issue," in *Party Policies in the South*, ed. Robert Steed, Laurence Moreland, and Ted Baker (New York: Praeger, 1980).

7. Calculations are based upon figures given in Allen Tullos, "Not So Simple Justice," *Southern Changes* 7 (May–June 1985), p. 4.

8. Fred Powledge, *Free At Last?* (New York: HarperPerennial, 1991), p. 613.

9. Chestnut and Cass, *Black in Selma*, pp. 262–263.

10. For a discussion of the variety of tactics used by whites in the Alabama Black Belt to thwart black participation, see *Hearings on Extension of the Voting Rights Act* before the Subcommittee on Civil and Constitutional Rights of the Committee on the Judiciary, 97th Cong., First Sess., 1982, pp. 751–768; 1511–1624.

11. *Ibid.*, p. 756.

12. Under local courtesy rules, a bill that applies only to a given legislative district or portions of a district are routinely passed by the full legislature if it has unanimous consent of the district's legislative delegation. This means that the senator or representative of a given county has almost unlimited legislative powers in such matters. White state legislators used this power extensively to frustrate black efforts in majority black counties.

13. See Thomas Bethel, *Sumter County Blues, The Ordeal of the Federation of Southern Cooperatives* (Washington, DC: National Committee in Support of Community-Based Organizations, 1982).

14. *Ibid.*, p. 14.

15. *Ibid.*, p. 15.

16. See Allen Tullos, "Crackdown in the Black Belt," *Southern Changes* (March–April 1985), pp. 1–5.

17. See *Hearings on Extension of Voting*, p. 1579. A fact sheet circulated by a defense committee for those charged with absentee voter fraud asserted that, in electoral contests between black and white candidates, the average margin of victory for black candidates was 200 votes and that the average number of black absentee ballots was around 400. "Fact Sheet on Federal Grand Jury Investigations of Black Leaders in Alabama for Voter Fraud" (Gainesville, AL: Alabama Black Belt Defense Committee, 1985), p. 41.

18. In a widely circulated letter calling for support, the group announced that the key to success was to "support good, responsible blacks and to keep whites out of the race," *Green County Democrat*, Eutaw, AL, June 13, 1984, p. 1.

19. Chandler Davidson and Bernard Grofman, "Editors' Introduction," in *Quiet Revolution in the South* (Princeton, NJ: Princeton University Press, 1994), pp. 14–15.

20. Peyton McCrary, Jerome A. Gray, Edward Still, and Huey L. Perry, "Alabama," in *Quiet Revolution in the South* (Princeton, NJ: Princeton University Press, 1994), p. 54.

21. Bernard Grofman, Lisa Handley, and Richard Niemi, *Minority Representation and the Quest for Voting Equality* (New York: Cambridge University Press, 1992).

22. Parity ratios greater than 1.0 indicate that a group is overrepresented relative to their population size. In the South as well as nationally, blacks are underrepresented in government.

23. Grofman, Handley, and Niemi, *Minority Representation*, pp. 17–18.

24. Parker, *Black Votes Count*, p. 113.

25. See William L. Clay, *Just Permanent Interests: Black Americans in Congress, 1870–1991* (New York: Amistad Press Inc., 1991).

26. Carol M. Swain, *Black Faces, Black Interests: The Representation of African Americans in Congress* (Cambridge, MA: Harvard University Press, 1993), p. 60.

27. Stokely Carmichael and Charles V. Hamilton, *Black Power* (New York: Vintage Books, 1967), p. 47.

28. Steven P. Erie, *Rainbow's End* (Berkeley, CA, and Los Angeles, CA: University of California Press, 1988).

29. William J. Grimshaw, *Bitter Fruit, Black Politics and the Chicago Machine, 1931–1991* (Chicago, IL: University of Chicago Press, 1992), p. 114.

30. Grimshaw, pp. 110–113.

31. Paul Kleppner, *Chicago Divided: The Making of a Black Mayor* (DeKalb, IL: Northern Illinois University Press, 1985).

32. Kleppner, pp. 148–149.

33. Grimshaw, p. 177.

34. Kleppner, p. 217.

35. Grimshaw, p. 200.

36. Rufus P. Browning, Dale Rogers Marshall, and David H. Tabb, *Protest Is Not Enough* (Berkeley, CA, and Los Angeles, CA: University of California Press, 1984), p. 25.

37. Dianne M. Pinderhughes, *Race and Ethnicity in Chicago Politics* (Chicago, IL, and Urbana, IL: University of Illinois Press, 1987).

38. William E. Nelson, Jr., "Cleveland: The Evolution of Black Power," in *The New Black Politics*, 2nd ed., ed. Michael B. Preston, Lenneal J. Henderson, Jr., and Paul L. Puryear (White Plains, NY: Longman, 1987).

39. Richard A. Keiser, "After the First Black Mayor: Fault Lines in Philadelphia's Biracial Coalition," in *Racial Politics in American Cities*, 2nd ed., ed. Rufus P. Browning, Dale Rogers Marshall, and David H. Tabb (White Plains, NY: Longman, 1997), pp. 65–93.

40. Huey L. Perry, "The Evolution and Impact of Biracial Coalitions and Black Mayors in Birmingham and New Orleans," in *Racial Politics in American Cities*, 2nd ed., ed. Rufus P. Browning, Dale Rogers Marshall, and David H. Tabb (White Plains, NY: Longman, 1997), pp. 179–200.

41. Carmichael and Hamilton, *Black Power*, p. 63.

42. John Mollenkopf, "New York: The Great Anomaly," in *Racial Politics in American Cities*, 2nd ed., ed. Rufus P. Browning, Dale Rogers Marshall, and David H. Tabb (White Plains, NY: Longman, 1997), pp. 97–115.

43. Dianne Pinderhughes, "An Examination of Chicago Politics," in *Racial Politics in American Cities*, 2nd ed., ed. Rufus P. Browning, Dale Rogers Marshall, and David H. Tabb (White Plains, NY: Longman, 1997), p. 129.

44. Robert T. Starks and Michael B. Preston, "Harold Washington and the Politics of Reform in Chicago 1983–1987," in *Racial Politics in American Cities*, ed. Rufus P. Browning, Dale Rogers Marshall, and David H. Tabb (White Plains, NY: Longman, 1990), pp. 88–107.

45. Pinderhughes, "An Examination of Chicago Politics," p. 131.

46. For an excellent collection of commentaries on the Gary Convention, see *Unity without Uniformity*, compiled by Senator Mervyan Dymally, California legislature (Sacramento, CA: 1972).

47. See "Dead End or New Beginning? National Black Assembly," *Black World* 25 (October 1975) pp. 2–46; Harold Cruse, "The Little Rock National Black Political Convention," *Black World* 23 (October 1974), pp. 10–17; 82–84; and William Strickland, "The Gary Convention and the Crisis of American Politics," *Black World* 21 (October 1972), pp. 18–31. See also Robert Smith, *We Have No*

Leaders: African American Leadership in the Post-Civil Rights Era (Albany, NY: State University of New York Press, 1996), Chapter 2.

48. See "NAACP Blasts Preamble," *Post-Tribune*, Gary, IN, March 11, 1972, p. 1.

49. The election of Jimmy Carter in 1976 on the heels of the Watergate scandal was thought by some to be more of a reaction to the scandal than an endorsement of Carter's philosophy. The thorough defeat of Carter by Reagan in 1980 lends credence to this supposition.

50. *ABC News/Washington Post* poll.

51. This discussion is drawn on Mack H. Jones, "The Political Thought of the New Black Conservatives: Analysis, Explanation and Interpretation," in *Readings in American Political Issues*, ed. Franklin Jones, et al. (Dubuque, IA: Kendall/Hunt, 1987).

52. Walter Williams, *The State against Blacks* (New York: New Press, 1982), p. xvi.

53. "Thomas Sowell on Meet the Press," *Manhattan Report*, special ed. 1, no. 8 (November 1981), p. 7.

54. Loury's thesis was first published as "A New American Dilemma," *The New Republic* 184 (December 31, 1984). It was published in a slightly different form in four other nationally circulated journals.

55. David Swinton, "The Economic Status of the Black Population," in *The State of Black America 1992* (New York: National Urban League, 1992), p. 92.

56. Robert Hill, "The Economic Status of Black Americans," in *The State of Black America 1981* (New York: National Urban League, 1981), pp. 1–59.

57. *Ibid.*, p. 15.

58. *Ibid.*, p. 18.

59. H. Paul Friesema, "Black Control of Central Cities: The Hollow Prize," *American Institute of Planners Journal* (March 1969), pp. 75–79.

60. Adolph Reed, Jr., "The Black Urban Regime: Structural Origins and Constraints," in *Power, Community, and the City*, vol. 1, ed. Michael Peter Smith (New Brunswick, NJ: Transaction Press, 1988); and Clarence N. Stone, *Regime Politics* (Lawrence, KS: University of Kansas Press, 1989).

61. Albert K. Karnig and Susan Welch, *Black Representation and Urban Policy* (Chicago, IL: University of Chicago Press, 1980); Peter K. Eisinger, "Black Employment and Municipal Jobs: The Impact of Black Political Power," *American Political Science Review*, vol. 76, 1982, pp. 380–392; Browning, Marshall, and Tabb, *Protest Is Not Enough*; Kenneth R. Mlandenka, "Blacks and Hispanics in Urban Politics," *American Political Science Review*, vol. 83, no. 1, 1989, pp. 165–192; and James W. Button, *Blacks and Social Change* (Princeton, NJ: Princeton University Press, 1989).

62. William Keech, *The Impact of Negro Voting* (Chicago, IL: Rand McNally, 1968), p. 94.

Chapter 5

The Supreme Court and the Politics of Uncertainty

I do not believe that the meaning of the constitution was forever "fixed" at the Philadelphia convention. Nor do I find the wisdom, foresight, and sense of justice exhibited by the Framers particularly profound. To the contrary, the government they devised was defective from the start, requiring several amendments, a civil war, and momentous social transformation to attain the system of constitutional government, and its respect for the individual freedoms and human rights, we hold as fundamental today.... What is striking is the role legal principles have played throughout America's history in determining the condition of Negroes. They were enslaved by law, emancipated by law. Along the way, new constitutional principles have emerged to meet the challenge of a changing society.

—Justice Thurgood Marshall[1]

Our task in this case, like any other case involving the construction of a statute, is to give effect to the intent of Congress. To divine that intent, we traditionally look first to the words of the statute and, if they are unclear, then to the statute's legislative history. Finding the desired result hopelessly foreclosed by these conventional sources, the Court turns to a third source—the "spirit" of the Act. But close examination of what the Court proffers as the spirit of the Act reveals it as the spirit animating the present majority, not the Eighty-eighth Congress.

—Justice William H. Rehnquist[2]

One legal scholar has suggested that the Supreme Court's principal duty in opinion writing is to make each decision "a coherent communication about the Constitution."[3] Nevertheless, it is clear that the Court's efforts to define the scope and requirements of the equal protection components of the Fifth and Fourteenth Amendments have not always been fully coherent and have, in fact, often engendered greater legal confusion and political controversy. Even when the Court decides an equal protection case in a seemingly clear and resolute voice, it has often found that the ultimate question about the definite contours of "equal protection" are still perceived by the lower courts and others as shrouded in ambiguity. This is not to suggest that this uncertainty robs the Court of power or authority. Indeed, it may be that the Court finds its greatest influence in politics and policy through the ambiguity and uncertainty recurrent in this ongoing conversation about the Constitution's meaning. The Court's approach to affirmative action questions is a prime example of the uncertainty of equal protection jurisprudence.

The 1964 Civil Rights Act spurred both federal and state governments to take affirmative measures to correct the lingering effects of past discrimination. When the government acted in such a remedial capacity, the Court's initial approach was to apply a less exacting level of scrutiny to such action. For example, in its 1980 decision in *Fullilove* v. *Klutznick*,[4] the Court accorded Congress great deference in creating race-based preferences in a remedial context. But in 1989, a deeply divided court took a more skeptical look at state and locally created affirmative action programs and applied strict scrutiny in rejecting Richmond, Virginia's minority contracts set-aside program.[5] In her decision for the Court in *City of Richmond* v. *J.A. Croson Co.*, Justice O'Connor reasoned that Congress could act where the states may not because Section 5 of the Fourteenth Amendment specifically gives Congress a "mandate" to enforce the Amendment's provisions. Consequently, Congress could act after making only generalized findings of historical discrimination but state and local actors, like the City of Richmond, may act only after justifying their programs by reference to concrete and particularized findings of state participation in past discriminatory activity. The Court's 1990 decision in *Metro Broadcasting Inc.* v. *F.C.C.*,[6] continued to accord higher deference to federal remedial programs. In this instance, the remedial program was a Federal Communications Commission policy giving preference to minority applicants for broadcast licenses. The Court upheld this use of affirmative action as serving the constitutionally permissible goal of furthering diversity in radio and television.

This 1990 *Metro Broadcasting* decision led to even more uncertainty and confusion in equal protection jurisprudence with respect to the status of affirmative action. And in 1995 the Supreme Court attempted to simplify the state of affirmative action law in *Adarand Constructors Inc.* v. *Pena*.[7] *Adarand* involved construction contracts for a federally funded highway project, based on a provision of the Small Business Act[8] that stated the federal government's policy of encouraging "socially and economically disadvantaged" individuals to participate in the performance of federally funded projects. A key provision of the act stipulated that contractors working on federally funded projects would be given financial incentives for hiring subcontractors certified as small businesses controlled by disadvantaged individuals. Regulations of the Small Business Administration presumed that all members of certain minority groups were "disadvantaged" for purposes of the Small Business Act.

In 1989, Mountain Gravel and Construction Company, a major contractor for a federally funded highway construction project in Colorado, solicited bids from subcontractors for the guardrail portion of the highway project. Although Adarand Constructors submitted the lowest bid for the project, the subcontract was ultimately awarded to Gonzalez Construction Company, which was certified as disadvantaged under federal rules. Adarand brought suit in federal district court to challenge both the federal policy of favoring minority-owned enterprises and the federal presumption that all minority-owned firms were controlled by socially and economically disadvantaged individuals.[9]

The District Court dismissed Adarand's complaint[10] and the Court of Appeals for the 10th Circuit affirmed.[11] The lower courts had relied on what they believed was the more lenient level of scrutiny that had been developed for congressionally created affirmative action programs by the high court in *Klutznick* and *Metro Broadcasting*. But a sharply divided Supreme Court reversed. It specifically overturned *Metro Broadcasting*, which had been decided only five years earlier, and held that congressionally enacted affirmative action programs must satisfy the same strict scrutiny that was applied to state and local governments in *Croson*. Although acknowledging a "lingering uncertainty" in its own equal protection jurisprudence, the Court interpreted its prior cases as standing for three propositions. First, "skepticism" (any preference based on racial or ethnic criteria must necessarily receive the strictest scrutiny); second, "consistency" (the standard of review should be the same whether the purpose of government classification was invidious or remedial); and third, "congruence" (equal protection analysis under the Fifth Amendment should be the same as that under the Fourteenth Amendment).[12]

Although the Court obviously hoped to use the *Adarand* case as a platform for making a clear and coherent statement about the place of affirmative action in equal protection jurisprudence, its analytically splintered decision only muddied the water still further. The picture that emerged from the six separate opinions generated by the case was that the Court was divided along three fractured lines.[13] Justices Scalia and Thomas were uncompromising in their stand against such affirmative action programs. In Scalia's view, "government can never have a 'compelling' interest in discriminating on the basis of race in order to 'make up' for past racial discrimination in the opposite direction."[14] Thomas wrote separately to attack what he viewed as the corrosive "paternalism" inherent in affirmative action programs and to argue that "[g]overnment cannot make us equal; it can only recognize, respect, and protect us as equal before the law."[15]

At the other end of the spectrum, Justices Breyer, Stevens, Ginsberg, and Souter agreed that all race-based preferences and classifications should meet the requirements of strict scrutiny. They believed, however, and with varying points of emphasis, that Congress enjoyed broad discretion when acting pursuant to Section 5 of the Fourteenth Amendment.[16] Consequently, they would have approved outright the affirmative action program in *Adarand* as consistent with federal power. In the middle, a prevailing coalition composed of Justices O'Connor, Kennedy, and Rehnquist believed that Congress's power to enact remedial affirmative action programs was no greater than that of state and local entities. Importantly, however, they sought to leave open the question as to whether affirmative action programs might survive strict scrutiny under certain limited circumstances. In the end, and with Thomas's and Scalia's acquiescence, O'Connor won five votes to remand the case to the lower courts for reconsideration under a strict scrutiny standard.

If anything, the decision represents a prime example of how the "politics of uncertainty" continues to haunt the fundamental political and social status of African Americans. As we discuss later, *Adarand* may also be seen as part of a more general change in the tone and substance of civil rights decisions that seems to have differentiated the Warren Court from the Burger Court, and now the Burger Court from the Rehnquist Court. And this more general shift has been furthered by lower court rulings espousing the formalistic color-blindness favored by the Rehnquist Court. In *Hopwood* v. *Texas* (1996), a three-judge panel of the Fifth Circuit Court of Appeals ruled that public universities were prohibited from using affirmative action in the admissions process, except where needed to remedy the school's own past discrimination. Despite the decision's direct attack on the Supreme Court's holding in *Bakke*, the Court chose to deny certiorari in *Hopwood*, thereby allowing the decision to stand. As a result, the ban on affirmative action in admissions applies only to public universities in the states contained within the Fifth Circuit (Louisiana, Mississippi, and Texas). The Fifth Circuit's ruling, however, emboldened leaders of anti-affirmative action movements in other states, most notably California. In a related development, the Ninth Circuit Court of Appeals, following the Supreme Court's lead as per *Croson* and *Adarand*, upheld California's widely publicized Proposition 209 (see *Coalition for Economic Equality* v. *Wilson* [1997]). This initiative, which became part of California's constitution, outlawed race and gender preferences in public employment, public education, and public contracting.

Additionally, and in a broader context, the *Adarand* case represents a prime example of the situation that Alexis de Tocqueville observed long ago. Sooner or later major political issues are translated into legal issues. This observation is certainly supported by the involvement of courts in racial problems. And this involvement has been anything but neutral—that is, above political interests. Indeed, because of the American belief in the "majesty of the law," courts and other participants in the legal process play a crucial role in determining who gets what, when they get it, and how they get it.[17]

This importance of courts and judges in the political process was made clear early in the nation's history in the classic case of *Marbury* v. *Madison*.

Chief Justice John Marshall's 1803 decision went a long way toward establishing the principle of judicial review: the authority of courts to declare legislative acts (e.g., acts of Congress) unconstitutional. Marshall made it clear that whether or not an act of Congress conflicts with the Constitution is, in the final analysis, a matter for the Court to decide. "It is emphatically the province and duty of the judicial department," said Marshall, "to say what the law is."

While there is no specific basis or authority in the Constitution for the Court's power to declare acts of Congress unconstitutional, the force of Marshall's argument in *Marbury* v. *Madison* is now fully imbedded in our constitutional system. Moreover, that power not only refers to the actions of the federal government but also to the actions of state and local governments. In short, it is the special province of courts and judges to authoritatively decide conflicts over constitutional interpretation. It is hardly surprising, then, that conflicting interests frequently turn to the Court for support. When, for example, the Supreme Court decided in *Plessy* v. *Ferguson* (1896) that "separate but equal" facilities were constitutional, it strongly supported the segregation policies of southern whites. It was a major setback to civil rights for African Americans. But when the Court decided in *Brown* v. *Board of Education* (1954) that "separate but equal" was unconstitutional, it strengthened the rising civil rights movement and dealt a severe blow to segregationists. In the 1978 *Bakke* case and the 1995 *Adarand* decision, the Court rendered decisions that gave some constitutional support to the major contending interests. Such decisions on major political issues tend to assure continued controversy and added opportunities for court involvement.

STATUTORY INTERPRETATION

Thus far we have focused on the highly visible role of the Court in interpreting the Constitution. This emphasis is quite understandable since the "interpretation of the Constitution … is the highest and most difficult responsibility that American judges are called on to perform."[18] Nonetheless, we should mention here that a major part of the workload of courts in America consists of cases dealing with statutory interpretation as opposed to constitutional interpretation. Statutory interpretation refers to the work of courts in applying and enforcing laws (statutes), such as those enacted by Congress. Constitutional interpretation refers to the role of courts in applying and enforcing various provisions of the Constitution.

In deciding conflicts concerning statutory law, the role of courts can become crucial in determining who wins or who loses as a result of specific legislative enactments. For example, in *Grove City College* v. *Bell* the Court interpreted Title IX of the 1972 Education Amendments so as to blunt its use as an effective weapon in monitoring federal grants to institutions that discriminated against persons on account of sex. The Court held that Title IX prevents such discrimination in particular programs or activities receiving federal grants, but not in the institution as a whole. This severely limited the scope of Title IX. In response, Congress passed the Civil Rights Restoration Act of 1987[19] to overcome the effects of *Grove City*.

But only two years later, in 1989, the Rehnquist Court decided five other cases that would interpret various civil rights laws and determine their application in the employment context.[20] These decisions were widely regarded as unfavorable to African Americans and other minority groups seeking judicial relief from employment discrimination. Congress was again compelled to pass legislation (the Civil Rights Act of 1991) to clarify its own understanding of previous civil rights laws and to reverse the effects of the Supreme Court's 1989 decisions in this regard.[21] Consequently, what a statute means is what the courts say it means. And the language inevitably found in statutes, which more or less reflects compromises needed to enact such legislation, obviously means that "the opportunities for the exercise of judicial discretion in statutory interpretation are both frequent and wide."[22]

When we combine the traditional function of courts in statutory interpretation with that of judicial review, we begin to see more clearly the enormous importance of courts and judges in the political process. We begin to see more clearly the influence of courts in determining who gets what, when, and how. This influence is undoubtedly enhanced by the strong attachment Americans have to doing things "legally" and "according to law." Under our system of government, courts exercise a crucial role in determining what is "legal" and "according to law." Accordingly, courts are the focal point of the legal process. However, we should not overlook the fundamental role of other participants in that process, especially that of lawyers.

Lawyers are important because it is from their ranks that judges are chosen or elected. They are the principal gatekeepers to the courts and to the legal process in general. Their special training gives them the knowledge needed to negotiate the details of the process on behalf of their clients. The legal process is indeed controlled by lawyers. Such control is stabilized by the strong influence and representation of lawyers in government as well as in the private sector. Again, it was de Tocqueville who observed that if he had to describe where the aristocracy lies in America, it would be in the lofty role and deference accorded lawyers. De Tocqueville's observation is even more valid today. Lawyers and the public alike acknowledge the importance of lawyers and the legal profession. This is remarkably consistent with de Tocqueville.[23] Unfortunately, since there are so few black lawyers,[24] it is also consistent with the very limited role and influence that blacks have, not only in the legal system but also in the political process generally.

COURTS AND JUDGES

Judges, like legislators, are also engaged in the business of allocating resources, making rewards, and imposing deprivations. The fact that a judge is so involved, as Peltason puts it, is "not a matter of choice but of function."[25] "Judicial participation," continues Peltason, "does not grow out of the judge's personality or philosophy but out of his position."[26] This position is entrusted with the authority to render decisions that support certain interests and don't support others—which leads us to describe judges as participants in the political process. Consequently, courts, the institutional structures in which judges operate, become important forums in managing and resolving conflict in the governing system.

To be sure, certain factors that tend to remove or insulate courts and judges from politics can sometimes obscure their crucial role in American politics. Consider our attachment to the belief in a "government of laws and not of men [individuals]." Consider, moreover, that courts stand as a constant reminder of this belief and are to rule according to law. While general public opinion and special interests may influence other decision makers, the judge's influence is believed to come from the law and what the law requires. In addition to public opinion, the methods of selecting judges, which increasingly emphasize their expertise in the law and their judicial temperament, are based upon the judges' accountability to no one except the law and their own consciences. In addition, consider the formal and informal expectations (norms) concerning how judges are to act, behave, and carry on their high duties. These jurists must show impartiality and neutrality.

Admittedly, these and other factors do shape judicial behavior and how courts function. They also shape our perceptions of courts and judges and how we think they should carry out their responsibilities. All this, however, does not change the crucial and often determining roles that courts perform in the business of governing. Rather than lessening their functions, these perceptions and expectations strengthen the judicial hand.

We are not attempting here to equate the functions of courts with legislatures, or judges with elected politicians. Rather, we suggest that courts, through proper judicial procedures, also make decisions that determine who gets what, when, and how. However, decision making in the judicial forum—unlike the legislature, for example—does not supposedly turn on numbers, wealth, or social standing. Rather it turns on the law. And though much of the law is itself influenced by these very factors (for example, wealth and social standing),[27] once enacted it may be subject to judicial interpretations that might or might not support interests that led to its original enactment. In any event, the structure of courts is such that they do not necessarily respond to the same interests as do other political institutions, such as legislatures. This element of discretion and the authority of his or her decisions place the judge in a position of power and influence in the American government system. How one gains such a position and what manner of person becomes a judge are of obvious importance to those interested in the allocation of values.

Few can forget the fierce and widely publicized controversies that accompanied President Ronald Reagan's nomination in 1987 of Judge

Robert Bork to the U.S. Supreme Court. Nor can we forget the furor and sensationalism that followed President George Bush's nomination of Judge Clarence Thomas to the high court. Indeed, at bottom, these nominations illuminate vividly and dramatically the various interests and stakes involved in selecting those who sit on the Court. Though few nominations are as controversial as those of Bork and Thomas, the close scrutiny given to judicial appointments serves to illustrate the important role that courts and judges play in American politics and society.

COURTS AND JUDICIAL SELECTION

Three main criteria stand out in the selection of federal judges. These selection variables are competence, party affiliation, and ideological considerations.[28] The latter two factors are primarily political. Thus, they will be determined largely by political officials, such as the president, U.S. senators, and state and local party officials. The potential nominee is almost always (90 percent of the time) a member of the president's party. In addition, the kinds of support he or she has given the party, as well as the "right" ideological positions on important policy issues, define more accurately the best nominee for a federal judgeship. However, the competence part, having to do with the legal ability, experience, and judicial nature of the nominee, are matters to be determined through institutionalized legal channels, such as the American Bar Association (ABA) Committee on Federal Judiciary. The role and influence of such key participants in the selection process vary widely depending upon a number of factors, for example, the particular judgeship to be filled (Supreme Court, court of appeals, district court) and the political context in which the appointment is being made.

The president makes all appointments to federal court judgeships, but the president's appointments must be confirmed by the Senate. While appointments to lower federal courts are very important, it is the appointments to the U.S. Supreme Court that are most visible and command public attention. This means that the stakes are very high in terms of who serves on the Court. Given the authority and prestige of the Supreme Court and since vacancies occur only occasionally, it is obvious that the president savors the authority and opportunity in making such appointments. While certain other factors, such as race, religion, ethnic affiliation, gender, and geographic balance may be considered, a president will perhaps be most concerned about the ideological and policy dispositions of potential nominees. Indeed, decisions of the Supreme Court have national implications. They can do much to promote, frustrate, or negate presidential policies and programs. Because of this power, other participants in the selection process—both official and unofficial—attach their own importance to Supreme Court nominations.

Consequently, senators and other public officials, the ABA and leaders of the bar, organized interest groups, and concerned citizens will all use the full range of their influence to make certain that the "right" person is selected. All it takes is a controversial appointment to bring the dynamics of selecting a Supreme Court justice into full focus. And there are some well-publicized examples. The story of one such appointment, that of Judge G. Harrold Carswell, is brilliantly told by Richard Harris in his description of the unsuccessful attempt of President Nixon to appoint Carswell to the Court.[29] The Carswell episode, it will be recalled, followed the earlier unsuccessful Nixon effort to place Judge Clement Haynsworth on the Court. Of course, the 1987 attempt of President Reagan to appoint and elevate federal appellate judge Robert Bork to the Supreme Court engendered one of the most bitter, divisive, and engulfing confirmation battles in history. Similar comments may be made about the highly controversial 1991 nomination of Clarence Thomas to the Supreme Court.

What kinds of judges have come out of this judicial selection process? The overwhelming majority of federal judges are white, Anglo-Saxon, Protestant males. The few who come from other racial (black), ethnic, and religious backgrounds (Jewish, Catholic) were mainly appointed by Democratic presidents. Clearly, President Bush's appointment of black conservative Judge Clarence Thomas to the Supreme Court indicates how, on occasion, Republicans might also select judges from these groups. In general, however, the proclivity of Democrats to appoint such persons may be explained in part by the attachment that economically disadvantaged and ethnic groups have to the Democratic party. Federal judges generally have been "politically active"; that is, they have been actively involved in politics prior to their appointment. However, appointments to the Supreme Court have gone in large measure to those who have either held important political or legal office (for example, U.S. senator or attorney general) or to those who have achieved prominence in the legal profession (for example, in the ABA or in prestigious law schools).

This discussion about courts and judicial selection leads to a major conclusion: Those who are selected as federal judges mostly represent the dominant political interests at any given time. Hence, those who are disadvantaged in political arenas will find, as far as representation is concerned, that they are similarly disadvantaged in the judicial forum. It should come as no surprise then that black representation, as well as representation of women and Hispanics in the third branch at all levels (national, state, and local) is very small. While tradition, structures, and insulation of the judicial office serve to hide these selection biases, their visibility becomes all too clear when one takes a closer look at the facts. In the late 1970s, before the appointment of new judges pursuant to the Omnibus Judgeship Act (see following), of the about 500 judges on the federal district courts and courts of appeals, the Justice Department estimated that there were 23 blacks, 11 women, and 7 Hispanics on these courts.[30] And, of course, the only 2 blacks to serve on the U.S. Supreme Court were Thurgood Marshall, appointed in

1967 by President Johnson, and Clarence Thomas, appointed in 1991 by President Bush. Yet, there are some other developments that could affect the number of minorities in the third branch, including the creation and addition of new courts and judgeships.

In 1978, for example, Congress passed the Omnibus Judgeship Act, which established 117 new federal district judgeships and 35 additional seats on the courts of appeals.[31] As an outgrowth of the new legislation, President Carter issued two executive orders providing for standards and guidelines for the merit selection of federal district judges and for the establishment of a Circuit Judge Nominating Commission for the selection of judges to the courts of appeals. The commission was designed to operate through panels in each circuit, which would be composed of lawyers, nonlawyers, persons of both sexes, and minority group members. The Carter administration had hoped that merit selection would increase the number of women and blacks in the federal judiciary.

It is somewhat ironic, but not surprising, that preliminary results of "merit selection" indicate the continued domination of white male nominees for judgeships. The use of criteria, such as long years of "prior legal experience," tend to limit possible minority nominees who have just recently entered the legal profession in any substantial numbers.[32] Indeed, even with the merit plans in operation, it was estimated in early 1979 that of 77 persons recommended for 54 judgeships under the 1978 legislation, only 5 were blacks (including 2 women), 3 were Hispanic males, and 3 were white women. Thus, the nominees still overwhelmingly tend to be white males. Yet, by October 1979, there were some encouraging signs. Of the 109 nominations that President Carter made under the new act, 16 had been white women, 14 had been blacks (including 4 black women), and 4 had been Hispanics. And of the 80 confirmed nominations, there were 13 white women, 8 blacks (including 2 black women), and 2 Hispanic men.[33] That these 23 appointments increased the representation of women and minorities on the federal bench by 56 percent (from 41 to 64) lends evidence to the continued sparsity of their numbers.

A CHANGING FEDERAL JUDICIARY: THE REHNQUIST COURT AND THE REAGAN-BUSH LEGACY

While many of President Carter's judicial appointments were undoubtedly "liberal," those of President Reagan and President Bush were of a clear conservative mold and not expected to further the interests of blacks and other minorities. In all, during the 1980s Reagan had the opportunity to fill almost 45 percent of the existing 900 federal judgeships, including the appointment of three new justices to the Supreme Court (O'Connor, Scalia, and Kennedy).[34] He also, of course, elevated Justice Rehnquist to the position of chief justice to replace Chief Justice Burger. Although particular appoint-

ments might not turn out as expected, by and large those selected as federal judges reflect fairly well the overall views and positions of the president,
and in view of their lifetime tenure, will continue to do so long after the
president leaves office. Should this pattern prevail, it seems unlikely, at least
in the next ten years or so, that blacks and other minorities will find strong
support for their interests in the federal judiciary.

This support certainly cannot be expected to come from black and
minority judges whose numbers remain small. By and large, appointments
to the federal judiciary reflect the relative strength of various interests
among those who make up the president's constituency, or those whose support the president would like to cultivate. Consequently, we saw more black
and minority judicial appointments under Carter than under Reagan or
Bush. Even so, the number of such judges remains woefully sparse, especially when viewed in relation to their proportions in the population. In the
federal courts, for example, between 1960 and 1989 a total of 50 African
Americans were appointed, and 28 of these were Carter appointees. As of
1988 there were 14 African Americans on courts of appeals, and as of 1992,
there have been 2 African Americans on the Supreme Court (Thurgood
Marshall, who retired in 1990, and Clarence Thomas who was appointed in
1991). While the number of African American judges fluctuates over time,
some idea of their relation to the total number of judges may be gleaned
from the fact that as of 1991, the total of authorized judgeships on district
courts was 649; on the courts of appeals 179 judgeships; and of course the
number of justices on the Supreme Court is 9. Overall, the fact that there are
still so few black judges is yet another example of the disproportionate representation and influence of blacks in the American political system. The
election of Bill Clinton in 1992, however, brought with it the promise of
greater ethnic and gender diversity in nominations to the federal bench. This
promise manifested itself in Clinton's appointment of Judge Ruth Bader
Ginsburg to the Supreme Court, as well as in his appointments to the lower
federal courts. As a centrist-minded president, Clinton has come under fire
from both ends of the political spectrum for his appointments. Conservatives
have criticized Clinton-appointed judges for their alleged liberalism, especially on crime; liberals, in contrast, have bemoaned what they view as a lost
opportunity to offset the more conservative judicial appointments of
Presidents Reagan and Bush. There is consensus, however, on the fact that
Clinton's appointments to the bench have generally been more liberal, and
certainly more diversified, in terms of race and gender than those of his
Republican predecessors.

At this point, we should reemphasize that courts play far too important
a role to perpetuate the romanticized notion that the judiciary is "above" or
"beyond" politics. Courts are a part, although a differentiated and specialized
part, of the political system. For, as stated earlier, "[Courts] are in the political process ... not as a matter of choice but as a matter of function."[35] Those

judges who do not wish to become involved (self-restrainers) are supporting certain interests as much as those judges (judicial activists) who do become involved. And this involvement, of course, concerns applying and enforcing statutes. Overall, the participation of courts in both constitutional and statutory interpretation has increased the visibility of the judiciary in politics. As a consequence, courts are of vital political importance to blacks and other minorities. Indeed, as we shall observe in more detail, courts can play important and sometimes crucial roles in the formulation of public policies, including policies relevant to blacks and other minorities.

COURTS, POLICY MAKING, AND CIVIL RIGHTS

Earlier in this chapter we discussed the role of law and courts in the political system. The uniqueness of that role is highlighted by the authority of American courts to exercise judicial review. How courts exercise their authority, and for what ends, inevitably brings them into the business of policy making. It also brings them into the thick of political controversy. The history of the Supreme Court in dealing with racial problems clearly shows these various factors. Particularly, it clarifies the role of the Court in the political system and the nature and limitations of the judiciary in forming public policy.

Prior to the Civil Rights Act of 1964, the political branches had done almost nothing to deal with the problem facing blacks in America. The Civil Rights Act of 1957—the first such legislation passed by Congress since Reconstruction—and the later Civil Rights Act of 1960 were little more than sympathetic gestures toward civil rights interests. It was not until the passage of the 1964 act that the political branches at last began to come to grips with the problem. But, as we shall see, the 1964 act did not just come about. Dire circumstances and enormous resources created the environment conducive to its passage. A crucial element in this environment was the strong support given blacks by the Warren Court, highlighted by the famous *Brown* decision of 1954. Indeed, the Warren Court did not shy away from the problem of race; unlike previous Courts, it met and directly addressed issues that had long been brushed aside and stymied in the political process.

In many ways courts are the forums of last resort, especially for those who are politically disadvantaged. The resources needed to achieve desired objectives through the judicial process are much more attainable and available to minorities than those needed to prevail in the political process. It stands to reason then that blacks who were (and are) certainly disadvantaged in the political system have for some time resorted to the judiciary rather than to the political branches to protect their interests. These efforts were primarily the work of the NAACP and later the NAACP Legal Defense staff. Here was a small group of lawyers whose only armor included the good will and help of a large lay organization (NAACP); a modest amount of money coming mainly from voluntary contributions; courageous litigants with good causes; and, most important, the keen intellect and endless devotion of the legal staff itself, which made good cases out of good causes. The successes achieved by the NAACP, although limited, give some hope to those who believe that the problem can be resolved through the system.

Yet, as we shall see, the records of the Burger Court and now the Rehnquist Court suggest that judicial victories, like political victories, are time bound and thus subject to change. The fact is, for example, that in some areas the Burger Court seems to have read the Constitution differently than did the Warren Court, illustrating anew that the meaning of the Constitution (and law) is not fixed and unchanging. That law and the courts stand as barriers to the tyranny of the majority is not at all certain. In fact, time and again we are reminded of the reverse—that law and courts are indeed instruments of majority rule. If judges interpret the law contrary to persistent majorities, sooner or later the judges (and the law) will change.

Whether this should be the case in a democratic government—as the government of the United States is described—is not of concern here. What does matter is that African Americans and others who place their hope and trust in courts should be aware that the nature of law and the judiciary is anything but static. Though blacks were greatly encouraged by the actions of the Warren Court, a sober reminder is that the Supreme Court of earlier years had much to do with legitimating and perpetuating the very racial inequities with which both the Warren Court and other branches of the national government had to deal. But, as we shall see, such progress made in these areas has once again been put in jeopardy by certain subsequent actions of the Burger-Rehnquist Courts and by the Reagan-Bush administrations. Let us take a brief look at history.

CONSTITUTIONALIZING RACISM: ITS BIRTH AND DECLINE

Decisions of the Supreme Court did much to constitutionalize and legitimize racism. They helped create a climate conducive to fostering rather than eliminating racial segregation. In the *Civil Rights Cases* (1883), for example, the Court effectively rebuffed attempts of the Reconstruction Congress to get rid of some of the badges and incidents of slavery. In 1875 Congress passed the first public accommodations statute in history. It forbade racial segregation in various places of accommodation open to the public, for example, hotels, inns, and theaters. But the Supreme Court ruled that neither the Thirteenth nor the Fourteenth Amendment provided constitutional support for the congressional action. A significant holding of the Court in that case was that the Fourteenth Amendment applied to "state" action and not to "private" action (that is, to action by individuals). Privately owned accommodations could discriminate among their customers without fear of constitutional restrictions. This state-private action distinction of the *Civil Rights Cases* has not been wholly abandoned. But its effect has been largely overcome by the 1964 Civil

Rights Act and by subsequent decisions of the Warren Court. Nonetheless, the decision in the *Civil Rights Cases* in 1883 reflected the waning of Reconstruction policies in the South and the return of white control/black subordination in that region.

An even more ominous decision was made by the Court in *Plessy* v. *Ferguson* (1896). In this case, the Court upheld a Louisiana statute that required racial segregation of passengers on trains as a valid exercise of state police power. Specifically, the Court held that segregation of the races was not the discrimination proscribed by the equal protection clause of the Fourteenth Amendment. In short, classification by race was not arbitrary and without reason and was within the state's authority. States, under this formula, could provide separate facilities for the races if they were equal. It is here that the Court sanctioned "separate but equal." In so doing, in effect, it constitutionalized racism. To be sure, state laws and practices certainly treated blacks separately, but not at all equally. The *Plessy* decision, in effect, legitimated racial segregation, not only in transportation but in every aspect of life, including education, voting, public accommodations, employment, and so on.

Take education, for example. Just three years after *Plessy*, the Court upheld the actions of a Georgia county school board in maintaining a high school for whites but discontinuing a high school for blacks because of financial difficulties (*Cumming* v. *Board of Education*, 1899). The Court reasoned that the black high school was discontinued temporarily for economic reasons and did not indicate that the school board was discriminating because of race. In this way, the Court skirted the constitutional issue of segregation. But once again blacks (and minorities) suffered because of the state authorities' (and now the Supreme Court's) decision. Similarly, the Court avoided the racial segregation issue in two other school cases. In *Berea College* v. *Kentucky* (1908), though Berea is a private college, the Court sustained a Kentucky law that required segregation of blacks and whites in both public and private institutions as a valid regulation by the state of corporate charters. In the second case, *Gong Lum* v. *Rice* (1927), the Court upheld Mississippi's exclusion of Asian Americans from white public schools. This Court action upheld Mississippi segregation laws generally and gave them constitutional legitimacy.

Some change in the Supreme Court stance toward racial segregation in public education began to surface in 1938 in a Missouri law school case (*Missouri ex. rel. Gaines* v. *Canada*). Missouri maintained a law school for whites but refused to accept blacks. Missouri did, however, offer blacks scholarships to attend law schools outside the state. This "out-of-state scholarship" arrangement became one of the many avenues used by southern states to foster racial segregation. However, the Court ruled that where the state did maintain certain educational opportunities for whites, it must furnish such opportunities to all of its residents "upon the basis of an equali-

of right." More importantly, the Court gave notice that it would begin to scrutinize more closely the "equal" part of the "separate but equal" doctrine (*Pearson* v. *Murray*, 1936). But Missouri and five southern states (Texas, Louisiana, Florida, North Carolina, and South Carolina) responded to the Court decision in *Gaines* by establishing separate law schools for blacks. This action quite naturally led to legal challenges as to the standard of equality required by the "equal protection clause" of the Fourteenth Amendment.

The Texas law school case (*Sweatt* v. *Painter*, 1950) provided the opportunity for the Supreme Court to explain the meaning of the "equal protection" provided by the "separate but equal" formula. While not overturning "separate but equal," the Court ruled that the legal education Texas had offered to blacks was not equal to that provided by the state to whites. And most importantly, the Court defined equality in such a way as to signal the end of "separate but equal." In terms of faculty, curriculum, size of student body, and scope of the library, the University of Texas law school was superior to the law school for blacks. Chief Justice Fred Vinson, who spoke for the Court, reasoned as follows:

> What is more important, the University of Texas Law School possesses to a far greater degree those qualities which are incapable of objective measurement but which make for greatness in a law school. Such qualities, to name but a few, include reputation of the faculty, experience of the administration, position and influence of the alumni, standing in the community, traditions and prestige. It is difficult to believe that one who had a free choice between the law schools would consider the question close.

That the "separate but equal" doctrine was being subjected to a more rigid test was also evidenced by another 1950 Supreme Court decision, *McLaurin* v. *Oklahoma*. The Court ruled that the Fourteenth Amendment (equal protection) required that black students (in this instance McLaurin) be accorded the same treatment as other students. In general, *Sweatt* and *McLaurin*, though at the professional and graduate school level, signaled the declining support of the Supreme Court for racial segregation. And, as we shall see later, while the Court finally declared "separate but equal" unconstitutional, it can never be forgotten that the Court (and the judiciary generally) initially supported and furthered racial segregation in education.

Political participation by blacks in voting provides another example of how decisions of the Supreme Court legitimated racism in America. It was not until 1944, for example, that the Court finally declared the white primary unconstitutional as a deprivation of rights secured by the Fifteenth Amendment (*Smith* v. *Allwright*). Though the focus of the litigation was in Texas, the white primary was one of the chief methods used by southern states to prevent blacks from voting and from participating in politics generally. Many other devices were used to disfranchise blacks, including the grandfather clause," the poll tax, and literacy tests. The grandfather clause was declared unconstitutional in 1915, but the poll tax and literacy tests were not overcome until the 1960s through the combined efforts of the Court and Congress. In addition, less formal devices were used to stifle black voting through physical intimidation and violence and ranged from loss of jobs to loss of life.

The "white primary" was as simple as it was effective. Since the Democratic party was the dominant party in the South and since the winner of that primary was inevitably the winner of the general election, the way to prevent blacks from having any real effect on the election of southern officeholders was to prevent them from joining the Democratic party and hence voting in that party's primary election. But in 1944, the Supreme Court overruled one of its earlier decisions and held that the primary was not the "private" affair of the Democratic party. The Court ruled that the party (and its primary) was so enmeshed in and supported by state law and state election machinery that it had become an agent of the state. Consequently, if the party engaged in racial discrimination, its actions amounted to "state action" forbidden by the Fifteenth Amendment.

Blacks suffered inequities and deprivations as a result of discrimination in other areas as well. In addition to education and politics, the plight of blacks and other minorities in their efforts to obtain jobs and housing and to gain service in places of public accommodations was similarly stymied by laws and legal action. As we shall see later, it was only after the 1954 *Brown* decision and well into the 1960s before the national government began to address the quality of life for blacks and other minorities in these areas. But even these actions, as we shall also see, have still not secured equality of treatment and opportunity for blacks in this country. Nonetheless, just as in the past, the Supreme Court (and the judiciary generally) continues to play an important role.

The importance of the Court's role for policy outcomes is demonstrated by the generally favorable position of the Warren Court toward racial problems and the much more uncertain positions of the Burger and Rehnquist Courts toward such problems. In the remainder of this chapter the role and implications of Court participation in dealing with racial policy will be examined.

THE WARREN COURT AND RACIAL DISCRIMINATION

The school segregation cases (*Brown* v. *Board of Education*, 1954) set the tone that the Warren Court was to follow in matters relating to racial segregation. The tone was one of "great policy pronouncement" followed by less grandiose and certainly less definite decisions to implement such policies. For example, the Court boldly declared that where racial segregation was based upon law, black schools were inherently unequal. In short, racial segregation in public school education was declared unconstitutional al. But the Court hedged in 1955 when it made its decision to implement the 1954 policy. The force of the Court's decision was blunted both by its remanding (sending back) cases to federal district courts and by the flexibility given those courts to implement school desegregation "with all deliberate speed." In later decisions, the Warren Court had to deal bit by bit with a variety of schemes and strategies designed to circumvent the decision, including freedom-of-choice plans, free transfer plans, and plans that integrated schools one grade at a time. More drastic measures included closing public schools entirely and the creation of white "private" academies that would then receive various forms of public funding.

Without a commitment from Congress or the executive branch, the Warren Court was left to walk a tightrope between its desire to condemn segregation and its desire to have court orders obeyed. While the Court let stand several lower court rulings that permitted the delaying tactics mentioned above,[36] it drew the line at more extreme forms of resistance to desegregation. In the famous Little Rock, Arkansas, desegregation controversy, the potential for violence was presented by state officials as a justification for defying a court order. The Court, however, made clear in *Cooper* v. *Aaron* [358 U.S. 1 (1958)] that defiance of court orders would not be tolerated. And in *Griffin* v. *Prince Edward County School Board* [377 U.S. 218 (1964)], the Court responded to an attempted school system closing by authorizing a federal district court to order the taxing authority to raise whatever funds were needed to maintain the public school system in a non-discriminatory fashion.

Moreover, the Court applied the principle of its 1954 *Brown* decision to other areas that involved public facilities. When the elective political institutions joined the battle in the 1960s, the Court found ways to legitimate the legislative response to civil rights demands. The Civil Rights Act of 1964, for example, was by far the most extensive rights legislation since Reconstruction. It forbade discrimination against persons in places of public accommodation and in employment. The act also provided substantial new weapons to fight against discrimination, including a mandate to cut off federal funds to agencies that practice discrimination. Nonetheless, despite strong constitutional challenges and precedents (especially the *Civil Rights Cases* of 1883), the Warren Court supported this congressional exercise of legislative authority.

Whereas *Brown* and other rulings on desegregation eventually created opportunities for equality in political education, the Warren Court's holdings on voting rights produced far-ranging effects on legislative apportionment and, as a result, on the balance of power within legislatures. In his memoirs, Earl Warren wrote that, contrary to popular belief, the most important case decided during his tenure as chief justice was not *Brown*, but *Baker* v. *Carr* [369 U.S. 186 (1962)].[37] *Baker* involved a case arising in Tennessee, which, like many states, had not reapportioned its state legislative seats for more than six decades, despite sizable population shifts during that period and a state constitutional requirement that districts be redrawn every ten years. As a result, legislative districts varied wildly in size, with the effect of benefiting rural areas at the expense of urban and suburban dwellers. A 7–2 majority, led by Justice Brennan, ruled for the first time that legislative malapportionment claims were justiciable. That holding led to the Court's enunciation in *Reynolds* v. *Sims* [377 U.S. 533 (1964)] of the "one person-one vote" principle requiring both houses of state legislatures to have equally populated districts.

The Warren Court addressed deviations from majoritarian principles in its *Baker* and *Reynolds* holdings, but it also set limits on the majority's power to shut racial and ethnic minorities out of the electoral arena. The Court invalidated "understanding" tests that were typically used by white southern registrars to prevent otherwise qualified blacks from registering to vote [*Louisiana* v. *United States*, 380 U.S. 145 (1965)]; struck down the poll tax on Fourteenth Amendment grounds [*Harper* v. *Virginia Board of Elections*, 383 U.S. 663 (1966)], and outlawed the use of literacy tests as a means of furthering racial discrimination [*Lassiter* v. *Northampton County Board of Elections*, 360 U.S. 45 (1959)]. Also deemed unconstitutional was the Alabama legislature's use of gerrymandering to exclude blacks from political participation [*Gomillion* v. *Lightfoot*, 364 U.S. 339 (1960)]. After Congress and President Lyndon Johnson teamed up to pass the Voting Rights Act of 1965, the Court upheld the act [*South Carolina* v. *Katzenbach*, 383 U.S. 301 (1966)] and read its preclearance requirements expansively [*Allen* v. *State Board of Elections*, 393 U.S. 544 (1969)].

The Warren Court clearly altered the landscape of educational policy and reshaped representative democracy, but it also abetted a social revolution extending into the most private of all settings, the home. At a time when interracial marriages are more commonplace, it is perhaps difficult to envision that such marriages were once illegal in many states. As recently as 1967, when the Court invalidated Virginia's anti-miscegenation statute in *Loving* v. *Virginia* [388 U.S. 1], 16 states prohibited interracial marriage, and 14 other states had invalidated their anti-miscegenation statutes only within the previous 15 years. The Court's prior record on such statutes was hardly a source of pride. In its first brush with cases involving interracial relationships, the Court in 1883 (*Pace* v. *Alabama*, 106 U.S. 583) upheld the convictions of a black man and a white woman charged with "living together in a state of adultery or fornication." Writing for a unanimous Court, Justice Field held that the equal protection clause was not violated because offenders, regardless of race, received the same punishment under the Alabama statute.

The Alabama law at issue in *Pace* did not address state anti-miscegenation laws squarely, but the Court's decision was generally understood as a validation of such laws. When Linnie Jackson, a black woman, challenged Alabama's miscegenation laws several decades later, one might have expected a more liberal Supreme Court to look to strike down such laws. But Jackson was a victim of unfortunate timing: Her case reached the Supreme

Court after *Brown I* but before *Brown II*. Given the controversy surrounding school desegregation, the Court was reluctant to take on another explosive issue. As Philip Elman wrote, "the last thing in the world the Justices wanted to deal with at that time was the question of interracial marriage."[38]

The Court denied certiorari in that case [*Jackson* v. *Alabama*, 348 U.S. 888 (1954)] and also declined to hear a Virginia case [*Naim* v. *Naim*, 350 U.S. 891 (1955)] involving a Chinese man and a white woman. Indeed, one sign that *Loving* v. *Virginia* represented a significant departure from precedent can be seen in the fact that Chief Justice Warren's opinion, written for a unanimous Court, made no mention of *Naim*. By the time *Loving* was decided in 1967, the Court had rendered a number of decisions regarding the special significance of marriage and various rights possessed by married couples, including the right to send children to private schools [*Pierce* v. *Society of Sisters*, 268 U.S. 510 (1925)], to teach them a foreign language [*Meyer* v. *Nebraska*, 262 U.S. 390 (1923)], and to receive birth control information and use contraceptives [*Griswold* v. *Connecticut*, 361 U.S. 479 (1965)]. The Court had also unanimously ruled in a Florida case [*McLaughlin* v. *Florida*, 379 U.S. 184 (1964)] that a state could not use a miscegenation statute to prosecute interracial couples for cohabitating, though it reserved for later judgment the question of whether interracial marriages could be banned. Thus, in *Loving* the Court used both the equal protection and due process clauses of the Fourteenth Amendment, unanimously overruled the state courts, and struck down Virginia's statute. Emphasizing the status of marriage as a fundamental right, the Court rejected Virginia's claim that its statute punished both whites and blacks equally, and thus should be subjected only to a rational basis test. Although it applied strict scrutiny, the Court seemed to indicate that the challenged law would not even withstand the more lenient rationality review.

CIVIL RIGHTS IN THE BURGER AND REHNQUIST COURTS

School Desegregation: Implementing Brown

Generally, the Burger Court tempered the trend and tone of the Warren Court in combating racial segregation and discrimination. To be certain, particular decisions of the Court supported many policies of the Warren Court. But when these individual decisions are viewed in terms of evolving judicial policy in broad issue areas, it becomes evident that the Court refused to extend or expand such policies. Rather, by imposing more strict evidentiary requirements and through various other strictures, the Court tended to narrow and limit the application of these very doctrines. Take the area of education. The Burger Court was still concerned with the implementation of the 1954 *Brown* ruling, which outlawed racial segregation in public schools. In 1969, for example, the Burger Court unanimously held against the attempts of the Justice Department to delay beginning integration plans in certain

Mississippi school districts. In so doing the Court stated again the formula established late in the Warren Court era that integration of public schools must begin "at once." Further, in *Swann* v. *Charlotte-Mecklenburg Board of Education* the Court approved busing as a judicial tool for integrating public school districts in which officials had deliberately created or enforced a "dual" system on racial lines. *Swann* granted federal judges wide discretion in establishing remedial measures to combat state-enforced segregation. At the same time, however, *Swann* was seen by lower courts as lessening judicial presence in this area, especially if in their view a unitary school system had been achieved. And, in *North Carolina* v. *Swann* (1971), the Court declared a state statute unconstitutional in that it limited the discretion of school authorities to overcome the effects of dual educational systems. Such a policy "must give way," said Chief Justice Burger, speaking for a unanimous Court, "when it operates to hinder vindication of federal constitutional guarantees."[39]

In *Keyes* v. *School District No. 1, Denver, Colorado* (1973), the Court began to tackle the tough problems of dealing with racial segregation northern style. But the Court declined to build on or expand the Warren Court's desegregation decisions. It continued to recognize the distinction between *de facto* and *de jure* segregation. However, *Keyes* did put northern school districts on notice that where intentional segregation occurred in particular units within a school district, those units must be desegregated. It also held that the burden of proving that a policy of intentional segregation in that unit did not demonstrate a segregative intent with respect to the entire district rested on the defendant school board. *Keyes* shows important legal support for improving the quality of education for minority school children in northern areas. But one cannot help but note the apparently gradual steps of the Court in judging constitutional rights of black and other minority children. Specifically, the Court's reluctance to abandon the *de jure/de facto* distinction in determining the constitutional rights of minority school children and the obligations of school districts seriously slowed down meaningful changes of racial balances in the North. Clearly, meaningful changes that could come about in large metropolitan areas might necessitate the use of busing. Earlier, it will be recalled, the Court had approved busing as a permissible tool to effect public school integration. However, it had left the extent to which this "tool" could be used somewhat unclear. In dealing with the city-to-suburbs busing issue, the position of the Burger Court toward busing became clearer. The Court called a halt to the Detroit metropolitanwide (interdistrict) busing plan.

The thorny issue concerns whether students may be bused across district lines to remedy the segregative effects of central city school districts, which are predominantly black. As is well known, the overwhelming black majorities in central cities, which exist because of the flight of whites to suburban areas, make it virtually impossible to effect an integration remedy o a central city school district even if that central city district were found have purposefully engaged in *de jure* segregation practices (for example, drawing of attendance zones, location of new school buildings). The black central city school district, hemmed in with a suburban ring of white school districts, is still a familiar pattern in America today. To break this pattern some have suggested a metropolitanwide solution (interdistrict busing) for what they consider a metropolitanwide problem (rigid segregation patterns in city and suburban schools).

As would be expected, this multifaceted issue eventually came to the Supreme Court. The first time around, however, in a 1973 Richmond, Virginia, case (*Bradley* v. *School Board*, 412 U.S. 92), the Burger Court left the issue essentially unresolved when the Court divided in a 4–4 deadlock. (Justice Powell did not participate in the case, apparently because of his involvement in the Virginia school situation prior to his appointment to the Supreme Court.) But it was not long before the issue was again before the Supreme Court. And this time, in the 1974 Detroit case *Milliken* v. *Bradley*, the Burger Court, with Justice Powell joining a five-man majority, made its position clear. A multidistrict remedy, said Chief Justice Burger who spoke for the 5–4 majority, could not be used to solve single-district *de jure* segregation unless other affected districts had engaged in constitutional violations. Since earlier rulings of the Court had been confined to violations and remedies within a single school district, Burger said that for the first time the Court was asked to decide "the validity of a remedy mandating cross-district or interdistrict consolidation to remedy a condition of segregation found to exist in only one district." In holding against such a remedy, the Chief Justice stated:

> Before the boundaries of separate and autonomous school districts may be set aside by consolidating the separate units for remedial purposes or by imposing a cross-district remedy, it must first be shown that there has been a constitutional violation within one district that produces a significant segregative effect in another district. Specifically, it must be shown that racially discriminatory acts of the state or local school district or of a single school district have been a substantial cause of interdistrict segregation.

Burger concluded that since the record contained evidence of *de jure* segregated conditions only in Detroit city schools, the remedy (of the lower courts) was inappropriate. "It is clear…," said Burger, "that the district court, with the approval of the court of appeals, has provided an interdistrict remedy in the face of a record which shows no constitutional violations that would call for equitable relief except within the city of Detroit." However, since "the constitutional right of the Negro respondents in Detroit is to attend a unitary school system in that district," and since that district had engaged in unconstitutional segregation policies, Burger remanded the case for "prompt formulation of a decree directed to eliminating the segregation found to exist in Detroit city schools."

Justices Douglas, White, and Marshall filed dissenting opinions, the latter two being joined by Justice Brennan. Justice Thurgood Marshall, who at one time led the NAACP's attack against segregation, bitterly attacked the Court's decision and called it a "giant step backwards." "The rights at issue in this case," he said, "are too fundamental to be abridged on grounds as superficial as those relied on by the majority today." Marshall continued:

> We deal here with the right of all of our children, whatever their race, to an equal start in life and to an equal opportunity to reach their full potential as citizens. Those children who have been denied that right in the past deserve better than to see fences thrown up to deny them that right in the future. Our Nation, I fear, will be ill-served by the Court's refusal to remedy separate and unequal education, for unless our children begin to learn together, there is little hope that our people will ever learn to live together.

In 1977 the Court took another look at the Detroit situation in *Milliken* v. *Bradley II* (1977) and ruled unanimously that federal courts have the authority to require school officials to employ a variety of remedial and compensatory programs in order to alleviate the effects of illegal racial segregation. This ruling, however, reinforced the Court's view requiring remedies to be fitted to the scope and nature of the discriminatory actions found.

As it has evolved, the position of the Court is that a finding of discrimination for which remedies may be fashioned must be based on particularized findings, on a determination of whether there was a "discriminatory intent." This more stringent requirement was articulated most forcefully by the Court in cases involving racial discrimination in the areas of employment and housing. For example, in *Washington* v. *Davis* (1976), blacks charged that testing and selection procedures used by the District of Columbia police department had a racially disproportionate impact against blacks. But the Court held that a mere showing of disproportionate racial impact of the selection procedures is not enough. Rather, where a constitutional claim is raised, aggrieved blacks must show that there was an "intent" to discriminate against blacks. Similarly, in the Arlington Heights housing case [*Village of Arlington Heights, Illinois* v. *Metropolitan Housing Development Corp.* (1977)] the Court ruled that merely showing that the "ultimate effect" of a zoning decision of the village board was racially discriminatory was not enough. Rather, the court made it incumbent on developers and proponents of low-income and public housing to shoulder the very strict burden of proving "discriminatory intent"—of showing that the "motivating factor" was purposefully and intentionally to discriminate on the basis of race.

Though articulated most forcefully in housing and employment cases, this more rigorous criterion was transported and applied to race discrimination cases on education, as well. For example, in *Dayton Board of Education* v. *Brinkman* (1977), the Court specifically cited its decision in *Washington* v. *Davis* and said it was not enough to base the remedy of a citywide busing plan on racial discrimination resulting from "cumulative violations" and that more particularized findings of official segregative acts were required before such a remedy could be implemented.

By 1979 the *Dayton* case was once more before the Court for decision.[40] And so was a similar situation from Columbus, Ohio.[41] In *Dayton*, the Court held that a systemwide remedy was justified to overcome racial segregation in the public school system. The segregation in question involved such practices and policies as faculty hiring and assignments, the location and construction of new and expanded school facilities, and the use of optional attendance zones and transfer policies. Justice White, who spoke for a 5–4 majority, first reviewed the history of the case. White stated that though the federal district court "conceded" that Dayton schools were "highly segregated," it ruled that "the Board's failure to alleviate this condition was not actionable absent sufficient evidence that racial separation had been caused by the Board's own purposeful discriminatory conduct."[42] However, the court of appeals reversed and "expressly held that 'at the time of *Brown I*, the defendants were intentionally operating a dual school system in violation of the Equal Protection Clause of the Fourteenth Amendment,'" and that the "'finding of the district court to the contrary is clearly erroneous.'"[43] Justice White said that the district court had "ignored the legal significance of the intentional maintenance of a substantial number of black schools in the system at the time of *Brown I*."[44]

The decision in the *Columbus* case commanded a larger 7–2 Court majority.[45] Unlike *Dayton*, the court of appeals and the Supreme Court majority in *Columbus* upheld the findings and conclusion of the district court. Indeed, Justice White, who also spoke for the majority in *Dayton*, agreed with the trial court's finding that the Columbus schools "were openly and intentionally segregated on the basis of race" at the time of the 1954 *Brown* decision and that the "Board of Education never actively set out to dismantle this dual system."[46]

The dissenting opinions in *Dayton* and *Columbus* warrant special attention, not only for what they said about those cases but also for what they might suggest for future cases and policy directions of the Court. Justices Rehnquist and Powell dissented in both cases, while Chief Justice Burger and Justice Stewart concurred in *Columbus* but dissented in *Dayton*. The reservations that the four justices had with the court majority focused on (1) the role of deference that should be accorded to the trial judge (the district courts) in school desegregation litigation; (2) the importance of linkages to the present and whether or not dual school systems existed at the time of the 1954 *Brown* decision; and (3) the need to follow appropriate legal standards in the determination of whether or not systemwide remedies are warranted.

Though varying in emphasis, there was a good deal of commonality and overlap in the views of the dissenters, especially among Chief Justice Burger and Justices Rehnquist and Powell. For example, Justice Rehnquist, in dissent joined by Powell, hit particularly hard at the lower courts' attempts to draw linkages, relationships, and inferences between pre-1954 violations and such current segregation as might exist in the school system. Rehnquist said that "the lower courts' methodology would all but eliminate the distinction between *de facto* and *de jure* segregation and render all school systems captives of a remote and ambiguous past." And by so approving this methodology, Rehnquist charged the following:

> [The Court majority itself] suggests a radical new approach to desegregation cases in systems without a history of statutorily mandated separation of races: if a district court concludes—employing what in honesty must be characterized as an irrefutable presumption—that there was a "dual" school system at the time of *Brown I* … it must find post-1954 constitutional violations in school board's failure to take every affirmative step to integrate the system. Put differently, *racial imbalance* [emphasis his] at the time the complaint is filed is sufficient to support a system-wide, racial balance school busing remedy if the district court can find *some* [emphasis his] evidence of discriminatory purpose prior to 1954, without any inquiry into the causal relationship between those pre-1954 violations and current segregation in the school system.[47]

Chief Justice Burger especially agreed with this aspect of Rehnquist's opinion and said that "nothing in reason or our previous decisions provides foundation for this novel legal standard."[48] Increased efforts to desegregate schools in the North led some northern congresspersons, not unlike their colleagues from the South, to reassess their support.

Increased efforts to desegregate northern public school systems, particularly through the "funds cutoff" provision of the 1964 Civil Rights Act, led to increased efforts in the Congress to restrict such enforcement. These efforts were supported by members of Congress from the North as well as the South and were intensified after President Nixon's election in 1968 and the *Swann* decision in 1971. Much of this activity was designed to curb busing as a remedy for school desegregation. One rather watered down anti-busing provision was attached to the massive Aid-to-Education Act of 1974. A more stringent provision, passed as a rider to the Commerce, Justice, and State Department 1981 appropriations measure, was vetoed by President Carter, who believed it would be a dangerous precedent for Congress to interfere in executive law enforcement responsibilities.

After his election in 1980, however, President Reagan, working through his assistant attorney general for civil rights (W. Bradford Reynolds), developed a "new leniency" in enforcing *Brown*. Compliance litigation was brushed aside for voluntary measures adopted through negotiated consent decrees. These decrees stressed such concepts as the "magnet school" to achieve acceptable racial mix and almost always relegated the view of mandatory busing as a remedy of last resort. And the administration worked to get lower-level federal courts to stop existing busing plans, but mostly to ño avail. (See for example, situations in East Baton Rouge Parish, Louisiana, and Nashville, Tennessee.)

Another strategy of anti-busing forces was to use the popular initiative and referendum as methods to restrict busing. These efforts, however, had mixed results in the courts. In a Seattle case, for example [*Washington* v. *Seattle School District No. 1*, 458 U.S. 457 (1982)], the Supreme Court found violative of the equal protection clause a statute that prohibited assignment of pupils to schools outside their neighborhood. Although the statute allowed exceptions for assignment outside the neighborhood for a number of purposes, it singled out racial desegregation as a "prohibited" purpose. As such, Justice Harry Blackmun, who spoke for the Court, viewed the statute as contrary to *Hunter* v. *Erikson* since it structured a "decision-making process" where subsequent "state action placed special burdens on racial minorities."

On the same day, however, the Court upheld a state constitutional provision adopted by California voters that limited the power of state courts to mandate busing only in the kinds of situations where federal courts would be required to use such a remedy to overcome a Fourteenth Amendment violation. In effect, the Court found that all California voters had done, unlike Seattle, was to decide that Fourteenth Amendment standards were more appropriate for state courts to apply than the more exacting standards of its own constitution. Justice Powell, who spoke for the 8–1 court majority, agreed with the lower court finding that there was no "discriminatory intent"; rather the measure was adopted to advance "legitimate non-discriminatory objectives."

But the Court did not agree with the Reagan administration's attempt to circumvent *Brown* by allowing the IRS to terminate its longstanding policy of denying tax-exempt status to schools that practice racial discrimination. The administration argued that Congress had not authorized the IRS to enforce such a policy, but was rebuffed in the *Bob Jones* case [461 U.S. 574, (1983)] when the Court rejected the efforts of two private schools to prevent the IRS from enforcing its policy of denying such exempt status to schools that practice racial discrimination. Chief Justice Burger, speaking for seven of the eight-member majority, declared that racial discrimination policies and practices in education are contrary to "fundamental national policy." But one year later, in *Allen* v. *Wright* [104 S. Ct. 3315 (1984)], the Court held that, due to lack of standing, parents of black children could not sue the IRS for granting exemptions to such schools. This, of course, underscored once more the uncertainty of the law as applied to African Americans.

Of course, for many persons the overriding question about school desegregation is whether federal court supervision should cease once districts have met requirements of *Brown*. In short, some school districts have sought to terminate such supervision arguing that they are now operating unitary school systems that fully comport with Brown. But some civil rights interests believe that without court supervision districts might well revert to policies and practices that could lead to resegregation. In *Pasadena City School Board* v. *Spangler* (1976), Justice Rehnquist, speaking for a 6–2 majority, stated that school officials in the instant case had complied with the district court's order to obtain racial neutrality with respect to attendance patterns and that the district court could not require school authorities to make year-by-year adjustments of its attendance zones. "Once the affirmative duty to desegregate has been accomplished and racial discrimination through official action is eliminated from the system," said Justice Rehnquist, "school officials are not obligated to make annual adjustments in the racial composition of schools caused by demographic changes." It should be noted that three years after the *Pasadena* case, the district court returned complete authority to the school board.

In general, the termination of federal court supervision met with mixed results in various jurisdictions. To be sure, it is reasonable to suggest that the Reagan-Bush "flavored" judiciary, including the Rehnquist Court, seemed inclined to increasingly allow state and local institutions more control over education as well as other matters, for example, abortion. To be sure, after years of federal court supervision, some local school boards sought to remove such scrutiny on the grounds that they had fully complied with *Brown* with respect to operating a unitary school system. In 1976 they began to meet with some success. For example, in *Pasadena* Chief Justice Rehnquist stated that the district court, "having once implemented a racially neutral attendance pattern in order to remedy the perceived constitutional violations on the part of the defendants ... had fully performed its function of providing the appropriate remedy for previous racially discriminatory attendance patterns."

Further, in *Board of Oklahoma City* v. *Dowell* [111 S. Ct. 630 (1991)], Chief Justice Rehnquist, speaking for the Court majority, emphasized the importance of moving away from federal court supervision of public school desegregation efforts once such schools had attained unitary status. Stating that school desegregation decrees "are not intended to operate in perpetuity," Rehnquist indicated the following:

> Local control over education of children allows citizens to participate in decision making, and allows innovation so that school programs can fit local needs.... Dissolving a desegregation decree after the local authorities have operated in compliance with it for a reasonable period of time properly recognizes that "necessary concern for the important values of local control of public school systems dictates that a federal court's regulatory control of such systems not extend beyond the time required to remedy the effects of past intentional discrimination."

The Chief Justice concluded that "in considering whether the vestiges of *de jure* segregation had been eliminated as far as practical, the District Court should look not only at the student assignments, but to every facet of the school operations—faculty, staff, transportation, extracurricular activities, and facilities."

Justice Thurgood Marshall, joined by Justices Blackmun and Stevens, issued a sharp dissent. He charged that the majority had veered away from the "central aim" of the Court's desegregation jurisprudence, the elimination of racially segregated schools, and prevention of their recurrence. He particularly argued that such supervision should not be withdrawn "so long as conditions likely to inflict the stigmatic injury condemned in *Brown I* persist," which he contended would by the majority acceptance of some "one-race schools." Marshall charged that the practical effect of the Court's decision was to allow the return of "many of its elementary schools to their former one race status," which to him "suggests that 13 years of desegregation was enough."

That removing federal court supervision would remain perhaps the crucial issue in the school desegregation controversy became more of a reality when the Court revisited the matter a year later in *Freeman* v. *Pitts*, the DeKalb County, Georgia, school case [112 S. Ct. 1430 (1992)]. The decision was rendered by eight justices, with Justice Thomas not participating since he had not been confirmed when the case was heard. All justices agreed that federal court supervision could end once a school district had complied with certain factors. But agreement stopped there as the justices sharply disagreed over the scope and timing of the application of the various factors, specifically over whether court supervision could be terminated in one category (student assignments). There was also sharp disagreement over whether full court supervision should be continued until each facet of the school operations had been desegregated. Justice Kennedy, joined by the Chief Justice and Justices White, Scalia, and Souter, thought that such supervision may be removed in some areas while continuing in others. Justice Scalia would accelerate removal of federal court supervision even more, saying that "plaintiffs alleging Equal Protection violation must prove *intent and causation* [emphasis added] and not merely the existence of racial disparity."

But Justice Blackmun, in an opinion joined by Justices Stevens and O'Connor, strongly cautioned that district courts should make a searching examination to ensure that actions of local school boards themselves had not in any way contributed to continued segregation. "It is not enough," said Justice Blackmun, "for [the school board] to establish that demographics exacerbated the problem; it must prove that its own policies did not contribute." Though unanimous in their view that at some point federal supervision could be removed, the sharp disagreement over how and when that point would be reached indicates that the controversy over the full implementation of *Brown* is likely to continue for some time to come. The complexity and conflictual nature of the issues involved in school desegregation clearly suggest that such matters remain difficult to handle, making it hard to predict with any degree of certainty how particular governmental institutions, especially courts, will rule. Of course, the 1990 Court decision in the Kansas City, Missouri, case (*Missouri* v. *Jenkins*) offers a prime example of the complexity of the questions involved in such cases. Here, a bare 5–4 majority ruled that under certain circumstances in a school desegregation case, a district court may well order property tax increases to implement a valid federal court desegregation order. Justice White, plus Justice Stevens and the three liberals on the Court (Brennan, Marshall, and Blackmun) constituted the majority while Chief Justice Rehnquist and Reagan appointees (Scalia, Kennedy, and O'Connor) were in the minority.

But in revisiting the Missouri case in 1995,[49] Chief Justice Rehnquist now spoke for a newly constituted Supreme Court majority consisting of himself, the other three dissenters in the 1990 case (Scalia, Kennedy, and O'Connor), and the more recently appointed Justice Clarence Thomas. And this time, unlike in the earlier case, the Court found that certain orders of the district court had exceeded the court's remedial authority. Indeed, district court orders had required (1) the Kansas City Metropolitan School District to give salary increases to virtually all of its instructional and non-instructional personnel, and (2) the state to continue to fund "quality education" programs because student achievement levels [are] still "at or below national norms at many grade levels."

After reviewing relevant precedents and speaking for a 5–4 majority, Chief Justice Rehnquist said that the "proper analysis of the District Court's orders ... must rest upon their serving as proper means to the end of restoring the victims of discriminatory conduct to the position they would have occupied in the absence of that conduct and their eventual restoration of state and local authorities to control of a school system that is operating in compliance with the Constitution." At bottom, Rehnquist viewed the orders as part of the "District Court's overall pursuit of 'desegregative attractiveness,'" a goal that the Chief Justice stated "cannot be reconciled with our cases placing limitations on the district court's remedial authority." Indeed, Rehnquist stated that the goal of "'desegregative attractiveness' results in so many imponderables and is so far removed from the task of eliminating the racial identifiability of the schools within the KCMSD that we believe it is beyond the admittedly broad discretion of the District Court."

It remains to be seen whether this change in judicial tone and policy in school desegregation and other areas may be slowed, even turned around, by changes in the composition of both the Supreme Court and lower federal courts that might come from judicial appointments made by President Clinton. Of course, other factors may also impact judicial policy change, including public opinion and the position of other elites in both the public and private sector.

To conclude, over 40 years have passed since the first *Brown* decision. Since that time, *Brown* has been credited with any number of developments: tolling the death knell of *Plessy* v. *Ferguson* and state-sponsored segregation; providing moral support to civil rights forces; demonstrating both the potential and the limitations of litigation-based civil rights strategy; and symbolizing the Supreme Court's commitment to racial equality. In addition, conventional wisdom holds that *Brown* eventually produced school desegregation, once Congress gave the decision teeth and state and local officials complied with its overarching principles.

But what is the state of school desegregation today? Currently, approximately one-third of black public school students nationwide, and one-half in the Northeast alone, attend schools that are at least 90 percent minority.[50] An increasingly conservative federal judiciary apparently has made it easier for local officials to terminate busing efforts. Hand-in-hand with the courts' willingness to end supervision of school systems has been a push in many locales to discontinue busing plans.[51]

One might expect these trends to be rooted in a diminished commitment to racially integrated schooling. However, the NAACP and other civil rights organizations have remained committed to desegregation. The NAACP still vigorously challenges attempts to roll back school desegregation plans, and in 1995 it suspended two branch chapter presidents for publicly criticizing busing efforts. But what about the public at large? Recent polling data offer a portrait of an American polity deeply at odds with itself concerning desegregation. This sentiment is also being reflected in civil rights organizations such as the NAACP (see Chapter 7).

On one hand, both blacks and whites increasingly believe that integration has been beneficial. According to a 1994 Gallup Poll,[52] 62 percent of whites and 75 percent of blacks surveyed agreed that school integration has improved interracial relations. A majority of each group believed that integration resulted in better education for black students (64 percent of whites, 70 percent of blacks), and a sizable number felt that white students received similar benefits (39 percent of whites, 59 percent of blacks). Furthermore, a majority of each group (52 percent of whites, 84 percent of blacks) believed that more should be done to integrate schools across the country.

On the other hand, many respondents were willing to accept proposals that would effectively resegregate schools. In that same poll, when asked about the best way to aid minority students, 48 percent supported more funding for minority schools, whereas only 32 percent favored redoubling efforts to integrate schools. Whites favored the increased funding solution by a 47–33 percent margin; more surprisingly, blacks did too, but by a wider margin (60–25 percent). What has produced the shift toward solutions that sound eerily like "separate but equal"?

For one, preferences for neighborhood schools have grown stronger in recent years. Opposition to busing one's children across town has sometimes been the rallying cry of parents seeking to avoid integration, but such opposition is not necessarily the product of racist sentiment. Having children attend nearby schools reduces transportation costs and facilitates parental involvement in their children's education. As schools become increasingly strapped for funds and parents become more concerned about the declining quality of public education, proposals that promise to offer lower costs and enhanced opportunities for parental involvement are likely to develop some appeal.

Furthermore, in some places the busing debate reflects class divisions as well as racial cleavages. When one thinks of the exodus of middle-class families from central cities to suburbs, the term "white flight" inevitably comes to mind. But in some communities, the flight is no longer exclusively white. In the Washington, DC area, for example, the black population has declined from 71 percent in 1970 to 66 percent in 1990, while Prince George's County in Maryland has gone from 14 percent black in 1970 to 52.2 percent in 1996.[53] While the newest suburbanites express some empathy for the black poor left behind, they also share white suburbanites' concerns about crime, taxes, governmental efficiency, and quality of public education.

In the desegregation debate, pragmatic questions concerning the means for achieving integration have been joined by ideological questions addressing the desirability of the ends themselves: racial integration or separation. Frustration with the gap between *Brown's* promise and its actual legacy has manifested itself in efforts by some educators and parents to seek change outside the traditional public school system. According to the Institute for Independent Education based in Washington DC, by 1996 almost 400 private, religious, and charter schools had been launched by blacks.[54] In addition, public school systems in cities such as Detroit and Milwaukee have created special academies based on Afrocentric principles, while many other schools across the country utilize African-centered curricula. Tendencies toward separatism have found expression in the view that since schools will never be truly integrated, regardless of what government does, civil rights groups should concentrate more on bringing heavily black schools up to par with predominantly white schools. But it is questionable whether even this goal can be reached. As Harvard sociologist Gary Orfield put it, "'Separate but equal' is the most well-tried experiment in American history. It was policy for 60 years, and we have no evidence that it can work, given the distribution of power and resources in our society."[55]

Affirmative Action: Employment Problems

The Supreme Court has also been confronted with the sensitive and emotion-laden issues embodied in the "affirmative action versus reverse discrimination" controversy. In 1978, the Burger Court decided the *Bakke* case relative to affirmative action programs in state university admissions.[56] The immediate issue involved in *Bakke* was the validity of the special admissions program as it related to the denial of Bakke's admission to the University of California-Davis Medical School. On June 28, 1978, the Court, on the one hand, supported the affirmative action interest by holding that it is lawful for race to be considered as a factor in a university's admissions process. On the other hand, the Court supported those who were fighting against "reverse discrimination" and "quotas" by holding that the particular Davis program was unlawful and by ordering Bakke's admission to the medical school. Both aspects of the decision were reached by 5–4 votes, with only Justice Powell agreeing to both outcomes. Thus, the Court was sharply divided: There was no majority opinion; instead there were six opinions totaling almost 160 pages.

Justice Powell announced the judgment of the Court and wrote what some refer to as the "prevailing" opinion in the case. There is no doubt that Powell's position did prevail. His vote proved decisive and broke the apparent stalemate between the two equally divided factions on the Court. Essentially, Powell's opinion was that while race may be considered a "plus" in a university's admissions process, the particular Davis program was unconstitutional. His view that race constitutionally may be considered as a factor in the university admission process was supported by four justices (Brennan, Marshall, Blackmun, and White). But whereas Powell thought the particular Davis program used race in such a way as to violate constitutional standards, the four other justices thought that the program did not violate the Constitution. However, Powell did find the needed support for this position among his four other colleagues (Chief Justice Burger and Justices Stevens, Stewart, and Rehnquist) who joined in an opinion written by Justice Stevens. The Stevens group agreed with Powell that the particular Davis program was invalid and that Bakke should be admitted to the medical school. But they disagreed with how Powell reached that conclusion. In short, unlike Powell (and the Brennan group of justices), the Stevens group thought that it was unnecessary to reach or decide the constitutional issue involved. The Davis program, in their opinion, violated the intent as well as the "plain language" of the Civil Rights Act of 1964 (Title VI) by excluding Bakke because of his race.

However, the *Bakke* case left a number of issues unanswered. Hence, and not unexpectedly, the issue was once again before the Court in 1979. However, this time the Court faced the issue in the area of employment[57] rather than in education. The Kaiser Aluminum and Chemical Corporation, in a national collective bargaining agreement with the United Steelworkers, instituted a voluntary affirmative action plan to ensure equitable representation in plant craft training programs. Under the plan, 50 percent of the openings in such programs would be reserved for black employees until the percentage of black craft workers in a plant became commensurate with the percentage of blacks in the local labor force. Brian Weber, a white plant worker, brought suit challenging the institution of an affirmative action program at the Kaiser plant in Grammercy, Louisiana, where he worked. Weber charged that the program violated the prohibition of Title VII of the Civil Rights Act of 1964 against racial discrimination in employment since he thought the program unfairly discriminated against him because he was white.

But Justice Brennan, writing for a 5–2 majority, held that "the very statutory words [of Title VII] intended as a spur or catalyst to cause employers and unions to self-examine and to self-evaluate their employment practices and to endeavor to eliminate, so far as possible, the last vestiges of an unfortunate and ignominious page in this country's history ... cannot be interpreted as an absolute prohibition against all private, voluntary, race-conscious affirmative action efforts to hasten the elimination of such vestiges."[58] "It would be ironic indeed," said Justice Brennan, "if a law triggered by a Nation's concern over centuries of racial injustice and intended to improve the lot of those who had 'been excluded from the American dream for so long' constituted the first legislative prohibition of all voluntary, private, race-conscious efforts to abolish traditional patterns of racial segregation and hierarchy."[59] However, Chief Justice Burger and Justice Rehnquist dissented. They concluded that "Kaiser's racially discriminatory admission quota is flatly prohibited by the plain language of Title VII."[60]

Overall, in *Weber* the Court decided that Title VII permitted voluntary affirmative action programs by private companies as long as the measures are temporary and do not unnecessarily restrict the rights of innocent persons. One year later, in *Fullilove* v. *Klutznick* [448 U.S. 448 (1980)], the Court upheld a congressional law requiring that state and local governments applying for grants under the Public Works Employment Act of 1977 give assurances that at least 10 percent of each grant would be for contracts with minority business enterprises. In upholding the "10 percent set-aside," as the program was called, the Supreme Court stressed the broad remedial powers of Congress to remedy the effects of past racial discrimination. The Court also noted the temporary nature of the program.

But the Reagan administration continued to push its position that under affirmative action each beneficiary must be required to establish that he/she was an actual victim of discrimination. Clearly, full acceptance of this standard would severely limit race-conscious group-based remedies and undermine the use of past and societal discrimination as a rationale for affirmative action. For the Reagan administration, the actual victim standard was the appropriate one to be followed in determining the constitutionality of both voluntary and court-imposed affirmative action programs.

In *Firefighters* v. *Stotts* [467 U.S. 561 (1984)], the Burger Court undoubtedly gave some support and hope to those who embraced the position of the Reagan administration. In *Stotts*, the Court rejected a federal court order (to effectuate an earlier consent decree) enjoining Memphis from following its seniority system in determining layoffs resulting from budgetary shortfalls, the effect of which would be to layoff whites with more seniority than blacks due to past racial discrimination. However, the Supreme Court held that "Title VII protects bona fide seniority systems, and it is inappropriate to deny an innocent employee the benefits of his seniority in order to provide a remedy in a pattern or practice suit such as this." But in *Firefighters* v. *Cleveland* [106 S. Ct. 3063 (1986)] the Court held that Title VII does not preclude "voluntary adoption (in a consent decree) of race-conscious relief that may benefit non-victims" of discriminatory practices. This view was reaffirmed in *Sheet Metal Workers* v. *EEOC* [106 S. Ct. 3014 (1986)] when the Court, focusing on powers of district courts to fashion affirmative action remedies, indicated that Title VII does not "say that a court may order relief only for the actual victims of past discriminations." The Court thus rejected the view that *Stotts* prevents a lower court from ordering affirmative action remedies that might benefit non-victims. "The purpose of affirmative action," said the Court, "is not to make identified victims whole but rather to dismantle prior patterns of employment discrimination and to prevent discrimination in the future." The Court made it clear that "such relief is provided to the class as a whole rather than to individual members," and that individuals entitled to relief "need not show themselves victims of discrimination."

Two important affirmative action cases gave the Rehnquist Court opportunities to consider affirmative action in both race and gender contexts. In *U.S.* v. *Paradise* [107 S. Ct. 1053 (1987)], black plaintiffs in prolonged litigation with the Alabama Department of Public Safety alleged that the state had followed racially discriminatory practices in its employment policies—hiring, promotions, and so forth. Eventually, a federal district court issued a "one-black-for-one-white" promotion order as an interim measure to increase rank and status of blacks in the department. Subsequently, on an equal protection challenge under the Fourteenth Amendment, the Court upheld the district court order saying that the relief was "narrowly tailored" to serve a "compelling governmental interest," thus making it unnecessary to apply the strict scrutiny test. Justice Brennan, who wrote the opinion for the Court majority, said that "the persuasive, systematic, and obstinate discriminatory conduct of the Department (of Public Safety) created a profound need and a firm justification for the race-conscious relief ordered by the district court." Justice O'Connor's dissenting opinion, joined by Chief Justice Rehnquist and Justice Scalia, charged that the "one-for-one" order would have failed the strict scrutiny test.

In *Johnson* v. *Transportation Agency* [107 S. Ct. 1442 (1987)], the Court upheld an affirmative action plan that stipulated "in making promotions to positions within a traditionally segregated job classification in which women have been significantly underrepresented, the agency is authorized to consider as one factor the sex of a qualified applicant." The case that triggered the Court's position was the promotion by the agency of a female employee who ranked slightly lower on test scores than a male applicant, the latter charging that her promotion was unlawful under Title VII of the 1964 Civil Rights Act. The plan did not set aside a specific number of positions or jobs for minorities or women but did provide for the "consideration of ethnicity or sex as a factor when evaluating qualified candidates for jobs in which members of such groups were poorly represented." Justice Brennan, who spoke for the Court, found it appropriate to consider the sex of applicants for skilled craft jobs when there is found to be a "manifest imbalance." Brennan said that employers should compare "the percentage of minorities or women in the employer's work force with the percentage in the area labor market or general population" and "where the job requires special training ... the comparison should be with those in the labor force who possess the relevant qualifications." Brennan took special note that the plan "expressly directed that numerous factors be taken into account in making hiring decisions, including specifically the qualification of female applicants for particular jobs." He also found that the plan did not necessarily trammel on "the rights of male employees" or create "an absolute bar to their advancement." Again, Chief Justice Rehnquist joined Justice Scalia's dissenting opinion, as did Justice White, in part.

Johnson is important since it filled much of the gap left open by *Bakke* and *Weber*. Specifically, the Court indicated clearly that public employers may institute affirmative action programs even though there has been no judicial, administrative, or legislative determination of discrimination and where there is no proof of prior discrimination on the part of the employer. In short, employers may adopt voluntary affirmative action plans that address the underrepresentation of blacks, women, and minorities "caused not only by their own and society's proven employment discrimination, but also by the effects of unconscious discrimination and internalized sexual and racial stereotypes that discourage women and minorities from seeking certain kinds of employment."[61] But it is clear that the Rehnquist Court plans to subject affirmative action plans to increasing scrutiny, clearly resulting in less judicial support for the issue. This is signaled in several major decisions of the Rehnquist Court. For example, the 1989 decision in *City of Richmond, Virginia* v. *J.A. Croson Co.* (109 S. Ct. 706) took much of the steam out of the Burger Court's *Fullilove* decision, which upheld a federal law designed to enhance the economic position of minority contractors by a "set-aside" provision that required that at least 10 percent of grants awarded under the Public Works Employment Act of 1977 be given to minority contractors. Following *Fullilove*, a number of state and local governments adopted their own "set-aside" programs, clearly patterned after the federal plan. The City of Richmond adopted one such plan that provided that, due to manifest past discrimination against minority contractors, 30 percent of future contracts awarded by the city would be set aside for minority contractors. White contractors who contested the plan were joined by the Reagan administration, which had generally launched major attacks on race-based affirmative action plans.

In a 6–3 decision, the Rehnquist Court dealt such plans a major setback when it held that governmental policies utilizing race-conscious numerical remedies are "suspect" and therefore subject to "strict scrutiny." Justice Sandra Day O'Connor, speaking for the majority, said that this kind of plan can only be constitutionally acceptable by showing a "compelling state interest" in order to redress specific "identified discrimination." By adopting the "strict scrutiny" standard, the Court indicated that it would be quite difficult for affirmative action plans of any sort to pass constitutional muster. This point was not lost on Justice Thurgood Marshall, the first African American appointed to the Court. In a strong dissent, Marshall lashed out at the majority for taking "a deliberate and giant step backward in the Court's affirmative action jurisprudence." Rather than employing the Court's most exacting standard of scrutiny (strict scrutiny), which almost always results in findings of unconstitutionality, Marshall would utilize an intermediate standard ("mid-level scrutiny") that would determine whether such plans "serve important governmental objectives" and are "substantially related to the achievement of those objectives." This would allow such plans to be subjected to adequate constitutional scrutiny without denying cities a potentially effective mechanism to overcome obvious patterns and practice of past race-based discrimination. Two other 1989 Rehnquist Court decisions also dealt severe setbacks to affirmative action interests. In *Wards Cove Packing Co. v. Atonio* (109 S. Ct. 2115), a developing conservative majority on the Court (White, Rehnquist, O'Connor, Scalia, and Kennedy) rejected challenges of employees of two Alaskan salmon cannery companies alleging discriminatory employment practices in violation of Title VII of the 1964 Civil Rights Act. The "burden-of-proof" requirements articulated by the five-person Court majority make it more difficult for a plaintiff in a disparate impact case to win. In *Wards Cove*, the plaintiffs had offered considerable evidence of discrimination in job assignments, with minorities disproportionately in lower positions and few of them in higher paying positions. While such evidence convinced the court of appeals of a *prima facie* case of disparate impact, it did not convince the Rehnquist Court majority. Justice White, who spoke for the majority, said that race-based statistical comparisons were not enough to prove disparate impact. Rather, said White, there must be a showing of disproportionality that looks at the "pool of qualified applicants" or the "qualified population in the labor force." And though employers are required to offer a "business justification" for using the challenged practice, said Justice White, "the ultimate burden of proving that discrimination against a protected group has been caused by a specific employment practice remains with the plaintiff at all times." The dissenters sharply criticized the majority. In a biting dissent, Justice Stevens charged the majority with "turning a blind eye to the meaning and purpose of Title VII." Stevens noted that the majority had misread a 1971 decision of the Court itself (*Griggs* v. *Duke Power Co.*), as well as ignored the practice of federal enforcement agencies, all of which had interpreted Title VII to ban practices that had discriminatory effects as well as those practices that indicated discriminatory intent.

In another major setback to affirmative action, the Court, just one week after *Wards Cove*, spoke through Chief Justice Rehnquist and held in *Martin v. Wilks* that, although a "consent decree" [the key tool for implementing affirmative action goals] could settle matters among the immediate parties to a lawsuit, such decrees could not "conclude the right of strangers [in this instance, white firefighters in Birmingham, Alabama] to those proceedings." The court decision, in effect, opened up the potentiality of a large number of lawsuits challenging consent decrees that have been concluded over the past two decades in a number of affirmative action contexts. Justice Stevens's sharp dissent recognized with dismay this possibility when he warned that the decision would "subject large employers who seek to comply with the law by remedying past discrimination to a never ending stream of litigation and potential liability."

But such court decisions, as indicated earlier in this chapter, may not necessarily be the last word. This is especially true in matters that turn on statutory interpretation (as affirmative action cases tend to do) where Congress has the opportunity to pass subsequent legislation that might overcome or otherwise circumvent adverse court decisions. In fact, it was these very Rehnquist Court decisions that gave impetus to congressional efforts to overcome adverse effects of these and related court actions. One standout example of this type of effort was made by a coalition of Democrats and Republicans in a rare show of bipartisan support. Engineered by moderate Republican Senator John Danforth of Missouri, this coalition succeeded in winning support from a reluctant President Bush and divided White House staff for the Civil Rights Restoration Act of 1991.

The 1991 statute was designed to reverse the effects of some eight court decisions, including *Wards Cove* and *Wilks*. But the act was deliberately silent on an important question: whether the law could be applied to cases arising prior to the act's passage. Democrats favored retroactivity; Republicans opposed it. Congress, which was then under Democratic control, left the issue ambiguous so as to ensure President Bush's signature. The Supreme Court eventually settled the issue in a pair of decisions, one involving sexual harassment [*Landgraf* v. *USI Film Products*, 511 U.S. 244 (1994)], the other concerning racial discrimination [*Rivers and Davison* v. *Roadway Express, Inc.*, 511 U.S. 298 (1994)]. By an 8–1 margin, the Court, in an opinion penned by Justice Stevens, held that the statute is not retroactive. The Court said that absent a clear statement by Congress on retroactivity, the usual presumption against retroactivity remains in force.

Overall, the Civil Rights Restoration Act of 1991 did little to stem the Court's increasing skepticism toward race-based legislation not narrowly designed to reverse the effects of clearly identifiable historical discrimination. In *Adarand Contractors* v. *Peña* [115 S. Ct. 2097 (1995)], the Court extended its *Croson* "strict scrutiny" holding to federal affirmative action programs, which, in *Fullilove*, the Court had previously distinguished from similar state programs. Unlike the Richmond, Virginia, program struck down in *Croson*, the Department of Transportation (DOT) in *Adarand* did not impose a rigid set-aside program to benefit minority contractors. Rather, along with many other federal agencies, DOT provided a financial incentive to prime contractors that hire subcontractors controlled by persons defined by the Small Business Association as "socially and economically disadvantaged individuals." What triggered the lawsuit was the use of race-based presumptions in identifying disadvantaged individuals. And a 5–4 Court majority, led by Justice O'Connor, held that the program failed to withstand the strict scrutiny that the equal protection component of the Fifth Amendment's due process clause requires of federal laws based on racial classifications. On this point, the Court thus renounced much, if not all, of its holdings in *Fullilove* and a more recent affirmative action holding, *Metro Broadcasting, Inc.* v. *FCC* [497 U.S. 547 (1990)].

Given the Court's attitudes toward affirmative action and the use of race for "benign" purposes, the majority opinion contained few surprises. The partial concurrences written by Justices Scalia and Thomas also lacked suspense, but they were striking in their strong support for color-blindness in state action. Said Scalia:

> To pursue the concept of racial entitlement—even for the most admirable and benign of purposes—is to reinforce and preserve for future mischief the way of thinking that produced race slavery, race privilege, and race hatred. In the eyes of government, we are just one race here. It is American.

Justice Thomas, criticizing Justices Stevens's and Ginsburg's dissents for their alleged premise that there is a "racial paternalism exception to the principle of equal protection," stated, "Government cannot make us equal; it can only recognize, respect, and protect us as equal before the law." Interestingly, Justice Thomas's statement is strikingly similar to the view expressed in the majority opinion in *Plessy* v. *Ferguson*; viz.; "The object of the [Fourteenth] [A]mendment was undoubtedly to enforce the absolute equality of the two races before the law, but in the nature of things it could not have been intended to abolish distinctions based upon color, or to enforce social, as distinguished from political equality."

In their dissents, Justices Stevens and Ginsburg each took aim at the view that no difference exists between a majority's decision to burden a racial minority and that same majority's decision to burden itself on behalf of that minority. Said Stevens, "There is no moral or constitutional equivalence between a policy that is designed to perpetuate a caste system and one that seeks to eradicate racial subordination.... The consistency that the Court espouses would disregard the difference between a 'No Trespassing' sign and a Welcome mat." The dissenters also held to the *Fullilove* distinction as to what the federal government can do to enforce the Fourteenth Amendment and what state governments are prohibited from doing by that amendment.

VOTING ARRANGEMENTS AND REAPPORTIONMENT

The Burger Court also faced issues related to attempts to dilute the increasing influence of the black vote as a source of political power. These discriminatory efforts included replacing single-member districts with multimember districts and the use of at-large elections; the annexation by central cities of white suburban areas to increase the white vote and to decrease black voting strength; and certain reapportionment actions involving the redrawing or restructuring of particular electoral districts. States covered by the Voting Rights Act of 1965, however, are subject to having such schemes reviewed by federal administrative officials and by federal courts. Specifically, Section 5 of the Voting Rights Act forbids changes that have "the purpose or effect of denying or abridging the right to vote on account of race or color."

In 1971, the Court was asked to rule on the use of a multimember district, at-large election scheme from a state (Indiana) not covered by the Voting Rights Act. Here, blacks alleged that the Indiana statutes that established Marion County (Indianapolis) as a multimember district for the election of state senators and representatives deprived them of a realistic opportunity to win elections. Specifically, they charged that the laws diluted their votes in the predominantly black inner-city areas of Indianapolis. A three-judge federal district court agreed with this position. But the Supreme Court overturned the lower court decision by a 6–3 vote (*Whitcomb v. Chavis*). Justice White, who wrote for the Court, said there was no suggestion that the multimember district in Marion County or similar districts in the state were "conceived or operated as purposeful devices to further racial or economic discrimination." Justice White maintained that "the failure of the ghetto to have legislative seats in proportion to its population emerges more as a function of losing elections than of built-in bias against poor Negroes." "The mere fact that one interest group or another concerned with the outcome of Marion County elections has found itself outvoted and without legislative seats of its own provides no basis for invoking constitutional remedies where, as here, there is no indication that this segment of the population is being denied access to the political system." Furthermore, reasoned Justice White, to uphold the position of one racial group would make it difficult to reject claims of any other group—for example, Republicans, Democrats, or organized labor—who find themselves similarly disadvantaged.

But Justice Douglas, joined by Justices Brennan and Marshall, filed a strong dissenting opinion in *Whitcomb*. Justice Douglas supported the position of the district court that "a showing of racial motivation is not necessary when dealing with multimember districts." Justice Douglas maintained that the test of constitutionality for multi-member districts is where there are "invidious effects." And in this case Douglas thought there were such effects, since the result of the plan was to "purposely wash blacks out of the system."

In *White* v. *Regester* (1973), the Court considered whether the election of state legislators from multimember districts in two Texas counties violated the equal protection rights of blacks and Mexican-Americans. After examining the history of the political participation of these groups in the two counties, a long history of official segregation including the small number of blacks (only two since Reconstruction) elected from the area, the persistence of white-dominated slate making, and technical rules of the electoral process, the Court concluded that within the context of the multimember scheme, the Texas legislative apportionment plan was invidiously discriminatory in violation of the equal protection clause.

Subsequently, in 1976 the Court approved a city reapportionment plan, this time in a case brought under Section 5 of the 1965 Voting Rights Act. In *Beer* v. *U.S.*, the Court reversed a federal district court ruling and upheld a New Orleans city council reapportionment plan that would increase black representation on a seven-member city council (five single members and two at-large) from none to one. Thus, the Court accepted a plan that seemingly still had a racially discriminatory effect (blacks constituted about 45 percent of the population). But it was important to the Court that the plan did not result in "retrogression," but rather in an improvement of the position of blacks in the exercise of the franchise. However, Justices White, Brennan, and Marshall filed strong dissents. White, for example, thought the Court majority failed to consider the twin realities of residential segregation and bloc voting, which, according to his interpretation of the Voting Rights Act (Section 5), would legitimately entitle blacks to an opportunity to elect at least three members of the city council. Marshall, in an opinion joined by Justice Brennan, concluded that it could very well be that this case represented a prime example for a plan that betters the electoral position of blacks but that remains "blatantly discriminatory."

In *Richmond* v. *U.S.* (1975), the Court approved a Richmond, Virginia, plan that, by the annexation of white suburban areas, reduced the city's black population from 52 percent to 42 percent. Initially, the city's request for approval of the plan under Section 5 of the Voting Rights Act was denied by the U.S. attorney general because of what he saw as a dilution of black voting strength. But at the suggestion of the attorney general, and in order to overcome the adverse racial impact of annexation, the city eliminated an at-large election structure and replaced it with a single-member district scheme. Nonetheless, a federal district court (District of Columbia) still found the plan defective under the Voting Rights Act. By a 5–3 vote, a Supreme Court majority overturned the district court since the subsequent electoral structure "fairly recognizes black political strength."[62] At present, Richmond has a black majority city council.

Still another electoral arrangement scheme was at issue in the 1977 case of the *United Jewish Organizations of Williamsburgh* v. *Carey*. Here, the Court interpreted Section 5 of the Voting Rights Act[63] in such a way as to uphold a New York state legislative reapportionment plan to increase black representation. The Hasidic Jewish community argued that the reapportionment plan, which restructured certain districts to produce black majorities, was done at the expense of diluting voting strength of the Hasidic Jews by dividing members of that community into two districts. Though no one opinion commanded majority support, the Court did agree, by a 7–1 vote, that the legislature had the authority to take race into account in its reapportionment scheme. The lone dissenter, Chief Justice Burger, said he was troubled by the semblance of a "racial gerrymander" and by what fragmented representation by race might do to the "American melting pot ideal."

By and large, however, the Court continued to press its more demanding standard requiring proof of purposeful discrimination in challenges to various electoral schemes, such as multimember at-large structures. In the much publicized *Mobile* v. *Bolden* (1980) case, for example, it was shown that blacks constituted 40 percent of the city's population but had never been elected to its three-member city commission, allegedly due to the at-large election scheme. The federal district court agreed that the scheme had discriminated against blacks. Nonetheless, the Supreme Court reversed the decision and reiterated the need to prove purposeful discrimination to sustain a Fourteenth or Fifteenth Amendment violation, as well as a violation of the Voting Rights Act.

But this more exacting standard of proof used by the Court in *Mobile* became a focal point of controversy in the 1982 battle to extend the Voting Rights Act. In the end, the act's supporters were successful in getting Congress to reject the more exacting "intent" standard of *Mobile* and to include in Section 2 the less exacting "effects or results" standards for proving a discriminatory violation.

At-large electoral schemes that dilute their vote and inhibit their chances of winning continue to raise the ire of black voters. Perhaps in its most definitive consideration of the issue, in *Thornburg* v. *Gingles* [106 S. Ct. 2752 (1986)], the Court held that vote dilution charges emanating from multimember district schemes were actionable under Section 2 of the Voting Rights Act of 1965. The Court said that in such cases the plaintiffs must show that the multidistrict scheme, "under the totality of circumstances," results in "unequal access to the electoral process." Specifically, plaintiffs in such cases must show that the multimember district mechanism "interacts with social and historical conditions to cause an inequality in the opportunities enjoyed by black and white voters to elect their preferred representatives." Among factors that are critical in showing such claims are (1) lingering effects of past discrimination; (2) the extent of racially polarized voting in the electoral jurisdiction; (3) appeals to racial bias in the election campaign; and (4) patterns of racial bloc voting over extended periods of time. Justice Brennan, who spoke for the Court majority, stated that the finding of illegal vote dilution violative of Section 2 was appropriate when the district court, after considering the "totality of circumstances," found that the above factors "acted in concert with the multimember districting scheme to impair the ability of geographically insular and politically cohesive groups of black voters to participate equally in the political process and to elect candidates of their choice."

But the Court has become more skeptical of efforts of state legislatures to draw district lines that enhance the ability of black voters to elect candidates of their choice. In *Shaw* v. *Reno* [113 S. Ct. 2816 (1993)], the Court held that white plaintiffs challenging North Carolina's congressional districting plan presented a justiciable claim under the equal protection clause. Vote dilution was not the issue in *Shaw*: The plaintiffs did not base their argument on it, and the majority, led by Justice O'Connor, stated that the Court's Section 2 precedents were not affected by the holding in *Shaw*. Rather, the harm alleged by the plaintiffs and recognized by the Court stemmed from the drawing of a district map that "is so extremely irregular on its face that it rationally can be viewed only as an effort to segregate the races for purposes of voting, without regard for traditional districting principles and without sufficiently compelling justification." As in affirmative action cases following *Croson*, it would no longer be assumed that all race-conscious redistricting aimed at benefiting ethnic minorities is "benign," since such assumptions may foster and reinforce stereotypes about how minority voters and legislators think and act in the political arena.

Shaw initially produced great uncertainty. The confusion resulted in conflicting lower court holdings, as federal judges held differing views on which governmental interests qualified as "compelling." The Supreme Court attempted to clarify *Shaw* in subsequent cases, but to no avail. In *Miller* v. *Johnson* [115 S. Ct. 2475 (1995)], for example, the Court struck down Georgia's congressional districting scheme on Fourteenth Amendment grounds. The Georgia plan at issue contained three majority-black districts out of 11 total, including one that stretched across rural areas to connect concentrations of African-American voters in Atlanta, Augusta, and Savannah. Previously, the state had twice attempted to design a plan containing two majority-black districts—an increase from one out of ten following the 1980 redistricting—but both attempts failed to receive Justice Department preclearance under Section 5 of the Voting Rights Act.

In striking down the Georgia plan, a 5–4 majority led by Justice Kennedy tried to specify what made certain types of districting constitutionally unacceptable. District shape mattered not because "bizarreness" was a necessary condition for impermissible racial gerrymandering, but because it can serve as persuasive circumstantial evidence that "race for its own sake, and not other districting principles, was the legislature's dominant and controlling rationale in drawing ... district lines." Therefore, districts that are more compact than North Carolina's District 12, which was the subject of *Shaw*, could be deemed constitutionally suspect and thus subject to strict scrutiny if plaintiffs can show that race trumped traditional districting principles, such as compactness, contiguity, and preservation of communities of interest.

Two subsequent decisions, *Shaw* v. *Reno* (*Shaw II* hereafter) and *Bush* v. *Vera*, struck down congressional redistricting plans in North Carolina and Texas, respectively. In *Shaw II*, the Court revisited the districting plan featured in its three-year-old landmark holding (*Shaw I*). The 5–4 majority, per Chief Justice Rehnquist, found that race was the "predominant factor" in the North Carolina legislature's decision to draw relatively non-compact majority-black districts. Applying strict scrutiny, the Court held that the plan was not narrowly tailored to serve any of the three claims advanced in defense of the plan: (1) combating the effects of past discrimination, (2) complying with Section 5 of the Voting Rights Act, and (3) avoiding impermissible vote dilution as defined by Section 2 of that act.

In *Bush*, a fractured Court applied similar analysis to three majority-minority districts in Texas and, as in *Miller* and *Shaw II*, found the state plan wanting. What made *Bush* unusual was that Justice O'Connor wrote both the lead opinion, in which she was joined by only two other justices, Rehnquist and Kennedy, and a separate concurrence in which she expressed the view that compliance with Section 2 qualifies as a compelling state interest, and as such can be reconciled with the Court's holdings in *Shaw I* and its progeny.

THE POOR IN COURT

The Burger Court also rendered decisions in another area that is of importance to blacks—poverty law. In general, these decisions indicate that the Court is not disposed to break new ground in order to expand rights of the poor. Consider, for example, the much publicized 1973 Court decision in *San Antonio Independent School District* v. *Rodriguez*. The Court rejected challenges to the local property tax system that provides a significant part of public school finances in 49 of the 50 states. The contention was that the Texas system of supplementing state aid to school districts by means of property tax levied within the jurisdiction of the individual school district violated the equal protection clause. Speaking for a 5–4 majority, Justice Powell said that the financing system, although not perfect, "abundantly satisfies" the constitutional standard for equal protection since the system "rationally furthers a legitimate state purpose or interest," namely, the maintenance of local control of public education. Justice Powell applied the traditional equal protection standard since "the Texas system does not operate to the peculiar disadvantage of any suspect class," and since education, although an important state service, is not a "fundamental" right because it is not "explicitly or implicitly guaranteed by the Constitution."[64] Justice Marshall, in dissent, charged the majority with a retreat from our historic commitment to equality of educational opportunity and an "unsupportable acquiescence in a system which deprived children in their earliest years of the chance to reach their full potential as citizens."

Rodriguez, while not posed in racial terms, has a direct impact on equality of opportunity for racial minorities, since minorities tend to be concentrated in areas where property values are lower and where, regardless of the willingness in some of these areas to pay a substantial rate of tax for education, less money can be made available for educational services.

But *Rodriguez* is not the last word. Indeed, a number of state supreme courts have ruled on the constitutionality of their states' school financing systems. While many state supreme courts have found their school financing systems constitutional, several other supreme courts have held that the system utilized in their state violates educational provisions in the state constitution.[65] To some extent, the trend toward litigating civil rights issues at the state, rather than the federal level reflects a response to a federal judiciary that, despite President Clinton's appointments, remained viewed as generally conservative resulting from Reagan-Bush appointments.

Among the state supreme courts that found their systems unconstitutional was the Texas Supreme Court. In *Edgewood Independent School District* v. *Kirby* [77 S.W. 2nd 391, Tex. (1989)], that body ruled unanimously that the state school financing system violated the state constitutional provision requiring "the support and maintenance of an efficient system of public free schools." Public schools are supported in Texas through state-provided revenues and revenues raised by the local school districts from *ad valorem* property taxes. The ability of the school districts to raise their share of school support is hindered by disparities in property wealth among the school districts; the property wealth per student in school districts varies between $14 million and $20 thousand. These disparities are reflected in each school district's spending per student, ranging from $2,112 to $19,333. The Texas Supreme Court rejected the state's claim that the word "efficient" suggests a "simple and inexpensive system," ruling instead that "efficient" connotes a system that is effective or produces results. Since the amount of money spent on a student's education has an impact on the education opportunity available to the student, the Texas Supreme Court held that the "efficiency" requirement mandates the equitable and even distribution of education funds. Rather than prescribe a school financing system, the Texas Supreme Court gave the legislature discretion within time limits to develop such a system of school financing.

Subsequent developments in state legislative politics make it clear, however, that the matter will be difficult to resolve.[66]

Overall, it seems clear that the Burger Court did not seem disposed to break new ground in poverty law and in shoring up the constitutional rights of the poor. This disposition of the Burger Court is reflected well in *Lindsey* v. *Norment*, a 1972 case that posed a challenge to Oregon's statutory procedures for evicting tenants who failed to pay rent. The tenants had argued that the Court support the view that the "need for decent shelter" and the "right to retain peaceful possession of one's home" are fundamental interests that require "strict scrutiny." But Justice White rejected the tenants' argument and, for a 5–2 Court majority, said that though the Court appreciates "the importance of decent, safe, and sanitary housing ... the Constitution does not provide judicial remedies for every social and economic ill."

The decisions examined in this section impact the ability of people with limited means to gain access to certain features of a good society, such as decent shelter and public education. A trend that is perhaps more significant, however, could further restrict access to the courtroom. Created in 1965 as a federal poverty program and incorporated during the Nixon administration, the Legal Services Corporation was intended to provide free civil legal aid to the poor. While the right to representation, regardless of income, is guaranteed in criminal cases, individuals bringing civil actions receive no such guarantee. Federal funding for the corporation has long been a target of many conservatives who believe that the corporation uses taxpayer money to subsidize liberal political causes. When Republicans gained control of both houses of Congress after the 1994 elections, conservatives gained an opportunity to drastically cut Legal Services, if not eliminate it entirely. In the end, they did succeed in slashing funding in 1996 by approximately 30 percent and restricting the kinds of cases and clients Legal Services attorneys may take.

The effect of these cutbacks has already been felt in places like Georgia, where a lack of funding has formed Georgia Legal Services to practice a form of triage. Some activities remain high priorities (helping women in violently abusive marriages, keeping tenants from being evicted from public housing, and helping clients sue for federally guaranteed entitlements), while others are no longer performed by Legal Services attorneys (intervening in private landlord-tenant disputes, pursuing consumer fraud cases, and preventing students from summary expulsion from school).[67] While the full impact of Legal Services cutbacks remains to be seen, it seems likely that the poor will continue to have very limited and unequal opportunity to defend their rights effectively in court.

In general, this overall review of judicial policies indicates a change in the tone and substance between decisional outputs of the Warren Court, the Burger Court, and now the Rehnquist Court. These changes vividly illuminate the intimate and continuing interaction among courts, laws, and politics, a matter that is the focus of the next chapter.

TOPICS FOR DISCUSSION

1. Do you feel that judicial support is important for the attainment of black policy objectives? Explain your position.

2. As quoted in the epigraph to this chapter, Justice Marshall "fears" that the Court has come "full circle." Do you share his belief? Why or why not? Justify your position.

3. The number of blacks in the legal profession is very small. Blacks comprise less than 3 percent of the legal profession in America. How and in what ways does this shortage of black lawyers work to the disadvantage of blacks in American politics?

4. The records of the Burger and Rehnquist Courts suggest that judicial victories, like political victories, are not etched in concrete and are subject to change. Do you agree or disagree? How and in what ways do "judicial" victories differ from "political victories"? Are they related? How?

SUGGESTED READINGS

See Chapter 6.

NOTES

1. Remarks of Justice Thurgood Marshall at the Annual Seminar of the San Francisco Patent and Trademark Law Association, Maui, HI, May 6, 1987.
2. Dissenting in *United Steelworkers et al.* v. *Weber* (99 S. Ct. 2752–2753, 1979).
3. Joseph Goldstein. *The Intelligible Constitution* (New York: Oxford University Press, 1992), p. 23.
4. 448 U.S. 448 (1980) (upholding a congressionally created set-aside program for minority business owners). For a fuller discussion of the *Fullilove* case, see *infra* pp. 118–119.
5. *City of Richmond* v. *J.A. Croson Co.*, 488 U.S. 469 (1989). (Justice O'Connor's opinion for the court engendered five separate concurring and dissenting opinions from her colleagues.)
6. 497 U.S. 547 (1990).
7. 115 S. Ct. 2097 (1995).
8. 15 U.S.C. Sec. 637(d)(1)(1993).
9. 13 C.F.R. Sections 124.105(b)(1), 124.106(b)(1995); 48 C.F.R. Sections 19.001, 19.703(a)2 (1994).
10. 790 F. Supp. 240 (1992).
11. 16 F. 3d 1537 (1994).
12. *Adarand*, 115 S. Ct., p. 2111.
13. O'Connor wrote for the Court and Scalia, Thomas, Stevens, Souter, and Ginsberg each wrote in partial concurrence or dissent.
14. *Adarand*, 115 S. Ct., p. 2118.
15. *Ibid.*, p. 2119.
16. Section 5 of the Fourteenth Amendment to the Constitution provides that "[c]ongress shall have power to enforce, by appropriate legislation, the provisions of this [amendment]."

17. Harold Lasswell, *Politics: Who Gets What, When, How* (Cleveland, OH: Meridian Books, 1958).
18. Walter Murphy and C. Herman Pritchett, *Courts, Judges and Politics*, 2nd ed. (New York: Random House, 1974), p. 442.
19. Codified at 29 U.S.C. Section 794(b).
20. *Hopkins* v. *Price Waterhouse*, 109 S. Ct. 1775 (1989)(holding that plaintiffs in "mixed motive" adverse action cases could not prevail in court if the adverse action taken against them could be justified on non-discriminatory grounds, notwithstanding the fact that the plaintiff's race, color, religion, sex, or national origin might also have been a factor in the decision); *Wards Cove Packing Co., Inc.* v. *Atonio*, 109 S. Ct. 2115 (1989)(requiring that plaintiffs in "disparate impact" cases prove a causal link between apparently neutral employment practices and statistical racial imbalances in the workplace; also holding that employers may prevail if they proffered "legitimate business reasons" for the challenged practices notwithstanding any racially disparate impact that they may cause). Prior to *Wards Cove*, the courts shifted the burden of proof to defendant employers after the plaintiffs showed disparate impact and excused employment practices with discriminatory effects only after the defendant showed that the employment practices were essential or necessary. Also, *Martin* v. *Wilks*, 109 S. Ct. 2180 (1989)(holding that white individuals who were not joined in litigation between employers and minority plaintiffs would not be bound by the provision of any resulting judicial consent decree and could challenge the decision in court subsequently); *Lorance* v. *AT&T*, 109 S. Ct. 2261 (1989)(holding that the period under Title VII of the Civil Rights Act of 1964 for challenging a facially neutral discriminatory seniority system begins to run from the date the system was adopted, not from when the system adversely affects a plaintiff); and *Patterson* v. *McLean Credit Union*, 109 S. Ct. 2363 (1989)(holding that Title 42 U.S.C. Section 1981, a post-Civil War statute prohibiting racial discrimination in the making or enforcement of contracts, did not apply to on-the-job racial harassment complaints).
21. Civil Rights Act of 1991, codified at 42 U.S.C. Section 1981(A).
22. Murphy and Pritchett, *Courts, Judges, and Politics*, p. 408.
23. Cf. Alexis de Tocqueville, *Democracy in America*, ed. J. P. Mayer and Max Lerner, trans. George Lawrence (New York: Harper & Row, 1966), pp. 242–248.
24. In 1994, out of a total of 861,000 lawyers and judges, only 3.3 percent were black. This figure, however, represents an increase from 2.7 percent in 1983. For Hispanics, the corresponding figures are 3.0 and 1.0 percent, respectively. See U.S. Bureau of the Census, *Statistical Abstract of the United States, 1995*, p. 411.
25. Jack W. Peltason, *Federal Courts in the Political Process* (New York: Random House, 1955), p. 3.
26. *Ibid.*
27. See John P. Heinz, Robert W. Getleman, and Morris A. Seeskin, "Legislative Politics and the Criminal Law," *Northwestern Law Review* 64 (1969), pp. 277–358.
28. For discussion of judicial selection and characteristics of members of the Court generally, see Lawrence Baum, *The Supreme Court*, 6th ed. (Washington, DC: Congressional Quarterly, Inc., 1998), Chapter 2.
29. Richard Harris, *Decision* (New York: Dutton, 1971).

30. See Nadine Cohodas, "Merit Selection Diversified Federal Bench," *Congressional Quarterly Weekly Report* 37 (October 27, 1979), p. 2418.
31. See Exec. Order No. 12059, May 11, 1978, 43 Fed. Register 20949; and Exec. Order No. 19097, November 8, 1978, 43 Fed. Register 52455. Also see Charles W. Hucker, "Report Card on Judicial Merit Selection," *Congressional Quarterly Weekly Report* 37 (February 3, 1979), p. 189ff; and Nadine Cohodas, "Merit Selection Diversifies Federal Bench," *Congressional Quarterly Weekly Report* 37 (October 27, 1979), p. 2418ff.
32. "Report Card," p. 194.
33. See generally, "Merit Selection," p. 2418ff.
34. For an overall and in-depth look at the politics and dynamics of the selection of federal district court judges, see Kevin L. Lyles, *The Gatekeepers: Federal District Courts in the Political Process* (Westport, CT: Praeger, 1997), Chapter 2.
35. Peltason, *Federal Courts*, p. 3.
36. See, for example, *Kelly v. Board of Education* [270 F. 2d 209 (CA 6)(1959)]; and *Shuttlesworth v. Birmingham Board of Education* [358 U.S. 101 (1958)].
37. Earl Warren, *The Memoirs of Earl Warren* (Garden City, NY: Doubleday & Co., Inc., 1977), p. 306.
38. Philip Elman, "The Solicitor General's Office, Justice Frankfurter, and Civil Rights Litigation, 1946–1960: An Oral History," *Harvard Law Review* 100 (1960), pp. 817, 845–847. For other comments regarding the Court's reluctance to tackle miscegenation laws, see Jack Greenberg, *Race Relations and American Law* (1959), p. 345; Walter F. Murphy, *Elements of Judicial Strategy* (1964), pp. 192–193; memorandum from Harvey M. Grossman, law clerk, to Justice William O. Douglas (November 3, 1954) (on file with Justice William O. Douglas Papers, Box 1156, Library of Congress). All of these works are cited in Peter Wallerstein, "Freedom: Personal Liberty and Private Law: Race, Marriage, and the Law of Freedom: Alabama and Virginia," *Chicago-Kent Law Review* 70 (1994), pp. 371, 415–416.
39. 402 U.S. 43 (1971), p. 45.
40. *Dayton Board of Education et al. v. Brinkman et al.*, 99 S. Ct. 2971 (1979).
41. *Columbus Board of Education et al. v. Penick et al.*, 99 S. Ct. 2941 (1979).
42. 99 S. Ct. 2976 (1979).
43. *Ibid.*
44. *Ibid.*, p. 2978.
45. 99 S. Ct. 2941 (1979).
46. *Ibid.*, p. 2944.
47. 99 S. Ct. 2954.
48. 99 S. Ct. 2952 (concurring in *Columbus*).
49. *Missouri v. Jenkins*, 115 S. Ct. 2038 (1995).
50. James S. Kunen, "The End of Integration: A Four-Decade Effort Is Being Abandoned, as Exhausted Courts and Frustrated Blacks Dust Off the Concept of 'Separate but Equal,'" *Time*, April 29, 1996, p. 38.
51. Examples from the mid-1990s included Cleveland, Denver, Hartford, Kansas City, Minneapolis, Pittsburgh, St. Louis, and Seattle.
52. Leslie McAneny and Lydia Saad, "America's Public Schools: Still Separate? Still Unequal?" *Gallup Poll Monthly*, May 1994, pp. 23–29.

53. Steven A. Holmes and Karen DeWitt, "Black, Successful, and Safe and Gone from Capital," *New York Times*, July 27, 1996, p. 1+.

54. American Political Network, Inc., "Taking the Bull by the Horns: African-American Charters," *Daily Report Card*, February 9, 1996.

55. Kunen, p. 39.

56. *University of California Regents* v. *Bakke*, 438 U.S. 265 (1978).

57. *United Steelworkers* v. *Weber*, 99 S. Ct. 2721 (1979).

58. *Ibid.*

59. *Ibid.*, p. 2740.

60. *Ibid.*

61. Quoted from Barker and Combs, "Civil Rights and Liberties in the First Term of the Rehnquist Court: The Quest for Doctrine and Votes," *National Political Science Review* 1 (1988), pp. 50–51.

62. The Court did, however, remand the case to the district court to consider whether purposeful discrimination was involved. Subsequently, the plan as approved by the district court contained nine wards—four with black majorities; four with white majorities; and one "swing" district with approximately equal numbers of blacks and whites. In the first election under the plan on March 1, 1977, blacks won five of the nine seats.

63. See reference to the Voting Rights Act in *United Jewish Organizations of Williamsburgh* v. *Carey*, 430 U.S. 144 (1977).

64. While education is not explicitly guaranteed in the federal Constitution, it is so guaranteed by many state constitutions. These provisions have provided the basis for relief against unfair property tax assessments and expenditures in several states.

65. In addition to the Texas case described, the list of state decisions condemning the reliance on local property taxes to fund public education includes cases from Arizona, Arkansas, California, Connecticut, Michigan, Montana, and New Jersey.

66. See *Washington Post*, May 1, 1990; May 2, 1990; and May 23, 1990.

67. William Booth, "Attacked as Left-Leaning, Legal Services Suffers Deep Cuts," *Washington Post*, June 1, 1996, p. A1+.

Chapter 6

Courts, Judges, and the Interaction of Law and Politics

Groups which find themselves unable to achieve their objectives through the ballot frequently turn to the courts. Just as it was true of the opponents of the New Deal legislation during the 1930s, no less is it true of the Negro minority today. And under the conditions of modern government, litigation may well be the sole practicable avenue open to a minority to petition for the redress of grievances....

—Justice William Brennan from his majority opinion in *NAACP* v. *Button*, 371 U.S. 415, pp. 429–430 (1963)

Stare decisis is the preferred course because it promotes the evenhanded, predictable, and consistent development of legal principles, fosters reliance on judicial decisions, and contributes to the actual and perceived integrity of the judicial process.... Adhering to precedent "is usually the wise policy, because in most matters it is more important that the applicable rule of law be settled than right."... Nevertheless, when governing decisions are unworkable or are badly reasoned, "this Court has never felt constrained to follow precedent." *Smith* v. *Allwright*, 1944. *Stare decisis* is not an inexorable command; rather it "is a principle of policy and not a mechanical formula of adherence to the latest decision." This is particularly true in constitutional cases, because in such cases "correction through legislative action in practically impossible."... Considerations in favor of *stare decisis* are at their acme is cases involving property and contract rights, where reliance interests are involved ... the opposite is true in cases such as the present one involving procedural and evidentiary rules.

Applying these general principles, the Court had during the past 20 terms overruled in whole or in part 33 of its previous constitutional decisions. Booth and Gathers were decided by the narrowest of margins, over spirited dissents challenging the basic underpinnings of those decisions. They have been questioned by members of the Court in later decisions, and have defied consistent application by the lower courts.... Reconsidering these decisions now, we conclude for the reasons heretofore stated, that they were wrongly decided and should be, and now are, overruled. We accordingly affirm the judgment of the Supreme Court of Tennessee.

—Chief Justice William Rehnquist from his majority opinion
in *Payne* v. *Tennessee*, 111 S. Ct. 2597 (1991)

Power, not reason, is the new currency of this Court's decision making. Four terms ago, a five-Justice majority of this Court held that "victim impact" evidence of the type at issue in this case could not constitutionally be introduced during the penalty phase of a capital trial. (*Booth* v. *Maryland*, 1987). By another 5–4 vote, a majority of this Court rebuffed an attack upon this ruling just two terms ago. (*South Carolina* v. *Gathers*, 1989) Nevertheless, having expressly invited respondent to renew the attack ... today's majority overrules *Booth* and *Gathers* and credits the dissenting views expressed in those cases. Neither the law nor the facts supporting *Booth* and *Gathers* underwent any change in the last four years. Only the personnel of this Court did.

In dispatching *Booth* and *Gathers* to their own graves, today's majority ominously suggests that an even more extensive upheaval of this Court's precedents may be in store.... The majority sends a clear signal that scores of established constitutional liberties are now ripe for reconsideration, thereby inviting the very type of open defiance of our precedents that the majority rewards in this case. Because I believe that this Court owes more to its constitutional precedents in general and to *Booth* and *Gathers* in particular, I dissent.

—Justice Thurgood Marshall from his dissenting opinion
in *Payne* v. *Tennessee*, 111 S. Ct. 2597 (1991)

As the above epigraphs suggest, this chapter attempts to delineate more concretely the interactive role and importance of courts, law, and politics in formulation and implementation of public policy. And nowhere is this interaction illuminated more vividly than in this chapter, which (1) gives a brief overview of the life and legacy of Justice Thurgood Marshall, and (2) offers an overall conclusion regarding how African Americans have fared with respect to courts and judges as policy institutions and actors.

THE THURGOOD MARSHALL STORY

President Lyndon Johnson's appointment of Justice Thurgood Marshall t the U.S. Supreme Court in 1967 was of great historical, political, and le significance. In terms of history, it marked the very first time that African-American had been appointed to the high court. Further, as t itics, it gave recognition to the fact that African-Americans had an becoming an important political force in the Democratic pa American politics generally, especially presidential politics.

In addition, Marshall's appointment clearly sought to give

representation in the Supreme Court to the very person who demonstrated dramatically how groups might well resort to courts and litigation to achieve policy objectives they had been unable to attain elsewhere. Indeed, it was Marshall, as Director-General of the NAACP-LDF, who engineered the litigation and successfully persuaded the Court to unanimously proclaim the principles announced in *Brown*, the 1954 school desegregation cases. And it was clear that the *Brown* decision clearly portended to bring about revolutionary changes not only in our law and jurisprudence, but in our overall politics and society as well. Obviously, then, Marshall's appointment stirred bitter and prolonged opposition, particularly from interests who felt threatened by the new legal regime spawned in *Brown*. In the end, however, Marshall was able to win Senate confirmation and join the Court.

But controversy erupted anew over many of the same issues when some 25 years later, in 1991, Marshall retired from the Court and Republican President George Bush nominated Judge Clarence Thomas to take his place. Indeed, the resignation of Justice Thurgood Marshall and President Bush's subsequent nomination of Judge Clarence Thomas as his replacement illumined once again the interrelation and importance of courts and judges to American politics and public policy. And the fact that Justice Marshall, a black liberal, was being replaced by Judge Thomas, a black conservative, stirred the debate even more.

It would indeed be difficult to find any two persons whose views differ as widely as those of Justice Marshall and Judge Thomas along both policy and jurisprudential dimensions. And it clearly would prove more difficult, but not impossible, as Thomas's very appointment shows, to find two African Americans whose views would prove as divergent on matters relating to problems of race and the role of government and courts in dealing with such problems.

Of course, Republican President Bush, not unlike Democratic President Johnson, nominated a person whom he thought would represent interests that appealed to him and his party. Thus, though blacks were not an important constituent group in the Republican party, President Bush's nomination of a black conservative potentially held double appeal. On the one hand, a Thomas appointment would give symbolic recognition to the interests represented by African Americans, and as a result, could possibly help to mitigate the generally negative image most blacks hold of the Republican party.

Simultaneously, however, it likewise seemed clear that the appointment of a well-known and proven conservative judge like Thomas to the Supreme Court would give strong support to major conservative interests held by President Bush and the Republican party. And as matters have played out thus far, Justice Thomas's performance on the Court has clearly met these presidential expectations.

But similarly, as suggested earlier, so did President Johnson have every expectation to believe that a Court appointment would give Marshall a key position and vantage point from which to safeguard and promote interests, particularly civil rights, that were strongly supported by the President. And, as we shall see following, Justice Marshall's performance on the Court certainly lived up to President Johnson's expectations.

THURGOOD MARSHALL, THE LAW, AND THE SYSTEM: TENETS OF AN ENDURING LEGACY[1]

LUCIUS J. BARKER[2]

[L]aw cannot only respond to social change but can initiate it, and ... lawyers, through their everyday work in the courts may become social reformers.

—Thurgood Marshall[3]

Few Americans have affected our nation's legal, political, and social lives as significantly as Thurgood Marshall. His contributions mark him as one of history's truly great jurisprudential leaders. While Marshall's work and reputation are best known in connection with the struggle to secure the civil rights of African Americans,[4] his influence is felt in other areas of the law as well.[5] His efforts—first as lawyer, then as judge, later as Solicitor General, and finally as Supreme Court Justice—have pushed the law to be more fair, more inclusive, more sensitive, and more responsive. His life's service challenges all Americans to join the battle for equal opportunity and justice.

Throughout his long career, Marshall directed this challenge with particular urgency to the practitioners and the interpreters of the law. Behind his eloquent legal arguments and incisive dissents is a philosophy of social fairness that required changing the dominant paradigm of power and privilege that exists throughout the political-social-economic order. And, as far as Marshall was concerned, courts had a central role to play in that effort, consistent with their constitutional role and legal competence. Marshall keenly understood that judicial opinions, resulting from the interplay of judges, lawyers, procedures, and principles, could never escape the shadow of politics.

It was this systemic perspective—a view of the American legal system as operating within a political governing structure, yet grounded in and restrained by enduring principles of law and equality—that allowed Marshall to forge a legal career that leaves as its legacy a philosophy of the aspirational role of law in society. This essay examines the roots of that philosophy and its operation in Marshall's jurisprudence.

The Making of an Enduring Legacy

Thurgood Marshall symbolizes what is best about our American society: the belief that human rights must be satisfied through the orderly process of law."

—President Lyndon B. Johnson[6]

Origins of a Social Reformer   Thurgood Marshall transformed the role of law in America by using the courts as vehicles of social transformation. Through a strategy of litigious confrontation he developed and perfected while Director-Counsel of the National Association for the Advancement of Colored People's Legal Defense Fund (NAACP-LDF), Marshall waged war against a system of racial segregation firmly embedded in the history and laws of the country.

Of course, much of Marshall's legal success stems from the fact that he was an extraordinary person. Very resourceful[7] and possessed of a keen intellect, Marshall was propelled by an undaunted courage and deep commitment to tearing down the nation's repressive, racist legal regime. Yet Marshall's ability to challenge the prevailing patterns of power can also be attributed to the life experience from which he came. Growing up black in segregated America forced Marshall to view the law as more than just a set of rules that excluded his race from citizenship. To Marshall, the law was animated by the aspirations enshrined in the Declaration of Independence; values that transcended law's temporal function of regulating the behavior of individuals vis-à-vis one another.

Marshall's sense that the law could and should reflect such egalitarian values had its origins in his early education. Born in 1908 into a world permeated by formal distinctions based on race, Marshall attended the segregated public schools in Baltimore, Maryland. It was in these schools that Marshall developed an interest in the federal Constitution. At Douglas High, the Negro high school in Baltimore, a favorite form of disciplinary actions was sending student offenders to the school's basement with "instructions to read and memorize sections of the Constitution."[8] "I went to the basement so often," recalls Marshall, "that I knew the whole thing by heart before I reached my senior year."[9]

Upon graduating from Douglas, Marshall entered Lincoln University with plans to study dentistry, but his interest in the area waned after he won a place on Lincoln's debating team. Debating rekindled the give-and-take on current issues that had been a favorite pastime in the Marshall household, particularly between Marshall and his father. "There were never any pros and cons on segregation,"[10] remembers Marshall. "Our only arguments on this subject were over the best methods of doing away with it."[11] This desire to be active in the affairs of the day, coupled with his success in debating, led Marshall to a career in law. In the fall of 1930, Marshall entered Howard University Law School in Washington, DC.

Shortly before Marshall's arrival, Howard University appointed a new dean of its law school, a young, black graduate of Harvard Law School named Charles H. Houston. For Houston, Howard could not be just another law school; rather, it had to be an institution devoted to social change. Keenly aware of both the need for black lawyers and the role that such lawyers could play in American society, Houston embarked on a crusade to train and develop legal minds who would devote their careers to improving the legal status and lives of African Americans. Said Houston: "The social justification for the Negro lawyer as such in the United States is the service he can render the race as an interpreter and proponent of its rights and aspiration[s]."[12] In addition to his demand that his students acquire a thorough technical competence in law, Houston, recalled one of his former students, kept "hammering at us all those years that, as lawyers, we had to be social engineers or else we were parasites."[13]

Marshall, excited by Houston's challenge, quickly fell under the dean's influence. That influence was evident years later, in Marshall's work and words as an Associate Justice of the Supreme Court. In 1968, for instance, in words that reflect Houston's own philosophy, Marshall warned that if the promise of the Fourteenth Amendment is to be kept, it is essential to have "a new kind of activism, and activism in the pursuit of justice."[14] Said Marshall, our "courtrooms are perhaps the most accurate barometers of the extent to which we have succeeded in building a just society."[15]

Three years after graduating from Howard, Marshall served as Houston's assistant at the NAACP, succeeding his mentor as NAACP special counsel when Houston resigned in 1938 due to ill health. When the separate NAACP Legal Defense Fund was established in 1940, Marshall became its first director-counsel. Marshall's efforts at the NAACP-LDF resulted in a number of court victories that bolstered the civil rights movement. His greatest victory came when the Supreme Court handed down its path-breaking decision, *Brown* v. *Board of Education*,[16] in which the Court declared racial segregation in public schools unconstitutional.[17] *Brown* was the culmination of a careful legal strategy developed by Marshall to lead the Court to repudiate the doctrine of "separate but equal" established in *Plessy* v. *Ferguson*.[18]

The Jurisprudence of Social Change: Viewing the Courts in Systemic Perspective   Part of Marshall's genius as a litigator was his willingness to view the federal judiciary in *systemic perspective*: as a branch of government not insulated from the whims and vagaries of the political process (as some might contend) but actively engaged in the day-to-day business of governance. Such a perspective recognizes that ours is a system in which various political and legal actors work interdependently, responding to one another within the constraints of their various constitutional roles. Thus, Supreme Court Justices, like other governmental actors, are an integral pa of the policy-making process.[19] This even includes those Justices who oste sibly refrain from judicial activism. "A judge who defers to the legislature," writes political scientist Jack Peltason, "is engaging in interest activity just as much as the judge who avowedly writes his own preferences into his opinions."[20]

Nevertheless, a systemic perspective also recognizes that federal judges, unlike other governmental actors, enjoy a large measure of institutional independence due to their life tenure. This is particularly true of the Supreme Court, which, through judicial review and statutory interpretation, has been able to tackle highly controversial issues that might otherwise lead to stalemate in the political arena. In such instances, the judiciary acts "as a safety valve for the elected political branches, providing leadership when it is reasonably ascertained that the elected institutions are either unwilling or unable to act."[21]

Indeed, "we might find ... that certain issues simply do not lend themselves to fair resolution by elective political institutions no matter how much we tell ourselves that they do."[22] As Justice Jackson wrote in *West Virginia* v. *Barnette*: "[T]he very purpose of a Bill of Rights [is] to withdraw certain subjects from the vicissitudes of political controversy, to place them beyond the reach of majorities and officials and to establish them as legal principles to be applied by courts."[23]

This does not mean, however, "that in every instance where elected institutions fail to act, the court must step in."[24] Nor does this mean that courts are super-legislatures whose freedom to act comes from their unaccountability in the political arena. "Such a notion simplifies too much, both the delicate operation of our governing system as well as the role of the court in that system. On the contrary, by deciding and fashioning policy on such issues, the court gives to the governing system that necessary viability and capacity needed to survive."[25] Clearly, the Bill of Rights and the other constitutional amendments serve to anchor judicial decision making to the bedrock of the Constitution. Indeed, it is this very constraint under which the Court operates, coupled with a strong American affinity for the rule of law, which gives judicial policies their unique character of authoritative potency. As Robert McCloskey has pointed out, these contradictory ideas—"the will of the people and the rule of law"—are reflected in our governmental structure, and the devotion of the American people to both ideas "insure[s] public support for the institution that represent[s] each of them."[26]

However, one need not overlook the competing reality that courts function within an overall political context from which they cannot be separated.[27] The most obvious example of this is the clear correlation between presidential appointments to the Supreme Court and the judicial outcomes that emanate from that body.[28] After the dramatic shift in Court personnel following the election of President Nixon in 1968, Marshall found himself increasingly in the Court's minority. He recognized this shift when, in a 72 dissent, he criticized the majority for departing from an earlier 1968

Justice Thurgood Marshall, shown here in a formal picture with the Rehnquist Court, found that though his views were generally in line with the more liberal Warren Court, they were increasingly at odds with the more conservative Burger and Rehnquist Courts. (*National Geographic Society*)

ruling. "But," acknowledged Marshall, "I am aware that the composition of this Court has radically changed in four years."[29]

The Supreme Court (and more generally the federal judiciary) fulfills a dual function: It is an adjudicating body as well as "a major maker of law and public policy." While this ironically "deviates from the normal conception of what a court is and ought to be" and leads paradoxically to the observation that the Supreme Court is *both* a court and *not* a court, or, at the least, "*more* than just a court,"[30] it is also true that judges recognize the constraints and limits of their constitutional role. If it is true that courts cannot escape the majoritarian thrusts of politics and public opinion, it is also true that judges respond to the rule of the law and to the timeless principles of an egalitarian social order.

It is this paradox that Marshall understood well. As a lawyer, viewing courts in systemic perspective enabled Marshall to craft legal arguments that addressed judges' political as well as legal concerns. As a Justice, it allowed him to vigorously argue for principled judicial activism based upon the enduring tenets articulated in the Bill of Rights. Marshall's jurisprudence regards courts and law as having a high calling, an aspirational quality, reflected in the Constitution, the Fourteenth Amendment, and the Court's decision in *Brown*. Therefore, while Marshall clearly acknowledge the political nature of courts and the law, he simultaneously understood need to rely on these institutions (and the aspirational principles underlie them) as restraints on unbridled majoritarian politics. The k an effective judiciary, in Marshall's view, is the delicate balance between its competing legal and political functions.

Perhaps there is no better evidence of this philosophy than Marshall's own dissents. Increasingly isolated ideologically by the appointment of younger, more conservative voices on the Court, Marshall, in the latter years of his term, used his words to warn against the danger of allowing politics to overshadow the jurisprudential function of the judiciary. In a 1991 dissent, Marshall charged that "power, not reason, is the new currency of this Court's decision making."[31] As the end of his tenure drew near, Marshall recognized the growing willingness of the Court to depart from precedent, particularly in the area of civil rights.[32]

Opportunities and Constraints of Office: Marshall as Dissenter Supreme Court dissents serve important functions. They allow a Justice to "state principled opposition" to the majority's position. In addition, they enable the dissenter to address competing ideas held by colleagues on the Court. Further, they offer lower court judges avenues by which to limit the majority's decision if they wish.[33] Most importantly, as "potential majority opinions of the future," dissents speak to future lawyers, judges, and Supreme Court Justices.[34] In addition to these functions, Marshall's dissents give readers a window through which they can observe the application of his philosophy of social change.

Marshall's dissents are rich, informative, and provocative. Through them, we view Marshall as historian-prophet, lawyer-jurist, politician-realist, and African American. Consider, for example, Marshall's dissent in *Milliken* v. *Bradley*,[35] where the Burger Court found that the scope of an interdistrict desegregation remedy for the Detroit public schools was not supported by corresponding evidence of interdistrict constitutional violations. Here, Marshall speaks to us in several roles: as a political-realist recognizing the difficulty of overcoming deeply ingrained racist attitudes; as a lawyer-jurist cautioning that despite popular opinion, the Court cannot be diverted from enforcing the Constitution and the rule of law; and as historian-prophet warning of the impending dangers should the Court fail to fulfill that unique role:

> Desegregation is not and was never expected to be an easy task. Racial attitudes ingrained in our Nation's childhood and adolescence are not quickly thrown aside in its middle years. But just as the inconvenience of some cannot be allowed to stand in the way of the rights of others, so public opposition, no matter how strident, cannot be permitted to divert this Court from the enforcement of the constitutional principles at issue in this case. Today's holding, I fear, is more a reflection of a perceived public mood that we have gone far enough in enforcing the Constitution's guarantee of equal justice than it is the product of neutral principles of law. In the short run, it may seem to be the easier

course to allow our great metropolitan areas to be divided up each into two cities—one white, the other black—but it is a course, I predict, our people will ultimately regret.[36]

Or consider Marshall's opinion in the highly controversial affirmative action case, *Regents of the Univ. of California* v. *Bakke*.[37] While agreeing with the majority's decision to uphold the use of race or ethnic background as a "plus" in admissions criteria, Marshall strongly disagreed with the majority's conclusion that the special admissions program at the University of California-Davis Medical School was unlawful. Marshall uses the opportunity not only to register disagreement; he carefully recounts an important history as well. In doing so, he touches on the frustration and anger African Americans have repeatedly felt when faced with the claim that the Constitution is colorblind and equal opportunity is a present reality:

> The position of the Negro today in America is the tragic but inevitable consequence of centuries of unequal treatment. Measured by any benchmark of comfort or achievement, meaningful equality remains a distant dream for the Negro....
>
> At every point from birth to death the impact of the past is reflected in the still disfavored position of the Negro.
>
> In light of the sorry history of discrimination and its devastating impact on the lives of Negroes, bringing the Negro into the mainstream of American life should be a state interest of the highest order. To fail to do so is to ensure that America will forever remain a divided society....
>
> While I applaud the judgment of the Court that a university may consider race in its admissions process, it is more than a little ironic that, after several hundred years of class-based discrimination against Negroes, the Court is unwilling to hold that a class-based remedy for that discrimination is permissible. In declining to so hold, today's judgment ignores that fact that for several hundred years Negroes have been discriminated against, not as individuals, but rather solely because of the color of their skins. It is unnecessary in 20th century America to have individual Negroes demonstrate that they have been victims of racial discrimination; the racism of our society has been so pervasive that none, regardless of wealth or position, has managed to escape its impact. The experience of Negroes in America has been different in kind, not just in degree, from that of other ethnic groups. It is not merely the history of slavery alone but also that a whole people were marked as inferior by the law. And that mark has endured. The dream of America as the great melting pot has not been realized for the Negro; because of his skin color he never even made it into the pot....
>
> I fear that we have come full circle. After the Civil War our Government started several "affirmative action" programs. This Court in the *Civil Rights Cases* and *Plessy* v. *Ferguson* destroyed the movement toward complete equality. For almost a century no action was taken, and this nonaction was with the tacit approval of the courts. Then we had *Brown* v. *Board of Education* and the Civil Rights Act of Congress, followed by numerous affirmative-action programs of the type used by the University of California.[38]

Perhaps Marshall's most eloquent dissents are those in which he revisits the case for which he is best known, *Brown*. In *Board of Education of Oklahoma Public Schools* v. *Dowell*,[39] the Court indicated that federal court supervision of school desegregation may be terminated in school districts that met certain "good faith" criteria in an effort to comply with desegregation decrees.[40] Though he agreed with the majority that "the proper standard for determining whether a school desegregation decree should be dissolved is whether the purposes of the desegregation litigation ... have been fully achieved," Marshall differed "on what must be shown to demonstrate that a decree's purposes have been fully realized."[41] In arguing his case, we catch a glimpse of Lawyer Thurgood Marshall, recalling the day he stood before the Court and, through his words, changed America. In Dowell, Marshall argued that a "standard for dissolution of a desegregation decree must take into account the unique harm associated with a system of racially identifiable schools and must expressly demand the elimination of such schools."[42] Recalling the theory he argued in *Brown*, Marshall wrote:

> Our pointed focus in *Brown I* upon the stigmatic injury caused by segregated schools explains our unflagging insistence that formerly *de jure* segregated school districts extinguish all vestiges of school segregation. The concept of stigma also gives us guidance as to what conditions must be eliminated before a decree can be deemed to have served its purpose....
>
> ... This focus on "achieving and *preserving* an integrated school system," stems from the recognition that the reemergence of racial separation in such schools may revive the message of racial inferiority implicit in the former policy of state-enforced segregation.
>
> ... Our jurisprudence requires ... that the job of school desegregation be fully completed and maintained so that the stigmatic harm identified in *Brown I* will not recur upon lifting the decree. Any doubt on the issue of whether the School Board has fulfilled its remedial obligations should be resolved in favor of the Afro-American children affected by this litigation.
>
> In its concern to spare local school boards the "Draconian" fate of "indefinite" "judicial tutelage," ... the majority risks subordination of the constitutional rights of Afro-American children to the interest of school board autonomy.[43]

Finally, one recalls Marshall's perennial debate with his Court colleagues over the use of discriminatory intent versus discriminatory impact as the proper standard to prove unconstitutional racial discrimination.[44] One of Marshall's best arguments in this regard is found in his dissent in *City of Mobile* v. *Bolden*,[45] where blacks, who made up about 40 percent of the population in Mobile, Alabama, had never been elected to the three-member city commission. This peculiar result was due to the city's at-large ·lection scheme. A plurality of the Court, however, finding no purposeful scrimination violating the Fourteenth or Fifteenth Amendments, upheld scheme.[46] In a strong dissent, Marshall writes as both political-realist historian-prophet:

It is time to realize that manipulating doctrines and drawing improper distinctions under the Fourteenth and Fifteenth Amendments, as well as under Congress's remedial legislation enforcing those Amendments, make this Court an accessory to the perpetuation of racial discrimination. The plurality's requirement of proof of *intentional discrimination*, so inappropriate in today's cases, may represent an attempt to bury the legitimate concerns of the minority beneath the soil of a doctrine almost as impermeable as it is specious. If so, the superficial tranquillity created by such measures can be but short-lived. If this Court refuses to honor our long-recognized principle that the Constitution "nullifies sophisticated as well as simpleminded modes of discrimination," ... it cannot expect the victims of discrimination to respect political channels of seeking redress.[47]

The increasing sharpness of Marshall's dissents reflected a growing apprehension about the Court's willingness to protect the rights of minorities, leading him to say in 1989 that recent Supreme Court decisions "put at risk not only the civil rights of minorities but the civil rights of all citizens."[48] Remembering the world to which he was born 80 years before, Marshall remarked, "We forget at our peril ... the historical lesson that 'civil rights and liberty rights' are 'inexorably intertwined.'"[49]

Tenets of an Enduring Legacy

Marshall's use of courts and the law has wrought fundamental change in our politics and society. He espoused principles and fought for causes of the highest order. His contributions give us a more thorough understanding of the political system and how that system may be made to work for the "have-nots" as well as for the "haves."[50] His was a strong belief in the capacity of courts to make real for all both the spirit and the letter of the Bill of Rights and the Fourteenth Amendment. And it is clear that Marshall believes courts must play a crucial role in this regard. Complex, difficult, and controversial issues, such as civil rights, often require "the artful use of judicial power no less than legislative and executive powers."[51]

Yet there must also be a balance between what the courts do legally and what they do politically. Marshall's work, particularly in the latter part of his career, cautions against the imbalance that has slowly overtaken the Court, resulting in a retreat from the Court's traditional role of protecting "discrete and insular" minorities.[52]

The Supreme Court played a major role in forging the national commitment to civil rights during the 1950s and 1960s. That commitment portended a framework in which heterogeneous racial and ethnic grou could both live and prosper together. As recent Court decisions indi however, that framework is now in jeopardy. For African American similar groups, these decisions suggest that relief must be sought in other than the federal courthouse—either through the state court toral politics.

SUMMARY

Overall, the Marshall story illuminates well several factors with respect to the relative role and interaction of law and politics. These factors include the following:

1. How the structure and functioning of our governmental system allow groups to use litigation as political strategy
2. The importance of judicial selection, since whoever sits on the Court determines in large measure what comes out of the Court
3. The capacity and limitations of courts and individual judges in the formation and implementation of public policy

We conclude our consideration of African-Americans and the courts, particularly the Supreme Court, with a general discussion of these and related matters.

CONCLUSION

Courts, Judges, and the Interaction of Law and Politics

Our discussion in this and the preceding chapter clearly suggests that changes in Court personnel have certainly brought with them changes in the judicial stance toward the rights of African Americans and other minorities. In short, it seems apparent that the legal fate of problems confronting African Americans was much more uncertain under the Burger Court than it was during the Warren Court, and the Rehnquist Court has moved in an even more openly negative direction.

What we have observed indicates the development and continuation of three somewhat interrelated trends in Supreme Court decision making during the Burger-Rehnquist Courts: (1) less inclination by the Court to expand Warren Court policies supporting racial justice; (2) less support for blacks and others who wish to use litigation to achieve objectives they cannot attain in political forums; and (3) less judicial support for individual or group claims against governmental authority.

These trends, if continued, hold important implications for blacks and for the political system generally. They could pose formidable barriers to one of the most vital points of access that blacks have in the political system. Indeed, one of the chief functions assumed by the Warren Court was to express and to respond to certain grievances of those who were unpopular, unrepresented, or underrepresented in the political system. The characteristics of the American judiciary, as opposed to Congress and the presidency, seem unique to this function. Particularly, the built-in insulation of the federal judiciary from conforming to various majoritarian pressures es judges in a very unique position to support the rights of "insulated colated" minorities.[53]

he problems that affect blacks and press the governmental system for are not trivial. They are the great issues of our time, which, as de Je observed long ago, sooner or later are converted into judicial issues. The American political system, as it has developed, tends to translate economic and social conflicts into legal conflicts. This, it seems, accounts for the unique significance of the Supreme Court. Consider the kinds of major issues that occupied the Warren Court and that remain with us today:

1. How to overcome problems of racial injustice
2. How to strengthen and extend political democracy—for example, fair and effective systems of representation
3. How to ensure fairness to all in administering criminal justice
4. How to safeguard the rights of the poor in distributing legal, political, and economic benefits
5. How to give maximum protection to individual freedoms

With all these problems, it was quite obvious that dominant interests during the Reagan-Bush era were unlikely to be in the vanguard of change. Those who are the victims of these problems—the politically disadvantaged—would quite naturally turn to the judicial system, where numbers, social status, wealth, and influence presumably have less bearing on the decision. In short, one of the important contributions of the Warren Court is that it was in a position to place items important to such groups on its agenda. It also could deal with them. These actions placed the symbol of constitutionalism and law on the side of particular issues relevant to such interests.

As a result, blacks were able initially to overcome many of the defects of coalition building and isolationism that so often characterize minority group politics. Coalition politics, for example, would appear to be necessary for a minority group to achieve favorable policies in the majority-rule electoral system. But to gain coalition support, a minority more often than not must soften its original objectives, since failure to do so lessens the possibilities of success in coalition building. Or a minority may hold to its original objectives and find itself isolated without the support necessary to achieve success. Then again, the minority group may subscribe to general, vague, though favorable policies. These policies either postpone the specific goals or shift their realization to another area. This is the more plausible course for a minority group to follow in elective-political arenas. But such policies are more likely to involve matters that affect the very self-esteem and dignity of individuals and the group itself. Hence, it would be most difficult for the group to soften its original objectives. But it could be equally difficult for the group to hold its original objectives in isolation without any viable chance of even limited success.

The judicial process can offer a minority group a way to overcome tain limitations that are part of the elective political process. In the ju process, a minority group may push its original objectives to obtain fu cific constitutional-legal guarantees. Moreover, the entire judicia though not separate from politics, is carried on in a strictly "nc manner; the language used addresses outcomes in terms o Constitution—and justice and fairness—"commands." "Reason and "legal principles" replace public opinion and majority rule as the "critical" determinants. The "myth" and structure of the judicial forum, unlike the practice and structure of elective political forums such as Congress, strengthen a minority group's chances of success. In addition, since courts also serve important functions for political elites and the political system generally—for example, resolution of conflict in terms of "law and order"—a victory for a minority group in the judicial system takes on added significance. Specifically, favorable court action may increase and constitutionalize (legitimize) pressures on and in elective political institutions to deal with the issues involved. Indeed, the minority group may now, as a result of victory in the courts, seek to give effect to legal constitutional rights, not mere interest group objectives. This, in large measure, is what happened during the Warren Court.

However, the situation began to change during the Burger Court. The Supreme Court's leadership and strong support for civil rights and civil liberties became much more uncertain. Nonetheless, the Burger Court did seem to follow the basic thrust of the Warren Court with respect to school desegregation and even extended increased constitutional protection to women. In general, however, decisions of the Warren Court included a creative use and application of the law to stimulate basic policy changes, whereas the Burger Court showed no such inclination. An off-the-bench comment by Chief Justice Burger illustrates this point. "Those [young people] who decide to go into law primarily on the theory that they can change the world by litigation in the courts," cautioned the Chief Justice, "may be in for some disappointment." Litigation, he said, is not "the route by which basic changes in a country like ours should be made. That is a very limited role for courts in this respect."[54] This seems to have characterized rather well the posture of the Burger Court, and now the Rehnquist Court. And given the nature and number of Reagan and Bush appointees to the Supreme Court, and lower federal courts as well, this posture is likely to manifest a strong presence in judicial policy making for some time to come. Hence, the problem for African Americans will not be how to forge new changes through litigation.[55] Instead, it will be how to prevent continuous "chipping away" of legal supports already gained.

With the 1992 election of Democratic President Clinton, and his reelection in 1996, this "chipping away" might be slowed or even turned around, given the general nature of the president's judicial appointments. ...deed, as suggested throughout our discussion, such change in judicial ...icy depends in large measure on *who* is appointed to the Court.

Importance of Judicial Support

...ove towards the twenty-first century, blacks and other minorities
...it even more difficult to achieve their objectives without strong
...ort—quality education, decent jobs, and adequate housing.

Notwithstanding the reelection of a more sympathetic president (Clinton), and given the nature of the political system, it seems unlikely that persistently strong leadership on civil rights and related problems can be expected from elective-political institutions, including the presidency.[56] In other words, elective-political institutions, in large measure, respond to constituencies that have the resources necessary to win elections. These resources include votes, financial wealth, support from influential groups, and so on. The only resource that blacks have historically had in some measure of supply is votes. However, even if blacks should achieve maximum voting strength, as a numerical minority it may not be enough to balance the scale, much less assure favorable action from elective-political institutions.

A higher degree of political participation among blacks, including voting and holding public office, might appear a desirable option. Yet it is unwise to build expectations regarding such activity beyond what we might reasonably expect. Reliance on political participation by "insulated and isolated" minorities to correct basic sociopolitical and legal problems must be tempered by an understanding of the limitations of American electoral politics. This latter point, as well as the overall inefficiency of elective-political institutions in dealing with racial problems, is illustrated in a study on black officeholders in the South by one of the co-authors of this volume, Mack Jones.[57] "While voting and holding office are necessary conditions," writes Jones, "they are not sufficient ones for realization of the democratic creed." This suggests, for example, that more than emergent black political majorities and elected officials in the nation's central cities may be needed for blacks to receive the full benefits of American society.[58] As the system presently operates, the authority and resources that cities need to deal effectively with urban problems make them greatly dependent upon institutions beyond their control, such as state and federal legislatures. This situation has led one scholar to conclude that future control of central cities appears to offer blacks "very limited" opportunities for gains and may well prove a "hollow prize."[59] But as we are beginning to see, this need not be the case. The dynamic character of American politics suggests that in certain situations, these "prizes" might not be that "hollow."

However, it could very well be that, given the nature and operation of the American political system, strong judicial support—similar to and even more than that given by the Warren Court—is one of the minimum conditions necessary for the full realization of the "democratic creed" by minority groups. The Court has had a long history of blocking and slowing down the constitutional rights of blacks, even when faced with strong congressional opposition. (An example is the *Civil Rights Cases* of 1883.) Even in r atively recent times, decisions of the Court offered only slight suppor black interests. As long as the Court impeded black interests or supp them only slightly, nothing much was done to improve blacks' stat once the Court began making decisions that strongly suppor expanded the constitutional rights of blacks, the situation began to change. Impetus was given to the civil rights movement. Support for its objectives was broadened. Congress and the president began to take action to deal with the problems of racial injustice. Initiatives taken by the Warren Court stand out as crucial in stimulating and developing policies designed to overcome these problems. However, the Burger Court did not appear so disposed and the Rehnquist Court has been even more inimical to concerns of blacks and minority groups.

Impact on Lower Courts and the Many "Others"

If the Supreme Court—the Burger Court and now the Rehnquist Court—continues to make uncertain, to narrow, or to negate the policies and posture of the Warren Court, we might expect such actions to have an important impact on lower federal and state courts. These courts, after all, perform crucial functions. They exercise a "gatekeeping" function to determine what issues enter the judicial arena. They determine, in large measure, how the few major issues that do finally reach the Supreme Court are phrased for decision by that body. Lower courts also implement Supreme Court mandates.[60] Moreover, decisions of lower courts are final in most cases. How lower courts exercise these functions may be determined largely by what they perceive to be, and what is, the actual posture of the Supreme Court. The same applies to the influence of the Supreme Court on the behavior of other institutions and officials in both the public and private sectors, including potential litigants and their lawyers.

Of course, the reverse is also true. Lower courts, for example, affect the substance and impact of Supreme Court decisions. These courts in large part sift and winnow the issues and arguments that constitute the record upon which the Supreme Court reaches its decision. Additionally, it is also lower courts who interpret and apply principles laid down in Supreme Court decisions to the bulk of cases and controversies that enter the judicial system.

These more generalized observations of the relative role and interaction of the Supreme Court and lower courts must be put in a more practical context. Indeed, as pointed out in Chapter 5, lower federal courts no less than the Supreme Court have come under the control and influence of Reagan-Bush judges. Though this could make for a high level of policy congruence between the Supreme Court and lower federal courts, that congruence could be disturbed, even turned around, in response to when and how President Clinton deals with the appointment opportunities that may ⊃me his way to shape and influence the federal judiciary.[61]

Not by Judges Alone: The Court in Political Perspective

`iscussion highlights the role of courts, primarily the Supreme Court, `ormation of racial policies. Indeed, the strong and persistent support `h policies by the Warren Court, in contrast to the uncertain posture of the Burger Court and now the Rehnquist Court, indicates that the position taken by the Court can prove crucial (even determinative) in gaining policy objectives. But court action in itself may not be enough to achieve the very goals and objectives expressed in court decision. Court pronouncements may be viewed as authoritative (and final) as to the law and the Constitution. Yet they are not necessarily authoritative and final as to ultimate policy and practice. This is especially true when dealing with the kind of tough political and social issues as those relating to race tend to be. Action from significant "others" is invariably needed to achieve benefits envisioned by court decisions. Specific and generalized support that the Court receives from other institutions, public officials, and various publics can prove crucial to the viability of particular decisions. This relates to specific support for a given court decision that might come from key officials such as the president, governors, mayors, and so on. It also relates very definitely to action taken by other political institutions—president, Congress, state legislatures—that might support and implement, or otherwise circumvent and impede, judicial policies.

There are, of course, other considerations that influence the importance of particular court decisions. But what we have suggested here is sufficient to illuminate the intimate interrelation of law, courts, and politics. This, however, is not meant to minimize the important, even crucial, role the courts play in the formulation of public policy and in the management of social conflict. Indeed, it may be suggested that the gross underrepresentation of blacks (and other minorities) in the legal profession accounts for their very limited influence not only in shaping judicial policies but also in shaping policies in other governmental institutions, such as in Congress, state legislatures, and administrative agencies.

TOPICS FOR DISCUSSION

1. Consider the relative nature and dynamics of the appointment and confirmation of Justice Thurgood Marshall, Justice Sandra Day O'Connor, and Justice Clarence Thomas to the Supreme Court. Point out the similarities and differences involved, especially as related to the interaction of law and politics.

Note: As to this question, you might wish to consult the popular press as well as relevant government documents (e.g., Senate Judiciary Committee hearings).

2. The article on Thurgood Marshall states that "the Supreme Court is *both* a court and *not* a court, or at least [it] is '*more* than just a court.'" Explain the meaning and significance of this statement especially as it relates to viability of the use of litigation as a political strategy.

SUGGESTED READINGS

Abraham, Henry J. *Justices and Presidents: A Political History of Appointmer*
    Supreme Court. New York: Oxford University Press, 1974.
———. *The Judicial Process*, 7th ed. New York: Oxford, 1998.

Armor, David J. *Forced Justice: School Desegregation and the Law.* New York: Oxford University Press, 1995.

Barker, Lucius J. "The Supreme Court from Warren to Burger: Implications for Black Americans and the Political System." *Washington University Law Quarterly* 4 (Fall 1973).

———. "Third Parties in Litigation: A Systemic View of the Judicial Function." *Journal of Politics* 29 (1967), p. 41.

Barker, T. W., and Michael Combs. "Civil Rights and Liberties in the First Term of the Rehnquist Court: The Quest for Doctrines and Votes." *National Political Science Review* 1 (1989), pp. 31–57.

Baum, Lawrence. *The Supreme Court,* 6th ed. Washington, DC: CQ Press, 1998.

Bell, Derrick, Jr. *Race, Racism and Law,* 3rd ed. Boston, MA: Little, Brown, 1992.

Bork, Robert H. *The Tempting of America.* New York: Free Press, 1990.

Caldeira, Gregory A., and John R. Wright. "Amici Curiae before the Supreme Court: Who Participates, When, and How Much?" *Journal of Politics* 52 (1990), p. 803.

———. "Organized Interests and Agenda Setting in the U.S. Supreme Court." *American Political Science Review* 82 (1988), p. 1109.

Caplan, Lincoln. *The Tenth Justice: The Solicitor General and the Rule of Law.* New York: Knopf, 1987.

Cardozo, Benjamin. *The Nature of the Judicial Process.* New Haven, CT: Yale University Press, 1921.

Casper, Jonathan D. *Lawyers before the Warren Court: Civil Liberties and Civil Rights.* Urbana, IL: University of Illinois Press, 1972.

Chayes, Abram. "Public Law Litigation and the Burger Court." *Harvard Law Review* 96 (1984), p. 4.

———. "The Role of the Judge in Public Law Litigation." *Harvard Law Review* 89 (1976), p. 1281.

Choper, Jesse. *Judicial Review and the National Political Process.* Chicago, IL: University of Chicago Press, 1980.

Dahl, Robert. "Decision Making in a Democracy: The Supreme Court as a National Policy Maker." *American Political Science Review* 70 (March 1976), p. 3.

Edley, Christopher. *Not All Black and White: Affirmative Action and American Values.* New York: Hill & Wang, 1996.

Ely, John Hart. *Democracy and Distrust: A Theory of Judicial Review.* Cambridge, MA: Harvard University Press, 1980.

Epstein, Lee. *Conservatives in Court.* Knoxville, TN: University of Tennessee Press, 1985.

Fried, Charles. *Order and Law.* New York: Simon & Schuster, 1991.

Goldman, Sheldon, and Austin Sarat, eds. *American Court Systems: Readings in Judicial Process and Behavior,* 2nd ed. White Plains, NY: Longman Inc., 1989.

Greenberg, Jack. *Crusaders in the Courts.* New York: Basic Books, 1994.

Guinier, Lani. *Lift Every Voice: Turning a Civil Rights Setback into a New Vision of Social Justice.* New York: Simon & Schuster, 1998.

Horowitz, Donald L. *The Courts and Social Policy.* Washington, DC: Brookings Institution, 1977.

Kennedy, Randall. *Race, Crime, and the Law.* New York: Pantheon, 1997.

Kluger, Richard. *Simple Justice: The History of Brown v. Board of Education and Black America's Struggle for Equality.* New York: Knopf, 1976.

Lyles, Kevin L. *The Gatekeepers: Federal District Courts in the Political Process.* Westport, CT: Praeger, 1997.

McCann, Michael W., and Gerald L. Houseman. *Judging the Constitution: Critical Essays on Judicial Lawmaking.* Glenview, IL: Scott, Foresman, 1989.

Murphy, Walter, and C. Herman Pritchett. *Courts, Judges, and Politics,* 3rd ed. New York: Random House, 1979.

O'Brien, David M. *Judicial Roulette: Report of the Twentieth Century Fund Task Force on Judicial Selection.* New York: Priority Press Publications, 1988.

Orfield, Gary, and Susan E. Eaton. *Dismantling Desegregation: The Quiet Reversal of Brown v. Board of Education.* New York: The New Press, 1996.

Peltason, Jack W. *Federal Courts in the Political Process.* New York: Random House, 1955.

Perry, H. W. *Deciding to Decide: Agenda Setting in the U.S. Supreme Court.* Cambridge, MA: Harvard University Press, 1991.

Rabkin, Jeremy A. *Judicial Compulsions: How Public Law Distorts Public Policy.* New York: Basic Books, 1989.

Rehnquist, William H. *The Supreme Court.* New York: Morrow, 1989.

Rosenberg, Gerald N. *The Hollow Hope: Can Courts Bring About Social Change?* Chicago, IL: University of Chicago Press, 1991.

Shapiro, Martin. *Freedom of Speech: The Supreme Court and Judicial Review.* Englewood Cliffs, NJ: Prentice Hall, 1966.

Simon, James. *In His Own Image: The Supreme Court in Richard Nixon's America.* New York: D. McKay, 1973.

Tribe, Laurence H. *God Save This Honorable Court: How the Choice of Supreme Court Justices Shapes Our History.* New York: Random House, 1985.

Warren, Elizabeth. *The Legacy of Judicial Policy-Making:* Gautreaux v. Chicago Housing Authority*: The Decision and Its Impacts.* Lanham, MD: University Press of America, 1988.

Wasby, Stephen L. *The Supreme Court in the Federal Judicial System.* New York: Holt, Rinehart & Winston, 1978.

NOTES

1. This article is reprinted with permission of the publisher from *Stanford Law Review* 44 (Summer 1992), pp. 1237–1247. The conclusion has been rewritten for inclusion in this text.
2. William Bennett Munro, Professor of Political Science, Stanford University. This essay is based on a larger study by the author on Thurgood Marshall. I wish to thank several people who read this essay and offered helpful suggestions, including professors H. W. Perry, Jr., of the University of Texas-Austin; Twiley W. Barker and Kevin L. Lyles of the University of Illinois at Chicago; and m˙ teaching and research assistant Roy Swan, Jr., who graduated from Stanfc Law School in June 1992. I absolve all of them, however, from any erro˙ fact and/or interpretation that remain; they are solely my responsibility.
3. Thurgood Marshall, "Law and the Quest for Equality," *Washington Univer Quarterly* 1, 7 (1967).
4. Marshall's legal contributions have influenced racial policies anᶜ throughout all major sectors of society. As director-counsel of t˙

Association for the Advancement of Colored People's Legal Defense Fund (NAACP-LDF), Marshall shaped the strategy and guided the forces that culminated in the path-breaking 1954 decision, *Brown* v. *Board of Educ.*, 347 U.S. 483 (1954).

5. See, for example, *Furman* v. *Georgia*, 408 U.S. 238, 314 (1972) (Marshall, J., concurring) (capital punishment); *San Antonio Indep. Sch. Dist.* v. *Rodriguez*, 411 U.S. 1, 70 (1973) (Marshall, J., dissenting) (the rights of the poor); *NAACP* v. *Alabama*, 357 U.S. 449 (1958) (First Amendment; Marshall, as Director-Counsel of the NAACP-LDF in 1958, filed the winning brief).

6. Ponchitta Pierce, "The Solicitor General," *Ebony*, November 1965, pp. 67, 68.

7. Marshall's "lifetime credo" was do "the best you can with what you've got." Sandra Day O'Connor, "Thurgood Marshall: The Influence of a Raconteur," *Stanford Law Review* 441 (1992), p. 217.

8. Ernest E. Goodman, "Portrait of Man of Law: Judge Thurgood Marshall," *Negro Digest* 12 (May 1963), pp. 3–4.

9. *Ibid.*, pp. 4–5.

10. *Ibid.*, p. 5.

11. *Ibid.*

12. Charles H. Houston, "The Need for Negro Lawyers," *Journal of Negro Education* 4 (1935), p. 49.

13. Richard Kluger, *Simple Justice: The History of* Brown v. *Board of Education and Black America's Struggle for Equality* (New York: Knopf, 1976).

14. Thurgood Marshall, "The Continuing Challenge of the 14th Amendment," *Wisconsin Law Review* (1968), pp. 979–980.

15. "Remarks of the Honorable Thurgood Marshall Upon the Occasion of His Acceptance of Honorary Membership in the Association of the Bar of the City of New York (Nov. 20, 1973)," *The Rec.* 29 (1974), pp. 15–16.

16. 347 U.S. 483 (1954).

17. In particular, *Brown* held that segregated public schools in the states violated the Fourteenth Amendment's guarantee of equal protection under the law. The Court extended that holding to public schools operated by the federal government in *Bolling* v. *Sharpe*, 347 U.S. 497 (1954).

18. 163 U.S. 537 (1896).

19. For example, there is research suggesting that the judicial policies that emanate from Supreme Court opinions are very much influenced by a variety of factors, such as the attitudes and actions of various system "elites"—actors like the President, Congress, and other political, economic, and social leaders; the reaction to Court decisions by lower court judges in both the federal and state judicial bureaucracies; and the social and political position of potential beneficiaries and supporters of particular judicial policies. See Lucius J. Barker, "Third Parties in Litigation: A Systemic View of the Judicial Function," *J. Pol.* 29 (1967), pp. 41, 53; Walter Murphy, "Lower Court Checks on the Supreme Court," *American Political Science Review* 53 (1959), p. 1017.

ck W. Peltason, *Federal Courts in the Political Process* (New York: Random House, 5), p. 3.

r, n17, pp. 64–65.

, 66.

624 (1943). But cf. *Department of Human Resources of Or.* v. *Smith*, 494

U.S. 872, 893 (1990) (Justice Scalia arguing "[v]alues that are protected against government interference through enshrinement in the Bill of Rights are not thereby banished from the political process").

24. Barker, n17, pp. 64–65.
25. *Ibid.*
26. Robert G. McCloskey, *The American Supreme Court* (1960), pp. 1, 13.
27. As one commentator has noted: "[C]oming to terms with the Supreme Court's legal and political nature is not easy, but to ignore or understate one or the other generally leads to an incomplete understanding of the Court." H. W. Perry, Jr., *Deciding to Decide: Agenda Setting in the United States Supreme Court* (1991), p. 5.
28. See Laurence H. Tribe, *God Save This Honorable Court* (1985), pp. 50–75; see also Kevin L. Lyles, *The Gatekeepers: Federal District Courts in the Political Process* (Westport, CT: Praeger, 1997).
29. *Lloyd v. Tanner*, 407 U.S. 551, 584 (1972) (Marshall, J., dissenting).
30. Martin Shapiro and Douglas Hobbs, *The Politics of Constitutional Law* (1974), p. 13 (emphasis added).
31. *Payne v. Tennessee*, 111 S. Ct. 2597, 2619 (1991) (Marshall, J., dissenting).
32. See *ibid.*, pp. 2621–2625.
33. See Stephen L. Wasby, *The Supreme Court in the Federal Judicial System*, 3rd ed. (1988), p. 235. For an excellent overview of the functions served by dissents, see *ibid.*, pp. 234–240.
34. *Ibid.*, p. 235. For a discussion of the use of dissent in a strategic context, see Walter Murphy, *Elements of Judicial Strategy* (1964), p. 60.
35. 418 U.S. 717, 787 (1974) (Marshall, J., dissenting).
36. *Ibid.*, pp. 814–815.
37. 438 U.S. 265, 387 (1978) (Marshall, J., concurring in the judgment).
38. *Ibid.*, pp. 395–402 (citations omitted).
39. 111 S. Ct. 630 (1991).
40. *Ibid.*, p. 638.
41. *Ibid.*, pp. 641–642 (Marshall, J., dissenting).
42. *Ibid.*, p. 642.
43. *Ibid.*, pp. 643–647 (footnotes omitted).
44. Marshall has vigorously advocated the adoption of an intermediate or mid-level standard of scrutiny to apply in equal protection analysis. See *City of Richmond v. J.A. Croson Co.*, 488 U.S. 469, 528 (Marshall, J., dissenting); *Craig v. Boren*, 429 U.S. 190 (1976) (Marshall, J., joining the opinion of the Court by Brennan, J.); *San Antonio Indep. Sch. Dist. v. Rodriguez*, 411 U.S. 1, 70 (1973) (Marshall, J., dissenting); *Dandridge v. Williams*, 397 U.S. 471 (1970) (Marshall, J., concurring in judgment).
45. 446 U.S. 55, 103 (1980) (Marshall, J., dissenting).
46. *Ibid.*, p. 58 (opinion of Blackmun, J.).
47. *Ibid.* p. 141 (Marshall, J., dissenting).
48. Linda Greenhouse, "Marshall Says Court's Rulings Imperil Rights," *New York Times*, September 9, 1989, p. 6.
49. *Ibid.*
50. For a thoughtful and challenging commentary on the role and limits of the l system as a "means for redistributive change," see Mark Galanter, "Wh 'Haves' Come Out Ahead," *Law & Society Review* 9 (1974), p. 95; see also

Chayes, "The Role of the Judge in Public Law Litigation," *Harvard Law Review* 89 (1976), p. 1281.

51. Barker, n17, p. 69.

52. See *United States* v. *Carolene Prod. Co.*, 304 U.S. 144, 152 n.4 (1938).

53. Jack W. Peltason, *Federal Courts in the Political Process* (New York: Random House, 1955).

54. *New York Times*, July 4, 1971, p. 24.

55. Yet state supreme courts may offer alternative judicial forums in which blacks may be able to continue to forge new changes through litigation. Justice Brennan, writing in 1977, saw signs of the development as perhaps an indication of increasing dissatisfaction with the Burger Court's construction of the federal Bill of Rights and the due process and equal protection clauses of the Fourteenth Amendment. See William J. Brennan, Jr., "State Constitution and the Protection of Individual Rights," *Harvard Law Review* 90, 489 (1977), esp. pp. 495–500.

56. For commentary on the inability of the political system to deal with these problems, see James M. Burns, *Uncommon Sense* (New York: Harper & Row, 1972); Theodore J. Lowi, *The End of Liberalism* (New York: W. W. Norton, 1969). See also Walter D. Burham, *Critical Elections and the Mainspring of American Politics* (New York: W. W. Norton, 1970), pp. 91–193.

57. Mack Jones, "Black Officeholders in Local Governments of the South: An Overview." Paper prepared for delivery at the Annual Meeting of the American Political Science Association, 1970.

58. For searing commentary on the problems that face a black mayor (and in many ways, problems common to elected executives generally), see Carl Stokes, *Promises of Power: A Political Autobiography* (New York: Simon & Schuster, 1972), pp. 118–120.

59. H. Paul Friesena, "Black Control of Central Cities: The Hollow Prize," *Journal of the American Institute of Planners* 35 (March 1969), pp. 75–79.

60. For a detailed and interesting account of lower court implementation of the school desegregation case, see Jack W. Peltason, *Fifty-Eight Lonely Men: Southern Federal Judges and School Desegregation* (Chicago, IL: University of Illinois Press, 1961). A more recent study of lower court implementation of federal law is found in Charles Hamilton, *The Bench and the Ballot: Southern Federal Judges and Black Voters* (New York: Oxford University Press, 1973). For a comprehensive study of the role and function of federal district courts in the political process, see Lyles, op. cit.

61. For more discussion in this regard, see Lyles, *The Gatekeepers*.

Chapter 7

Change through Politics: Interest Groups

The new black politics demands a reevaluation of this age-old concept. Those who embrace the new black politics must couch their thinking in the fundamental concept that "what is good for minorities is good for the nation." This position out of necessity requires the development of a new philosophy that must be practical and selfish—the same as all others that presently exist in this country. Black politics must start on the premise that we have no permanent friends, no permanent enemies, just permanent interests. In matters strictly of a political nature, we must be determined to "take what we can, give up what we must." Those in politics who disagree with this approach should first analyze the composition of their own philosophy and if it does not parallel ours—they are qualified to disagree.

The second qualification for the new black politics is a relative degree of political independence. Those black politicians who are subservient to white controlled political machines cannot possibly stand the kinds of pressures which will come when the new black politics launches the campaign for total black equality in all areas of American life. This is not to say that blacks in politics cannot have a reasonable, legitimate coalition with white politics. To think otherwise would be absolute folly. But the kinds of techniques necessary to employ at this stage in black politics must be abrasive, retaliatory, obstructionist—all of which may be offensive to whites, even white liberals. The question is—can the white liberal follow the lead of blacks who have followed them for so many years?

—Congressman William Clay (D-Missouri)[1]

Armed with ambitious plans and strategies, the premiere civil rights organizations have issued a clarion call to a new civil rights arena—economic empowerment. But before they can win back the hearts, minds, and pocketbooks of those who have defected, today's leaders must convince African-Americans that their decision is right for the 21st century."

—Roz Ayers-Willian

The two epigraphs on page 181, though made in 1971 and 1997, respectively, are very much related and interwoven with each other. Indeed, Representative Clay's comments remain relevant today and capture quite well two strategic premises needed to maximize the effectiveness of black politics in the context of the overall nature and practical operation of the American political system. Those two premises are (1) that groups who champion black political interests must operate on the premise that "we have no permanent friends, no permanent enemies, just permanent interests" and (2) that groups must be able to function with a "relative degree of political independence."

Economic empowerment becomes quite relevant here for it can determine the "relative degree of political independence" needed by interest groups to maximize chances for achieving particular policy objectives. The resources and access required to penetrate and achieve success in American politics are enormous, and give advantage to those who function from a strong economic base, essentially freeing them from too much dependence on others. And this becomes particularly salient when groups such as those that champion black interests are challenging policies and practices that continue to accord positions of privilege and influence to entrenched established interests in every socioeconomic sector of our politics and society.

Our discussion in the previous two chapters indicates that the transition from the Warren to the Burger and now to the Rehnquist Court vividly illustrates that policies and policy changes emanating from the judiciary are very much influenced by the kinds of support and policies that come from the "political" arena. It is precisely in such situations where interest groups (i.e., civil rights groups) can prove important, even determinative, in fashioning the kinds of supports and policies needed to achieve their objectives.

In this chapter we focus on (1) the nature of groups and factors that determine the relative success of interest groups in the political process; (2) the history, development, and present operations of black civil rights groups; and (3) some overall observations with respect to how blacks fare in interest-group politics and in American pluralism generally. In the next chapter we discuss blacks and political parties.

INTEREST GROUPS AND THE POLITICAL PROCESS

Factors Determining Success in Group Conflict

In general, the relative effectiveness of interest groups in the political process may be explained by a number of factors. Perhaps the most important factor the *nature of the membership* of the particular group. This includes the basis group membership; that is, why people belong to certain groups; the commitment and attitude of group members toward group goals; and the position and standing of the group and its members in the socioeconomic structure. Clearly, the nature of leadership is an important factor (and resource) in determining group effectiveness. In large measure, the quality of the leadership determines the quality of the organization. Leaders have to be constantly on top of things—managing the day-to-day operations of the organization, carrying out its policies and programs, promoting consciousness and self-awareness among its members, and constantly devising ways to deal with and overcome persistent "free-rider" problems that may well affect the group's ability to recruit and maintain its membership. The "free-rider" problem is particularly vexing—leaders have to convince members and potential members that in addition to "collective benefits" there are indeed certain "selective benefits" that one gains from formal membership.

The *resources* that groups can bring to bear in achieving their goals is another factor to consider in assessing their influence in the political process. These resources relate to such elements as leadership, money, size of group membership, and how the group is organized (structured) to carry on its business. Of course, in this respect strategy and tactics, that is, how and in what manner groups actually use their resources, are directly and crucially related to group effectiveness. Groups utilize a number of ways to achieve objectives. They try to stimulate a favorable public opinion, for example, through the use of "propaganda" or "educational campaigns." Through electioneering groups seek to influence election outcomes by supporting candidates who are favorable (or at least not opposed) to their goals. Group participation in elections may take several forms. It may range from outright endorsement and support of particular candidates to outright opposition in other situations. This, of course, leaves other options in between.

In this connection, *political action committees (PACs)* have come to take on increasing importance as a way for interests to promote their objectives. Organized labor has long had its political action committees, which offer support to "friendly" political candidates, mostly Democratic. In 1974 legislation was passed to make PACs altogether legal for corporations, professional groups, or any other groups who wished to solicit money and give it to candidates who support their interests. As a result, the number of PACs has skyrocketed from about 600 in 1974 to more than 3,500 in 1984. The growth has occurred primarily among corporate, business, and trade association PACs, although a number of ideological PACs—such as the National Conservative Political Action Committee (NCPAC)—have also burst on the scene. While there are limits on the amounts PACs may donate directly to federal candidates in a given year, PACs may spend any amount they wish on behalf of particular candidates so long as they do not contribute directly to candidates or coordinate their spending with the candidate's campaign.

Groups also *lobby* to influence public policy. Much of this activity focus es on Congress, where groups spend large amounts of money each yea protect and promote their interests.[3] But a number of factors, includin inability or unwillingness of Congress to deal with particular problem centralization and bureaucratization of power in Washington, and t

eral structure of our governmental system has led to a renewed interest in the role and authority of state and local governments. As a result, interest groups and lobbyists are increasingly looking to these governmental units as additional avenues through which to achieve their objectives.

Groups also use the *judicial process* to influence public policy. The two principal ways by which groups do this are by sponsoring (initiating, financing, and conducting) litigation, and by filing *amicus curiae* (friend of the court) briefs. For example, the NAACP has been quite vigorous in using litigation to achieve its goals. And the U.S. Supreme Court has held that such vigorous advocacy is constitutionally grounded in the First Amendment. As Justice Brennan put it:

> In the context of NAACP objectives, litigation is not a technique of resolving private differences; it is a means for achieving the lawful objectives of equality of treatment by all government, federal, state and local for the members of the Negro community in this country. It is thus a form of political expression. Groups which find themselves unable to achieve their objectives through the ballot frequently turn to the courts. Just as it was true of the opponents of the New Deal legislation during the 1930s, no less is it true of the Negro minority today. And under the conditions of modern government, litigation may well be the sole practicable avenue open to a minority to petition for redress of grievances.[4]

In general, the success of the NAACP and other such groups in this respect has been well documented elsewhere.[5] We will not repeat it here except to reemphasize that litigation remains a chief avenue by which groups seek to accomplish their objectives.

Direct action (marches, demonstrations, sit-ins, and violence) has long been used by groups to promote their causes. This is particularly true of groups that lack the traditional resources (money, skill, votes) needed to influence public policy. The more recent and widespread use of direct action occurred during the civil rights movement of the 1950s and 1960s. But even though these methods have long been part of the American political scene, they have never really been accepted as consistent with American beliefs and traditions of resolving conflict through peaceful (even nonobstructive) means. But accepted or not, the potential use of such methods may yet be determined by whether politically disadvantaged groups gain a greater share of the traditional and accepted resources (for instance, money, political offices) that they need to protect and promote their interests in the American political system.

CIVIL RIGHTS ORGANIZATIONS:
QUEST FOR SURVIVAL AND ROLE

1960s were the high point of the civil rights movement. The unity and ion that characterized that movement no longer exist; the focus of civil ctivity has changed. In the 1960s the push for formal recognition of legal rights provided a broad base around which civil rights groups and their white allies could rally. But in the 1970s, 1980s, and 1990s, the push for the actual implementation of those rights has commanded far less appeal and support. This situation has been caused by a number of factors. Perhaps the most significant factor is the belief that with the passage of major civil rights legislation in the 1960s, America's racial problems have been solved and civil rights need no longer be a priority on the nation's agenda.[6] To be sure, some very real, notable, and visible progress has been made by blacks and other minorities. This can be noted in both broad socioeconomic terms (e.g., income and education differentials) and also in the number of blacks elected or appointed to government positions. Such progress, however, has not had much effect on the circumstances of most blacks, and the progress that has been made, and especially the publicity that has accompanied such progress, serves, ironically, to lessen interest in civil rights.

Clearly, such visible signs of progress bolster the view that our civil rights problems are behind us and that ours is a society free from racism. This is the viewpoint that was nurtured and perpetuated by the Reagan administration, resulting in civil rights occupying low priority during Reagan's eight years. This should come as no surprise, however, given the comparative constituency support for civil rights between the two major parties. A similar situation prevailed during the Bush administration.

The small amount of attention paid to civil rights and racial problems in national politics is commensurate with the attitudes of the American electorate. In October 1965, for example, 27 percent of all Americans considered civil rights the most important problem facing the country. In September 1972, that figure had dropped to only 5 percent. And by 1978, race had all but vanished from the national conscience as one of our "most important problems."

During the past two decades that trend has continued. Other issues such as the state of the economy (unemployment, inflation, energy, and most recently, taxes), crime, and international crises (such as the Iranian hostage crisis in 1979, the Soviet invasion of Afghanistan in 1980, the Iran-Contra scandal of 1987, the end of the Cold War in 1989, and the Persian Gulf crisis of 1990) have eclipsed the importance of civil rights in the minds of many Americans. In addition, public disinterest in civil rights was only reinforced by the Nixon, Reagan, and Bush administrations. Each of these Republican presidents relegated civil rights concerns to the back burner, exhibiting attitudes that were at best insensitive and at worst deliberately hostile to the interests of African Americans. By contrast, Democratic president Bill Clinton has clearly been more supportive of black interests, even if his support has been somewhat inconsistent. In June 1997, President Clinton sought to refocus national attention by appointing an advisory board to engender a national conversation on race and advise him accordingly.

But it is clear that concerns of civil rights organizations today beyond race-specific issues and embrace the whole range of economic concerns consistent with the significant problems that continue to disproportionately and negatively influence the overall quality of life of blacks and minorities. These problems include persistently high levels of unemployment; the dire need for more jobs, better educational systems, and job training; the continuing high incidence of poverty; inadequate health care and delivery; and the lack of decent housing. The mounting challenge for traditional civil rights groups in the future is how effectively they can garner the resources needed to deal with these socioeconomic problems. Their relative success and survival depend on how well they can meet this challenge.

Another very important factor complicating the life of civil rights organizations has been the general posture of the president, Congress, the Supreme Court, and other governmental institutions toward civil rights and racial problems. The position of these institutions and officials, of course, is closely related and responsive to changing events and changing moods of public opinion. Indeed, what is perceived as the "most important problem" will undoubtedly affect the agendas of these various institutions of government. The posture of the president is a good example. As intimated earlier, the Nixon administration, for the most part, projected a hostile attitude toward the problems of blacks, the poor, and minorities. Neither Nixon's campaigns for the presidency nor his administration were disposed to encourage or seek support from civil rights interests. And quite obviously, that support was not forthcoming. In addition, the Ford presidency did little to change the overall posture of the Nixon era toward blacks. Of course, Gerald Ford was somewhat preoccupied with the spillover effects of Watergate. Though not viewed as being as hostile to civil rights as Nixon, the Ford administration could well be characterized as a "benign" continuation of the Nixon years.

The 1976 campaign and election of Jimmy Carter as president undoubtedly rekindled the hopes and aspirations of blacks and civil rights interests. But this renewed hope was rather short-lived. Indeed, many believe that the low-key performance of Carter simply did not live up to his glowing rhetoric and visible symbols, that is, his appointment of blacks to administrative positions. This view was openly and straightforwardly articulated by Vernon Jordan, executive director of the National Urban League and, at the time, one of the major black civil rights leaders.[7] In his opening address to the 1977 annual meeting of the Urban League, Jordan stated flatly that the Carter administration had "fallen short of blacks' expectations in terms of policies, program, and people."[8]

But two days later, in response to an earlier invitation by Jordan to address the convention, President Carter had his opportunity to react to Jordan's criticism, and the president reacted sharply. The president said he ̲ad "no apologies" for his administration's record with respect to blacks and ̲or people. In fact, Carter said that Jordan's criticism itself damaged "the ̲es and aspirations of those poor people."[9] However, despite the president's stirring defense of his record, there is little doubt that Jordan's criticism became an increasingly shared view among blacks. This was reflected by the immediate support for his position that Jordan received from other major civil rights leaders.[10] But by 1980 the Iran and Afghanistan situations directed attention away from domestic concerns, and President Carter gave his priority to foreign policy matters.

Black dissatisfaction with the Carter administration was mild compared to their open dissatisfaction and anguish following Ronald Reagan's victory over Carter in the 1980 elections. Time and again, through word and deed, the Reagan administration demonstrated its lack of concern and generally negative position toward matters that greatly affected blacks and minorities. Likewise, Reagan's overwhelming reelection victory over Mondale in 1984 sent ominous signals for the future of black progress.

The actions of the Reagan administration were clearly and concretely inimical to the continued progress of blacks and minorities (e.g., budget cutbacks in social welfare programs, lack of sensitive and systematic efforts to deal with severe and disproportionate unemployment and poverty among these groups, and hostile interpretations and enforcement of civil rights laws). Moreover, Reagan's appointments, including those to the federal judiciary, clearly reflected the president's negative attitude toward blacks, minorities, and civil rights interests generally.

Overall, the attitudes and actions of the Reagan administration illustrate vividly how the work and effectiveness of interest groups, in this instance civil rights organizations, can be affected greatly by the posture and policies of governmental officials and institutions. Black elected officials, as well as black interest group leaders, were quite unified and vocal in complaining about lack of access and influence with the Reagan administration.

The Bush administration, despite attaining the highest sustained approval rating among blacks for a Republican president, continued its opposition to certain civil rights issues, most notably affirmative action. In 1989, the Supreme Court issued six decisions that further eroded affirmative action.[11] In one of these rulings (*Patterson* v. *McLean Credit Union*), statutory provisions prohibiting discrimination in the formation and enforcement of contracts were read as applying only to hiring agreements and not to later conduct by the employer. Other rulings also included (1) placing the burden of proving discriminatory intent on the individual claiming employment discrimination and (2) eroding the effect of consent decrees by allowing persons not involved in the discrimination lawsuit to subsequently challenge the consent decree.

In response to these Supreme Court decisions, a Democratic Congress passed a bill to amend the Civil Rights Act to reverse the effect of these court decisions. Shortly after the bill's introduction, Attorney General Dick Thornburgh wrote the Senate Labor and Human Resources Committee that he would recommend that President Bush veto the bill. Bush stated that he wanted to sign a civil rights bill and met with black leaders to reach a compromise on the bill. However, the Bush administration continued to oppose the civil rights bill, and, in the end, the president vetoed the measure, alleging that the bill was an attempt to impose racial hiring quotas. Attempts to resurrect the legislation in 1991 by moderate Republican Senator John Danforth of Missouri continued to encounter rebuff and resistance from the White House.[12] In the end, however, Danforth's strong commitment paid off and the Civil Rights Act of 1991 was approved.

The presence of a number of other forces seems to indicate that civil rights groups and their objectives are in for hard times. The mixed posture of the Burger Court toward civil rights has become increasingly negative in the Rehnquist Court. Although the increasing influence of blacks and minorities in politics clearly found expression in the Senate's 1987 rejection of President Reagan's nomination of conservative Judge Robert Bork to the Supreme Court, in the end the president succeeded in bolstering the conservative position on the Court through the appointment of Justice Anthony Kennedy. Similarly, President Bush's judicial appointments, highlighted by his nomination of black Judge Clarence Thomas to the Supreme Court, also strengthened conservative trends in the federal judiciary. After 12 years of Republican administrations, civil rights groups and many others greeted the election of President Clinton in 1992 with much relief and enthusiasm. But the hope and expectations generated by Clinton's election, especially on the part of African Americans, has been tempered by the nature and realities of the policy process and American politics in general.

To be sure, Clinton has appointed a record number of African Americans to positions in both the judicial and political arenas. He has also taken other actions and initiatives that demonstrate his concern for race and race-related problems, such as his appointment in 1997 of a relatively small advisory board of seven persons to organize and engender a national Conversation on Race. However, Clinton has made other moves that signal his continuing commitment to follow "mainstream-centrist" politics—for example, withdrawal of the nomination of Lani Guinier as assistant secretary for civil rights and his signing of welfare reform legislation that included provisions that may disproportionately hurt blacks and other minorities.

Mention should also be made of another factor that seems to be influencing the general political-social climate as well as public policy. This is the increasing volume of published views—in books, pamphlets, the press, and other media—that foster an "outlook forged in reaction to sixties turbulence … fierce in its attachment to political and cultural moderation, committed to stability as the prerequisite for justice rather than the other way around, pessimistic about the possibilities for long-range, or even short-range, change in America, and imbued with a foreboding sense of our civilization's decline."[13] And though dressed in sophisticated garb, much of this outlook has been informed by views that have been generally critical of government intervention and of policies designed to overcome problems faced by blacks and other minorities. A great deal of this effort has been made by scholars—referred to by author Peter Steinfels as "neoconservatives"—whose credentials and reputations lend considerable prestige to their views and positions.[14] "The neoconservatives," says Steinfels, "are a *powerful* [emphasis his] party of intellectuals."[15] "Their reputations are solid; they speak from the elite universities—Harvard, Berkeley, MIT, Chicago, Stanford."[16] Steinfels warns that it would be risky and unwarranted to dismiss their significance as many are wont to do simply because they are intellectuals. Steinfels writes:

> Intellectuals serve as advisers to officeholders and political candidates, write speeches, propose programs, draft legislation, serve on special commissions. The mass media amplify their ideas to a wider public, though not without considerable distortion. In all this the intellectuals have two functions. As experts in particular fields relevant to public policy they work out the details of political measures. But as traffickers in society's symbols and values, as keepers of memories, as orchestrators of its spectacles and images, and, in Tocqueville's words, as political theorists and shapers of general ideas, intellectuals are legitimators. What will be the agenda of public concerns? Where will one set the outer limits of the "responsible" opinion to which busy decision-makers should attend? Will credibility of this or that set of policies, or of the schools of thought behind them, be eroded or maintained—or will they be eliminated from serious consideration altogether? The dueling in intellectual journals, the rallying of like-minded thinkers at conferences or in new organizations, the shifts of power within the disciplines are all elements in this process of legitimation. So, one might add, is the quality of scholarship and the cogency and eloquence of argument."[17]

But not all current activity comes from the pens of white scholars; a few black scholars also de-emphasize the importance of race as a barrier to enjoying the benefits and opportunities of the American political-social system. The influence of such scholars, especially those whom Steinfels calls the "neoconservatives," on public opinion and public policy is evidenced not only by their access to communications media but also by "their direct access to officeholders and the political elite generally." It is clear, for example, that repeated Republican control of the White House (1968–1992, with the exception of the Carter years, 1976–1980) has considerably strengthened the visibility and influence of black conservatives. This strengthening occurred mainly through the appointment of black conservatives to certain highly visible positions, such as Judge Clarence Thomas to the Supreme Court.

This overall "conservative" and "neoconservative" trend of the 1980s and the early 1990s seems to have been increasingly supported by attitudes and actions of not only Republicans but Democrats as well. To become more competitive in presidential elections, for example, a broad array of Democratic party leaders (conservatives, moderates, and "neo-liberals") now apparently want to make once "liberal" party principles more palatable to "mainstream" politics and the current popular mood. And Clinton's successful presidential campaigns in 1992 and 1996, as well as his overall administration, clearly demonstrate Democratic efforts to channel and institutionalize "centrist-mainstream" politics into the molding of a "New" Democratic party.

Overall, when one considers the various changes in the political-social climate, it becomes somewhat more understandable why civil rights organizations, whose major purpose is to promote the interest of blacks and minorities, have come upon hard times. These hard times have also had their impact on the internal politics and operations of civil rights groups. To these matters we now turn.

CIVIL RIGHTS GROUPS: PROBLEMS AND PROSPECTS

Civil rights groups continue to face a number of problems. These problems include (1) the nature of the groups' organizations and leadership and the problem of leadership succession; (2) the need to define continuously the group's role, objective, and tactics consistent with changing circumstances; (3) the ability to attract and maintain unity and support of group membership; and (4) the ability to attract financial support. In one way or another, these are the types of problems that can threaten not only civil rights organizations but any organizations or interest groups. It seems clear that SNCC and CORE have not been able to weather these problems and that the SCLC faces an uphill battle for survival. Even the more established groups, such as the NAACP and the Urban League, have also felt the crunch of hard times.

Whether a civil rights organization can survive hard times largely depends on the extent to which the group can integrate and function in the present political system. Figure 7-1 provides a yardstick by which to measure the relative influence and chances for success of various civil rights groups past and present. Let us consider these and related matters in more detail.

From Early Success to Later Problems

At the time of their founding, civil rights groups had little difficulty in defining their role and objectives and in recruiting and maintaining flourishing memberships. The primary purpose of such organizations was clear—to overcome the problems and pains of racial segregation and discrimination. The symbols and practices of racism were pervasive and were supported by a rigid system of laws, customs, and traditions. White racism was crudely blatant and openly visible: For example, public accommodations and educational opportunities were separate and inferior, if indeed they existed at all, and restrictions and pressures (physical if need be) against blacks voting and holding public office were pervasive. But civil rights groups and their allies were able to meet these blatant practices head-on, and their success in these efforts is evidenced by Court decisions (e.g., *Brown*) and civil rights legislation (e.g., the Civil Rights Act of 1964 and the Voting Rights Act of 1965). Simultaneously, a number of programs and policies supported and advanced black progress in a number of areas, for example, the War on Poverty.

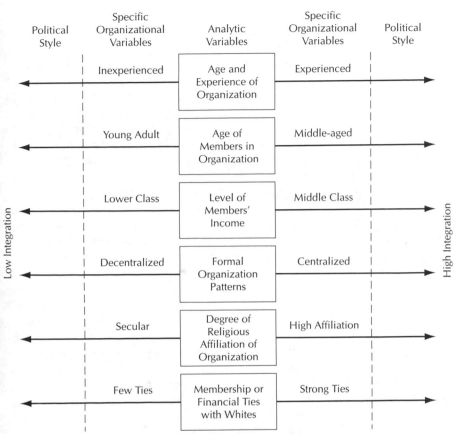

Figure 7-1   Factors Contributing to the "Integration" of Civil Rights Groups in the Existing Political System

Source: From Lucius J. Barker and Donald Jansiewicz, "Coalitions in the Civil Rights Movement," in *The Study of Coalition Behavior: Theoretical Perspectives and Cases from Four Continents*, ed. Sven Groennings, E. W. Kelley, and Michael Leiserson. Copyright 1970 by Holt, Rinehart & Winston. Reprinted by permission.

Hence, in terms of their original objectives, civil rights organizations had indeed met with a great deal of success.

But it is this very success that has led to some of the problems that civil rights organizations now face. Indeed, while the more blatant and visible forms of racism have been overcome—at least legally—there remains a great deal of racism that is much more subtle, more complex, and much less visible. In addition, a number of the socioeconomic problems that impact disproportionately on blacks and minorities remain, for example, dilapidated and overcrowded housing and rising unemployment. Under such circumstances, it is clear that civil rights groups must redefine their role and objectives. Simultaneously, their strategy and tactics must be tailored to meet this more subtle discrimination and to attack these more complex problems.

Some civil rights organizations, such as CORE and SCLC, have obviously encountered severe problems with respect to redefining their role and objectives in the light of changing circumstances. The extent to which the NAACP and Urban League retain a measure of viability is related directly to their programs and objectives that meet these new and more complex problems.

The ability of particular groups to adapt to changing circumstances depends greatly on the nature of the group's organization and leadership. It seems clear, for example, that the fortunes of the SCLC were closely tied to Martin Luther King, Jr. He founded the organization, articulated its purposes and programs, and provided the leadership. Charismatic personality, stirring oratory, and undaunted commitment to a noble cause held the organization together and attracted many followers. King was the very embodiment of the SCLC. He dominated the organization and shaped its character, and his leadership was as unquestioned as it was cherished. However, just about the time of King's tragic assassination, the overall civil rights movement was meeting a crucial turning point. Indeed, most of the major civil rights legislation, except for the Fair Housing Act of 1968, was on the books.

More importantly, by 1968 we began to see a few tangible effects of the 1964 Civil Rights Act; for example, the opening up of places of public accommodation and the impact of the cutoff threat of federal funds with respect to increasing desegregation of public schools. Moreover, mainly as a direct consequence of the 1965 Voting Rights Act, blacks began to register and to vote in increasing numbers: They began to run and be elected to public offices.

However, between 1965 and 1968, we were also experiencing massive urban rebellion and unrest that dramatically illuminated the wide gaps that remained between the lofty promises of laws on the books and the painful and cold reality that the overall effects of the civil rights movement—including these laws—had brought about little if any change in the everyday life of African Americans.

Changes in Climate and Priorities: Struggle for Survival

By 1968, we began to experience a shift in the political climate and in the nation's priorities. Ending the war in Vietnam and wiping out crime (restoring "law and order") replaced race and poverty as the most pressing problems facing the country. This shift in priorities brought about drastic changes in the political climate. President Lyndon Johnson, for example, who had strongly championed civil rights and socioeconomic programs, found himself in a quagmire that proved to be his political downfall. Johnson's undaunted courage and support for civil rights was not enough to satisfy liberals. They say his dogged prosecution of the Vietnam War was not only detrimental to finding a peaceful solution but also detrimental to harnessing the resources (money) necessary to deal with serious domestic problems, including civil rights and the socioeconomic programs that the president supported. Even so natural a supporter of the president as Martin Luther

King, Jr., found it necessary to speak out against the Vietnam War. Thus, with his natural support (e.g., liberals) eroding, Johnson shocked the nation by announcing that he would not be a candidate for reelection. The ensuing politics saw Hubert Humphrey win the presidential nomination in a party that, though united on civil rights, was badly divided by the Vietnam conflict. And Humphrey himself was viewed by many as being too avid a supporter of Johnson's Vietnam policies.

The Republican party undoubtedly stood to benefit greatly from these strong divisions among the Democrats. By nominating Richard Nixon for president, the Republicans were obviously determined to take full advantage of both the antiwar and the "law and order" (get tough on blacks) moods of the country. The Nixon campaign and his successful election only illuminated that the pro-civil rights mood of the country had indeed changed.

Given these markedly changed conditions in the nation's overall political-social climate, we began to see more clearly the extreme difficulties and problems that faced civil rights organizations. These organizations now had to survive in a hostile climate. They felt pressures from within the black community ("deliver on your promises") as well as pressure from the outside (e.g., an unsympathetic president and a strong current of public opinion that believed enough had been done for blacks). How could civil rights organizations bring about effective implementation of civil rights legislation in this sort of environment? How could they maintain the unity and spirit of their memberships? How could they attract necessary funds for survival? In short, how would or could civil rights organizations adapt their roles, objectives, and tactics to meet these changed conditions?

These were not easy questions, and they posed difficult problems even for organizations that enjoyed a stable leadership. But for an organization like the SCLC—whose founder and personal leader was swept away without warning—these problems undoubtedly proved disillusioning and divisive. A loosely structured group such as SCLC needed a charismatic leader to nourish those factors that make for an effective organization—viable goals and objectives, a unified membership, and sufficient financial resources. Of course, we can only speculate as to whether Dr. King would have been able to surmount these problems had he lived. But it is unquestionable that if any one person could have done so, King would have been that person. It is even more speculative whether SCLC—without King—can overcome such problems. Nonetheless, the SCLC leadership continues to give it a try and make the organization more responsive to the changing opportunities and realities of the present political-social climate.

The NAACP: Retrospect and Prospect

Similarly, we find that the more established organizations such as the NAACP and the Urban League have not been immune from problems. The changed political-social circumstances have also affected the operations of these groups. The NAACP, for example, has had a long tradition of centralized leadership and control, with power being wielded by a well-entrenched, middle-class national board of directors and by a strong executive director, since changed in 1995 to president/CEO. Local chapters of the organization (more than 2,200 as of 1998)[18] operate under guidelines and charters of the national organization. In general, this organizational structure has apparently worked rather well in defining and achieving the goals and objectives of the group. But the group's viability also depends upon mutual understandings of the relative role expectations and authority of the various officials and structures within the organization. For example, for the effective operation of an NAACP-type organizational structure, it is important to reach certain kinds of understandings with respect to the role expectations that exist (1) between and among the national board of directors, the national president/CEO, and the permanent professional and administrative staff and (2) between the centralized national structures (e.g., board of directors, president/CEO) and the local units or chapters.

The sheer survival and vitality of the NAACP serve to confirm that the organization's structure has worked rather well. Much of this, of course, has undoubtedly been due to the fact that the NAACP has traditionally had a national board of directors and executive directors who have enjoyed rather long tenures. This has not only promoted stability but has also institutionalized working relationships. The long tenures of Walter White and Roy Wilkins (when combined with their leadership skills and visibility) especially served to quiet and overcome internal differences. But some internal differences, which involved a combination of elements that generally concerned the relationship and authority of various structures at the national level, did become more evident near the end of Wilkins's tenure. These elements included a leadership vacuum mainly created by Wilkins' impending retirement (which was somewhat filled by the board of directors, especially in defining the agenda and articulating the position of the organization on various issues); the politics involved in the selection of a new executive director to replace Wilkins; and the accommodations and relations that had to be worked out between the new executive director and the national board of directors. In terms of NAACP leadership patterns, one could say that most of these tension points or elements should have become quieted and synchronized once a new executive director was chosen. But the problems appear more deep-rooted. The selection of Benjamin Hooks as executive director did not quiet the internal problems. At the time of his selection in 1977, Hooks's experience and background as a lawyer, judge, Federal Communications Commission commissioner, and a Baptist minister would seem to combine the talents necessary for the position. But some two years later, apparent problems remained in the national leadership structure. Some suggested, for example, that though Hooks had done a good job, he "made the mistake of underestimating the power of the national board of directors." In this regard, one writer described the 1979 NAACP annual convention as follows:

> While Mr. Hooks's popularity with the members is unquestioned, scores of interviews indicate that he has made less of an impact on the long-entrenched board of directors and that he has been quietly discouraged about the slow-to-change bureaucracy he inherited. "I don't want to give the impression that the organization does not function," one staff official said. "It does, but it could function so much, much better with fewer personal agendas at the top and a broadening of leadership base, as well as better communications within and without the organization—and more money, of course."

This quote points up several other problems that have plagued the NAACP. There has long been concern that the power of the organization was so centralized in the national organization and its board of directors that initiatives, programs, and activities of local branches have been thwarted. Thus, during the 1960s the national "establishment" (and even local establishments) had to deal with frustrations and petitions from NAACP youth groups who wanted to be more "militant." Since that time, friction between the national office and the local chapters became evident when local chapters (e.g., Atlanta) sought to work out school desegregation problems in ways that did not meet the approval of the national office. In general, however, the general membership seems to approve of this centralization of power and authority. A defeat of a resolution in the 1979 annual meeting to restrict the power and influence of the national board of directors by limiting the terms of its members to 12 years, as one writer put it, "is yet another indication of the board's strength and of the general membership's distrust of sudden change."

Lack of adequate financial resources is another problem confronting the NAACP. Just like other civil rights groups, the NAACP faces the situation of trying to cope with increasingly complex problems with decreasing financial resources and in a political-social climate that ranges from indifference to hostility.

It is clear, however, that the NAACP retains a measure of viability and is making attempts to improve its stature and standing. For example, though suffering some decreases in membership, the organization continues to have a relatively large mass membership of a reported 310,000 (reported in 1995). This number is down from about 500,000 who belonged to the organization in the 1960s and 1970s, closer to the time of the Civil Rights Movement.[19] (At the NAACP's annual board meeting in 1996, Kweisi Mfume, the organization's newly appointed president and chief executive officer, estimated the group's mass membership at 500,000 volunteers. Mfume did express some uncertainty about these estimates, though.)[20] It has an organizational structure that allows for centralized authority to be exercised by state and strong national leadership. It maintains an array of programs and activities that show an attempt to keep its agenda continuously consistent with the chang ing nature of problems and of the political-social climate. And it is clear that the organization is also taking steps to see that its operations and procedures are congruent with modern practice and technology. This is exemplified concretely by the infusion of younger, more aggressive, and better-trained staff personnel into the organization.[21] As we discuss later, the organization's progress is exemplified in structural and personnel changes in the organization's leadership that led to the election of Myrlie Evers-Williams in 1995 as Chair of the national Executive Board; and the appointment of then Representative Kweisi Mfume in 1996 as the new President/Chief Executive Officer of the organization. (In 1998, Julian Bond, civil rights activist and former Georgia state legislator, was elected as Chair of the Executive Board, replacing Evers-Williams, who had chosen to step down.)

To be sure, these actions may be viewed as responses to critics who over time had charged that both the NAACP agenda and its operations were out of step with current needs and requirements. In a 1991 interview, for example, NAACP Board Chairman Dr. William Gibson "acknowledged that the organization had been complacent in recent years but said it was becoming more active in areas like legislative redistricting, with an aim of increasing minority political representation and influence." This and similar efforts were spurred by the younger personnel (exemplified by the organization's 40-year-old general counsel—Dennis Hayes) and the modern technology (e.g., computers) that now occupy the NAACP's national headquarters in Baltimore.

Both Dr. Gibson and Hazel Dukes, then-NAACP president, saw these moves as reflecting both organizational goals and strategy. "We plan to be more firm and aggressive with corporate America over economic empowerment," said Gibson. "If negotiations fail, we will be prepared to use economic clout through boycotts. We're restructuring ourselves," he continued, "to lobby at the local, state, and federal levels, using new technology and communications, whatever it takes." And this "restructuring" was reflected in comments by Dukes, who said that "we're bringing in new people who, while they know how the NAACP operates, they're not from our tradition. They believe in the NAACP values, but are able to see beyond traditional approaches."

At the time, the organization's executive director, Benjamin Hooks, responded more directly to critics who suggested that the NAACP's agenda and priorities were out of step with current reality. In a 1991 interview, for example, Hooks joined the issue in sharp perspective:

> There are so many things we try to do with meager resources because the problems are so deep.... But one thing we won't do is to abandon the fight against racism. If we do, who's left?
>
> I don't know if our critics understand; our charter is to fight discrimination. If they're telling me there's no longer a problem with police brutality, no more job and housing discrimination and most people are not worried about it, they're wrong. We're not struggling to find a mandate; we've got one.

Overall, and despite its continuing struggles and its critics, the oldest civil rights organization, the NAACP, has developed an image and strong allegiance and tradition among blacks and Americans generally as a moderate organization that is stable yet flexible, sensitive yet rational in its approaches to problems. In recent years, however, the NAACP has suffered from leadership problems. The extent to which it might be able to maintain this role in the future will depend in great measure on what type of leader the organization selects to succeed Benjamin Hooks, who in 1992 stated his intention to retire as soon as a replacement could be found. And in April 1992, that replacement was found when the NAACP announced that Dr. Benjamin Chavis, a 45-year-old black minister and long-time civil rights activist, would replace Hooks as executive director.[22] But the dynamics leading to Chavis's selection were anything but tranquil; in many ways they reflected the overall tensions that had for some time been affecting the organization. For example, some on the 64-member national Board of Directors, the body that actually selects the executive director, thought that the organization needed a more active, visible, and aggressive leader; in particular they apparently wanted Jesse Jackson.

Jackson's candidacy perforce commanded attention. Indeed, despite being the focal point of repeated criticism and controversy, Jackson remains one of the most widely known and popular leaders in the black community, having waged two highly publicized and in many ways largely successful campaigns for the Democratic presidential nomination in 1984 and 1988.

Even so, controversy continued to swirl about Jackson—this time in his candidacy for the position of executive director. To be sure, Jackson on occasion has openly suggested that the organization should become more aggressively involved in issues such as those reflected by the 1992 Rodney King incident and the subsequent Los Angeles riots. In this way, Jackson and others reasoned that the NAACP could thus attract the interest and support needed to cope with today's problems.

But others on the Board of Directors were opposed to, or at least a bit wary of, Jackson. They were apprehensive, for example, that Jackson might be more disposed to follow his own "agenda" rather than that of the national board or organization generally. More directly, some "expressed grave concern over the administrative ability and temperamental compatibility" of Jackson with the NAACP. As the selection process evolved, however, any impending battle over such concerns was averted when in the end Jackson decided to withdraw his name from consideration.

However, Jackson's comments on his withdrawal continued to fuel the controversy. In explaining his withdrawal, for example, Jackson charged that the national board was "considering reducing the powers of the executive director," thus making the job less attractive and less doable. Other board members, however, were quick to counter Jackson. They indicated Jackson never was the "frontrunner" on the short list of four finalists,

was wont to believe. In fact, the charge was made that Jackson withdrew "because he almost certainly would have lost if he had stayed in the race."

Whatever the situation regarding Jackson's candidacy and withdrawal, several things can be said. First, as we have discussed earlier in this chapter, on occasion the NAACP has been confronted with tensions and disputes over the relative role and authority between the national board of directors and its executive director. Secondly, Jackson's withdrawal apparently smoothed the way for the selection of Chavis over the other two candidates that remained on the short list.

For his part, and as indicated earlier, Chavis, a long-time member of the NAACP and veteran of the civil rights movement, was not unaware of the problems surrounding both the organization and his own selection. In his acceptance speech as executive director, for example, Chavis took note of criticisms that had been leveled by Jackson and others against the organization. Indeed, Chavis acknowledged that he wanted to "sharpen the focus of the organization" consistent with the changing nature of the issues and the times. Moreover, Chavis in stating that he was no "stranger in the 'hood,'" similarly acknowledged that "I know we need to reach out and embrace our young people."

On the other hand, Chavis summarily dismissed criticisms that the NAACP has become "irrelevant" or "ossified." Indeed, said Chavis, "I think we need the civil rights movement more in '93 than [we did] in '63."

For his part, Chavis took on criticisms about the NAACP's obsolescence by restructuring the organization. In addition to downsizing the main administrative offices, Chavis advocated the expansion of a new chapter in South Africa. Substantively, Chavis embarked on an agenda that focused on policy issues affecting young minorities. The NAACP was principally responsible for initiating Toys-for-Guns programs both in New York and Houston, and the group increased its recruitment among young black Americans. By 1994, the organization reported an increase of about 100,000 members under its new Executive Director. But Chavis's tenure was not without its share of controversy; part of the youth-outreach program included meetings and affiliation with gang members. Additionally, Chavis sought to forge a link between the NAACP and Nation of Islam Minister Louis Farrakhan. His presence at a meeting where white board members were excluded was the source of much criticism and controversy.

Perhaps the final blow came when an independent audit revealed that the NAACP was deeply in debt. For the year that Chavis had held office, the organization's deficit had grown from $2.7 million to $3.2 million. Even more alarming was the discovery that Chavis had, without the Executive Board's knowledge, privately settled a lawsuit filed against him for more than a quarter-million dollars. These problems led the Board to fire Chavis ugust 1994.

Turmoil in the organization continued during the election for Chair of the Board and was perhaps the most contentious battle in the NAACP's history. Board members were evenly split between re-electing Chair William Gibson and choosing Myrlie Evers-Williams, the widow of the late civil rights worker Medgar Evers. A Board member herself, Evers-Williams had experience as a Commissioner on the Los Angeles Board of Public Works and on other corporate boards. As her platform, Evers-Williams promised to embark on a revitalization drive for resources, which included raising $10 million to erase the budget deficit. In the end, Evers-Williams was elected as the board's new chair by a single vote.

After the election, the NAACP sought to revamp its leadership structure by appointing an independent Chief Financial Officer and modifying the Executive Director's title to President/CEO. In February of 1996, Representative Kweisi Mfume (D-Maryland) announced his resignation from Congress to accept the position as president/CEO of the NAACP. Elected by a unanimous vote, Mfume was regarded as the appropriate leader for the organization at this particular juncture.

Unlike Chavis, Mfume was not closely associated with the NAACP; indeed some wondered how a relative outsider such as Mfume would do in this particular position. It was clear, however, that Mfume was an experienced, seasoned leader. And from the outset he signaled a leadership style, that though aggressive, was not likely to arouse conflict with his Executive Board.

As the new executive leader of the organization, Mfume inherited a number of problems, perhaps the most serious of which was what might be referred to as an "image" problem—a problem that seems to be affecting civil rights groups generally. It involves notions suggesting that the NAACP (and similar organizations) are no longer "relevant," that they are not attacking major problems affecting most black Americans, and that they do not want to alienate major sources of funds that might come from wealthy white or corporate donors.[23]

In general, it seems clear that Mfume and other NAACP leaders are attempting to deal with such problems. Ironically, however, to do so involves discussions or even debates on issues that appear at odds with longstanding traditional principles and positions of the organization. It is clear, for example, that there is growing dissatisfaction in the black community within and outside the NAACP over the nature and quality of education being offered to today's black youth. This in turn is leading some to call on the NAACP to reevaluate the continuing viability of its longstanding commitment to racial integration in accord with what is undoubtedly the organization's most heralded Supreme Court victory—the 1954 *Brown* case. Some semblance of this disquiet was clearly reflected in discussions leading up to and during the 1997 NAACP Convention.

Very directly, the issue boils down to whether to pursue integration (*Brown*) as the chief method for achieving equal education opportunity o whether experience under the *Brown* regime suggests that such opportunity might best be achieved through "quality education," even if in predominantly black schools. The mere discussion of the issue, of course, is important in that it suggests, at least implicitly, that the NAACP as the original and continuing driving force behind racial integration may be weakening its resolve for racial integration as the method by which to deal with the continuing problem of race. Cues from such activity might lead policy makers and others, including judges, to intuit that blacks and others might be willing to resort once again to the long discredited "separate but equal" doctrine.

But these cues could prove misleading if based primarily on actions or discussions in the national organization.[24] Given its financial difficulties and the increased costs of litigation, the national office is no longer a major player in school desegregation. As Gary Orfield, a leading expert on school desegregation, put it: "The NAACP is a large organization, and there are many local chapters who are still fighting the resegregation of schools that is going on.... But the national NAACP office has not been a major actor in this area for years." Even so, however, the sheer symbolism of any retreat by the NAACP in any form could hold enormous implications for all concerned.

The Urban League: A Changing Civil Rights Posture

The National Urban League has long been concerned with problems (e.g., housing, job opportunities) that strike at the very heart of the real everyday problems that affect blacks and other minorities. But given its nature—"an interracial, non-profit community service organization" with its main sources of financial support from corporate donations and federal grants—one would perhaps expect the Urban League to be among the more moderate civil rights groups; it is and has been. This is exemplified vividly by the League's decision to remain neutral on the controversial nomination of Clarence Thomas to the Supreme Court. Nonetheless, during the height of the civil rights movement, and also today, the League has somehow been able to project a relatively strong civil rights posture without alienating the kinds of support it needs from the private and public sectors.

This has been due in large measure to the leadership skills and resourcefulness that the League has enjoyed in its executive directors, including the late Whitney M. Young, Jr., Vernon Jordan, and John Jacob. During the civil rights movement, for example, Young found a way for the Urban League to be a cooperative partner in direct-action activities, for example, the 1963 March on Washington. And in 1979, Jordan became the first leader of a major black civil rights organization to openly criticize the Carter administration for its record and lack of achievements with respect to blacks. It is true, of course, that during the 1960s the League was not in the forefront of the battle; but neither were other organizations. They generally followed the leadership of Martin Luther King, Jr.

Today, however, the situation is somewhat different. Jordan initiated, in

During the 1960s, civil rights organizations generally followed the leadership of Martin Luther King, Jr. King took an active part in rallying various organizations, such as the NAACP, SNCC, CORE, SCLC, NALC, and the Urban League, for the August 1963 March on Washington, DC, which was the high point of coalition activity among civil rights groups and their allies up to that time. (*AP/Wide World Photos*)

terms of national visibility, the criticism of the Carter administration, and other civil rights leaders rallied to his support. And under John Jacob, the Urban League, through its annual state of the union reports, continued to systematize and crystallize the overall assessment of the progress or lack of progress that has been made to overcome the problems facing blacks. While these increased Urban League initiatives may be attributed to a number of factors, there is little doubt that they provide commentary on a changing leadership structure and perhaps on an apparent leadership vacuum or void that seems to have existed among civil rights groups and leaders since Martin Luther King, Jr. The Urban League, not unlike others, has acted to fill this void.

Following Jacob in 1994 is the current League president, Hugh Price, a Yale Law school graduate with wide experience in the public and private sector. Though concerned with a broad range of issues, under Price the Urban League, not unlike other civil rights groups, has highlighted its "economic agenda." This emphasis was clearly reflected in the theme for the organization's 1997 convention—"Economic Power: The Next Civil Rights Frontier."[25] Price particularly wants to focus on placing bright, young, highly educated blacks in tracks that can lead to corporate senior managerial positions. Said Price: "The corporations, I think, know the demographics of the country and realize that over the next 20 or 30 years, they will increasingly have to look to a talent pool largely comprising minorities and women for their senior and middle managers." If corporations take "a hard look at the resumes of their current managers," said Price, "they would see that their levels of education and the caliber of the schools they attended aren't quite up to those of a lot of today's African-American graduates." Still, Price concluded, these young, well-qualified African-Americans are "having difficulties getting comfortable" in the corporate "culture," and companies are "slowly becoming sensitive to this." The underlying assumption of Price, of course, is that placing African-Americans and minorities in such key positions will pave the way for others.

The Changing Structure of African American Leadership

The changing leadership structure among civil rights groups, and African Americans generally, may be attributed to a number of factors. For one thing, a number of other groups and organizations are now on the scene and are also seeking ways to deal with problems that affect blacks and minorities. Until the late 1980s, one of the most visible of these groups was Operation PUSH (People United to Save Humanity). Operation PUSH was founded by the Reverend Jesse Jackson, a former close associate of Martin Luther King, Jr., and former national director of SCLC's Operation Breadbasket. But apparent differences between Jackson and the Reverend Ralph Abernathy, King's immediate successor as president of SCLC, led Jackson to launch a new organization initially devoted mainly to the economic development of blacks and other minority groups. PUSH subsequently expanded its programs and activities to reach into a number of areas, especially voter registration and education.

Undoubtedly, PUSH profited greatly from the charismatic personality and the fiery oratory of Jesse Jackson. In many ways, Jackson was the life of PUSH, just as Martin Luther King, Jr., was the life of SCLC. Through the organization's programs and his own charisma, Jesse Jackson was able to command a role and presence in the civil rights leadership structure that did not seem possible for him within the existing structure of the SCLC. That role was clearly enhanced by his forays into Democratic presidential politics in 1984 and 1988. Inevitably, however, Jackson's presidential campaigns increasingly limited his role in PUSH—forcing him to turn over the active running of the organization to others in 1990. Subsequently, Jackson moved from Chicago to Washington, where he ran for and was elected as the "shadow" senator from the District of Columbia. This effectively removed Jackson from the Chicago national headquarters of PUSH, and since that time PUSH, like many other traditional civil rights organizations, has been struggling to survive. Without Jackson, PUSH was not the same.

But in 1996 Jackson acted to revive PUSH. He returned to Chicago to become national president of a new civil rights organization, which he formed by merging Operation PUSH with his Washington-based National Rainbow Coalition.[26] The new organization, called the Rainbow/PUSH

Action Network, is headquartered in Chicago, with several bureaus planned for Washington and elsewhere. By merging the black economic empowerment thrusts of PUSH with the political emphasis of the Rainbow Coalition, combined with Jackson as its president, the new organization appears well placed to hold a viable leadership position as it moves into the next century. Given his high visibility and talents, Jackson's move serves a number of purposes. It clearly reestablishes his base in Chicago politics and ensures his continuing viability as a major player in civil rights, in the black community, and in American politics generally. It also serves to bolster the present and future career aspirations of Jackson's son, Jesse Jackson, Jr., who now represents Illinois' second congressional district as a member of the U.S. House of Representatives.

Traditional civil rights groups, however, like the NAACP, the Urban League, SCLC, and Rainbow/PUSH are no longer the only major players in civil rights and in the black community. The Nation of Islam (or Black Muslims)—through their outspoken leader Minister Louis Farrakhan—offers a philosophy and an approach that appeals to a number of African-Americans, especially younger persons, and serves to differentiate the Muslims from traditional civil rights groups. That differentiation was aptly captured by a young black professional who, in reacting to Jesse Jackson's new effort to revitalize his organization, made remarks suggesting that PUSH had failed them. Said this young black professional:

> "We tried to march. We tried to get along. We tried to work within the system.... But it's not working.... Operation PUSH is saying, let's work with the system, and Farrakhan is saying, *let's build our own system. The Nation of Islam appeals to a lot of young people today.*" [emphasis added][27]

Though made in specific reference to PUSH, the thrust of this quote may also be made of other civil rights groups.

The Nation of Islam commands a membership in size and commitment that gives it an appealing and formidable presence in the black community. During the 1960s, the Muslims were one of the most separatist and feared groups in American society.[28] A religious organization dedicated to the complete cultural and spatial separation of the races, the Muslims were strongly anti-Christian and anti-white, regarding all white people as "devils." Its membership was (and to a large degree still is) concentrated in the black urban areas of the northern and western United States, and its membership mostly consists of black students, workers, and poor people. Unlike many of the other groups discussed here, the Nation of Islam continues to enjoy increasing visibility and membership. Much of this, as mentioned earlier, is due to one of the Nation's most vocal, charismatic, and controversial leaders, Minister Louis Farrakhan, and to the group's unwavering commitment to black separatism and black economic self-determination.

Farrakhan and the Muslims have done much to fill the apparent leadership vacuum that has existed for some time (and to an extent still does) in the black community. The height of Farrakhan's efforts in this regard was his well-orchestrated and obviously successful "Million Man March" on Washington, DC, in 1995. The March was conceived and developed at a time when African Americans sorely needed a way to show their determination to overcome the many retrenchments and hostile actions that were and are coming from both the public and private sector. Farrakhan responded to this felt need, and as a result enhanced his standing and support in the black community. Even so, the continuing influence of Farrakhan and the Muslims among blacks will depend largely on how effective current revitalization efforts of traditional civil rights organizations will prove in the future.

But the growing conservative trend evident since the 1970s has spurred the development of organizations that differ from the Muslims or the more traditional civil rights groups in their appeals to the black community. One such group, the National Center for Neighborhood Enterprise (NCNE), preaches the tenets of self-help and supports grass-roots, community-based efforts in low-income communities to combat such problems as economic underdevelopment and youth crime. Interests of the NCNE in such matters as economic empowerment do overlap in certain respects with those of the Muslims and other previously discussed groups. On the other hand, the NCNE's founder and current president, Robert Woodson, has drawn differences between these groups and his organization. For example, he has derisively characterized the work of the more traditional black groups, such as the NAACP, the Urban League, and the Congressional Black Caucus, as that of "bitchin', begging, and busing."[29]

Since 1965 there has been an increase in the number of organizations that retain offices in Washington and that deal with issues of primary interest to blacks and minorities. In general, these organizations, such as the Children's Defense Fund, focus on program implementation as a way of influencing public policy. Individually, these groups tend to be rather specialized, but collectively they cover a variety of policy areas of interest to blacks and minorities, such as housing, community development, day care and child development, food stamps and social services, business, and labor. The emergence of such groups symbolizes both the growth and increasing complexity of the problems facing blacks and other minorities. They also bring about a change in the overall leadership structure and influence affecting blacks and minorities. In this regard, mention should be made of the Joint Center for Political and Economic Studies, a think tank that houses policy analysts, scholars, and former government officials to investigate public issues that particularly affect African Americans. Yearly, the Joint Center publishes reports that assess the impact of legislation on the black community, as well as tracks the success of minority candidates in the political arena. This organization manages a multimillion dollar annual budget to inform policy makers and the general public about public policy issues.

The success of blacks in the political arena is another factor that has affected both the role of established groups—such as the NAACP—as well as influenced the general leadership structure among blacks and the civil rights community generally. Local voter leagues and other civil rights groups have been spurred and energized by the growing number of local black candidates and elected officials who view these groups as a way to solidify and expand their careers and influence in the black community and in politics. Undoubtedly, these local groups and organizations tend to vie for attention and serve as a viable substitute for some who might otherwise support—or at least support more fully—national civil rights groups and organizations such as the NAACP and Urban League.

By 1995 there were some 8,500 black elected officials—mainly at the state and local levels—and by virtue of their office, each of these officials has a leadership opportunity. Those in more visible positions, such as blacks in Congress and those who serve as big city mayors, are obviously in positions to have more influence. Those at the state and local levels are especially important to the leadership structure since they have greater chances for day-to-day, face-to-face contact with more persons in the black community.

Those in appointive positions also exercise political influence. Interestingly, many other black appointed officials gained experience with civil rights interest groups; the late Commerce Secretary Ron Brown, for example, served for years as counsel for the National Urban League before becoming chairman of the Democratic National Committee. This broadening of opportunity for African Americans could be understood as a product of increased black political influence of the more established leadership structures.

Blacks and minorities now widely recognize the importance of those in administrative roles as well as those who hold legal-judicial positions. Although the requirements and expectations of office vary and impose constraints somewhat different from those in elective office, it is undoubtedly the case that persons who hold appointive positions, be they high administrative officials or federal judges, are perceived as leaders by and in the black community. They are also obviously leaders in the general American community by virtue of their office and authority. In any event, when one combines the increasing leadership base in the public-political arena with the established and developing leadership structures (church, business), it is abundantly clear that the leadership base among African Americans has been considerably broadened with various persons "leading" from various vantage points. This broadening of the leadership base, to be sure, is indicative of the concrete advances that have been made. And it is this very success that makes it more difficult for blacks to have one leader or to speak with one voice (which in fact has never been the case) when there are so many different leaders and voices.

Several comments may be made about what seem to be the consequences of blacks gaining success in various leadership arenas. First, how to keep pressure on the system: From a practical standpoint, as blacks become more integrated into the "system" and the "establishment," they will tend to use more traditional and systematic means to achieve their objectives. The effectiveness of these efforts, however, will continue to depend upon the resources (leadership, money) that black organizations and their allies can develop and muster. Second, the inability of the black community to have one leader or speak with one voice: From a practical standpoint, it stands to reason that as the number of blacks in leadership positions increases, it will become much more difficult to harness the black community under any one leader. To put it another way, it will become increasingly difficult to have any one black leader who can speak for the black community. But it could very well be that in the future there could be events, circumstances, and common sense that will force the new "collective" black leadership to act with extraordinary unity on issues that tend to affect the self-esteem and life chances of blacks as a group.

INTEREST GROUPS: SOME CONCLUDING OBSERVATIONS

This discussion of interest groups permits us to make several conclusions and observations about these forums, especially as they relate to black politics.

1. American politics may well be described as a process that attempts to manage and accommodate the demands of conflicting and competing interests. Two dominant theories—pluralism and elitism—are most often advanced by political scientists to explain how politics works—for what ends and for whose benefit. Pluralist theory suggests that the number and diversity of interest groups and the competition among them place government in the role of a broker whose major function is to balance competing demands through compromise policies and actions. Under this theory no one group or coalition dominates; rather, in due course, competing interests will realize some but not all of their objectives.

On the other hand, those who hold to the elite theory of American politics also recognize the presence of interest groups, but they suggest that such groups are in the main controlled by an elite corps of leaders. Elite theorists posit that these leaders share similar goals, values, and directions and, as a result, reach compromises among themselves with little or no influence or input from the masses. While these two theories offer conflicting interpretations, clearly, elements of both are reflected in the political process. Thus, plural elitism may prove a more apt and perhaps more accurate description of American politics.

But whether pluralism, elitism, or some combination of the two exists, those who are on the lower rung of the socioeconomic ladder—as most African Americans are—tend to be disadvantaged by the nature and operation of the American political process whatever its definition.

Socioeconomic inequities in such resources as money, wealth, education, and expertise, mainly a result of racism and discrimination, continue to seriously impede effective black political participation. And these are the very resources that groups must have in order to maintain the kind of sustained presence needed to meaningfully participate, compete, and achieve their objectives in the political process.

2. Staff and money, as we have seen, are important resources that groups need in order to promote their objectives in the political process. However, black interest groups have such resources in relatively small measure, if at all. The possible effects of the lack of such resources are vividly portrayed by Harold Wolman and Norman Thomas in their study of black influence in the federal policy process regarding two policy areas that are of crucial importance to blacks—housing and education.[30] Wolman and Thomas found that "the civil rights movement did not result in extensive involvement by black groups in the federal policy process" in these two areas. Indeed, black groups suffer from problems such as small staffs, lack of technical expertise, and the resulting inability to influence policy at crucial stages of its formulation. When such groups do attempt to influence policy, say Wolman and Thomas, they do so in largely "formal and visible" ways, such as testifying before congressional committees. Moreover, these attempts occur "fairly late in the policy process, particularly at the stages of legislative consideration and implementation." "At those stages," the authors conclude, "certain actions can be prevented and marginal changes in policy outputs affected, but the major thrust of policies cannot substantially be altered, for they have been shaped in the earlier innovative and formulative stages when the basic agenda is set." In general, however, the lack of staff and money have forced black groups to concentrate what meager resources they have in ways and areas that they believe to be most useful. This might call for activities that are open and visible rather than those of the behind-the-scenes, low-profile variety, which ordinarily might be the most effective. In sum, black leaders and interest groups are in short supply of the kind of resources and muscle needed to bargain in such day-to-day, behind-the-scene negotiations.

3. "Social solidarity" and "expression of opinion" might best characterize black interest groups. Yet the stability and viability of these groups are related directly to the material benefits they can secure for the causes they represent. Hence, the successes of the Urban League in employment have kept this organization more viable than those where tangible successes are less continuously evident (e.g., SCLC and CORE). Nonetheless, both the NAACP and the Urban League have had to modify or broaden the posture of their "nonmaterial" benefits (such as participation in direct activity) to retain support and increase interaction with various segments of the black community.

4. Blacks can count on neither mass membership organizations (labor)

nor high socioeconomic status groups (such as the American Bar Association or the American Medical Association) to support their goals. And it is these groups that wield significant influence in American politics. Though less influential than in earlier times, the political arsenal of the AFL-CIO continues to remain quite formidable. That arsenal includes a large potential vote, a good amount of money, and lots of manpower to supplement and expand those things money can buy—for instance, time. To be sure, there are elements among labor that apparently still offer strong support to black interests. But racial friction and apprehension between labor's rank-and-file and blacks over such issues as school integration, job competition, and job security (e.g., affirmative action), have tended to lessen labor's traditional support for blacks and other minorities. This phenomenon has many implications, including the problems it could cause for black candidates who now enjoy labor support in elections. No longer can it be assumed that the policy positions of blacks and organized labor are compatible or closely related. That they should be compatible or related is another matter.

The high socioeconomic status groups—for example, the American Bar Association and the American Medical Association—have money and standing as their major resources. While there is an increasing number of black lawyers and doctors, their numbers and standing do not yet have a significant impact on these organizations and the policies they support. But the increasing growth and vitality of black professional and social organizations—National Bar Association, National Medical Association, and black Greek letter sororities and fraternities—could prove of potential value to black politics and to the black community in terms of providing relevant resources.

5. As we enter the year 2000, civil rights groups are in a precarious bind. They must function in an increasingly conservative climate that is not at all favorable to their sheer survival, much less their growth and vitality. These groups, such as the NAACP, must demonstrate that while the more visible barriers have been overcome and much progress has been made, there remain many less visible though no less formidable barriers that continue to stifle black representation and progress in every major socioeconomic sector of American life.

At the same time, however, civil rights groups must function in a climate where landmark civil rights milestones, such as the 1954 *Brown* decision, are now being openly questioned by friend and foe alike, including blacks. They must in fact operate in an environment where obvious major retrenchments in policies and actions seem on the increase from both the Congress and the Supreme Court. And while Democratic President Clinton is clearly more sympathetic and supportive of civil rights interests, his position at times is also somewhat uncertain. It is clear, for example, that not unlike the Congress and the Court, the strong conservative trends engulfing the nation since the 1970s have likewise influenced the president, leading him to fashion a posture consistent with "mainstream-centrist" politics, effectively tempering liberal rhetoric and policies long associated with the Democratic party. Thus, it is doubtful that blacks can expect much support for their interests from the federal government. Nor are they likely to meet much success at the state level, in view of the sparse representation in councils of state government. Though blacks enjoy more effective interest representation at local levels, these are precisely the areas that depend greatly on federal and state support, since urban and rural areas simply do not command the funds or resources needed to deal with the most difficult problems faced by women, minorities (such as blacks), and many others.

To be sure, at base many of these problems are economic, and it is thus not surprising that "economic empowerment" is the most common theme that permeates the objectives of civil rights groups. And though both can play important roles in this regard, the political climate described above makes it more understandable why civil rights groups would focus their efforts in seeking redress from the private sector rather than from the public sector (government).[31]

In addition, civil rights groups must function in a climate where the increasing friction between "race" and "class" makes it more difficult for such groups to maintain and increase membership and to solicit funds and other resources needed to function effectively.

This is just the kind of climate, however, in which civil rights groups are most needed in order to protect important and relevant policy interests of blacks and minorities. As suggested throughout this volume and elsewhere, it is significantly the matter of *race* that continues to thwart the life chances and opportunities of African Americans, no matter their class or social standing.

Whether existing civil rights groups are able to meet the challenges involved is unclear. What is clear, however, is that the interests facing African-Americans are so fundamental that they will find representation one way or the other, and that the nature and quality of that representation could well determine the future course of our overall politics and society.

TOPICS FOR DISCUSSION

1. Do you agree with the view that civil rights groups, such as the NAACP, are no longer relevant or needed? What seems to be the basis of this view? What is your position—are such groups "relevant or needed"? Discuss thoroughly.

2. The text states that "the changing civil rights leadership structure may be attributed to a number of factors." What are these factors? Do you agree that these factors have brought about changes in the civil rights leadership structure? Discuss.

3. The authors state that changes in the political-social climate have brought about "hard times" for civil rights organizations. Discuss these changes and describe how and in what ways they have complicated the life of civil rights organizations. Can these "changes" and "hard times" be overcome? Discuss.

SUGGESTED READINGS

Bentley, Arthur. *The Process of Government*. Chicago, IL: University of Chicago Press, 1908. A classic work on the whole body of literature on group analysis and interest group theory.

Blair, Thomas L. *Retreat to the Ghetto: The End of a Dream?* New York: Hill & Wang, 1977. A critical analysis of how relevant the "Black Power" movement and the "Black Revolution" were to the crisis of survival faced by urban blacks.

Button, James W. *Blacks and Social Change: Impact of the Civil Rights Movement in Southern Communities*. Princeton, NJ: Princeton University Press, 1989.

Carmichael, Stokely, and Charles V. Hamilton. *Black Power: The Politics of Liberation in America*. New York: Vintage Books, 1967. Pioneering work on the explanation and formulation of the meaning of the concept of black power.

Cigler, Allan J., and A. Loomis Burdett, eds. *Interest Group Politics*, 2nd ed. Washington, DC: Congressional Quarterly Press, 1986.

Epstein, Lee. *Public Interest Law*. New York: Garland Publishers, 1992.

Greenwald, Carol S. *Group Power: Lobbying and Public Policy*. New York: Praeger Publishers, 1977. Describes the importance of interest groups in the development and application of general policies in the public policy process.

Harmon, Robert B. *Interest Groups and Lobbying in American Politics: A Bibliographic Checklist*. Monticello, IL: Council of Planning Librarians, 1978. An extensive bibliography of sources dealing with the role of lobbying and interest groups in the American political system.

Hilliard, David. *This Side of Glory: The Autobiography of David Hilliard and the Story of the Black Panther Party*. Boston, MA: Little, Brown, 1993.

Jennings, James. *The Politics of Black Empowerment*. Detroit, MI: Wayne State University Press, 1992.

Key, V. O. *Parties, Politics and Interest Groups*. New York: Crowell, 1958. An examination of American politics in light of the activities of parties and interest groups.

McCartney, John T. *Black Power Ideologies: An Essay in African-American Political Thought*. Philadelphia, PA: Temple University Press, 1992.

Mundo, Philip A. *Interest Groups*. Chicago, IL: Nelson-Hall Publishers, 1992.

Olson, Mancur, Jr. *The Logic of Collective Action: Public Goods and the Theory of Groups*. Cambridge, MA: Harvard University Press, 1965. Explores the nature of interest groups, the behavior of members, the importance of size, and how these and other factors interact in realizing groups' objectives.

Salisbury, Robert. "Interest Groups." In *Handbook of Political Science*, vol. 4, ed. Fred I. Greenstein and Nelson Polsby. Reading, MA: Addison-Wesley Publishing Co., 1975. Analysis of interest groups over a broad spectrum.

Schattschneider, E. E. *The Semi-Sovereign People*. New York: Holt, Rinehart & Winston, 1975. A forceful commentary on the role of the people in the American political system.

Tate, Katherine. *From Protest to Politics: The New Black Voters in American Elections*. Cambridge, MA: Harvard University Press, 1993.

Walker, Jack L. *Mobilizing Interest Groups in America*. Ann Arbor, MI: University of Michigan Press, 1991.

NOTES

1. *Congressional Record,* February 19, 1971, p. E-936.
2. Roz Ayers-Williams, "The New Rights Agenda," *Black Enterprise,* August 1997, p. 85. Reprinted by permission.
3. See, generally, *New York Times,* October 19, 1979, p. 49; *Congressional Quarterly Almanac* (Washington, DC: Congressional Quarterly, Inc., 1978), p. 770; and John Felton "The Wealth of Congress," *Congressional Quarterly,* Report 35 (September 2, 1978), p. 2326.
4. *NAACP* v. *Button,* 371 U.S. 415 (1963), pp. 429–430.
5. See Lucius J. Barker, "Third Parties in Litigation," *Journal of Politics* 29 (1967), pp. 41–69, and sources cited therein.
6. See *The Gallup Poll: Public Opinion* (Wilmington, DE: Scholarly Resources), 1982, p. 222; 1988, p. 166; 1990, p. 149; 1992, p. 160.
7. Ernest Holsendolph, "Jordan Urges Carter to Visit Looted Areas," *New York Times,* July 26, 1977, p. 43.
8. *Ibid.;* Adam Clymer, "President Rejects Jordan's Criticism," *New York Times,* July 26, 1977, p. B-8.
9. Adam Clymer, "President Rejects Jordan's Criticism," *New York Times,* July 26, 1977, p. 1.
10. *Ibid.,* p. B-8.
11. *Price Waterhouse* v. *Hopkins,* 490 U.S. 228 (1989); *Wards Cove Packing Co.* v. *Atonio,* 490 U.S. 642 (1989); *Martin* v. *Wilks,* 490 U.S. 755 (1989); *Lorance* v. *AT&T,* 490 U.S. 900 (1989); *Patterson* v. *McLean Credit Union,* 491 U.S. 164 (1989); *Independent Federation of Flight Attendants* v. *Zipes,* 491 U.S. 754 (1989).
12. For a background overview of the situation, see *New York Times,* July 28, 1991, p. 10, cols. 1–4.
13. Peter Steinfels, *The Neoconservatives: The Men Who Are Changing America's Politics* (New York: Simon & Schuster, 1979), p. 1.
14. *Ibid.*
15. *Ibid.,* p. 7.
16. *Ibid.*
17. *Ibid.,* p. 6.
18. http://www.naacp.org/about/factsheet.html
19. See Steven A. Holmes, "Affirmative Action Reaction: For the Civil Rights Movement, a New Reason for Living," *New York Times,* July 9, 1995, Sec. IV, p. E-5, col. 2.
20. Bruce Lambert, "Incoming Leader of N.A.A.C.P. Vows That 'Change Is at Hand,'" *New York Times,* February 19, 1996, p. A-16.
21. For an overview of these matters, see Paul Delaney, "Called Complacent, NAACP Looks to Future," *New York Times,* June 10, 1991, p. C-10. Materials and quotes in the next two paragraphs are drawn from the Delaney article.
22. Quotes and background materials for this section may be found in Neil A. Lewis, "Veteran of Rights Movement to Lead N.A.A.C.P.," *New York Times,* April 10, 1993, p. 6, cols. 3–6. For an informative biographical profile on the new executive director, see Neil A. Lewis, "Deep Civil Rights Roots—Benjamin Franklin Chavis, Jr.," *New York Times,* April 11, 1993, p. 12, cols. 1–2.

23. See Michael Eric Dyson, "Ben Chavis Wasn't the Problem," *New York Times*, September 1, 1994, p. A-27.

24. Information in this section, unless otherwise noted, is taken from *New York Times*, June 23, 1997.

25. Unless otherwise indicated, quotes are taken from *Fortune*, August 4, 1997, p. 67.

26. For more information in this regard, see *Chicago Tribune*, September 20, 1996 and October 9, 1996, North Sports Final Ed., Metro Chicago, p. 3 and p. 1, respectively. Also see *Chicago Sun-Times*, September 17, 1996, Late Sports Final Ed., NWS Sec., p. 4.

27. *Ibid.*

28. Lomax, "Crisis of Leadership," pp. 178–192; Monsen and Cannon, "Negroes," pp. 145–146; Lomax, *When the Word Is Given*.

29. See the biography of Robert Woodson in *Contemporary Black Biography*, vol. 10, 1995, Gale Research, Inc.

30. Harold Z. Wolman and Norman C. Thomas, "Black Interests, Black Groups, and Black Influence in the Federal Policy Process: The Cases of Housing and Education," *Journal of Politics* 32 (1970), pp. 875–897.

31. See *Black Enterprise*, op. cit., August 1997.

Chapter 8

Change through Politics: Political Parties

U ndoubtedly the most striking feature of politics in America is the two-party system. Bringing about change through politics in the American political system necessarily involves change in and through political parties. Political change can only occur through the major role that the Democratic and Republican parties play—the recruitment and election of public officials at all levels of government. The lifeblood of parties is to control government by electing its members to office. This is the overriding preoccupation of parties, of their every move; every other function they provide is geared toward this central concern.

Since 1964, the vast majority of blacks have supported the Democratic party. And, in fact, blacks are the Democratic party's most loyal voting bloc, as Table 8-1 shows. Although party defections and split-ticket voting are on the rise, blacks have generally not crossed party lines. In fact, in five of the last six presidential elections, blacks have voted more consistently Democratic than all other voters who claim to be Democrats! But does the Democratic party serve as a real vehicle for blacks' political aspirations, or are their votes being taken for granted by the party?

THE AMERICAN TWO-PARTY SYSTEM

That two parties and only two parties have dominated the American political scene for more than 160 years has been explained by several factors.[1] Originally, scholars sought to explain the two-party system in terms of deeply rooted and widespread American consensus on fundamental beliefs. But the fact of the matter is that this "consensus" is very much the product of the symbiotic relationship that has developed between parties and the constitutional-legal system. As part of their effort to win and maintain polit-

Table 8-1   Percentage of Democratic Vote in Presidential
Elections, 1976–1996, by Key Social and Political Groups

	1976: Carter/ Mondale	1980: Carter/ Mondale	1984: Mondale/ Ferraro	1988: Dukakis/ Bentsen	1992: Clinton/ Gore	1996: Clinton/ Gore
National	50	41	41	46	43	49
Black	83	83	91	89	83	84
Democratic	80	67	74	83	77	84
Republican	11	11	7	8	10	13
Independent	48	31	36	43	38	43
Liberal	74	60	71	82	68	78
Moderate	53	43	46	51	47	57
Conservative	30	23	18	19	18	20
Men	52	38	38	42	41	43
Women	52	46	42	49	45	54
White	48	36	34	40	39	43
Hispanic	82	56	66	70	61	72
Asian	—	—	—	—	31	43
Union	62	48	54	57	55	59
Non-union	48	36	—	—	41	46

Sources: As reported in *The Public Perspective*, December 1996/January 1997. Exit polling conducted by CBS News/*New York Times* of 15,199 voters in 1976; CBS News/*New York Times* of 12,782 voters in 1980; CBS News/*New York Times* of 8,671 voters in 1984; CBS News/*New York Times* of 11,645 voters in 1988; Voter Research and Surveys of 15,490 voters in 1992; and Voter News Service in 1996 of 14,651 voters.

ical control, the Democrats and Republicans have actually written election laws governing the activities and functions of parties, that in turn block the emergence of more than two parties and ensure their own dominance as the two major parties.[2]

In particular, the U.S. plurality vote, winner-take-all method of elections, as opposed to a proportional representation system of government, greatly discourages the emergence of third parties. This is known as Duverger's Law—the plurality-vote, single-ballot system (where there are no run-offs or second ballot elections) favors the dominance of two political parties.[3] To win the presidency, for example, the party must win an absolute majority of the electoral votes, and electoral votes of each state are awarded on a winner-take-all basis. Thus, to remain viable, parties must possess tremendous financial and organizational resources; new or locally based parties are at a tremendous disadvantage to the major party. Texas billionaire H. Ross Perot got an astonishing 19 percent of the popular vote in 1992, but none of the states' electoral votes. And it took millions of his own money (about $7 million) for Perot to build the organization necessary to get his name on the ballot in all 50 states. In 1996, Perot would receive federal matching funds because of his promising showing in the 1992 presidential election, but be denied the opportunity to participate with the Republican and Democratic candidates in the nationally televised presidential debates.

In addition, Democrats and Republicans have also constructed complicated and lengthy procedures in order for new third-party or independent candidates to be listed on ballots. The perception that independent parties can't possibly win becomes self-fulfilling, influencing not only the voters who don't want to "waste" their votes on candidates who have little chance of winning but the media and their coverage of the campaign as well. Electoral laws, therefore, help perpetuate the dominance of the two major parties.

The two-party system affects the political psychology of voters. Americans have more deeply attached and stable identifications with the two major parties than citizens in multi-party systems. Since the 1950s, Gallup polls have found that there are more Democrats than Republicans nationally. Over the past 40 years, in fact, Americans identified with the Democratic party over the Republican party by a balance ranging from 60/40 to 55/45. By the 1960s, this coalition began to fall apart as white southerners, Catholics, and labor union members began defecting to the Republican party. The advantage that Democrats had enjoyed in partisan loyalties has narrowed. In a 1992 Gallup survey, 45 percent of those surveyed labeled themselves Democrats, while 42 percent identified as Republican. In 1952, by comparison, 56 percent surveyed were Democrats while only 35 percent were Republican.[4]

Finally, the two-party system affects the form and management of political conflict in the United States. As majority-seeking parties, the Democrats and Republicans must construct electoral coalitions of diverse, even competing, interests. The parties must somehow manage and overcome societally based divisions of class, race, religion, or ideology. The two-party system fosters consensus, real or temporary, lasting until after the election. The Democratic and Republican parties can thus be described as "grand coalitions."

For decades following the Great Depression of the 1930s, the Democratic party has performed better than the Republican party in fashioning a majority coalition from the diverse political interests in the United States. African Americans are part of the Democratic party's electoral coalition, also known as the New Deal coalition, which includes southern whites, Catholics, Jews, labor union members, and the poor. Since the 1930s, feminists, Hispanics, gays, and lesbians have become prominent groups active within the Democratic party coalition. The Republican party's traditional base of support comes from the business community, professionals and white-collar workers, Protestants, and suburbanites. Since 1980, the "Religious Right" has become a prominent part of the GOP's grand coalition. Table 8-2 shows the distribution of Republicans,

Table 8-2 Party Identification by Race, 1952–1996 (Percentages)

	Democrats		Independents		Republicans		Apolitical	
	Black	*White*	*Black*	*White*	*Black*	*White*	*Black*	*White*
1952	62	56	4	6	17	35	17	2
1956	59	56	5	7	22	34	15	2
1958	55	49	7	9	20	39	18	2
1960	58	55	4	8	22	34	16	3
1962	64	53	6	8	15	37	15	3
1964	82	58	6	8	8	32	4	1
1966	72	53	14	12	11	32	3	1
1968	92	53	3	11	3	37	3	1
1970	82	50	12	13	5	35	1	1
1972	75	49	12	13	11	36	2	1
1974	81	48	12	15	3	33	4	3
1976	84	47	8	15	5	37	1	1
1978	81	50	9	14	8	34	2	3
1980	81	49	7	14	8	37	4	2
1982	91	51	5	11	3	36	1	2
1984	77	44	11	11	7	44	2	2
1986	84	45	7	12	6	42	2	2
1988	81	40	6	12	11	46	3	1
1990	79	47	8	11	12	40	2	1
1992	78	45	12	12	8	42	2	1
1994	82	42	8	10	9	47	1	1
1996	80.5	48	10.5	8	8.5	44	0	0

Sources: National Election Studies, 1952–1996. The figures shown for 1952 to 1992 were calculated from Tables 8-2 and 8-3 in Abramson, Aldrich, and Rohde (1994), pp. 228–231. The percentages shown for 1994 and 1996 were added by the authors. The percentage supporting another party, usually less than 1 percent, is not shown.

Democrats, Independents, and those not interested in party politics (the apolitical) by race.

The diverse set of interests that comprise the two major parties makes it highly unlikely (although not unknown) that any one group or interest will have its way. Put another way, party conventions as forums of decision making, similar to other national forums, are not likely to come up with sharp, clear, concise actions that might jeopardize their mass broad support base. Consequently, compromise and moderation, rather than conflict and clarity, usually characterize the operation of parties at the national level. As such, the character of the national party tends to support those interests who favor the status quo or those who believe in gradual change.

Given the way the American two-party system works, it becomes obvious why black participation in national party politics has, for the most part, been frustrating. Let us take a brief look at black experience with the two major parties.

BLACKS AND THE REPUBLICAN PARTY: FREEDOM, BETRAYAL, AND ABANDONMENT

Abraham Lincoln's Emancipation Proclamation and the policies of the Republican Reconstruction Congress stand out as historic benchmarks in African Americans' struggle for freedom. The circumstances surrounding these actions have led some to ascribe various motivations for them. But the fact remains that these actions were taken by Republicans. Lincoln's Proclamation did free the slaves. Moreover, the support given blacks by Republicans during Reconstruction was symbolized not only through legislation, such as the Civil Rights Act of 1866, but also through the eventual enactment of the Civil War Amendments—the Thirteenth, Fourteenth, and Fifteenth Amendments. Quite naturally, these historic polices benefited the Republican party by attracting the newly emancipated and newly enfranchised black voters. By 1868, more than 700,000 blacks were registered to vote under the supervision of federal troops.

During Reconstruction, blacks, all serving as Republicans, held 15 percent of the elected seats in the South, including lieutenant governor and U.S. senator. Their presence in the southern electorate and in government was short lived. In the disputed election of 1876, Republican candidate Rutherford B. Hayes, in exchange for southern electoral votes, agreed to withdraw federal troops from the South and in effect adopted a "hands-off" policy toward the newly-freed blacks. This agreement, called the Compromise of 1877, led to a widespread feeling among blacks that they had been abandoned by the Republican party and once again offered up to the whims of their former slaveholders. Consequently, black Republicans who had prospered during Reconstruction were brushed aside both by the reemergence of the Democratic party as well as by southern white Republican leaders who wanted to rid the party of its black image. This led to warfare between two factions of the party: the white faction, known as the Lily White Republicans, and the black faction, known as the Black and Tan Republicans. And although national Republican leaders sought to overcome this factionalism and effect a viable and racially integrated party organization in the South, they were unable to do so.

Southern whites took full advantage of the situation. They solidified their control of state governments through the Democratic party. They instituted various devices that disfranchised black voters and generally relegated blacks to a subordinate status. In 1928, President Hoover squashed any hope that the Republican party would once again come to the rescue of blacks. Sensing an increasing wave of race prejudice throughout the country, Hoover sided with the Lily White Republicans and, through his economic policies, dealt a severe blow to the Black and Tan faction in the South. By 1938 this move by Hoover, coupled with the attractive economic policies of President Franklin D. Roosevelt's New Deal, had most blacks (those who could vote) voting Democratic in presidential elections.[5] But though Democrats controlled national politics until 1952, they did little to unravel the web of subordination that enveloped the life of blacks in the South.

However, the national Republicans did even less to alleviate the plight of blacks and of the poor. The GOP was pictured as the party of the rich and well-born WASPs. Led by General Dwight D. Eisenhower, the Republicans recaptured the White House from 1952 to 1960—crucial years in the civil rights movement. It was during this time that the Supreme Court handed down its decisions on public school desegregation, the Montgomery bus boycott, and the Little Rock school integration crisis. These were all situations that provided opportunities for the Republicans to regain its image as the "Party of Lincoln" and recapture the national black vote. But, as is well known, President Eisenhower refused to endorse the Court's 1954 *Brown* decision that mandated desegregation of public schools. He remained aloof and uninvolved in the expanding civil rights controversy, limiting his role to one of enforcement, using federal troops to enforce federal court orders during the Little Rock crisis only as a last resort. But there was little meaningful difference between the Republicans and Democrats on racial issues during this period. Although blacks had voted Democratic during the 1930s and 1940s in support of Roosevelt's New Deal legislation, Eisenhower still received about 40 percent of the black vote in 1956. Republican candidate Richard Nixon netted almost one-third of the black vote in the 1960 presidential election.

The Republicans did not regain the White House until 1968, when Richard Nixon was elected president. By this time, the vast majority of blacks had left the Party of Lincoln to become loyal Democrats. The Democratic party had captured the black vote through its support of black civil rights, and, more specifically, its passage of civil rights legislation during the Kennedy-Johnson administration. Senator Barry Goldwater's 1964 campaign for president also enhanced the appeal of the Democratic party among blacks. Goldwater had been one of six Republican senators who voted against the 1964 Civil Rights Act. His campaign turned race into a highly partisan issue, with Democrats now squarely occupying the pro-civil rights side and Republicans in the anti-civil rights camp. The public, who until 1964 had seen no real difference between the parties on civil rights now recognized the Republican party as the more racially conservative.[6]

Richard Nixon's early record on civil rights was moderate. In 1968, however, he won the presidency with a campaign crafted to appeal exclusively to white America and its fears about the rapid pace of racial change. The "law and order," "anti-busing," and "southern strategy" themes that characterized his 1968 and 1972 campaigns—as well as his administrations—were not directed toward black voters, but against them. Nixon had written off the black vote. President Nixon and leading figures of his administration, including his chief law enforcement officer, Attorney General John Mitchell, became trapped in their own "law and order" rhetoric, in word and in (mis)deed. This, of course, included Vice-President Spiro Agnew, who, along with Mitchell, symbolized the antipathy of the Republican administration toward blacks, minorities, and the poor.

Then came Watergate. The Watergate scandal led not only to the conviction of the leading officials of Nixon's administration but also to the resignation of the president himself. Predictably, the elevation of Gerald Ford to the presidency did little to improve the civil rights image of the Republican party. This may well have been Ford's undoing. In his 1976 presidential campaign, Ford did little if anything to win the black vote. In fact, a key strategist in Reagan's unsuccessful attempt to win the GOP nomination said that "Ford made so little effort [among blacks] it was an insult." An Urban League official put the matter even more vividly, saying that "if Ford had gone to black churches in Ohio, he might still be president." But Ford did not do so. And as matters turned out, it was the overwhelming black vote (over 90 percent) that provided Democratic nominee Jimmy Carter's margin of victory in the 1976 election. In addition, the black vote also proved crucial in other races. For example, former Senator William Brock of Tennessee inferred that it was the "awesome" black vote that perhaps led to his own defeat. Brock was defeated by some 77,000 votes, while his Democratic opponent, the eventual winner, received some 130,000 or 93 percent of the black vote.

In any event, the 1976 election taught Brock and other Republican party leaders about the importance of the black vote. So, in 1977, when Brock became chairman of the national Republican committee, he was in a position to do something to regain black support. In outlining the Republican strategy to attract blacks, Brock indicated that he wanted to provide blacks with alternatives to the Democratic party. Said Brock:

> I'm not sure it is realistic to establish goals with any degree of reason.... Fundamentally, I want this party to earn the support of the black community, to provide it with an honest and realistic alternative. How fast they seize the opportunity depends on how effective our efforts are.

The Republican alternative focused on three areas: "symbolic action, involvement of blacks in the party as policy makers and candidates, and legislation." Although "symbolic action" involves mainly rhetoric, some blacks believe that it is nevertheless "a step in the right direction." But, as Brock himself put it, "It is going to take tangible results; we're going to have to prove the rhetoric." He thought Republicans must pay close attention to problems that especially impact blacks and minorities, for example, unemployment, taxation, housing, and small business.

Although the Republicans took several concrete and highly visible steps in their attempt to attract blacks in the late 1970s, these efforts were short-lived. The election and reelection of Ronald Reagan in 1980 and 1984 and the hostile attitudes and actions of his administration all but obliterated most efforts by the party to attract black support. Black Republican votes dropped to their lowest level ever—into the single digits—in the 1984 election and would remain there through the 1990s. Ronald Reagan and his two administrations negated any new prospects for a rapprochement between blacks and the Republican party.

Despite the antagonism of the Reagan administration toward black interests, the Republican party once again attempted to reach out to blacks under the leadership of President Bush and Republican National Committee Chairman Lee Atwater. After Bush's victory in 1988, Atwater publicly announced that he would like to see black support for the Republican party in future presidential elections increase to the double digits. Republicans believed that blacks were more likely to look for an alternative to the Democratic party since the Democrats appeared to take their black support for granted.

George Bush's support among blacks, however, remained low. His 1988 campaign against Democratic nominee Michael Dukakis bore a close resemblance to Nixon's law and order campaign in 1968, which some thought was a coded message that capitalized on whites' racial prejudices against blacks. During the 1988 campaign, a conservative group independent of the official Bush campaign organization mailed fliers bearing the picture of Willie Horton, a black Massachusetts resident convicted for raping a white woman. The flier claimed, "Dukakis's election would set murderers and rapists free across the country." The Bush campaign organization had publicized the case of Willie Horton, but had not revealed his race. For all of the national party organization's rhetoric of reaching out to blacks, many other Republicans, especially those in the South, ran highly racialized campaigns that exploited racial divisions.[7] Although the national Republican party withheld its support from former Klansman David Duke of Louisiana, who twice ran statewide for governor and for the U.S. Senate as a Republican in 1990 and 1991, the racial tactics employed by the white Republican candidate helped reinforce the party's general image as anti-black. Duke lost to his democratic opponents by a narrow margin.

The Republican party, however, made a serious effort to open its door to blacks in the 1996 presidential race. Several African Americans are prominently involved in national party politics. Alan Keyes, a former ambassador during the Reagan administration, ran for the party's presidential nomination in 1996. At their 1996 national convention, Republicans gave prime air-time to campaign speeches by two black men, retired General Colin Powell and Oklahoma Congressman J. C. Watts. If these Republicans can participate as meaningfully as black Democrats have in national party politics, perhaps the GOP can sway a number of blacks back to the party in the near future.

BLACKS AND THE DEMOCRATIC PARTY: LOYALTY AND NEGLECT

The experience of blacks with the Democratic party can be seen, at its best, as mixed. Blacks' ties to the Democratic party can be traced in large part back to the economic benefits that accrued during Franklin Roosevelt's New Deal era. But although widely seen as the champion of the poor and the down-trodden, Roosevelt actually had a dismal record on race. During his administration, not one of the more than 150 civil rights bills introduced in Congress passed into legislation. It was only in his third term of office that Roosevelt issued an executive order making discrimination in government employment illegal and establishing a Committee on Fair Employment Practices to enforce a nondiscrimination policy in defense programs. Even then, Roosevelt acted only in response to the threat of a march on Washington that A. Philip Randolph would organize if the Roosevelt administration continued to ignore blacks' demand for civil rights legislation.

Although surely grateful for their black support, Democratic presidents feared supporting black demands for civil rights protection would antagonize white southerners, the most populous group in its New Deal coalition. President Truman learned of the dangers of supporting black interests first-hand. In 1946 he created a commission on civil rights that issued a report, "To Secure These Rights," that recommended, among other things, the protection of black voting rights. But efforts by Truman to push a civil rights bill (the first sent to Congress since Reconstruction) that would implement the commission's recommendations through Congress spurred southern Democrats to walk out of the party's 1948 national convention. In what became known as the Dixiecrat revolt, these southern delegates then formed a States' Rights party and nominated Strom Thurmond as their candidate for president. Although reelected, Truman's civil rights action cost him the electoral votes of Alabama, Mississippi, Louisiana, and Thurmond's state, South Carolina.[8]

President Kennedy, like Roosevelt before him, had initially adopted the strategy of ignoring blacks' demands for civil rights legislation. For example, he refused to endorse a civil rights bill introduced in May 1961 that he himself had asked be drafted. Finally, in the summer of 1963 in response to widespread racial violence, demonstrations, marches, and boy-cotts, Kennedy announced on national television his intention to submit sweeping civil rights legislation to Congress. Kennedy's successor, Lyndon Johnson would sign into law three landmark civil rights bills—the 1964 Civil Rights Act, an omnibus bill that included a mandate for implementing school desegregation; the 1965 Voting Rights Act; and the 1968 Civil Rights Act, which targeted housing discrimination. Johnson would also initiate the

War on Poverty, a set of federal programs aimed at creating new social services structures that would work to reduce poverty among blacks, which was twice that of whites.

With major differences between the parties on civil rights and racial issues readily apparent by 1964, the vast majority of blacks became Democrats. Blacks, however, were not proportionately represented within the party's ranks. In the South, they were effectively locked out of party politics altogether. As the 1964 national elections approached, the Mississippi Freedom Democratic Party (MFDP), a multi-racial civil rights group, challenged the all-white primary delegation in Mississippi to the Democratic party's national convention. Johnson was initially against the challengers, fearing that seating them would endanger his support among southern white Democrats. But after Fannie Lou Hamer movingly testified on national television how she and other blacks were savagely beaten in their attempt to register and vote, the President changed his mind.

At the convention, the MFDP was offered two at-large seats and promised the passage of future party rules that would prevent the seating of groups that discriminated against minority groups, while the all-white delegation retained their seats as representatives of the state of Mississippi. Most political observers and activists outside the MFDP, including Martin Luther King, Jr., welcomed these steps as a fair compromise. MFDP members, however, felt betrayed and only at the end bitterly took these two seats.[9] All-white delegations from Mississippi continued to be sent to the Democratic party's national conventions until 1976, even though the national party refused to seat these delegations, recognizing instead the alternative, biracial group from the state that was organized by the NAACP. Finally, in 1976, the governor of Mississippi persuaded the two groups to merge, ending black isolation from Democratic party politics in that state.[10]

Although by 1964 blacks represented 12 percent of the party's base support, they constituted fewer than 6 percent of the delegates at the 1968 convention. By 1972, the percentage of black delegates at the national convention had increased to 15 percent, but this figure was still out of line with the 25 percent black share of the party's voting base. As a result of the MFDP challenge and later events, the Democratic party had revised its delegate selection rules to include language in support of affirmative action policies to increase minority representation at the national conventions. The rule changes included a statement that "minorities, young people, and women" should be represented in state delegations to the national conventions in "reasonable relationship to their proportion in the state." The new affirmative action language, however, was controversial, and a debate continued within the party over whether or not the party should impose a quota system on the state parties in their selection of national convention delegates. In 1973, new delegate selection guidelines were issued that shifted the burden of proving that discrimination existed at the state level from the state party to the challengers. The draft proposal read, "If a State Party has adopted and implemented an approved Affirmative Action Program, the Party shall not be subject to challenge based solely on delegation composition or primary results."[11]

Black Democrats mobilized during this time in an effort to increase their numbers and influence within the party. A black caucus had already existed in the Democratic party, but in 1973, a new Black Democratic Caucus (BDC) was formed. Responding to what the BDC members perceived as a weakening resolve to bring black representation in line with their proportion in the electorate, the BDC issued a statement in 1974 that read, "If the Party leadership continues to insist on further compromises on Party Affirmative Action provisions, *we have no alternative but to reassess our involvement in and support of the Democratic party.*"[12]

In many respects, BDC's threat was a hollow one. The alternatives to the Democratic party that African American voters have are limited by the two-party system and by their ideological liberalism. Blacks, in other words, are *structurally dependent* on the Democratic party.[13] In a two-party system in which blacks are ideologically to the left of both parties, blacks would gain little politically by strategically relocating to the right. Thus political independence, or moving to the center of the two major parties, is not an option for a group as politically liberal as blacks.

A second option—third-party formation—is also of limited utility for blacks because the American party system works against the emergence of third parties. Moreover, third-party candidates rarely possess the financial resources needed to compete effectively against major-party candidates. Given their liberalism and the structure of the American two-party system, blacks therefore are "structurally dependent" on the Democratic party.

JACKSON'S PRESIDENTIAL STRATEGY IN 1984 AND 1988

By 1983, blacks had achieved substantial integration within the Democratic party. Black membership on key standing committees of the party increased on average from 7.7 percent in 1972 to 20 percent in 1984.[14] But their new involvement within party affairs had not yielded the level of influence they sought in presidential nominations. It had been assumed by black Democrats that political integration into the national Democratic party would automatically yield greater influence in the political decision-making process within the party. Even in 1980, however, bargaining results between black Democrats and party leaders were not satisfactory. In particular, black Democrats were angered by Senator Edward Kennedy's endorsement of Mayor Jane Byrne for reelection and Vice-President Walter Mondale's endorsement of Richard Daley, Jr., in Chicago's mayoral primary election in 1983. The absence of a major party endorsement for black Congressman Harold Washington, the eventual winner of the Chicago mayoral race, symbolized the lack of support by party leaders toward black candidates and black interests. Blacks were also dissatisfied with the weak and ineffective response of Democrats in Congress to President Reagan and his policies. Black Democrats felt that their vote was being taken for granted, while the national party was in pursuit of the Reagan Democrats. Thus, although blacks were generally successful in their efforts to achieve greater representation within the party, many black party activists felt that their loyalty and numbers had not translated into real influence within the party.

At the grassroots level as well, frustration with the party began to swell during this period. Blacks began to feel that their vote was being taken for granted by the Democratic party. In a 1983 *Los Angeles Times* survey, while 44 percent of the blacks interviewed felt that "most Democrats are sincerely committed to helping blacks get ahead," a nearly equal percentage thought that "most Democrats don't really care much about black people."[15]

Jesse Jackson's announcement of his intention to seek the presidency caused considerable consternation among Democratic party leaders, both black and white. Many felt that Jackson's candidacy would hurt the party's chances of winning the presidential election, feeling that conservative and moderate white Democrats will not vote for a party that is seen as a captive of Jackson and black interests. Many white Democrats feared that Jackson's candidacy would help drive more whites into the Republican party. As Lorenzo Morris put it: "[Jackson] seemed to be rocking the party's boat at a time when it could barely stay afloat."[16] Jackson's candidacy was also not favored by many black elected officials because it was not seen as credible. They pledged their support instead to the eventual frontrunner, Walter Mondale.

The majority of blacks, however, welcomed Jackson's entry into the 1984 race. Many saw him as the candidate who would speak to those outside national politics, especially black Americans. Jackson's presidential candidacy was also viewed as a way for blacks to bargain more effectively with the Democratic party. In his mobilization of blacks voters, Jackson hoped to activate blacks politically. At the same time, he hoped to establish a different, more reciprocal relationship—a "new covenant, as he puts it" between blacks and the Democratic party, states Lucius Barker in his account of his participation at the 1984 Democratic national convention as a Jackson delegate.[17]

Jackson was not the first black American to run for president, but he was able to mobilize a much higher percent of the black community in support of his candidacy than had past black presidential contenders, including New York Congresswoman Shirley Chisholm, who ran in 1972. Jackson sought the party's nomination at exactly the right moment. Since the civil rights struggle of the 1960s, blacks had become an important and formidable voting bloc. The defection to the Republican party of white southern

Protestants, who had originally been the largest and most important con-stituent group member of the New Deal coalition, sharply increased the party's dependence upon the black vote. Although blacks still represented a minority voting power, the Democratic party stood to lose every presiden-tial election if it did not receive the lion's share of the black vote in each election year. Moreover, just as the Supreme Court decision on *Brown* had encouraged early black civil rights activists, the successive gains in the num-ber of blacks elected, and especially the election of black mayors in cities like Chicago, helped generate widespread feelings of new political optimism among blacks. Blacks felt more politically effective in 1984. In a 1984 national survey, 72 percent of blacks strongly agreed with the statement that "if enough blacks vote, they can make a difference in who gets elected President." Only 11 percent disagreed. They were also mobilizing during this period, registering to vote at record rates. Jackson's campaign took on the form of a political movement, especially since it was viewed as an attempt to restructure politics and government to bring about the inclusion of the powerless and politically disadvantaged.

According to political scientist Ronald Walters, the benefits of a black presidential strategy are several. First, black presidential candidates can expand the political influence and strength of blacks within the Democratic party by denying the black vote to any of the other candidates and posing a threat to the nomination for the frontrunner. Black presidential candi-dates can also assist the institutionalization of black politics, for not only will such a campaign organize the black vote every four years, but a black presidential contender can issue policy statements that could become part of the party's policy platform at the quadrennial national conventions.

Jackson's leverage was further enhanced by his decision to run with-in the Democratic party. Historically, black presidential campaigns were ineffective as bargaining vehicles for blacks because, as representatives of minor parties, black candidates did not carry much influence at the nation-al level. As a major party presidential contender, however, Jackson was able to compete in a number of nationally televised debates involving all the Democratic candidates. Jackson's participation in such debates made it pos-sible for him to acquire more media attention for his campaign issues, and enabled him to make direct appeals to the public in competition with other presidential contenders.

THE IMPACT OF JACKSON'S PRESIDENTIAL CAMPAIGNS

Jackson's political victories in 1984 and 1988 can be divided into the tangi-ble and the symbolic. His tangible achievements were few. Even though Jackson had captured the lion's share of the black Democratic vote in the two primary contests, his leverage strategy failed miserably. He obtained over 3 million votes in the Democratic primary, but entered the convention unable to wrest concessions from the party. All of the minority planks proposed by the Jackson camp were overwhelmingly defeated by the Mondale-Hart forces at the 1984 convention.[18]

One of the issues that Jackson raised at the 1984 convention, which was soundly defeated, concerned the Democratic party's delegate selection system. The 1984 system allocated delegates only to those candidates able to achieve a 20 percent threshold of votes in each congressional district. Moreover, one-seventh of the delegates at the 1984 convention were "super delegates," elected officials and party leaders who were selected by the party and not elected by the rank-and-file membership. Jackson pointed out that the threshold requirement unfairly penalized minority and urban voters, who were more likely to be concentrated in a few congressional districts. Such a scheme, Jackson also charged, distorted the one-person one-vote principle. The party responded by committing a few of its at-large delegate slots to Jackson, but the delegate allocation procedures and threshold rule remained in place. Thus, although Jackson won 18.3 percent of the total primary vote in 1984, he ended up with only 10 percent of the convention delegates.

Another equally important issue for the Jackson camp in 1984 was the run-off primary. The run-off primary system, used primarily in some southern states, is perceived as one of the lingering obstacles to increased black political representation. Because one of his stated objectives was to increase the number of black elected officials, ending the run-off system was important to Jackson. To win the party's nomination in a run-off primary system, a candidate must receive 50 percent or more of the vote. This system has traditionally worked to the disadvantage of black candidates, since whites would combine their votes to defeat a black candidate who had won with the plurality of the vote in the initial contest. This plank, however, like all the rest of Jackson's planks was defeated in 1984.

Another Jackson objective was to increase black and minority representation in the campaign organization for the party's nominee. Again, Jackson was not especially successful in this endeavor. Mondale hired one Jackson aide in August and pledged to hire more. In addition to having been penalized by the 20-percent threshold rule in the allocation of party delegates, Jackson's bargaining power with the party had been greatly undermined by two factors in 1984. First, Mondale advisors, fearing that early concessions to Jackson would cost the Democrats the election, only wanted to work with Jackson after the convention. Second, black leaders and delegates to the convention were divided over Jackson's candidacy. Jackson's 1984 candidacy had not been welcomed by prominent black elected officials who thought that the best candidate to defeat the incumbent Republican President Ronald Reagan was Walter Mondale.

Jackson's use of his presidential bid as a bargaining vehicle was somewhat more successful in 1988 than in 1984. In 1988, Jackson and Dukakis forces reached agreement in advance of the convention on several policies contained in the party's platform. They included the party's endorsement for the designation of South Africa as a terrorist state, same-day voter registration, DC statehood, and increased set-asides for minority contractors in federal contacts. Two of the three issues that Jackson supporters would still bring to the floor for discussion and amendment to the party platform at the convention—the call for a tax increase for the wealthy and a U.S. pledge against first use of nuclear weapons—were soundly defeated by a 2 to 1 margin. The third issue, favoring Palestinian self-determination, was never voted on. Finally, Jackson was able to revise the delegation selection rules for 1992. The threshold rule was lowered from 20 percent to 15 percent, but the number of super delegates was increased to 1 in 5 for the 1992 national convention. Finally, the selection of Ronald H. Brown, a black American, as the party's national chairman in 1988, was interpreted as a move by the party to appease black Democrats and a reaffirmation of the party's long-term commitment to blacks.

Jackson's presidential strategy was more successful in 1988 because he had significantly increased his base of support. Jackson was the second-place finisher out of a field of eight in the 1988 nominating contest, as opposed to the 1984 contest in which he placed third. Moreover, in 1988 he was able to increase his support among white Democrats even as he consolidated his base among blacks. In 1984, 77 percent of blacks voted for Jackson in the primary; in 1988, 92 percent had. Thus, in 1988, he doubled his primary vote from 3.3 to 6.7 million, constituting 29 percent of the total primary vote. Furthermore, Jackson delegates represented a force of 27 percent at the 1988 convention. And, in contrast to 1984, many black elected officials endorsed his bid. Jackson did better in 1988 because he and Illinois Senator Paul Simon were the only candidates who represented the "liberal, New Deal, Great Society tradition" in the Democratic party.[19] In 1984, half of the Democrats who ran represented that tradition. Jackson was able, therefore, to expand his base among traditional liberal Democrats with little effective competition. Table 8-3 shows the proportion of the vote Jackson received in the 1984 and 1988 Democratic primaries by state and the number of delegates he was awarded.

While neither of Jackson's presidential campaigns resulted in clear bargaining successes for black Americans, both nevertheless achieved important symbolic victories for blacks. Jackson's campaigns and his convention addresses gave voice to black Democrats who felt shut out from party politics. In the end, Jackson's presidential bids sent an important message to the party that blacks will no longer play a passive role in party politics. However, the means by which blacks can best exert influence over the nominating process and party politics are still not clear. In 1992, the party would nominate a "new Democrat," Bill Clinton, who campaigned against the old-style liberalism of his party, which is a major basis of black support.

Table 8-3   Jackson's Primary Vote and Delegates
at Democratic Convention, by State in 1984 and 1988

	1984		1988	
State	*Percentage of Primary Vote*	*Number of Delegates*	*Percentage of Primary Vote*	*Number of Delegates*
Alabama	19.6	9	43.6[a]	28
California	19.6	30	35.2	122
Connecticut	12.0	1	28.3	16
District of Columbia	67.3[a]	13	80.0[a]	18
Florida	12.4	1	20.0	35
Georgia	21.0	17	39.8[a]	42
Idaho	5.7	2	15.7	3
Illinois	21.0	7	32.3	57
Indiana	13.7	0	22.5	18
Louisiana	42.9[a]	24	35.5[a]	33
Maryland	25.5	17	28.7	25
Massachusetts	5.0	3	18.7	19
Mississippi[c]	—	—	44.4[a]	26
Nebraska	9.1	1	25.7	8
New Hampshire	5.3	0	7.8	0
New Jersey	23.6	9	32.9	19
New Mexico	11.9	1	28.1	8
New York	25.6	51	37.1	97
North Carolina	25.4	15	33.0	35
North Dakota	0	0	15.1	3
Ohio	16.4	10	27.5	46
Oregon	9.5	1	38.1	18
Pennsylvania	16.0	18	27.3	23
Rhode Island	8.7	0	15.2	3
South Dakota	5.2	0	5.4	1
Tennessee	25.3	15	20.7	20
Vermont	7.8	3	25.7	9
Virginia[c]	—	—	45.1[a]	42
West Virginia	6.7	0	14.0	0
Wisconsin	9.9	5	28.2	25
Puerto Rico	0	0	29.0[a]	8
Total	**18.3**	**384[b]**	**29.0**	**1,218[b]**

[a]Winner
[b]Includes delegates he won through state caucuses as well as primaries.
[c]Held caucus in 1984.
Source: Congressional Quarterly Inc.

THE END OF THE REBELLION?

In 1992, Bill Clinton captured the lion's share of the black vote, both in the primary and presidential elections, and he had done very little to recruit it. In 1996 he would be rewarded with a second term in office, winning, again, not only solid black support, but Jesse Jackson's endorsement as well. It would appear that more than a decade after 1984 the period of black rebellion within the Democratic party has ended.

Even Jesse Jackson, who picketed the White House after Clinton had pledged to sign into law a bill ending the federal guarantee to welfare benefits for poor families, fell in line between party leaders to strongly endorse Clinton for reelection at the 1996 Democratic convention. There was none of the rebellious spirit and little chastising language in Jackson's convention floor speech, as had been the case at the 1992 Democratic National Convention. In his 1992 speech, Jackson had given Clinton an indifferent endorsement; he also publicly rebuked those in the party, like Clinton, who had engineered the party's move to the political center, stating, "History will remember us not for our positioning, but for our principles. Not a move to the political center, left or right, but rather for our grasp on moral and ethical center of wrong and right." He then pointedly devoted the rest of his speech to outlining a liberal policy agenda, one that corresponded with the liberal interests of black Democrats, but one that the delegates had rejected in the drafting of their party's platform.

Compared to his 1992 address, Jackson had kinder words for Michael Dukakis in his 1988 convention speech than for Clinton, crediting Dukakis for having run a "well managed and dignified campaign," and for not having stooped to "demagoguery." Clinton, however, fared somewhat better than Walter Mondale had in 1984. Jackson's 1984 convention speech was perhaps his finest. Nonetheless, in it he made no mention of Walter Mondale by name, tersely pledging at the beginning of his the speech that he would be "proud to support the nominee of this convention for the Presidency of the United States."

Jackson's 1996 convention speech differed radically from his past three speeches insofar as there was little of his own political agenda in it. This speech's theme was party unity. He pointed out that 30 years earlier in Chicago, the Democrats were divided and lost the election to the Republicans. Pointing out that the "stakes are high" because the Republicans now control Congress, Jackson then went on to praise the President for his support of an assault weapons ban, a higher minimum wage and earned income tax credit, affirmative action and voting rights, concluding that Clinton deserved another four years.

It is difficult to reconcile Jackson's support for Clinton in 1996 with his indifference and even disdain for Clinton in 1992. Some political observers

Colin Powell, shown here addressing the Republican Convention, received highly positive ratings in the 1996 National Black Election Study. (*Greg Gibson/AP/Wide World Photos*)

might credit Bill Clinton and his legendary charm for Jackson's change of heart. Others, and specifically liberals critical of Clinton's policy record, have suggested that Jackson's shift was motivated by a personal agenda; his desire to maintain his access to the White House for his own political purposes, including helping his son who was recently elected to the House of Representatives from a Chicago district. Still others take Jackson at his word, that the stakes were profoundly high in 1996, while others would argue that what has happened to Jackson is only what has happened to countless insurgent leaders of the past; they become co-opted by the mainstream.[20]

The fact is that most blacks would not have supported a third presidential bid by Jesse Jackson in 1996. While over 80 percent in 1984 thought it had been a *good idea* for Jackson to run for president, 65 percent thought it would have been a *bad idea* if Jackson had run in 1996—even though Jackson's popularity among blacks remains as strong as it was in 1984. In fact, both Jackson and Powell received highly positive ratings, well in the 70s on a scale from 0 to 100, in the 1996 National Black Election Study. For comparison purposes, blacks were asked if it would have been a good idea or a bad idea for Colin Powell to run for the Republican party's presidential nomination. Most blacks, 56 percent, thought it would have been a bad idea as well.

Blacks' satisfaction with Bill Clinton's performance and their desire to maintain their representation in the executive branch of government also help explain why black Democrats were no longer at odds with their party.

Clinton's support among blacks has remained consistently strong. One reason for Clinton's strong showing among blacks is the economy, as we shall see in the next chapter. Many blacks felt that the economic conditions had improved for themselves and in general, and these attitudes shape their evaluation of Clinton's performance as president. In addition, blacks have become more conservative. The majority support Clinton's welfare reform law that imposes a five-year lifetime limit for welfare benefits for poor families. Blacks' shift to the political center is an important factor that explains why the rebellion has ended. Finally, the Republican party has not increased its appeal to blacks since the Reagan years, which reduced black GOP support to the single digits. Newt Gingrich's leadership of the House and its far-right Republican freshmen have reinforced the view among blacks that the GOP remains hostile to blacks and their interests.

The new political conservatism among blacks and the growth in the number of black Republicans, including J. C. Watts and Colin Powell, provide new opportunities for the GOP to restore some of its support among African Americans. However, nothing succeeds like success, as President Clinton has found. Black Democrats have enjoyed the benefits of having a Democrat in the White House, even a moderate one, and it would appear that their loyalties are as strongly attached to the Democratic party as ever.

TOPICS FOR DISCUSSION

1. It has become obvious that both the Democratic and Republican parties have not been very responsive to political aspirations of African Americans. What alternatives do blacks have to the major parties? What would be the advantages and disadvantages to blacks forming their own national third-party organization?

2. Jesse Jackson ran twice for the Democratic party's presidential nomination, in 1984 and 1988, in an effort to make the party more responsive to black interests. Were his bids successful or unsuccessful toward that end? Should Jackson pursue the presidency a third time? Should he run as a Democratic or as an independent?

3. Suppose you were a consultant to the Republican party whose job was to attract more blacks to the party. What would you propose?

SUGGESTED READINGS

Baer, Denise L., and David A. Bositis. *Elite Cadres and Party Coalitions: Representing the Public in Party Politics.* Westport, CT: Greenwood Press, 1988.

Barker, Lucius J. *Our Time Has Come.* Urbana, IL, and Chicago, IL: University of Illinois Press, 1989. A firsthand account of a political scientist's experiences as a Jackson delegate at the 1984 Democratic party's national convention.

Barker, Lucius J., and Ronald W. Walters, eds. *Jesse Jackson's 1984 Presidential Campaign.* Urbana, IL, and Chicago, IL: University of Illinois Press, 1989. Contains essays that analyze the significance of Jesse Jackson's 1984 campaign for president.

Beck, Paul Allen. *Party Politics in America,* 8th ed. New York: Longman, 1997. Considers the nature, role, and functions of political parties in the American political system.

Burnham, Walter D. *Critical Elections and the Mainsprings of American Politics.* New York: W. W. Norton & Co., 1970. An excellent analysis of aggregate electoral behavior in historical perspective.

Carmines, Edward G., and James A. Stimson. *Issue Evolution, Race, and the Transformation of American Politics.* Princeton, NJ: Princeton University Press, 1989.

Glaser, James M. *Race, Campaign Politics, and the Realignment in the South.* New Haven, CT: Yale University Press, 1996. Case studies of special congressional elections in the South that reveal the different ways Democratic and Republican candidates have handled the race issue.

Marable, Manning. *Black American Politics: From the Washington Marches to Jesse Jackson.* London: Thetford Press, 1985.

Morris, Lorenzo, ed. *The Social and Political Implications of the 1984 Jesse Jackson Presidential Campaign.* New York: Praeger, 1990.

Pinderhughes, Dianne. "Political Choices: A Realignment in Partisanship among Black Voters?" In *The State of Black America.* New York: National Urban League, 1986. Pinderhughes discusses political alternatives to the Democratic party for blacks.

Reed, Adolph, Jr. *The Jesse Jackson Phenomenon.* New Haven, CT: Yale University Press, 1987. A highly negative assessment of Jackson's 1984 presidential bid that also characterizes it as a phenomenon of the post-civil rights era of black politics.

Robinson, Pearl T. "Whither the Future of Blacks in the Republican Party?" *Political Science Quarterly* 97, 2 (1982), pp. 207–231.

Rosenstone, Steven J., Roy L. Behr, and Edward H. Lazarus. *Third Parties in America.* Princeton, NJ: Princeton University Press, 1984.

Sundquist, James L. *Dynamics of the Party System.* Washington, DC: The Brookings Institution, 1983. A study of the alignments and realignments of political parties.

Tate, Katherine. "Structural Dependence or Group Loyalty? The Black Vote in 1992." In *Democracy's Feast: Elections in America,* ed. Herbert F. Weisberg. Chatham, NJ: Chatham House Publishers, Inc., 1995, pp. 179–194. An empirical examination of blacks' extraordinary allegiance to the Democratic party and their presidential vote in 1992.

Walters, Ronald W. *Black Presidential Politics in America: A Strategic Approach.* Albany, NY: State University of New York Press, 1988. Based both on historical analysis and his role as a Jackson campaign strategist, political scientist Ron Walters outlines a model of how blacks, as a numerical minority, can expand their power and influence in party and presidential politics.

Walton, Hanes, Jr. *Black Political Parties: An Historical and Political Analysis.* New York: Free Press, 1972. Traces the historical development of black political parties.

Weiss, Janet J. *Farewell to the Party of Lincoln.* Princeton, NJ: Princeton University Press, 1983.

NOTES

1. Paul Allen Beck, *Party Politics in America,* 8th ed. (New York: Longman, 1997), Chapter 2.
2. Steven J. Rosenstone, Roy L. Behr, and Edward H. Lazarus, *Third Parties in America* (Princeton, NJ: Princeton University Press), see Chapter 2.

3. Maurice Duverger, *Political Parties: Their Organization and Activity in the Modern World*, trans. Barbara and Robert North (New York: Wiley, 1963).

4. Paul R. Abramson, John H. Aldrich, and David W. Rohde, *Change and Continuity in the 1992 Elections* (Washington, DC: Congressional Quarterly Press, 1994), pp. 224–230.

5. Nancy J. Weiss, *Farewell to the Party of Lincoln* (Princeton, NJ: Princeton University Press, 1983).

6. Edward G. Carmines and James A. Stimson, *Issue Evolution* (Princeton, NJ: Princeton University Press, 1989).

7. James M. Glaser, *Race, Campaign Politics & the Realignment in the South* (New Haven, CT: Yale University Press, 1996).

8. Carmines and Stimson, *Issue Evolution*, p. 34.

9. Fred Powledge, *Free At Last?* (New York: HarperPerennial, 1991), pp. 595–600.

10. Parker, *Black Votes Count*, pp. 147–151.

11. Walters, *Black Presidential Politics*, p. 58.

12. Walters, *Black Presidential Politics*, p. 61. Emphasis in original.

13. See Katherine Tate, "Structural Dependence or Group Loyalty? The Black Vote in 1992," in *Democracy's Feast: Elections in America*, ed. Herbert F. Weisberg (Chatham, NJ: Chatham House Publishers, Inc., 1995), pp. 179–194; Hanes Walton, Jr., "Black Presidential Participation and the Critical Election Theory," in *Social and Political Implications of the 1984 Jesse Jackson Presidential Campaign*, ed. Lorenzo Morris (New York: Praeger, 1990); and Walters, *Black Presidential Politics*; Dianne Pinderhughes, "Political Choices: A Realignment in Partisanship among Black Voters?" in *The State of Black America* (New York: National Urban League, 1986).

14. Walters, *Black Presidential Politics*, p. 65.

15. I. A. Lewis and William Schneider, "Black Voting, Bloc Voting, and the Democrats." *Public Opinion* 6, 5 (1983), pp. 12–15, 59.

16. Lorenzo Morris, ed., *The Social and Political Implications of the 1984 Jesse Jackson Presidential Campaign* (New York: Praeger, 1990), p. 11.

17. Lucius Barker, *Our Time Has Come* (Chicago, IL, and Urbana, IL: University of Illinois Press, 1989), p. 183.

18. Barker, *Our Time*, p. 156.

19. Paul R. Abramson, John H. Aldrich, and David W. Rohde, *Change and Continuity in the 1988 Elections* (Washington, DC: Congressional Quarterly Press, Inc., 1990), Chapter 1.

20. Robert C. Smith, "Black Power and the Transformation from Protest to Politics," *Political Science Quarterly* 96, 3 (1981), pp. 431–443; Frances Fox Piven and Richard A. Cloward, *Poor People's Movements: Why They Succeed, How They Fail* (New York: Pantheon Press, 1977).

Chapter 9

Black Voters
and Electoral Politics

Anybody that really wants to vote could have done that without welfare offices getting into the business of registering people to vote.... The essence of it is: Are we going to protect the precious right to vote in America or are we going to open up the floodgates?

—Kirk Fordice, Governor of Mississippi: His response to the recent Supreme Court's ruling against his state's failure to fully implement the 1993 federal Motor-Voter Law.[1]

The 1965 Voting Rights Act struck down a host of legal barriers, including literacy tests and poll taxes, that southern states adopted at the turn of the century to keep blacks from registering and voting.[2] The 1965 law's effectiveness was impressive; in a relatively short period of time—less than three years after the law took effect—black registration in the 11 southern states covered under the act shot up from an average of 12 percent in 1947 to 62 percent in 1968.[3] Table 9-1 shows the considerable progress blacks have made in registration and voting. Twelve percent of the population, blacks would cast 10 percent of the nation's vote for president by 1984.

Four decades have now passed since the Voting Rights Act was signed into law by President Lyndon B. Johnson. And, in fact, unless Congress decides otherwise, the Voting Rights Act is set to expire in 2007. Has the strategy of black voting lived up to its promise? Are blacks finding that their votes make a difference in their politics and in their lives?

Determining the benefits of black voting and of black elected officials is a complicated and arduous endeavor. As discussed in Chapter 4, the election of blacks to political office has yielded mixed results. In this chapter, we examine this question from the vantage point of blacks themselves. What do blacks think of electoral politics? Do blacks feel that they are benefiting from voting, or is disenchantment with electoral politics spreading? In *An*

Table 9-1   Reported Voter Registration and Turnout among Blacks

	Reported Registered			Reported Voting		
	Voting-Age Population (Thousands)	Number Registered (Thousands)	Registration Rate (Percentage)	Total Votes Cast (Thousands)	Votes Cast by Blacks (Thousands)	Proportion of Total Votes Cast by Blacks (Percentage)
1966	10,533	6,345	60.3	62,518	4,398	7.0
1968	10,935	7,238	66.2	78,964	6,300	8.0
1970	11,472	6,971	60.8	65,888	4,992	7.6
1972	13,493	8,837	65.5	85,755	7,032	8.2
1974	14,175	7,778	54.9	63,164	4,786	7.6
1976	14,927	8,725	58.5	86,698	7,273	8.4
1978	15,636	8,921	57.1	69,587	5,812	8.4
1980	16,423	9,849	60.0	93,066	8,287	8.9
1982	17,624	10,411	59.1	80,310	7,581	9.4
1984	18,432	12,223	66.3	101,878	10,293	10.1
1986	19,020	12,166	64.0	81,564	8,225	10.1
1988	19,692	12,700	64.0	102,223	10,144	10.0
1990	20,371	11,968	58.8	83,480	7,978	9.6
1992	21,039	13,442	63.9	113,866	11,371	10.0
1994	21,779	12,762	58.5	87,386	8,095	9.3
1996	22,483	14,267	63.5	105,017	11,386	10.8

Source: Current Population Reports.

Economic Theory of Democracy,[4] Anthony Downs argues that rational citizens won't vote if the costs of voting outweigh the benefits of it. Thus, who votes in the black community? How are they voting, and on what basis? Finally, given the impact of the 1965 act on rates of black officeholding, what do blacks think of their elected representatives in Washington?

WHO VOTES IN THE UNITED STATES?
THEORIES OF POLITICAL PARTICIPATION

After the Civil War, laws in the South were designed to prevent blacks from going to the polls. The South, however, was not alone in limiting its franchise to certain groups. The Constitution had left voting requirements for the states to devise. Initially, voting was limited to property owners in the original 13 colonies. In addition to race, states assigned the right to vote on the basis of gender, economic status, literacy, religion, age, and other criteria. By 1972, however, states had moved closer to accepting citizenship as the universal criterion for voting rights.

Though suffrage was extended to a wider and more inclusive pool of citizens, Americans have always favored an electoral system where full participation by all of its citizens is discouraged. One way the American system discourages voting is by requiring all voters to be registered to vote prior to election day, before interest in the campaign can develop for most. Registration laws vary state to state. In 1992, the average closing date for registration was three weeks before election day.[5] More states now allow voters to register on the same day they vote and, increasingly, states permit voters to register by mail. Most would-be voters, however, must generally travel to inconveniently located state and county offices in order to register. Thirty states, in fact, have no facilities for weekend or evening registration. While the 1993 National Voter Registration Act, known as the Motor-Voter law, will ease some of the restrictions states place on the act of voting, registration is a burden, a hurdle that prevents a large proportion of Americans from voting. Registration is also a burden that falls unevenly on certain classes of voters. Research has established that the young, the poor, the least educated, and those who rent are less likely to participate in elections than older, wealthier, college-educated, and home-owning citizens.

The impact of registration laws on voting participation is but one reason why America lags so far behind other developed democratic states in voter turnout. Those who study voting participation offer two reasons other than electoral laws for the generally low participation rates in this country, one of which is related to election itself. Politics has its own effect on political participation. People who ordinarily don't participate are more likely to vote in competitive races. Hotly contested elections can inspire more people to vote. The money spent by candidates on advertisements can attract the interest of the typical non-voter. Parties can initiate get-out-the-vote drives to mobilize their supporters on election day. While 20 million people registered in motor vehicle and social service departments in the first year that the Motor-Voter law took effect, voter turnout in the 1996 presidential election dropped to its lowest level of this century. Fewer than half (49 percent) of Americans eligible to vote participated in this election. One important reason why turnout was so low was because the presidential race between Bill Clinton and Bob Dole was not competitive, as Clinton led Dole by a comfortable margin in the polls over many months in advance of the election.

While some scholars have emphasized the effects of the campaign, the election, and the institutional and legal electoral structures that regulate political participation on voting participation, the dominant theories of political participation put greater emphasis on the individual. The social characteristics of citizens and their political attitudes have been identified as the key determinants of voter participation,[6] as have education and money. Formal education is positively related to participation, as one set of researchers point out, because "schooling increases one's capacity for understanding and working with complex, abstract, and intangible subjects, that is, subjects like politics."[7] Educated Americans are more likely to be familiar with the political process, to know how to register to vote, and to follow politics and learn the names of the candidates who are running for public office.

Income, by comparison, generally has a smaller, though still significant, effect on voter turnout. Personal finances are tied to participation because poor people have less time and energy for the "nonessentials" in life, including politics and voting. Steven J. Rosenstone and John Mark Hansen explain the link between income and participation this way:

> Citizens with lots of income can simply afford to do more—of everything—than citizens with little money. The wealthy have discretionary income that they can contribute directly to political parties, candidates, political action committees, and other causes. Moreover, money is fungible—it can be freely converted into other political resources that make it easier for people to take part in politics. A car is not a necessary condition for political action, for example, but having one makes it much easier to get to a school board meeting, a political rally, or a candidate's campaign headquarters. Money can be used to hire someone to do the daily chores—to clean the house, buy the groceries, cook dinner, babysit the kids—and free up time for politics. Thus, if people want to participate in politics, money makes it easier for them to do so.[8]

Moreover, those with a strong sense of civic duty and faith in the system, as well as in their own abilities to influence politics, are more likely to participate. Not surprisingly, people who are interested in politics and are strongly attached to the political parties are also more likely to participate. These political and psychological attitudes are related to socioeconomic status as well. Higher-status individuals are more likely to feel a civic obligation in participating; they are more efficacious and more politically aware. Not only do affluent and educated Americans express more confidence in their ability to influence government (this attitude is known as "internal efficacy"), they are also strong in "external efficacy," believing that the government is generally responsive to the interests of average Americans.

BLACK PARTICIPATION AND GROUP-BASED RESOURCES

The implications of the theories of political participation for black political participation are clear: Given that registering and voting are so strongly tied to socioeconomic status, black Americans are expected to participate in politics at lower levels than whites. Blacks are not only "resource poor" in that many lack the necessary political skills, money, and levels of education that whites generally possess, but like the poor in general, many blacks lack the basic motivation and incentives essential for political participation. Given their long history of exclusion from politics, blacks are more alienated and less efficacious than whites. Blacks, in short, are weak across most of the individual attributes (education, income, political trust, external and internal efficacy, political interest) that researchers have identified as promoting political participation.

Nevertheless, while blacks are clearly handicapped by their social status in politics, empirical studies conducted in the late 1960s found blacks to be more politically active than whites once differences in socioeconomic status were taken into account. For blacks, something other than election laws, election-specific forces, and socioeconomic status is related to their participation rates. Researchers have established that blacks are able to participate at high levels in politics in spite of their political disadvantages through the utilization of nontraditional group-based political resources.[9] These resources are the same ones that were critical to explaining the emergence of the modern-day civil rights movement. They include the development and maintenance of a racial ideology that encourages political action, as well as membership in indigenous community and political organizations.

Race consciousness has been shown to promote black political participation. Blacks' self-awareness as a discriminated and disadvantaged group in society leads them to be more politically active than other disadvantaged groups who lack a comparable collective identity. Membership in black political organizations and institutions, including the black church, has been identified as crucial to the success of the modern-day black civil rights movement. While these organizations gave structure to the protest movement, many, operating well before the passage of the 1965 Voting Rights Act, also helped register and mobilize black voters. Although religious groups, such as those affiliated with the Christian Right, have recently become active in national politics, black churches have traditionally been involved in politics. Contrary to their depiction as separate spheres, black religious life and politics have traditionally commingled. Aldon Morris labeled the black church as the "institutional center" of the black civil rights movement.[10] Black churches have also been active in electoral politics. Jesse Jackson's 1984 bid for the Democratic party's presidential nomination was greatly aided by the black church. Jackson relied upon a network of black ministers and churches to raise campaign funds and mobilize black voters. Churches have also been instrumental in the election of blacks to local governments.

In general, organizational membership has been shown to be one of the most powerful predictors of political participation. Members of voluntary associations, both political and social, are more likely to be politically active than nonmembers. Participation is promoted by organizations either through the dissemination of political information or, as in the case of political organizations, through the involvement of members in activities that are explicitly political. Black organizations, especially, have the potential for offsetting the disadvantages that individual blacks carry within the political arena. Black organizations can pool scarce resources, such as money and time, educate their members about political matters, and provide additional incentives for getting involved in politics.

In spite of the church's historically documented role in the civil rights struggle, as well as its activism in the 1984 and 1988 presidential candidacies of Jesse Jackson, the notion of the black church as a base of black political activity has always been questioned by some social analysts. Beginning in the 1930s, a number of sociologists, including E. Franklin Frazier, have argued that the black church's "pie-in-the-sky," other-worldly orientation and its emotionalism work against the development of a black political consciousness and "this-world" concern with social change. Most recently, political scientist Adolph Reed, Jr., has asserted that the black church is at odds with the principles of democracy.[11] He claims that despite the church's involvement in Jackson's presidential bids, church political activism is incompatible with modern, democratic political processes, given that the black church is intrinsically "nonpolitical," authoritarian, and conservative.

Critics of the black church base their arguments on the claim that religion is often depoliticizing, that is, "the opiate of the masses." Gary Marx's book, *Protest and Prejudice*,[12] published in 1967, is frequently cited as empirical documentation of the antithetical relationship that exists between religion and politics for blacks. Marx found that religious blacks were less likely to be supportive of black civil rights militancy than nonreligious blacks. This negative association between religiosity and militancy held even when other factors, such as age, region, and social class, were taken into account. More surprising than this, however, was his discovery that pro-militant blacks were more likely to belong to conventional religious denominations, including interracial churches, such as Episcopal, Presbyterian, and Catholic churches. Marx concluded that the nature of religion found in independent black churches is "an important factor working against the widespread radicalization of [blacks]."

In spite of the fact that his study is frequently presented as empirical evidence that the black church has a strong depoliticizing effect, Marx did not actually examine the effects of religiosity and church membership on black voting behavior. It has not been established in any published account that religious blacks are less likely to be active in politics than nonreligious blacks. In their book, *The Black Church in the African American Experience*,[13] C. Eric Lincoln and Lawrence H. Mamiya seriously challenge the sociological studies of the black church that characterize it as a nonpolitical, conservative institution. Throughout the period of slavery, they argue, many black clergy were active in the cause of emancipation. Moreover, the church has also served as a training center for black leaders and has always stressed to its congregates participation in the political process in order to fulfill their duties as "responsible American citizens."

A further problem with Marx's analysis is that it failed to differentiate between the sectlike and churchlike dimensions of religiosity. Sectarianism or the dimension of religious beliefs that embodies a strong other-worldly orientation, tends to depress civil rights militancy and political activism, while religious beliefs are not in conflict with a protest orientation. Black religious sectarianism is in decline. According to Lincoln and Mamiya, black Pentecostals, such as the Church of God in Christ, have moved closer to black mainstream churches in doctrine and teachings. In their 1983 survey of 1,894 black clergy, Lincoln and Mamiya found an almost absolute majority to be supportive of social change achieved through political action. Nine out of ten clergy whom they interviewed said that they would approve of clergy in their churches taking part in protest marches on civil rights. Furthermore, 92 percent felt that churches should express their views on day-to-day social and political questions. Though a slightly smaller percentage, fully 80 percent of the Church of God in Christ clergy responded positively to these questions as well.

One major difference between the civil rights era and the new electoral phase of black politics is the absolute numbers of blacks seeking office. Black officeseeking, particularly in elections involving blacks as political newcomers, seems to be associated with astoundingly high black turnouts. During the late 1960s and 1970s, blacks registered in unprecedented numbers. Not only did this encourage blacks to seek office for the very first time, but the presence of black candidates further inspired additional numbers of blacks to register. For example, in 1967, when Carl Stokes was elected mayor of Cleveland, roughly 80 percent of blacks who were eligible to vote did vote. In the 1983 general election of Harold Washington in Chicago, approximately 82 percent of voting-eligible blacks turned out. Blacks presumably turn out and vote in greater numbers when a black is running for office because of (1) greater group loyalty and pride and (2) greater interest, given the historic nature of the event (the candidate may be the first black to seek such an office). Black turnout may also be higher in such elections because black candidates often campaign more intensively and spend greater resources in black communities precisely to get out the black vote. Clearly, then, black officeseeking should be viewed as a collective political resource of blacks.

PREDICTING BLACK CAMPAIGN ACTIVISM

Table 9-2 displays the determinants of campaign activism among blacks in the 1984 and 1996 elections. The effects of both types of determinants as discussed above are shown: (1) the conventional measures of socioeconomic status or SES and attitudinal variables, such as political trust, and (2) three measures of the group-based political resources (race consciousness, political activism in churches, and membership in black organizations).

Campaign activism is measured as the total number of campaign actions a respondent engaged in during the election year; it ranges from zero (no acts) to four (engaged in all four acts). These acts are (1) canvassing for votes for certain candidates, (2) attending political meetings and rallies, (3) helping with voter registration and turnout drives, and (4) donating money. Most people do not participate directly in campaigns; the average number of acts engaged in by the black respondents in 1984 was less than one. Table 9-2 shows the estimated effects of the predictor variables and their standard errors in parentheses. The superscript letters (a, b) indicate whether the relationship is statistically valid or not. Coefficients without these letters are indistinguishable from zero, indicating that no independent relationship between the predictor measure and campaign activism likely exists. The results shown in Table 9-2 establish that, in contrast to the group-based resource measures, only a few of the standard predictors of political participation are associated with black campaign activism.

Of the attitudinal variables, the two most strongly and consistently related to black campaign activism were also the most explicitly election-

Table 9-2   Demographic and Attitudinal Determinants of Campaign Activism among Blacks in 1984 and 1996

| | Campaign Activism (0 to 4 scale) | | | |
| | 1984 | | 1996 | |
Independent Variables	B	(SE)	B	(SE)
Constant	−.39	(.39)	.78[a]	(.34)
SES and Attitudinal Predictors				
Gender (male)	.10	(.09)	.25[a]	(.09)
Age (young-old)	.003	(.003)	−.005	(.003)
Education (low-high)	−.03	(.02)	.09	(.05)
Family income (low-high)	.02	(.02)	−.02	(.02)
Region (the South)	−.18[a]	(.09)	−.10	(.08)
Homeowner (yes)	.16	(.10)	.05	(.09)
System responsiveness (low-high)	.09[a]	(.04)	−.02	.01
Political trust (low-high)	−.07	(.04)	−.05	(.05)
Political interest (low-high)	.10[b]	(.03)	.19[b]	(.03)
Partisan (yes)	.13[a]	(.05)	.17[a]	(.08)
Group-Based Resources				
Racial identification (low-high)	.07[a]	(.03)	.04[a]	(.02)
Black organization (member)	.50[b]	(.11)	.33[b]	(.09)
Political church (member)	.49[b]	(.10)	.14	(.09)
Total cases	**605**		**574**	
R Square	.25		.21	

[a] p < .05
[b] p < .01
Source: The 1984 and 1996 National Black Election Studies.

specific: political interest and partisanship. Those who expressed a strong interest in politics were more likely to be campaign activists. Similarly, partisans—those who expressed a strong psychological attachment to either the Republican or Democratic party—tended to be the most active. Among the demographic variables, black men were more likely to be involved in campaigns in 1996, although not significantly more so than black women in 1984. Southerners were less involved in political campaigns in 1984, but region was not related to campaign involvement in 1996.

All three group-based measures—race identification and membership in either black organizations or politically-active churches—strongly affected the level of campaign activities that blacks engaged in in the 1984 and 1996 elections. Their effects are somewhat less in 1996 than in 1984, however. Moreover, being a member of a politically active church, one where voting is encouraged, was not related to campaign activism in 1996. Nevertheless, even in the 1996 election, which was a low-key affair (lacking the drama and excitement of 1984 that was generated by Jesse Jackson's entry into the presidential race), these black political resources helped promote political participation.

Given the fact that education and income were unrelated to campaign activism in both years, it would be tempting to conclude that class does not matter. That would be wrong. First, black political participation is greatly affected by social status, albeit indirectly, through its effect on factors such as political interest and partisanship. For example, college-educated blacks, in particular, were more likely to be interested in political campaigns and to feel that they have voice and representation in government. For example, 57 percent of black college graduates reported being "very much interested" in the 1984 political campaigns, in comparison to 34 percent of black high-school graduates. Secondly, while the group-based political resources can reduce the racial disparities found in voting and other forms of political participation, they may not help much to reduce the class-participation gap in the black community. College-educated blacks were found to be more race conscious and more likely to be members of black organizations than those with less education. And while membership in black organizations and politically active churches promotes political participation, such institutions are rare in ghetto communities. In fact, a study of the Detroit area found that, even taking into account individual differences in income, education, and political interest, blacks living in poverty-stricken neighborhoods were less likely to participate in politics than blacks in working-class and middle-income communities.[14] Poverty, therefore, packs a double whammy: Being poor makes blacks less likely to vote and living among the poor deprives them of social networks and institutions that have been shown to facilitate participation.

To conclude, the traditional correlates of political participation—socioeconomic status, political interest, and faith in the political system—affect black political participation. In general, the poorest and least-educated blacks are less likely to participate than affluent and college-educated blacks. But just as important as SES and political attitudes are the collective political resources blacks possess that can offset the disadvantages blacks have as individual actors. These group-based resources include race consciousness, membership in black organizations, and in churches that are politically active. The fourth group resource is black officeseeking. Black participation can be markedly higher in elections having black candidates.

RACE AND VOTER TURNOUT: A SECOND LOOK

As stated at the beginning of this chapter, racial differences in political participation have greatly diminished as a result of the 1965 Voting Rights Act. However, beginning with the 1988 elections, the racial gap in voter turnout in national elections has re-emerged with increasingly fewer blacks than whites going to the polls (see Table 9-3). In 1984, the racial gap in voting was at its lowest ever of −5.6; by 1994, this gap grew by an additional 4 percentage points to −9.6. In 1996, however, the racial gap in voting narrowed as white voter participation dropped sharply in this election.

Notably, in spite of the large rate of increase in voting in 1992 from 1988, racial differences in turnout in the 1992 election increased the racial gap by two percentage points. Also, the racial gap in voter registration nearly doubled in size from −3.4 percent in 1988 to −6.2 percent in 1992. The 1984 presidential elections remains the highwater mark of black voter turnout.

Since 1968, nonvoting among registrants has been substantially higher among blacks than among whites. In fact, among blacks who claimed to

Table 9-3   Voting and Registration by Race in Presidential Elections, 1964–1996

	Registration			Voting		
	Black	*White*	*Racial Gap*	*Black*	*White*	*Racial Gap*
1964	—	—	—	58.5*	70.7	−12.2
1968	66.2	75.4	−9.2	57.6	69.1	−11.5
1972	65.5	73.4	−7.9	52.1	64.5	−12.4
1976	58.5	68.3	−9.8	48.7	60.9	−12.2
1980	60.0	68.4	−8.4	50.5	60.9	−10.4
1984	66.3	69.6	−3.3	55.8	61.4	−5.6
1988	64.5	67.9	−3.4	51.5	59.1	−7.6
1992	63.9	70.1	−6.2	54.0	63.6	−9.6
1996	63.5	67.7	−4.2	50.6	56.0	−5.4

*Includes blacks and other races in 1964.
Source: *Current Population Reports.*

244

Chapter 9

be registered voters, 15.4 percent reported not voting in the 1992 election. In contrast, only 9.3 percent of white registrants reported not having voted in this election. Nonvoting among black registrants was especially pronounced during the 1972 and 1988 presidential elections, as was nonvoting among white registrants during these elections. The 1972 and 1988 elections were similar in that the Democrats were organizationally weak and divided in their effort to unseat incumbent Republican presidents. But indifference among black voters to presidential politics ran particularly high in the 1988 presidential election. Many blacks who failed to vote in 1988 had solidly backed Jesse Jackson in the 1988 Democratic presidential primaries and caucuses.[15] The nonvoting among black registrants in this election, in fact, exceeded 20 percent.

The racial gap in voter participation may signal black dissatisfaction with electoral politics. There appear to be substantial minorities of blacks who are indifferent to their choices for president on election day, and who choose not to vote. Who are these "nonvoting" black voters? Although black women are more likely than black men to be registered voters, they are not more likely to turnout to vote. As shown in Table 9-4, among registered voters, the black gender gap in turnout among registrants is fairly negligible (under two percentage points). Generational differences in participation rate, in fact, are more striking than gender differences. Younger blacks are less likely to vote than older blacks, and even among those registered to vote, blacks under 35 years of age are less likely to turn out.

Gender-generational interactions also relate strongly to the propensity to vote among black registrants. Of these registered to vote, young black males, those 25 years old and under, are the least likely to turn out to vote on election day. Over 30 percent of black men, 18–24 years of age and registered to vote, failed to vote in the 1992 presidential election, in contrast to 21 percent of black women in the same age category.[16]

Table 9-4   Percentage of Registered Voters Who Did Not Vote
by Race and Hispanic Origin, 1968–1996

	Blacks	Whites	Hispanics
1968	13.0	8.4	—
1972	20.4	12.2	15.7
1976	16.7	10.8	16.7
1980	15.9	10.9	17.8
1984	15.8	11.8	18.5
1988	20.1	13.0	18.9
1992	15.4	9.3	17.5
1996	20.2	17.3	25.0

Source: Calculated from Tables 1 and 2 in *Current Population Reports*, P-20, no. 192, 253, 370, 405, 440, 466, and 504.

THE ECONOMY AND ITS EFFECT ON THE BLACK VOTE

In the previous section, we saw that the lower economic standing of blacks vis-à-vis whites means that their rates of political participation are lower, even while they have some resources that promote voter participation. The income gap between blacks and whites also greatly affects their politics. Empirical studies have confirmed that there is a relationship between macroeconomic conditions and support for incumbent presidents—that the economy largely predicts the outcome of presidential elections.[17] Put simply, incumbent presidents are rewarded in economic good times and punished in economic bad times. Blacks and whites had very different evaluations of the economy during the 1980s, while they shared a common assessment of it in the 1990s. The gulf between black and white economic assessments explains the wide divergence in their evaluations of Ronald Reagan during the 1980s, and their common rejection of George Bush in 1992 and preference for Bill Clinton.

A comparison of blacks' and whites' perceptions of economic conditions, shown in Table 9-5, indicates that blacks and whites perceived their personal economic situation in like terms, even as they disagreed sharply in their assessments of the economic situation. Whereas 46 percent of whites thought that the economy had improved in 1984, only 20 percent of blacks saw improvement. In fact, blacks had the opposite assessment; nearly half (48 percent) of the blacks surveyed thought the economy had gotten worse in 1984. Blacks and whites also disagreed significantly over how blacks as a group were faring economically in 1984. The vast majority of whites, 83 percent, thought blacks' economic situation had either improved or stayed the same from 1983 to 1984. In contrast, 35 percent of blacks thought the group's economic position had worsened during this period. Blacks had suffered the most in the early 1980s, especially as a result of the 1982 recession. Poverty and unemployment had increased in the black community under the Reagan administration. The number of black families living below the poverty line increased during this period, and, even though real earning power dropped throughout the nation, economic conditions were more severe in the black community.

As Table 9-5 shows, the economic picture changed in 1992; nearly everyone, both black and white, thought that the national economy was in poor health. A whopping 80 percent of whites and about 84 percent of blacks said that the economy had gotten worse over the past year. These evaluations shaped their votes in 1992. Bill Clinton's dual success with blacks and whites owed much to the fact that not only did increasing percentages of both groups feel that their own economic situation had deteriorated over the past year, but also both groups were in relative agreement about the state of the nation's economy. A scant 3 percent of blacks and a mere 5 percent of whites thought that the economy had gotten better in 1992.

Four years after the first Clinton administration, blacks gave their most positive assessment of their personal economic well-being ever. In contrast to previous presidential election years, a large majority (58 percent) said that their economic situation had gotten better over the past year, while only one-fifth of the respondents said that their economic situation had deteriorated. The fact of the matter is that black family incomes have improved since 1992. Black poverty has dropped to its lowest level ever. According to the U.S. Census Bureau, which monitors poverty rates, black poverty dropped to its lowest level ever in 1996.

Survey data have shown that voters' evaluations of their personal economic situation explain little about their voting preferences, while their perceptions of the health of the general economy explain a great deal. Among blacks, however, their assessments of the economy combine with how they are faring economically as a group to affect their presidential vote. In fact, their perceptions of group's economic position has a stronger effect on the direction of the black vote in presidential elections than their attitudes about the health of the national economy. Even taking into account party membership and ideology, blacks who thought that group's position became worse over the past year were more likely to cast votes for the Democratic candidates challenging incumbent Republican presidents. African Americans use their perceptions of the interests of African Americans as a group as a "proxy" for their own interests because the two are perceived as strongly intertwined.[18] Many African Americans feel that their individual fates are tied to that of the group's. Viewing politics from an economic-group lens, therefore, can simplify politics for

Table 9-5   Black and White Economic Assessments,
1984, 1988, 1992, and 1996—Personal and National (Percentages)

	1984		1988		1992		1996	
	Black	White	Black	White	Black	White	Black	White
Personal economic situation:								
got better	46.0	45.0	41.0	43.0	26.0	31.0	58.0	39.0
stayed the same	21.0	29.0	28.0	33.0	33.5	36.0	21.0	44.5
got worse	33.0	26.0	32.0	24.0	41.0	34.0	21.5	16.0
Total Number Polled	**1,136**	**1,912**	**264**	**1,689**	**316**	**2,066**	**1,166**	**1,446**
National economy:								
got better	20.0	46.0	10.0	20.0	3.0	5.0	31.0	44.5
stayed the same	32.0	33.0	51.0	50.0	11.0	17.5	39.0	24.0
got worse	48.0	21.0	39.0	30.0	84.0	80.0	30.0	31.5
Total Number Polled	**1,127**	**1,883**	**248**	**1,639**	**316**	**2,048**	**1,162**	**1,449**

Sources: The 1984 National Black Election Study, 1996 National Black Election Study, and the 1984, 1988, 1992, and 1996 American National Election Studies.

black voters. Blacks can simply support presidents whose policies benefited blacks economically and reject those whose policies or agendas hurt blacks' economic interests and standing.

BLACK ATTITUDES TOWARD THEIR
ELECTED REPRESENTATIVES IN CONGRESS

In 1928, Oscar DePriest would become the first black elected to the House of Representatives in the twentieth century. Seventeen years would pass before two blacks would simultaneously serve in Congress. No black from the South would be elected to Congress until 1972 when Barbara Jordan of Texas and Andrew Young of Georgia were elected. By 1992, 39 blacks, including the non-voting delegate from the District of Columbia, served in the U.S. House of Representatives. The 1992 elections increased black representation in the House by 50 percent—up from 26. Of the 13 new black lawmakers who were elected in 1992, all won in newly drawn majority-black or minority-majority districts in the South under the 1982 extension of the Voting Rights Act. During the 1980s, only 4 new black congressional districts were created, and none existed at all in 5 southern states: Alabama, Florida, North Carolina, South Carolina, and Virginia.

What do blacks think of their new black representatives in Washington? While research on Congress and congressional elections has emerged to become a large and lively research domain in American politics, only scant attention has been paid to black voters in this field. Recently, scholars such as Carol Swain and Kenny Whitby have begun to systematically examine the type of representation that blacks have won in Congress,[19] but no work has systematically examined the attitudes that blacks have toward Congress and their representatives.

Simply comparing blacks' attitudes toward their representatives in Congress to whites' attitudes in 1994, one finds that blacks were neither more nor less satisfied with their representatives in Congress than were whites. In the 1994 survey, about 87 percent of blacks as opposed to 81 percent of whites approved of their House legislator's performance in office (the 6 percentage point difference is not statistically significant). Trend data from as far back as 1980 support this pattern; black approval ratings of their incumbent House legislators were consistently high and closely tracked those of whites.

Obviously, public evaluations of their representatives are strongly influenced by the party affiliations of these legislators as well as their legislative record. All things being equal, Republican constituents are going to give higher marks to Republican representatives over Democratic legislators. What about the race of the member of Congress? Are blacks more satisfied with the performance of their representatives when their representative is black? What about the behavioral effect of the race of the representative? Are blacks more knowledgeable about Congress and more participatory when residing in districts represented by an African American?

The 1996 National Black Election Study was designed to explore this issue. The congressional districts of 36 of the 39 black members of the 104th Congress fell into the pre-election study sample. In all, 31 percent of the black respondents were represented by these black legislators. These black members of Congress enjoyed the highest approval ratings relative to their white, Asian, and Latino counterparts. Table 9-6 presents a cross-tabulation of black political attitudes toward their congressional representatives by the racial group and party memberships of these elected officials. While blacks represented by blacks did not appraise Clinton or Congress any differently from those not represented by blacks, they generally were far more knowledgeable about Congress and more active in politics than their counterparts. Most striking is the effect that the race of the representative has on voter recall. Although few blacks could spontaneously recall the name of their House representative, 30 percent of those with black representatives could name their representative, while only 19 percent of those not represented by blacks could. Moreover, 82 percent of those with black representatives who said that they knew who their representative in Washington was could correctly name their representative, in contrast to only 49 percent of those not represented by blacks.

These findings lend additional support to Lawrence Bobo and Franklin D. Gilliam, Jr.'s black empowerment theory—blacks represented by blacks are more participatory and politically efficacious than blacks who are not.[20] The results establish that black political representation matter; that blacks express high levels of satisfaction with their political representation when represented by blacks; and that they are more likely to be engaged in politics when represented by blacks as opposed to whites. Beyond the symbolic benefits that the elections of blacks to Congress bestows to blacks, there are important political benefits attached to black representation as well.

SUMMARY

The 1965 Voting Rights Act eliminated the most egregious barriers to black voting and ushered in a new phase of black politics that emphasized voting and the election of blacks to public office. The Voting Rights Act, however, did not eliminate all barriers to black voting. A study released by the Sentencing Project, a Washington, DC-based, nonprofit group organized in the aftermath of the Million Man March, estimated that nearly 1.46 million, or nearly 15 percent of all black males have lost their right to vote through imprisonment for a felony conviction (a crime such as murder, rape, or burglary).[21] All but four states (Maine, Massachusetts, Utah, and Vermont) bar felons from voting. However, 15 of these states restore voting rights to convicted felons once released from prison. Thirteen states deny voting rights to felons for life. These 13 states are Alabama, Arizona, Delaware, Florida, Iowa, Kentucky, Maryland, Mississippi, Nevada, Tennessee, Virginia, and Wyoming. When southern states rewrote their state constitutions to prevent the newly-freed slaves from voting, they often included provisions that disfranchised persons convicted of certain crimes, including felonies. During the 1970s the

Table 9-6 Respondent Attitudes and Behavior
by Race and Party of Their House Representative

	Black Democrat	White/Other Legislator	White/Other Democrat	White/Other Republican
Percent who approve of Clinton	85.0	81.0	79.0	82.0
Percent who approve of Congress	32.0	26.5	25.0	33.0
Percent who approve of House representative	84.0	63.0*	72.0	56.0
Percent who correctly named both senators	12.0	10.0	11.0	9.0
Percent who correctly named one senator	12.0	10.0	11.0	13.0
Percent who correctly named their House representative	23.0	9.0*	10.0	8.0
Percent who recognized the name of their House representative	89.0	76.0*	78.0	75.5
Percent who correctly identified the party of their House representative	57.0	35.0*	36.0	34.0
Percent who correctly identified the race or ethnicity of their House representative	79.0	61.0*	64.0	59.0
Percent who are very interested in political campaigns	36.0	27.0*	30.5	25.0
Percent who care a good deal who wins presidential election	88.0	80.0*	79.5	80.0
Percent who said they voted in 1994 House race	57.0	45.5*	45.0	46.0
Percent who said they voted in 1992 election	79.0	69.0*	67.0	71.0

*Chi-square sig. at .001
Source: 1996 National Black Election Study.

Supreme Court affirmed the right of states to deny voting rights to felons. Since 1993 black House Representative John Conyers of Michigan has introduced a bill into Congress to force states to let felons vote in federal elections once released.

Furthermore, states can erect new barriers to the vote, as Mississippi attempted to do when it implemented the Motor-Voter law that Congress passed in 1993. This law allowed citizens to register to vote in state motor vehicle and welfare departments. Mississippi chose to establish a dual registration system in which those who registered under the new federal law were registered to vote only in federal elections. To vote in state and local elections, however, citizens had to register separately. The dual registration system was challenged in court on the basis that Mississippi failed to win approval from the Justice Department as required by Section 5 of the 1965 Voting Rights Act. While a three-judge panel initially found the State not to be in violation of the Voting Rights Act, in a unanimous decision (*Young* v. *Fordice*), the Supreme Court held that Mississippi needed to have sought pre-clearance from the Justice Department. The Justice Department is expected to withhold its approval, and Mississippi will be forced to permit those registered under the 1993 National Voter Registration Law to vote in its state and local elections as the other 49 states have already done.

Elections laws, campaigns, and the limited socioeconomic resources of citizens all can make it difficult for those eligible to vote to take part in politics. African Americans, however, have several key community-based resources that enable them to overcome these barriers as individuals and participate at higher levels than expected. These resources are the same as those used during the civil rights movement and include race consciousness, church activism, and membership in black civic and political organizations.

Since 1984, black voter participation in presidential elections has declined. Why fewer blacks are going to the polls to elect presidents is presently unclear. It could be that the electoral choices offered to blacks in presidential elections simply fail to excite some enough to make the effort to vote. This continued racial gap in participation in national elections merits close watch, since it could signal black dissatisfaction with electoral politics.

Most blacks, nevertheless, continue to express strong optimism about their ability to effect change through the electoral process. Clearly, their faith in the political process is tied to the tremendous gains blacks have achieved since passage of the 1965 Voting Rights Act. The number of black elected officials has skyrocketed since the 1960s, and a 1996 survey found that blacks represented by blacks in Congress expressed greater satisfaction with their legislator's performance than those represented by whites.

TOPICS FOR DISCUSSION

1. Identify the barriers to black registration and voting that still exist. Which resources do blacks have collectively that help them overcome these barriers to political participation?

2. Even among registered voters, black voter turnout is lower than among whites. What would it take for registered blacks to turn out at the same rate as whites? Consider in your answer the three general theories of political participation: (1) electoral laws, (2) election-specific factors, and (3) the attitudes and demographic characteristics of the voters themselves.

3. What effect, if any, will the 1993 National Voter Registration Act have on the racial gap on voter registration and turnout in presidential elections?

4. What are the advantages and disadvantages for blacks to vote according to how their racial group is faring economically?

SUGGESTED READINGS

Davidson, Chandler, and Bernard Grofman, ed. *Quiet Revolution in the South.* Princeton, NJ: Princeton University Press, 1994. The authors in the edited volume present detailed data and methodologically sophisticated analyses of the impact of the Voting Rights Act on the southern states it covered from 1965 to 1990.

Dawson, Michael C. *Behind the Mule: Race and Class in African-American Politics.* Princeton, NJ: Princeton University Press, 1994. See Chapter 7, "Racial Group Interests, African-American Presidential Approval, and Macroeconomic Policy," which was co-authored with Cathy Cohen and Ronald E. Brown.

Kousser, J. Morgan. *The Shaping of Southern Politics: Suffrage Restriction and the Establishment of the One-Party South, 1880–1910.* New Haven, CT: Yale University Press, 1974.

McAdam, Doug. *Political Process and the Development of Black Insurgency, 1930–1970.* Chicago, IL: University of Chicago Press, 1982. This book outlines a model that explains the rise and decline of the black protest movement in the United States.

Morris, Aldon. *The Origins of the Civil Rights Movement.* New York: The Free Press, 1984.

Parker, Frank. *Black Votes Count.* Chapel Hill, NC: University of North Carolina Press, 1990.

Piven, Frances Fox, and Richard A. Cloward. *Why Americans Don't Vote.* New York: Pantheon Press, 1988. These authors present their controversial argument that our electoral system was reformed at a critical moment in American history to keep poor people from participating.

Rosenstone, Steven J., and John Mark Hansen. *Mobilization, Participation, and Democracy in America.* New York: MacMillan, 1993.

Tate, Katherine. *From Protest to Politics: The New Black Voters in American Elections,* expanded ed. Cambridge, MA: Harvard University Press and the Russe Sage Foundation, 1994. See Chapter 4 on group resources and black el toral participation.

Verba, Sidney, Kay Lehman Schlozman, and Henry E. Brady. *Voice and Equality.* Cambridge, MA: Harvard University Press, 1995. Based on a survey of 15,000 Americans, the authors identify the key social attributes linked to political participation.

NOTES

1. Quoted in Reed Branson, "Mississippi's Use of Motor-Voter Law in Jeopardy," *Commercial Appeal*, April 1, 1997, p. A-5. Reprinted by permission.
2. J. Morgan Kousser, *The Shaping of Southern Politics: Suffrage Restriction and the Establishment of the One-Party South, 1880–1910* (New Haven, CT: Yale University Press, 1974).
3. James E. Alt, "The Impact of the Voting Rights Act on Black and White Voter Registration in the South," in *Quiet Revolution in the South*, ed. Chandler Davidson and Bernard Grofman (Princeton, NJ: Princeton University Press, 1994), pp. 351–377.
4. Anthony Downs, *An Economic Theory of Democracy* (New York: Harper & Row, 1957).
5. The states allowing same-day registration in 1997 are Minnesota, Wisconsin, Wyoming, Idaho, Maine, and New Hampshire. See also Richard J. Timpone, "Structure, Behavior, and Voter Turnout in the United States," unpublished manuscript, State University of New York.
6. Sidney Verba and Norman H. Nie, *Participation in America* (Cambridge, MA: Harvard University Press, 1972); Raymond E. Wolfinger and Steven J. Rosenstone, *Who Votes?* (New Haven, CT: Yale University Press, 1980).
7. Wolfinger and Rosenstone, *Who Votes?* p. 18.
8. Steven J. Rosenstone and John Mark Hansen, *Mobilization, Participation, and Democracy in America* (New York: MacMillan, 1993), pp. 12–13.
9. Katherine Tate, *From Protest to Politics* (Cambridge, MA: Harvard University Press and the Russell Sage Foundation).
10. Aldon Morris, *The Origins of the Civil Rights Movement* (New York: Free Press, 1984), p. 4.
11. Adolph Reed, Jr., *The Jesse Jackson Phenomenon* (New Haven, CT: Yale University Press, 1986).
12. Gary T. Marx, *Protest and Prejudice* (New York: Harper & Row, 1967).
13. C. Eric Lincoln and Lawrence Mamiya, *The Black Church in the African American Experience* (Durham, NC, and London: Duke University Press, 1990).
14. Cathy J. Cohen and Michael C. Dawson, "Neighborhood Poverty and African American Politics," *American Political Science Review* 87, 2 (1993), pp. 286–302.
15. Tate, *From Protest to Politics.*
16. See Katherine Tate, "Structural Dependence or Group Loyalty? The Black Vote in 1992," in *Democracy's Feast: Elections in America*, ed. Herbert F. Weisberg (Chatham, NJ: Chatham House Press, 1995), pp. 179–194.
17. Douglas A. Hibbs, Jr., *The American Political Economy* (Cambridge, MA: Harvard University Press, 1987).

18. Michael C. Dawson, *Behind the Mule: Race and Class in African-American Politics* (Princeton, NJ: Princeton University Press, 1994), p. 60; see also Tate, *From Protest to Politics*, Chapter 6.

19. Carol M. Swain, *Black Faces, Black Interests: The Representation of African Americans in Congress* (Cambridge, MA: Harvard University Press, 1993); Kenny J. Whitby, *The Color of Representation: Congressional Behavior and Black Constituents* (Ann Arbor, MI: The University of Michigan Press, 1997).

20. Lawrence D. Bobo and Franklin D. Gilliam, Jr., "Race, Sociopolitical Participation, and Black Empowerment," *American Political Science Review* 84, 2, pp. 379–393.

21. Fox Butterfield, "Many Black Men Barred from Voting," *New York Times*, January 30, 1997, p. A-12.

Chapter 10

African Americans and the Congressional Arena

In the orderly process of government, success of an issue often depends on the skill of its advocates in understanding who holds the key to power on that issue, and how to approach that person in a friendly or persuasive manner....

... Congress evidently gave little thought to the fact that if the poor people had the means to do things the right way—to hire a full-time lobbyist to touch the vital pressure points, to provide position papers, inserts for the Congressional Record, steaks and wine for the congressmen—they wouldn't be poor.

—Nick Kotz, *Let Them Eat Promises: The Politics of Hunger in America*[1]

Perhaps the gravest distortions in congressional representation come from the extraordinary difficulty of defeating incumbents, and the great dependence of congressional campaigns on large contributions from interests with very specific legislative objectives. The slow turnover of members causes Congress to be always dominated by members with a vested interest in the organizational status quo. Sometimes it also isolates the legislative branch from changes in public attitudes. The members' dependency on business, unions, and the more affluent professions greatly increases the difficulty of enacting legislation to reform these institutions.

—Gary Orfield, *Congressional Power: Congress and Social Change*[2]

Congress is the chief law-making institution in our governmental system. The legitimacy of this law-making function is enhanced by the fact that all of its 535 members (100 senators and 435 representatives) are elected directly by the people. Consequently, they are the people's representatives in Washington. And if there is anything about the principles of democratic government that undergirds our overall constitutional system, it is that our government is based upon the concept of popular representation. That is, the people (the governed) have the right and obligation to directly select those who represent them in the government (the governors).

Hence, our government may be referred to as a *representative government*. This contrasts with the "town-meeting," or "direct democracy," idea in which all citizens participate directly in the governing process. But in a country as large as ours, direct democracy is both unworkable and impossible. Hence, our Constitution provides for a representative government with fixed terms and periodic elections for elected officials. This allows us to hold to the principle of *popular sovereignty* without suffering the pains and problems of direct democracy. In short, representative government makes popular sovereignty a practical, operational concept.

However, the idea of representative government, while a noble concept, continues to pose some perennially troubling questions. What defines "representativeness"? By what procedures should voters be aggregated for the purpose of electing representatives, and who gets to perform the aggregation? The Supreme Court answered some of these kinds of questions in *Reynolds* v. *Sims*, when it held that legislative apportionment had to conform to a "one person-one vote" standard. "The fundamental principle of representative government in this country," said the Court, "is one of equal representation for equal numbers of people."[3] Rejecting an implicitly group-oriented conception of representation, the Court went on to state:

> Legislators represent people, not trees or acres. Legislators are elected by voters, not farms or cities or economic interests. As long as ours is a representative of people, the right to elect legislators in a free and unimpaired fashion is a bedrock of our political system.[4]

While the Court subsequently permitted minimal variations from strict population equality in state and local districting,[5] the one-person one-vote standard remained firmly in place for congressional districting. Of course, representation in the U.S. Senate is a paradigmatic example of malapportionment, since all states, whether heavily populated (California) or sparsely populated (Wyoming), receive the same number of senators. The Court, in *Reynolds*, acknowledged that its holding would make the Senate an anomaly, but it concluded that the Senate's apportionment was justifiable as a compromise necessary for "the birth of the nation." In any case, the issue of Senate apportionment is mooted by Article V of the Constitution, which states that "no State, without its Consent, shall be deprived of its equal Suffrage in the Senate." Absent a constitutional amendment, the Senate's apportionment will remain the same, regardless of changes in population.

The concept of popular representation, however, encompasses much more than an automatic formula that apportions legislative representation according to strict population equality. Indeed, Congress has been criticized for its overrepresentation of particular socioeconomic strata within the American population. More specifically, Congress, relative to the population at large, has disproportionate numbers of whites[6] (473 out of 535), males (475 out of 535), and educated individuals from professional occupations

Table 10-1   **"Representativeness" of the 105th Congress: Members' Occupations***

	House			Senate			Congress
	D	R	Total	D	R	Total	Total
Actor/Entertainer	0	1	1	0	1	1	2
Aeronautics	0	1	1	1	0	1	2
Agriculture	8	14	22	2	6	8	30
Artistic/Creative	1	1	2	0	0	0	2
Business or Banking	55	126	181	8	25	33	214
Clergy	1	0	1	0	1	1	2
Education	40	33	74	5	8	13	87
Engineering	1	7	8	0	0	0	8
Health Care	1	1	2	0	0	0	2
Journalism	4	7	12	2	7	9	21
Labor Officials	1	0	1	0	0	0	1
Law	87	85	172	26	27	53	225
Law Enforcement	8	2	10	0	0	0	10
Medicine	3	9	12	0	2	2	14
Military	0	1	1	0	1	1	2
Miscellaneous	0	5	5	0	0	0	5
Professional Sports	0	3	3	0	0	0	3
Public Service	54	46	100	9	17	26	126
Real Estate	3	20	23	2	3	5	28
Technical/Trade	0	1	1	0	0	0	1

*Because some members have more than one occupation, totals are higher than total membership.
Source: *Congressional Quarterly Weekly Report* 55, 1 (January 4, 1997), p. 29.

(see Table 10-1). Although the number of women in Congress has risen from 8 in 1947 to 27 in 1989 to 60 in 1997, Congress remains a predominantly white male institution.

With regard to black representation in Congress, Table 10-2 shows a steady climb from 2 black members in 1949 to 25 in 1991, and then a sharp increase to 39 in 1993. This increase reflects the impact of the Voting Rights Act of 1965, as the 1990 round of redistricting produced increased numbers of majority-black districts in various southern states. The Voting Rights Act's initial impact came decades earlier, as newly registered black voters changed the tenor of southern elections, pushed Democrats toward more moderate positions on racial issues, and in 1972 helped elect the first black members of Congress from the South in the twentieth century—Barbara Jordan (D-Texas) and Andrew Young (D-Georgia). The 1992 elections represented a watershed change that neither the Republican takeover of Congress in 1994 nor the judicial repeal of majority-minority districts in North Carolina, Texas, Georgia, and Louisiana has been able to reverse. Contrary to predictions that a series of Supreme Court decisions on race-based districting

Table 10-2   African American Members of Congress, 1947–1998 (by Numbers)

Congress	Senate	House	Congress	Senate	House
105th			93rd	1	15
1st sess.	1	37	92nd	1	12
104th	1	39	91st	1	9
103rd	1	38	90th	1	5
102nd	0	25	89th	0	6
101st	0	23	88th	0	5
100th	0	22	87th	0	4
99th	0	19	85th	0	4
98th	0	20	84th	0	3
97th	0	17	83rd	0	2
96th	0	15	82nd	0	2
95th	1	15	81st	0	2
94th	1	16	80th	0	2

Sources: Adapted from *Congressional Quarterly Weekly Report* 49 (January 2, 1993), p. 10; *Congressional Quarterly Weekly Report* 49 (January 16, 1993), p. 12; *1995 Congressional Quarterly Almanac* 51, pp. 1–14; and *Congressional Quarterly Weekly Report* 55 (January 4, 1997), p. 28

would result in a purge of minority membership, in the 105th Congress blacks managed to hold 37 House seats and 1 Senate seat.

Even so, the percentage of blacks and women in Congress still falls short of each group's share of the population at large. The implicit, and sometimes explicit, assumption is that blacks and women, for example, would be represented better if more representatives hailed from these groups. But whether enhanced *substantive* representation (electing members who will advance the group's political interests) necessarily follows from increases in *descriptive* representation (electing members from one's group) remains a hotly contested question. This chapter focuses on black members of Congress and how various electoral and institutional structures affect their roles and aspirations.

BLACKS IN CONGRESS

In 1997, there were 38 blacks in Congress, all of whom (except 1) were serving as members of the House of Representatives. Only 2 blacks have served in the Senate since 1880—Edward Brooke (R-Massachusetts), who was defeated in his reelection bid in 1978, and Carol Moseley-Braun (D-Illinois), who was elected in 1992 (see Table 10-3). This represents a net increase of 12 blacks from the 26 who served in the 101st Congress, with most new House members coming from largely black districts created through redistricting. While fewer than half of the 26 blacks in Congress in 1992 had prior experience in elective office, all of the 17 elected in 1992, except for 1 (Me▪

Table 10-3 African American Members of Congress, 1870–1997 (by Year)

Senate

Hiram R. Revels (R-Miss.)	1870–71	Edward W. Brooke (R-Mass.)	1967–79
Blanche K. Bruce (R-Miss.)	1875–81	Carol Moseley-Braun (D-Ill.)	1993–present

House

Joseph H. Rainey (R-S.C.)	1870–79	George W. Crockett, Jr.	
Jefferson F. Long (R-Ga.)	1870–71	(D-Mich.)	1981–91
Robert B. Elliott (R-S.C.)	1871–74	Mervyn M. Dymally (D-Calif.)	1981–93
Robert C. De Large (R-S.C.)	1871–73	Gus Savage (D-Ill.)	1981–93
Benjamin S. Turner (R-Ala.)	1871–73	Harold Washington (D-Ill.)	1981–83
Josiah T. Walls (R-Fla.)	1871–76	Katie Hall (D-Ind.)	1983–85
Richard H. Cain (R-S.C.)	1873–75	Charles A. Hayes (D-Ill.)	1983–93
	1877–79	Major R. Owens (D-N.Y.)	1983–present
John R. Lynch (R-Miss.)	1873–77	Edolphus Towns (D-N.Y.)	1983–present
	1882–83	Alan Wheat (D-Mo.)	1983–94
James T. Rapier (R-Ala.)	1873–75	Alton R. Waldon, Jr. (D-N.Y.)	1986–87
Alonzo J. Ransier (R-S.C.)	1873–75	Mike Espy (D-Miss.)	1987–93
Jeremiah Haralson (R-Ala.)	1875–77	Floyd H. Flake (D-N.Y.)	1987–present
John A. Hyman (R-N.C.)	1875–77	John Lewis (D-Ga.)	1987–present
Charles E. Nash (R-La.)	1875–77	Kweisi Mfume (D-Md.)	1987–95
Robert Smalls (R-S.C.)	1875–79	Donald M. Payne (D-N.J.)	1989–present
	1882–83	Craig Washington (D-Tex.)	1990–94
	1884–87	Maxine Waters (D-Calif.)	1991–present
James E. O'Hara (R-N.C.)	1883–87	Gary Franks (R-Conn.)	1991–96
Henry P. Cheatham (R-N.C.)	1889–93	William Jefferson (D-La.)	1991–present
John M. Langston (R-Va.)	1890–91	Barbara-Rose Collins (D-Mich.)	1991–96
Thomas E. Miller (R-S.C.)	1890–91	Lucien E. Blackwell (D-Pa.)	1991–94
George W. Murray (R-S.C.)	1893–95	Earl F. Hilliard (D-Ala.)	1993–present
	1896–97	Walter R. Tucker (D-Calif.)	1993–95
George H. White (R-N.C.)	1897–1901	Corrine Brown (D-Fla.)	1993–present
Oscar De Priest (R-Ill.)	1929–35	Alcee L. Hastings (D-Fla.)	1993–present
Arthur W. Mitchell (D-Ill.)	1935–43	Carrie Meek (D-Fla.)	1993–present
William L. Dawson (D-Ill.)	1943–70	Sanford Bishop (D-Ga.)	1993–present
Adam C. Powell, Jr. (D-N.Y.)	1945–67	Cynthia McKinney (D-Ga.)	1993–present
	1969–71	Bobby L. Rush (D-Ill.)	1993–present
Charles C. Diggs, Jr. (D-Mich.)	1955–80	Mel Reynolds (D-Ill.)	1993–95
Robert N. C. Nix (D-Pa.)	1958–79	Cleo Fields (D-La.)	1993–96
Augustus F. Hawkins (D-Calif.)	1963–91	Albert R. Wynn (D-Md.)	1993–present
John Conyers, Jr. (D-Mich.)	1965–present	Bennie Thompson (D-Miss.)	1993–present
Louis Stokes (D-Ohio)	1969–present	Eva Clayton (D-N.C.)	1993–present
William L. Clay (D-Mo.)	1969–present	Melvin Watt (D-N.C.)	1993–present
Shirley Chisholm (D-N.Y.)	1969–83	James E. Clyburn (D-S.C.)	1993–present
George W. Collins (D-Ill.)	1970–72	Eddie Bernice Johnson (D-Tex.)	1993–present
Ronald V. Dellums (D-Calif.)	1971–present	Robert C. Scott (D-Va.)	1993–present
Ralph H. Metcalfe (D-Ill.)	1971–78	J. C. Watts (R-Okla.)	1995–present
Parren J. Mitchell (D-Md.)	1971–87	Chaka Fattah (D-Pa.)	1995–present
Charles B. Rangel (D-N.Y.)	1979–present	Sheila Jackson-Lee (D-Tex.)	1995–present
Yvonne B. Burke (D-Calif.)	1973–79	Juanita Millender-McDonald	
Cardiss Collins (D-Ill.)	1973–96	(D-Calif.)	1996–present
Barbara C. Jordan (D-Tex.)	1973–79	Jesse Jackson, Jr. (D-Ill.)	1996–present
Andrew Young (D-Ga.)	1973–77	Elijah Cummings (D-Md.)	1996–present
Harold E. Ford (D-Tenn.)	1975–96	Danny K. Davis (D-Ill.)	1997–present
Julian C. Dixon (D-Calif.)	1979–present	Julia Carson (D-Ind.)	1997–present
William H. Gray III (D-Pa.)	1979–91	Carolyn Cheeks Kilpatrick	
George T. Leland (D-Tex.)	1979–89	(D-Mich.)	1997–present
Bennett McVey Stewart (D-Ill.)	1979–81	Harold E. Ford, Jr. (D-Tenn.)	1997–present

Sources: *Congressional Quarterly Weekly Report* 49 (Jan. 2, 1993), p. 10; *Congressional Quarterly Weekly Report* 49 (Jan. 16, 1993), p. 12; and *Congressional Quarterly Weekly Report* 53 (Jan. 24, 1997), p. 28. In addition to the members listed above, John W. Menard, R-La., won a disputed election in 1868 but was not permitted to take his seat in Congress. Walter E. Fauntroy, D (1979–1991) and Eleanor Holmes Norton, D (1991–present) have served as non-voting delegates from the District of Columbia; and Victor Frazer, I (1993–96) and Donna Christian Green, D (1997–present) have served as non-voting delegates from the Virgin Islands.

Reynolds of Illinois, who replaced Gus Savage),[7] come with a rich background of experience in state government or local office.[8]

A brief review of the socioeconomic characteristics of blacks in the House indicates a variety of career background patterns with no one pattern predominating (see Table 10-4). Overall, however, the fact that blacks in Congress come from a variety of career patterns may reflect a general trend away from any particular career avenue to Congress. If this is true, then Congress may become more "representative," at least in terms of broadening the range of occupational interests now represented in Congress.

In addition, a look at the congressional districts represented by blacks reveals a striking homogeneity in the types of districts represented by blacks in terms of race, urbanization, and poverty. Of the 37 congressional districts represented by blacks, 24 were majority-black, and several additional districts were majority-minority (black plus Latino).[9] Eighteen districts were classified as 100 percent urban, and 9 others fell between 95 and 100 percent. Finally, of the 25 congressional districts with the highest rates of families in poverty, 11 were represented by blacks. Overall, then, the constituencies represented by black members of Congress tend to be mostly black, poor, and urban.

There is another dimension on which congressional districts represented by blacks are homogeneous. That is the degree to which black representatives come from what are called "safe" districts. In this context, "safe" refers to the probability that an incumbent will continue to be reelected. A "safe" seat is one in which a candidate receives a high proportion (at least 60 percent) of the votes cast. Using vote share as a yardstick, we see that in the 1990 elections, all but one of the winning black candidates received at least 68 percent of the vote. The one exception, Gary Franks (R-Connecticut) received 52 percent of the vote in a mostly white district. More recently, the lowest margin of victory for a black incumbent member of Congress in 1994 was the 54 percent share received by Bennie Thompson (D-Mississippi).[10] And in 1996, only 6 of the 37 winning black candidates received less than 60 percent of the vote. Two of these candidates—J. C. Watts (R-Oklahoma) and Julia Carson (D-Indiana)—came from majority-white districts, while three others—Sanford Bishop (D-Georgia), Cynthia McKinney (D-Georgia), and Eddie Bernice Johnson (D-Texas)—came from districts that had recently been redrawn to comply with the dictates of the Supreme Court.

An alternative measure of the safeness of a district for black representatives is the extent to which blacks replace blacks (or contest black incumbents) in a specific seat. For example, in the 1992 elections, of the 16 newly elected blacks, only 3 come from districts previously represented by blacks, the other 13 coming from mainly new black districts resulting from 1990 state reapportionment policies. Since 1992, the trend has been for districts to replace black representatives with black representatives. Of the 11 House seats vacated by black members between 1994 and 1996, 8 were subse-

Table 10-4   Blacks in Congress: Socioeconomic Characteristics

Name	Age	Education	Religion	Career
Sanford Bishop (D-Ga., 2)	49	B.A., 1968, Morehouse College; J.D., 1971, Emory University	Baptist	Attorney; state legislator
Corrine Brown (D-Fla., 3)	50	B.S., 1969, Florida A & M University; Ed.S., 1974, University of Florida	Baptist	College guidance counselor; state legislator
Julia Carson (D-Ind., 10)	58	Martin University 1994–95	Baptist	Clothing store owner; human resource manager; congressional aide
William L. Clay (D-Mo., 1)	65	B.S., 1953, St. Louis University	Catholic	Real estate; life insurance; union business representative
Eva Clayton (D-N.C., 1)	62	B.S., 1955, Johnson C. Smith University; M.S., 1962, North Carolina Central University; 1967, University of North Carolina Law School	Presbyterian	Consulting firm owner; nonprofit executive; county commissioner
James E. Clyburn (D-S.C., 6)	56	B.S., 1962, South Carolina State College	African Methodist Episcopalian	State human affairs commissioner
John Conyers, Jr. (D-Mich., 14)	67	B.A., 1957, LL.B., 1958, Wayne State University	Baptist	Legislative assistant; workman's compensation referee; attorney
Elijah Cummings (D-Md., 7)	45	B.A., 1973, Howard University; J.D., 1976, University of Maryland	Baptist	Attorney
Danny K. Davis (D-Ill., 7)	55	B.A., 1961, Arkansas A. M. & N. College; M.A., 1968, Chicago State University; Ph.D., 1977, Urban Institute	Baptist	Health care consultant; teacher
Ronald V. Dellums (D-Calif., 9)	61	A.A., 1958, Oakland City College; B.A., 1960, San Francisco State College; M.S.W., 1962, University of California	Protestant	Social worker; city councilman
Julian Dixon (D-Calif., 32)	62	B.S., 1962, Los Angeles State College; J.D., 1969, Southwestern Law School	Episcopalian	Special legal counsel; legislative assistant; state legislator

Table 10-4, continued

Name	Age	Education	Religion	Career
Chaka Fattah (D-Pa., 2)	40	A.A., 1976, Community College of Philadelphia; M.A., 1986, University of Pennsylvania	Baptist	Public official
Floyd H. Flake (D-N.Y., 6)	51	B.A., 1967, Wilberforce University; Payne Theological Seminary, Northeastern University	African Methodist Episcopalian	Marketing analyst; college administrator; minister
Harold E. Ford, Jr. (D-Tenn., 9)	26	B.A., 1992, University of Pennsylvania; J.D., 1996, University of Michigan	Baptist	Law clerk
Alcee L. Hastings (D-Fla., 23)	60	B.A., 1958, Fisk University; 1958-60, Howard University; J.D., 1963, Florida A&M University	African Methodist Episcopalian	Federal judge
Earl F. Hilliard (D-Ala., 7)	54	B.A., 1964, Morehouse College; J.D., 1967, Howard University; M.B.A., 1970, Atlanta University	Baptist	Attorney; insurance; state legislator
Jesse Jackson, Jr. (D-Ill., 2)	31	B.S., 1987, North Carolina A&T University, Greensboro; M.A., 1990, Chicago Theological Seminary; J.D., 1993, University of Illinois	Baptist	Attorney
Sheila Jackson-Lee (D-Tex., 18)	46	B.A., 1972, Yale University; J.D., 1975, University of Virginia	Seventh-Day Adventist	Attorney; congressional aide
William J. Jefferson (D-La., 2)	49	B.A., 1969, Southern University; J.D., 1972, Harvard University	Baptist	Legislative aide; attorney; state legislator
Eddie Bernice Johnson (D-Tex., 30)	61	B.S., 1967, Texas Christian University; M.P.A., 1976, Southern Methodist University	Baptist	Business consultant; state legislator; regional director of Department of Health, Education and Welfare

Table 10-4, continued

Name	Age	Education	Religion	Career
Carolyn Cheeks Kilpatrick (D-Mich., 15)	51	A.A., 1965, Ferris State University, B.S., 1968, Western Michigan University; M.S., 1972, University of Michigan	Baptist	Teacher
John Lewis (D-Ga., 5)	56	B.A., 1961, American Baptist Theological Seminary; B.A., 1963, Fisk University	Baptist	Civil rights activist; city councilman
Cynthia McKinney (D-Ga., 4)	41	B.A., 1978, University of Southern California; 1981, Georgia State University; 1984, Wisconsin, Fletcher School of Law and Diplomacy, Ph.D. candidate	Catholic	Professor; state legislator
Carrie Meek (D-Fla., 17)	70	B.S., 1946, Florida A&M University; M.S., 1948, University of Michigan; 1979, Florida Atlantic University	Baptist	Teacher; education administrator; state legislator
Juanita Millender-McDonald (D-Calif., 37)	58	B.S., University of Redlands; M.A., California State University, Los Angeles; University of Southern California	Baptist	Teacher
Carol Moseley-Braun (D-Ill.)	48	B.A., 1967, University of Illinois-Chicago; J.D., 1972, University of Chicago	Catholic	Attorney
Eleanor Holmes Norton (D-Wash., D.C.)*	59	B.A., 1960, Antioch College; M.A., 1963, LL.B., 1964, Yale University	Episcopalian	Assistant legal director of ACLU; head of EEOC; professor
Major R. Owens (D-N.Y., 11)	60	B.A., 1956, Morehouse College; M.S., 1957, Atlanta University	Baptist	Library administrator; community development official; state legislator
ɔnald M. Payne Ɔ-N.J., 10)	62	B.A., 1957, Seton Hall University	Baptist	Teacher; businessman; city councilman

Table 10-4, continued

Name	Age	Education	Religion	Career
Charles B. Rangel (D-N.Y., 15)	66	B.S., 1957, New York University; LL.B., 1960, St. John's University	Catholic	Attorney; state legislator
Bobby L. Rush (D-Ill., 1)	50	B.A., 1973, Roosevelt University; 1975–77, University of Illinois-Chicago	Protestant	Civil rights activist; insurance; college administrator; alderman
Robert C. Scott (D-Va., 3)	49	A.B., 1969, Harvard University; J.D., 1973, Boston College	Episcopalian	Attorney; state legislator
Louis Stokes (D-Ohio, 11)	71	1946–1948, Western Reserve University; J.D., 1953, Cleveland-Marshall Law School	Methodist	Attorney
Bennie Thompson (D-Miss., 2)	48	B.A., 1968, Tougaloo College; M.S., 1972, Jackson State University	Methodist	Teacher; alderman; mayor
Edolphus Towns (D-N.Y., 10)	62	B.S., 1959, North Carolina A&T University; M.S.W., 1973, Adelphi University	Presbyterian	Teacher; social worker; hospital administrator; deputy borough president
Maxine Waters (D-Calif., 35)	58	B.A., 1970, California State University	Christian	State legislator
Melvin Watt (D-N.C., 12)	51	B S., 1967, University of North Carolina; J.D., 1970, Yale University	Presbyterian	Attorney; sate legislator
J. C. Watts (R-Okla., 4)	39	B.S., 1981, University of Oklahoma	Southern Baptist	Property management company owner; professional football player
Albert R. Wynn (D-Md., 4)	45	B.S., 1973, University of Pittsburgh; 1973–74, Howard University; J.D., 1977, Georgetown University	Baptist	Attorney; state legislator

*Non-voting member.

Sources: Michael Barone, et al., *The Almanac of American Politics 1992* (New York: Dutton, 1992); *Congressional Quarterly Weekly Report* 49 (Jan. 2, 1993); *Congressional Weekly Report* 49 (Jan. 16, 1993).

quently filled by blacks. This suggests that there is a fairly stable number of congressional districts that will continue to elect black representatives. The "safeness" of these districts, insofar as electing blacks, seems very much related to the size of the black population in that particular district. That is, the larger the black population, the greater the chance a black has of being elected. There are signs that the incumbency advantage can protect candidates whose districts have lost their majority-minority status. In 1996, five black candidates—Sanford Bishop (D-Georgia), Corrine Brown (D-Florida), Sheila Jackson-Lee (D-Texas), Eddie Bernice Johnson (D-Texas), and Cynthia McKinney (D-Georgia)—managed to hold their seats despite losing sizable numbers of black voters as a result of Supreme Court decisions limiting the use of race-based redistricting. Nonetheless, the probability of black representation still seems directly related to the size of the black population.[11]

In addition, it should be mentioned that particular court decisions on discriminatory voting procedures may also help aid the election of blacks to Congress and other offices. It is true, of course, that the Supreme Court, in *City of Mobile, Alabama* v. *Bolden* [446 U.S. 55 (1980)], rejected a case challenging Mobile's at-large districts for city commissioners on the ground that such districts diluted the black vote. But in response to this decision, Congress passed an amendment to the Voting Rights Act of 1965 that prohibited any voting procedure that abridged the right to vote on account of race or language minority status. And in *Thornburg* v. *Gingles* [478 U.S. 30 (1986)], the Supreme Court held that a district containing a majority of minorities should be created when, among other factors, (1) effects of discrimination are evident and the area has a sufficiently large and geographically compact minority population; (2) the minority is politically cohesive; and (3) minority candidates have been previously defeated due to bloc voting by whites. *Gingles* had an enormous effect on legislative districting at all levels, as lawmakers sought to draw plans that complied with Section 2 of the Voting Rights Act as interpreted by the Supreme Court in *Gingles*. While the Court's subsequent restrictions on race-based districting have created some ambiguity regarding the contours of Section 2 and the viability of *Gingles* as precedent, it remains clear that at least for now, the shadow of *Gingles* will continue to loom over redistricting efforts.

THE CONGRESSIONAL ARENA

"All legislative Power herein granted," says the Constitution, "is vested in a Congress of the United States...." But the Constitution says much more. It makes similar statements about the executive power being vested in the president and the judicial power being vested in the federal courts. However, as discussed in Chapter, the Constitution follows the separation of powers doctrine only so far. After coming to delegate total power to each of the three branches, the Constitution goes on to give each branch just enough of the other's powers to make it *interdependent* with, rather than independent of,

each other. Accordingly, it is not accurate, either in theory or in practice, t‹
say that the whole of any of these powers resides in any one branch exclusively. But exclusiveness aside, the fact is that Congress is the chief reposito-
ry of legislative power under our system of government. As such, Congress
has been and remains a major forum in the formation of public policy.

For one thing, the composition of Congress enhances its role in the
policy-making process. Congress, as we know, is a *bicameral* legislature consisting of the House of Representatives and the Senate. The members of the
House are closest to the people because they are from smaller districts.
House members are elected for two-year terms from 435 single-member
districts into which the various states are apportioned. This apportionment
is figured on the basis of population[12] by the respective state legislatures. No
state has less than one member in the House. While there are 435 members
of the House, there are only 100 senators, each elected for 6-year terms
with 2 senators from each state. The Senate elections are staggered so that
one-third of the Senate members are elected every 2 years.

COMMITTEES

The basic organizational and working unit in both houses is the *standing committee*. The main work of Congress, both legislative formulation and legislative oversight, takes place in these committees. How they function in large
measure determines what Congress actually does.

Standing committees are generally organized along subject matter
lines, such as agriculture, finance, science, foreign policy, and the budget.
The Senate currently has 18 such committees, while the House has 20. In
addition, there are a number of joint committees, with membership from
both houses. Finally, there are select committees, which are created for special purposes and have limited tenure. Three select committees were opera-
tive in the 105th Congress—the Senate Ethics Committee, the Senate
Intelligence Committee, and the House Select Intelligence Committee.

Committees differ with respect to the perceived status and prestige
conferred on their members. This variation among types of standing committees is reflected in the rules of the House that separate committees into
three groups: exclusive, semi-exclusive, and nonexclusive. A member of an
exclusive committee cannot sit on any other committee. These are the really important and prestigious committees that have impact on the work of all
other committees and the entire House. There are three exclusive committees in the House: (1) Appropriations, (2) Rules, and (3) Ways and Means.
Next in order of prestige are the semi-exclusive committees; these include
Agriculture, Banking and Financial Services, Budget, Commerce, and
Judiciary. Members can sit on no more than one semi-exclusive committee,
though they may also sit on one nonexclusive committee. A bit lower in
rank and prestige, but not in terms of their particular functions, are the
nonexclusive committees, such as House Oversight and Government

Reform and Oversight. A member may serve on two nonexclusive committees. These restrictions, however, apply only to standing committees and not to select or joint committees.

Membership on the major working committees—the standing committees—is bipartisan, with each party represented roughly in proportion to its strength in the particular chamber. In the House, each party uses its own Steering Committee to assign members to committees. In the Senate, Republican assignments are made by the party's Committee on Committees, while Democrats are assigned by the party's Steering and Coordination Committee. House Republicans, following their 1994 takeover, passed several institutional controls on House offices. Among these controls were the following:

1. Term limits for the speaker (four consecutive terms) and committee and subcommittee chairs (three consecutive terms)
2. Limits on committee assignments (maximum of two standing committee and four subcommittee assignments per member)
3. Cuts in committee staff by one-third from the number employed in the 103rd Congress
4. Shift over control of staff hiring from subcommittee chairs and ranking minority members to committee chairs[13]

The political jockeying for what are considered "plum" committee assignments is particularly intense. This is because committees are the focal point of congressional work and because congressmen perceive that committee assignments can make or break their careers. Representatives fight for the committee assignments that can do the most to further their interests. Interests of congressmen can be distinguished as influence within the House, ensuring reelection through aiding constituents, and making good public policy.[14]

Different committees allow representatives to attain these goals in various ways. For example, Appropriations and Ways and Means are seen as committees that bestow influence and prestige on their members. The Veterans' Affairs and Transportation and Infrastructure committees are the type that aid a member's reelection through constituency service. In contrast, committees such as International Relations and Judiciary are more policy-centered. To be sure, committees can and do serve multiple purposes for individual members. Membership on Ways and Means, for example, provides both prestige and an opportunity to formulate tax policy. What is clear is that one factor behind committee assignment is the representative's desire to have at least one of these purposes met.

However, even if the desires of a representative are known and that representative gets the committee assignment, it is sometimes difficult to establish a direct causal relationship between the two. Take, for example, the case of the black representative from Texas, the late Mickey Leland.[15] Leland wanted to be on the Interstate and Foreign Commerce Committee to work on health issues, which were his main area of interest while serving in the Texas state legislature. He was, however, only one of a number of new representatives who wanted to fill one of the few vacancies on that committee. In fact, both Leland and another newly elected Texas representative (now Senator, Phil Gramm) sought membership on the Commerce Committee. This was possible since two of the seats open on the Commerce Committee had been vacated by Texans. Most important, however, is that the Commerce Committee has jurisdiction over oil and gas matters, a subject very dear to the hearts of Texans. Consequently, Texas representatives thought that their delegation and interests should be well represented on the committee. In any event, both Leland and Gramm lobbied for support among members of the Texas delegation to fill the two seats vacated by departing members of the delegation. (It should be pointed out that both Leland and Gramm had earlier received the endorsement of the Texas freshman representatives, who numbered seven in all.) However, some members of the delegation felt that Leland was soft on energy issues, but Gramm was not so viewed. While consumer groups were concerned with Gramm's stand on issues such as his strong opposition to government regulation, the oil industry was pleased by his prospective membership on the Commerce Committee. Eventually, both Leland and Gramm received the support of the full Texas delegation, including Jim Wright, the House Majority Leader. Leland, in addition, also had the support of the Congressional Black Caucus (CBC) and Ralph Nader's Congress Watch Organization. The CBC supported Leland by expressing that he should be given the seat on the committee left vacant by the death of Ralph Metcalfe, a black representative from Illinois. In the end, both Leland and Gramm won seats on the committee. And though they did not lobby or campaign as a team, Leland thought that "Gramm's candidacy assisted him because … many welcomed them as representatives of diverse viewpoints."[16] Thus, Leland received the committee assignment he wanted, but primarily for reasons not included in his original desire to seek the appointment.

This example serves to show, to some extent, the political maneuvering necessary to get a valued committee assignment. Although it is difficult to state with certainty the factors responsible for gaining a particular assignment, a large part of Leland's success was due to his own lobbying efforts. He thus gained support from his own state congressional delegation. This support undoubtedly provided the key to Leland winning a seat on the committee he preferred.

By way of summary, we have suggested that the major working units of the Congress are its standing committees. Describing the limits to the exclusive, semi-exclusive, and nonexclusive committees are classified as number of committees on which an individual representative may serve. These categories reflect the general perception of the prestige and imporance of given committees, but there remain difficulties in attempting to attach importance and prestige to any particular committee except as it relates to the needs and desires of individual congressmen. In short, how and why members gain particular committee assignments is apparently a very dynamic process subject to the push and pull of a number of factors. Despite the complexities involved, however, it is possible to make several observations on committee assignments of black representatives. To begin with, a number of black representatives serve on the exclusive committees that are perceived as the most influential and prestigious assignments. In the 105th Congress, black representatives held three seats on the House Ways and Means Committee and three seats on the House Appropriations Committee. This membership included both veterans [Charles Rangel (D-New York) on Ways and Means, Louis Stokes (D-Ohio) on Appropriations] and relative newcomers [William Jefferson (D-Louisiana) on Ways and Means, Carrie Meek (D-Florida) on Appropriations].

COMMITTEE CHAIRPERSON

What comes out of the committee, as well as how the committee conducts its work, depends largely upon the committee chair. The power of an individual chairperson, of course, depends upon many factors—his or her personal prestige and standing among colleagues, the tradition and norms of the particular committee, and so on. Nonetheless, the committee chair occupies a central position in the work of the committee. He or she controls the committee staff, schedules or postpones committee meetings, determines the agenda, and generally sets the pace of the committee. Though recent rule change have somewhat diminished their powers, chairpersons retain a great dei of influence over the committee's operations.

Hist ically, the only way in which a member could become a committee cha was through *seniority*. This tended to favor southerners from safe district However, because of the changes in Democratic party rules, seniority, the h still an important factor, is not the only way to become a committee ch 17 While a number of factors operated in concert to break the seniority s m, a primary reason was the number of new representatives elected to gress in the 1970s. The turnover rate in Congress reached the point that in 8 more than half of the House members had been elected since 1974. 18 result was a steady and large influx of new members who did not owe thing to the House senior establishment. But the seniority system re ded in the 1980s with a dramatic reduction in the turnover rate. For ex e, the return rate for the current Congress—those who were members o previous Congress—was 92 percent. In fact, 97.5 percent of those who reelection in 1988 won. In 1990, the rate for the House was 96 perc Black incumbents have been particularly successful in winning reele much so that although blacks make up only 5 percent of the 435 votir bers of the House, they chaired 25 percent of the standing and select committees in the 100th (previous) Congress.[20] These gains have come largely as a result of the seniority of black members. For example, in the 103rd Congress (1993–94), two black members chaired key House committees—John Conyers, Jr. (D-Michigan), chair of the Government Operations Committee (now the Government Reform and Oversight Committee), and Ron Dellums (D-California), chair of the Armed Services Committee (now the National Security Committee). In addition, William Clay (D-Missouri) chaired the now-defunct House Post Office and Civil Service Committee. This represents quite a departure from the situation in 1978, when Dellums was the only black serving as a committee chair (the now-defunct District of Columbia Committee). He had replaced another black, Charles Diggs (D-Michigan), who became chair in 1972. Diggs was forced to resign the chairmanship following his conviction in October 1978 on felony charges relating to the diversion of his congressional employees' salaries to personal use.[21]

The two men who became committee chairmen prior to Diggs are names familiar to many of us—Representatives William L. Dawson (D-Illinois) and Representative Adam Clayton Powell (D-New York). Dawson was elected to Congress in 1942 and served as chairman of the House Committee on Government Operations from 1955 until his retirement in 1970. Powell was elected to Congress in 1944 and became chairman of the very important House Committee on Education and Labor in 1961. Powell remained as chairman of the committee until 1967, when he was ousted from that position and eventually from Congress. Let us take a more detailed look at the politics and chairmanships of Dawson and Powell.

Since the depression there has always been at least one black member in the House. But until Dawson and Powell came on the scene, blacks did not hold positions of significant influence in congressional policy making. Dawson's situation is especially important, we believe, since he seemed *so* enmeshed in the Chicago political machine that it was difficult, if not impossible, for him to attend to black interests. However, it should be stated that Dawson's committee did not at the time handle matters of salient interest to blacks. The jurisdiction of the committee has been described as follows:

> [b]udget and accounting measures other than appropriations, reorganization in executive and legislative branches of government, studying intergovernmental relations between U.S. and the states and municipalities, general legislative oversight of executive branch.[22]

Possessing institutional power in this instance did not lead to generalized political gains for blacks. In this regard, Hanes Walton has stated:

> Dawson used his institution and personal power to enhance his political position and influence in Congress and did not serve blacks in general.[23]

he time Dawson became chairman, he had reached an advanced age and his health was deteriorating. Effective use of power requires a degree of vigor and energy that he did not possess. And, finally, the amount of bargaining with colleagues for the interest of a black constituency was limited since Dawson's position furnished fewer resources with which to negotiate. Unlike his colleague from Chicago, Adam Clayton Powell, Jr., was a maverick. The minister of the largest black Protestant congregation in New York City, Congressman Powell exploited this resource in fighting the Tammany machine of New York. Powell emerged at an opportune time. The influence of political machines was declining, but of equal importance was a growing political consciousness among northern urban blacks. This consciousness partly resulted from longstanding frustration over unresponsive government institutions. African Americans were becoming increasingly resentful of the continued discrimination and other forms of social injustice to which they were subjected.

Because of his flamboyant style and the explicit emphasis that Powell placed on race, he has generally been criticized by political commentators and scholarly analysts. James Q. Wilson, for example, characterized Powell as a political leader who substituted "personal charisma and bellicose militancy" for organization.[24] We agree that Powell had charismatic appeal and that he was (for his time) militant. But personalizing leadership is a characteristic of black ministerial style, especially in the Baptist denominations. And in the absence of more tangible rewards, charisma is a functional substitute for holding a constituency together. It should also be kept in mind that a religious congregation is similar to a political machine; it provides welfare services to members. This function is, of course, more limited in scope in a church.

As a political base, Powell's congregation was both durable and large enough to return him to office repeatedly. In consequence, he became chair of the House Committee on Education and Labor when Graham Barden resigned from Congress in protest against packing the committee with new members who favored more liberal legislation. Powell's tenure as chair was important since it spanned the period during the development of legislation needed to wage the War on Poverty. His committee was a focal point for many of the crucial legislative debates in this effort. Powell's committee leadership, however, has not been evaluated favorably. Unlike some of the other chairpersons, Powell was not considered an "expert" in his assigned responsibilities. Much of the work of Education and Labor, as with other House committees, was done by subcommittee chairs. The flamboyant style that characterized Powell's leadership also worked against his effectiveness as committee chair. In addition, he could not be attentive to the business of the committee because of his high rate of absenteeism from Congress.

Perhaps Powell's fall from power was an inevitable consequence of his behavior. He was never a popular figure in Congress. His troubles grew in New York and Washington, as well. Powell had gone against congressiona norms, including what a special House committee found to be a misuse federal funds. As a result, the House fined Powell and stripped him of seniority and his chairmanship. The racial themes that he espoused offended the white majority at the same time that they gained him widespread admiration among blacks. But in the end, it was Powell's Harlem constituents who did what his House colleagues wanted to do but could not: deprive him of a seat in Congress.[25] Powell was defeated in the 1970 primary and died soon thereafter.

Subcommittees: Their Increasing Influence

While standing committees retain their role as the chief working units of both houses, subcommittees are increasingly being looked upon as the chief working units of the standing committees themselves. Indeed, the committee structure of Congress provides members with the opportunity to gain expertise and visibility in discrete areas of public policy. This is important both for a member's efforts at reelection through constituency service and for the development of innovative and important policy initiatives. Almost all work done in Congress begins in a subcommittee. This is also the place where much of the investigation pursuant to legislative oversight occurs. Thus, because of their rather small size and discrete areas of jurisdiction, it is possible for one or a few members of Congress to exert significant influence in both the larger standing committees and in the legislative process generally.

Subcommittees exist under the jurisdiction of committees. In the House of Representatives, for example, there were 104 subcommittees during the 105th Congress. As with committees, subcommittees vary with size, jurisdiction, and prestige. Historically, subcommittees existed as the personal fiefdoms of powerful committee chairmen. But no more. Along with changes to lessen the power of committees and committee chairs have come changes that have increased the role and authority of subcommittees and their chairs.

The major changes occurred in 1973 and have come to be known collectively as the "*subcommittee bill of rights.*"[26] These reforms, for example, now allow committee caucuses, rather than committee chairs, to select chairs of the subcommittees, establish their jurisdictions, provide for adequate subcommittee budgets, and ensure all members of a major subcommittee assignment. They also require committee chairs to refer legislation to appropriate subcommittees within two weeks. This, of course, prevents committee chairs from killing bills by not scheduling them for action. Furthermore, the changes allow subcommittee chairmen and their ranking minority members to hire one staff person each to work for them on the subcommittee. Such staff assistance allows subcommittees more independence from committee chairmen. Thus, subcommittees are becoming an increasingly important stage in the legislative process.

How do blacks fare in subcommittee assignments? Do they serve on subcommittees that can have a significant impact on the social welfare policies affecting African Americans? As with full committee assignments, answers to such questions can prove difficult, but we can suggest that black representatives, not unlike others, tend to serve on at least one subcommittee that addresses the interests of their constituents, for example, health, education, and social welfare policy.

Subcommittee Chairpersons

The reforms of the Democratic party and House rules that changed the committee and subcommittee structures also affected the power of subcommittee chairs. Decreasing the power of committee chairs over subcommittees provided subcommittee chairs with more autonomy. Again, as with committee chairs, seniority has ceased to be the only factor in selecting chairpersons. Thus, there has been an element of unpredictability added to who will become subcommittee chairs. The Democratic Caucus of each committee, established in 1973, typically decides who the subcommittee chair will be. However, one qualification to this general rule occurs with the Appropriations Committee, in which all subcommittee chairs are approved by the Democratic Caucus of the House.

How successful have black representatives been in becoming subcommittee chairs? Just as in other areas, as black representation grows in numbers and seniority, so does its role and influence in chairing subcommittees. For example, probably the most influential subcommittee chaired in the 103rd Congress by a black member was the Select Revenue Measure Subcommittee of the House Ways and Means Committee, which was chaired by Charles Rangel (D-New York). However, changes in partisan control of Congress affect opportunities for subcommittee control as well as committee control. In the Republican-controlled 105th Congress, for example, the lone black representative in the majority—J. C. Watts, of Oklahoma—did not chair any subcommittee.

Other Congressional Leaders

In addition to committee and subcommittee chairs, there are other key positions in Congress. In the House there is the Speaker of the House, the majority *floor leader*, and the minority floor leader. Though each of these officials is selected by his party *caucus*, only the Speaker (the presiding officer) is officially elected by the entire House. The Speaker is by far the single most important official in the House. He wields great influence in his party, the House, and the Congress generally. Together, the Speaker and the majority and minority floor leaders significantly influence the outcome of business in the House. Similarly, the majority and minority leaders in the Senate set the pace of business in that house.

In general, the party leadership and various party committees decide standing committee assignments and committee chairs and control the operations and flow of business in each house. For these reasons, to be active in the party is extremely important to a congressional career.

Thus, another role for members of Congress has been identified. In addition to proposing legislation, engaging in oversight activities, providing services to constituents, and serving as members of committees and sub-committees, legislators must also attend to important party business that influences the inner workings of the House. If congressional careers can be made or broken by the type of committee assignment a member receives, a source of considerable power must be the bodies that decide committee assignments. Thus, it is in the interest of black members in furthering their careers and dealing with the problems of their constituents to gain leadership roles and membership in various congressional party structures.

In the 105th Congress, many black members held party committee assignments. Among the positions held by black members were Deputy Whip [John Lewis (D-Georgia)], Democratic Policy Committee Vice-Chair [Eva Clayton (D-North Carolina) and Jesse Jackson, Jr. (D-Illinois)], and Democratic Steering Committee member [Maxine Waters (D-California) and Charles Rangel (D-New York)]. In addition, several blacks serve in the Democratic Party's Leadership Advisory Group. Service on these committees and in these roles gives black members opportunities to shape policy, to influence the composition of House committees and subcommittees, and to perform party-building functions.

The Legislative Bureaucracy: Congressional Staffs

The executive bureaucracy and administrative agencies bear the brunt of studies, investigations, and humor about what all those "faceless" federal bureaucrats do and how they operate. And, since this bureaucracy operates primarily under the direction of the president and his cabinet, it plays an important role not only in the implementation of public policies but also in the development of those policies. Thus, attention is properly focused on what and how these officials operate. However, similar attention has not been given to another group of staff persons who work for the federal government—*the legislative bureaucracy*. This bureaucracy includes (1) professional staff persons who work for congressional committees and (2) those persons who serve as staff for individual members of Congress. These persons assist the Congress in carrying out day-to-day operations. Their work runs the gamut from research and data collection needed for hearings, investigations, and bill drafting to the kind of things needed to nurse a constituency, such as responding to letters from the people back home.

In short, the work of Congress is greatly dependent upon the work of various staffs. As such, legislative bureaucrats –just like bureaucrats in the executive branch—play a crucial and influential role in the legislative process. They provide ideas, information, and insight that help to shape legislation and congressional decision making. As such, the work effectiveness standing, and influence of individual members of Congress and of congressional committees depend in large measure upon the work and resourcefulness of the various staffs.

This apparent and increasing role of legislative bureaucrats in the work of the Congress is (or at least should be) of obvious interest to blacks and minorities. And just as attention is focused on the "representativeness" of Congress and the executive bureaucracy in terms of minority representation, so must we devote similar attention to the "representativeness" of the legislative bureaucracy. And, in this regard, blacks and minorities remain woefully underrepresented and unrepresented both on congressional committee staffs and on staffs of individual members of Congress. The situation differs little, and in fact may be worse, than it was some 20 years ago. A 1979 *National Journal* study of congressional committee staffs, for example, found that committee staffs were "dominated by white males."[27] The study indicated that blacks and other minorities constituted only about 5 percent of the staffs (85 out of 1,669). Moreover, the study pointed up that the few blacks who were on committee staffs were "often" selected by black members who served on these committees.[28] Consider, for example, the following excerpt from the *National Journal* study:

> Of the 50 committee staff directors, not one is a woman. The only black holding the job is the staff director of the House District of Columbia Committee, which is chaired by a black member. No women or blacks are to be found heading any of the major administrative support offices and (at the time of the 1979 study) the only woman filling an important post in the legislative bureaucracy is Alice Rivlin, director of the Congressional Budget Office.[29]

Staffs of individual members, of course, are selected by and work for the various members of the Congress. Here again, the 1979 *National Journal* study indicated that, just as on committee staffs, blacks constituted only about 5 percent of the staff personnel in members' offices. Moreover, a breakdown by staff position shows that blacks were clustered in the lower prestige and salaried jobs. Almost one-half (49 percent) of all blacks in members' offices were in "clerical" positions, with 75 percent clustered in the bottom three categories. By contrast, whereas only 25 percent of the blacks employed in staff positions were in the top four categories, more than 50 percent of the whites in staff positions (54 percent) held jobs in these top categories.

Overall, little has changed in terms of the continued paucity of black and minority representation in legislative staffs and the congressional bureaucracy. According to surveys conducted in 1993 and 1994 by the nonprofit Congressional Management Foundation, minorities make up 22 percent of the nation's workforce, yet they held only 16 percent of the jobs in legislators' personal offices in the House and 15 percent in the Senate. The numbers declined to 12 percent in the House and 4 percent in the Senate when only the top legislative and administrative jobs were considered.[30] In addition, the number of black professionals has dropped sharply since the GOP takeover of Congress in 1994. A 1995 survey by congressional researcher Jeffrey Cooper identified only 12 black professionals working for House committees, or one-sixth the number employed in the last Congress. In the Senate, the decline was approximately one-half.[31] These declines have occurred despite the lack of change in black membership on Capitol Hill between the 103th and 104th Congresses.

"Power jobs" are defined as including administrative assistants, legislative assistants, press secretaries, and senior committee staff. The 1991 report indicates that in the Senate blacks hold some 68, or 2.5 percent, of these 2,700 most important positions. The situation is only a little better in the House, where blacks hold about 240, or 4.4 percent, of the 5,500 most important staff jobs. Mention is made, however, that more than half of these black staffers at the time worked for the 26 black members of the House.[32]

Various explanations, of course, are offered for the small number of blacks in the legislative bureaucracy. One may be that Congress (and the judicial branch) was not covered by the anti-discrimination provisions of earlier civil rights legislation, such as the Civil Rights Act of 1964, even though both houses subsequently adopted policies against such discrimination.[33] It is true, of course, that the 1991 Civil Rights Act offers congressional (and White House) employees protection against job discrimination, but neither house is required to follow affirmative action guidelines. The 104th Congress, in one of its more publicized accomplishments, did pass a law requiring legislators to comply with the same laws it imposes on other actors. The Congressional Accountability Act, however, possessed several shortcomings that have rendered it ineffective in protecting staffers.[34]

In short, there is a lack of any effective enforcement mechanism to ensure greater representation of blacks and minorities among congressional staffs, and litigation as a way of enforcing rights remains a long and tortuous process. Thus, the lack of more blacks and other minorities in congressional staff positions might very well be due to the lack of any effective anti-discrimination or affirmative action policies. It is indeed ironic that the Congress that passed so much civil rights legislation should itself be found wanting in giving full effect to the kinds of policies that it has imposed on others.

On a more practical level, the lack of blacks in staff positions can also be explained by the fact that it is hard to find blacks who have the qualifications and experience needed for such positions. This, of course, is a time-worn excuse that is used in many contexts. Qualifications are often so nebulous that they can easily be tailored to permit or prevent certain persons from gaining particular positions. And while it is true that experience can be an important asset for given jobs, this explanation becomes somewhat circular and self-fulfilling since blacks, by not being employed initially, have not had the opportunity to gain such experience.

Since blacks are grossly underrepresented both in the membership of Congress and in the various congressional staffs, it follows that very few blacks participate in the fashioning of laws by which they, and all other Americans, are governed. This could prove of major consequence since such staff positions "tend to become springboards to even more powerful positions."[35] Indeed, some current members of Congress, as well as persons in other branches [such as Justice Clarence Thomas, a former aide to Senator John Danforth (R-Missouri)], got their starts by working on congressional staffs.

Legislation and Legislative Oversight

The main business of Congress is legislating, or passing laws. Congress, however, is concerned with more than passing laws; it is also interested in how those laws, once enacted, are carried out. The enactment of laws and their implementation are obviously dynamic processes, involving as they do the interaction of the president, Congress, interest groups, administrators, and others. A discussion of these dynamics is reserved for the next chapter. Our purpose here is to give a brief overview of the process by which Congress passes laws and how Congress goes about finding out what happens once such laws are enacted.

Generally, the initiative in law making comes from the president, although a myriad of legislative proposals comes from the Congress. Nonetheless, before any proposals (bills) can become laws, they must run the legislative gamut in Congress, which includes (1) introduction and referral to committee; (2) committee consideration, including the full range of options open to the committee: for example, whether or not to hold public hearings; whether the bill should be amended, redrafted, or substituted altogether; or whether or not the bill should be reported out; and (3) consideration, or debate, and vote by the entire house. If passed by one house, the bill is sent to the other house, where basically the same procedures are followed. If both houses pass the bill in identical form, then the bill is sent directly to the president. However, if a similar but slightly different version of the bill is passed by one house, a conference committee made up of members of both houses convenes to resolve the differences. If such differences are resolved, the identical measure worked out by the conference committee is presented to both houses. If passed in this identical form, the bill is then sent to the president for his approval or disapproval (veto). If the president approves and signs the bill, it becomes law; if he disapproves (vetoes) the bill, it might still become law if two-thirds of both houses of Congress vote to override the president's veto. The overriding of a presidential veto, however, is seldom accomplished. Or, if the president does not take action on the bill within ten weekdays, the bill becomes law without his signature. However, if the Congress adjourns within this ten-day period, the president—by not taking any action—can kill the bill.

The activities of Congress do not stop once a bill becomes law. Indeed, there is an increasing interest in Congress to determine whether particular laws are being implemented by the executive branch in accord with congressional intent. This continuous review by Congress of the executive branch is generally known as *legislative oversight*.

Legislative oversight is on the increase. A major reason for this increase is perhaps due to a belief that certain implementation activities of government bureaucrats—such as the issuance of rules, regulations, and guidelines—violate legislative intent or otherwise abuse executive discretion. Moreover, many Americans believe that the government, especially the executive bureaucracy, has become too big and insensitive to their needs, and therefore, constant surveillance is required if adequate control on legislative implementation is to be maintained. Members of Congress, ever sensitive to voters in their quest for reelection, have increased their oversight of the bureaucracy to meet this perceived need.

The efforts of Congress to oversee the activities of executive agencies were dealt a blow when the U.S. Supreme Court held the legislative veto unconstitutional in *Immigration and Naturalization Service* v. *Chadha* [462 U.S. 919 (1983)]. The legislative veto, a mechanism whereby either house of Congress could overturn an executive agency's decision, was included in hundreds of laws to provide Congress with a weapon to combat bureaucratic decisions that it opposed. The Immigration and Nationality Act included a provision that allowed either the House of Representatives or the Senate to pass a resolution rejecting the decision of the attorney general and the Immigration and Naturalization Service to suspend a deportation proceeding. Through the use of a resolution, it was not necessary to present the action to either the other chamber or the president. In *Immigration and Naturalization Service* v. *Chadha*, the House of Representatives overturned the attorney general's decision to suspend the deportation of an East Indian, Jagdish Rai Chadha, and to allow him to remain in the United States. Chadha had a nonimmigrant student visa, but he remained in the United States after its expiration. The Supreme Court struck down the legislative veto because the resolution was not presented to the president for his approval. The result of this decision was to lessen Congress's ability to check the actions of executive agencies.

The brunt of the oversight function is carried on by various committees and subcommittees. A variety of methods are used by Congress in its oversight activities. The most prevalent of these methods are *hearings*,[36] wherein executive branch personnel appear before committees to give testimony on administrative implementation of legislative mandates.

Insofar as blacks and minorities are concerned, the increase in oversight activities by Congress can cut both ways. On the one hand, the time spent on oversight is time not spent on developing creative legislation and policy initiatives to deal with the problems of blacks and other minori-

On the other hand, it may be argued that legislative oversight activities are necessary to protect and make more effective programs such as those embodied in the mass of legislation passed during the 1960s, for example, the Civil Rights Act of 1964. Indeed, such activities might point to the need for corrective or supplemental legislation to profit from new information.

However, the continuing inequities (e.g., in housing and employment) suffered by blacks and other minorities lend credence to the view that minorities do not appear to derive much benefit from the oversight activities of the Congress. Indeed, in the past few years Congress has done little, if anything, to fill in the "gaps" (in legislation) and come to grips with the persisting problems of racism. But, as we shall see, one of the major objectives of the Congressional Black Caucus is to push Congress to deal with these persistent problems.

DISTRICT REPRESENTATIVES WITH A NATIONAL CONSTITUENCY: THE CONGRESSIONAL BLACK CAUCUS

"When we started the Caucus [in 1969]," said Representative Louis Stokes, "we had no idea that it would have the kind of impact on black America that it's had....[37] All we were trying to demonstrate was that nine blacks, given the responsibility to be in the U.S. Congress, could come together to try to work on behalf of black people as best as we knew how."[38] Stokes's remarks capture well the notion that blacks in Congress represent more than just their district constituencies; in a very real sense, they also represent what Matthew Holden would call the "Black Nation."[39] This is indeed a tremendous burden, and it is one that is shouldered by (or that haunts) black leaders in various contexts. In short, whether individual blacks want to or not, those in visible leadership positions—such as black members of Congress— are perceived by many Americans, not only blacks but whites as well, as representing the hopes and aspirations of all blacks. In the main, blacks in Congress have accepted this additional responsibility and have sought ways to carry it out. In this sense, the Congressional Black Caucus (CBC) symbolizes, in a very formal way, the commitment and concern that black members of Congress have toward their "national" constituency.

The formative years of the CBC, 1969–1971, saw the organization searching for its role and identity. At times, the organization served as an investigative body calling nationwide attention to everyday problems and perils faced by blacks. At other times, the CBC served as an information agency, collecting and dispensing data on black concerns. But, according to one source,[40] the incident that gave the CBC national visibility and stature was its protracted battle with President Nixon. Essentially, the CBC was concerned and disturbed, as were many others, over Nixon's negative posture toward blacks. In February 1970, the organization requested a meeting with president to discuss its concerns. But Nixon ignored the request. Apparently, this upset CBC members to the extent that they let it be known that they would boycott Nixon's 1971 State of the Union message, and they did. Obviously, the boycott created some concern and embarrassment to the president. In any event, some two months after this incident, on March 25, 1971, Nixon met with the CBC, and the group had done its homework. The organization "confronted" the president with 61 recommendations covering the range of problems facing blacks and other minorities, including health, welfare, poverty, and civil rights. Not unexpectedly, the president's response was anything but encouraging. However, the "confrontation" meeting with Nixon was not without benefits. It served to bring the CBC to the fore as a major force in black politics. Perhaps, also, it served to crystallize the common dislike that blacks generally had for Nixon's policies. This, in turn, undoubtedly helped to overcome or quiet stresses and divisions not only within the CBC but also among the CBC and other civil rights groups and leaders.

In 1971, the CBC sharpened its focus and direction and mushroomed as a force in national politics. This was symbolized by a number of things— a highly successful fund-raising dinner; the shaping of a permanent CBC staff; and more systematic attention to and study of black problems. Even so, the CBC had to define carefully its role and purpose so that it would supplement, not duplicate, the work of other groups. Eventually, the CBC decided that it would abandon some of its "national forum" functions—such as conferences and hearings—and would instead concentrate on matters consistent with the role and expertise of its members. Thus, the primary focus of the CBC would be on legislation and the legislative process.

This new direction was well reflected in the workshops, speeches, and other activities connected with the group's third annual fund-raising dinner in 1973. As Caucus Chairman Stokes put it, the primary purpose of the CBC is to "utilize the legislative process to help bring about full equality of opportunity in American society." The CBC, continued Stokes, is now at the point where it hopes to put "the black perspective into all legislation."[41]

In February 1974, Representative Charles Rangel (D-New York) became the new chairman of the CBC, replacing Stokes. Rangel cited the successful passage of "home rule" for the District of Columbia as evidence of the Caucus's acting with a new "sophistication." He reemphasized that the CBC must limit itself to legislative concerns. Said Rangel:

> I plan to present to the Caucus a legislative agenda that we can work on that will get us more realistic support rather than the spiritual support we have already. We have no permanent friends, no permanent enemies, just permanent interests of blacks and minority constituents.[42]

In looking to the future, Rangel indicated his intention to strengthen the CBC staff and to stimulate more participation from black elected officials in the national black convention movement.[43]

But perhaps the biggest challenge and opportunity that faced Caucus involved its relations and access to the then-new president, Ge

Ford. As a U.S. representative from Middle America (Grand Rapids, Michigan), Ford's record was far from sympathetic to the needs and goals of blacks. But as president, Gerald Ford made the first move.[44] Within three days after assuming the presidency, Ford called Congressman Rangel directly, indicating his desire to meet with the CBC. Rangel admitted that different interpretations had and would be made of the president's initiative in calling the meeting. But, said Rangel:

> Whatever interpretation you choose, both sides undeniably reaped benefits. Clearly, the President's initiation of the meeting just three days after taking office means he saw it in his own self-interest. Our quick acceptance reflected the majority view that we could only gain by making this effort at establishing communication with the new national administration.

The meeting between the president and the CBC took place on August 21. Although disappointed that Ford's very first speech to the Congress indicated little if any sympathy for black concerns, the Caucus nevertheless decided "to give him the benefit of the doubt and approach the meeting in good faith as an effort to communicate." Accordingly, the CBC agreed "to meet the President halfway" and to structure its presentation for the meeting around "double digit inflation," the "domestic enemy number one" that the president had identified in his speech to Congress. Such emphasis, said Rangel, "did no violence to our own priorities, for it is the poor and minority communities that have suffered most because of runaway inflation." In keeping with the inflation theme, the CBC "warned" the president that budget cuts in such areas as housing, health, and education would be counterproductive, saying that "those who can least afford to lose federal aid will be hurt the most."

The Caucus also asked the president to appoint blacks and other minorities who would be "sensitive" to the needs of poor and minority communities "at every level of his administration." As to this request, the president responded that he "fully intended" to make such appointments. Rangel called this the "most important commitment" to come out of the meeting. Indeed, said Rangel, "the best and most lasting way to achieve institutionalization of communication between the executive branch and the CBC is to have the type of executive agency appointees in this administration who will be sympathetic to the needs of the poor and minorities because of their ideological and philosophical commitment and, equally important, because of who they are." Overall, there appeared to be some optimism that the meeting would lead to improved relations between the CBC and "The Man" in the White House. But, as Rangel put it, "optimism cannot be sustained unless it is fed by concrete accomplishment, and although we stand ready to work with the President if he proves his good will, we stand equally ready to oppose him if he does not."

Subsequently, Ford took some actions that undoubtedly caused the

Caucus to be "less optimistic" about future relations with him. For one thing, his "full and unconditional" pardon of former President Nixon did nothing to convince blacks and other minorities that all men are equal under the law. Moreover, in an October 1974 news conference, the president served to provoke rather than quiet racial friction when he indicated sharp disagreement with "forced busing" (and a federal court order) at the very time that the Boston school situation was erupting in violence over the issue.[45] Consequently, his attitude toward "forced busing" greatly overshadowed his announced intention to enforce the law (the federal court decision). In any event, actions such as these were definitely not calculated to improve relations between the president and the CBC.

Carter and the CBC

Jimmy Carter won the 1976 presidential election, and the CBC—from all apparent indications—now had a more friendly president in the White House. For one thing, Carter was a Democrat, as were all members of the CBC. Moreover, Carter received some of his strongest support during the election from particular members of the CBC, especially Representative Andrew Young (D-Georgia). And, perhaps most important of all, Carter won the presidency with overwhelming support from African Americans—more than 90 percent of blacks voted for Carter. Hence, along a number of dimensions, the CBC and African Americans had reason to be optimistic about the new president.

Generally, however, relations between the CBC and Carter, just as with African Americans generally, were mixed and fluctuated greatly. To be certain, the president did appoint blacks to a number of positions throughout the federal government, including the appointment of two blacks to cabinet-level positions: Patricia Harris, Housing and Urban Development (HUD) and Andrew Young, U.N. Ambassador. In addition, the president consistently expressed sympathy and support for the hopes and aspirations of blacks and other minorities. On the other hand, many blacks—including some members of the CBC—did not think he lived up to his campaign promises. As discussed in Chapter 2, many blacks saw little if any improvement in the everyday problems that affected blacks (e.g., unemployment and poor housing). Consequently, though relations between Carter and blacks remained friendly, they were also somewhat strained.

An example may serve to illustrate this friendly yet uncertain relationship. The CBC, pursuing its new legislative focus, adopted the passing of the Humphrey-Hawkins bill as one of its major legislative objectives. This bill, co-sponsored by CBC member Augustus Hawkins (D-California) and the late Senator Hubert Humphrey (D-Minnesota), was aimed at unemployment, an all-too-common status among blacks and other minorities. Simply put, the Humphrey-Hawkins bill sought to reduce unemployment by 4 percent by 1983. But there was a great deal of

whether or not the bill should be passed. It took an incident, not unlike the CBC confrontation with President Nixon, to provide the impetus necessary to get the bill through Congress.

The CBC met with President Carter to discuss the status of the bill. During the meeting, CBC member John Conyers, Jr. (D-Michigan), charged that the president was not doing enough to support passage of the bill. When Vice-President Mondale objected to this assessment, Conyers walked out of the meeting. Obviously, it is difficult to ascribe motivation to any one particular incident, but apparently after this incident the president lobbied intensively in support of the bill.[46] Conservative opposition, however, loaded the measure with what many viewed as crippling amendments. Eventually, with Carter's help, the bill did pass, but in a form that made its lofty goals difficult, if not impossible, to achieve. Nevertheless, both the president and many civil rights leaders hailed the new law as an important victory for blacks and for all the poor. And in many ways the passage of the bill was a victory, even if primarily along symbolic lines. One thing seems clear, however. The unity and feeling of the CBC in its meeting with the president did much to spur the bill's passage.

The CBC in the Reagan Years

After winning the 1980 presidential election, Ronald Reagan met with the CBC during his first year in the White House. The relationship got off to a remarkably smooth start and continued that way through the first months of the Reagan presidency. The president even met personally with then-CBC chair Mickey Leland (D-Texas) in December 1982 to discuss famine relief in Africa. "He (Reagan) immediately upon our request diverted a ship that was going to India with food to Ethiopia," Leland said. "I was really happy—for the first time proud—that President Reagan was our President. He was far more concerned than I had seen him on any issue dealing with human beings."[47] But Reagan's relationship with the CBC soon soured. The president rejected further meetings with the CBC, leading Leland to describe the relationship as "non-existent." Refusing to meet with the CBC "is past being just insensitive," Leland said. "It is an evil character who refuses to spend time with people who have a deep abiding concern about humanity when we are in severe jeopardy."[48]

It was the latter sentiments, expressed by Leland, that most character-d Reagan's relationship with the CBC during his two terms in office. ral issues polarized the White House and the CBC, including Reagan's ng of South Africa, his economic policies, which reduced inflation at dous costs in terms of unemployment (especially among young nd his opposition to civil rights legislation. Although the balance of veen the CBC and the White House obviously favored the presi-C won some significant victories over the Reagan administration. the CBC led the fight in Congress to pass legislation calling for economic sanctions against South Africa. After Reagan vetoed the bill, Congress overrode the president and enacted the Anti-Apartheid Act of 1986, which was sponsored in the House by the CBC's Ronald Dellums (D-California).[49]

The CBC also built coalitions with like-minded groups in Congress—such as the Hispanic and Women's caucuses[50]—to oppose Reagan's widely perceived hostility to civil rights legislation. The strategy paid off in passing the Civil Rights Restoration Act over Reagan's veto, with the CBC's Augustus Hawkins (D-California) playing a prominent role in the House override. The act was designed to overturn the effects of the 1984 Supreme Court *Grove City* v. *Bell* decision, which limited the reach of federal anti-discrimination laws in institutions that receive federal funds.[51]

Beyond the battle over specific pieces of legislation, however, some CBC members considered the Reagan years a big setback in general for blacks and other minorities. This sentiment was succinctly expressed during the 1988 presidential campaign by former U.S. Representative and CBC member [...] ell (D-Maryland): "Even if Reagan gets kicked out, what you have in this country is a whole new mindset. There is an antiblack mood and an economic problem that we must address. The question for us is who will best cushion bl[...] Reagan did not get "kicked out" in 1984, and his vice-president, George Bush, won the 1988 presidential election after running what some observers considered a racially divisive campaign.[53]

The CBC and the Bush Administration

The Bush administration, in contrast to the Reagan administration, seemed more open to contacts with the Congressional Black Caucus. In May 1989, President Bush met with the CBC and agreed to a schedule of regular meetings and instructed administration officials to meet with CBC members.[54] In their meeting with Bush, CBC members urged the president to tackle the problems underlying the drug crisis, such as the system for caring for the poor, and to shape military policy on the changing relations with the Soviet Union.

This willingness to consult with the CBC, however, did not mean an absence of conflict between members of the CBC and the Bush administration. An early conflict arose over the nomination of William Lucas to hea[...] the civil rights division of the Justice Department.[55] Lucas, a former [...] agent, sheriff, and county executive, had little trial experience or knowl[...] of civil rights issues. Some members of the CBC, such as William H. G[...] (D-Pennsylvania), felt that his inexperience in civil rights issues dis[...] him for the job. On the other hand, other members of the CBC, [...] John Conyers (D-Michigan), supported the nomination. In th[...] Lucas nomination was defeated. Similarly, in 1991 the CBC [...] black organization to openly oppose President Bush's nomin[...] Clarence Thomas to the U.S. Supreme Court. To the CB[...]

Thomas was an African American was not as important as his policy positions, especially those taken in his role as director of the Equal Employment Opportunity Commission. Representative Gary Franks (R-Connecticut) was the only member of the CBC to vote against the Caucus position.

The CBC and the Clinton Administration

The 1992 elections appeared to place the Congressional Black Caucus in its most promising political position since its formative years in 1969–1971. The number of black members in the House grew from 26 to 39, a 50 percent gain, and Carol Moseley-Braun (D-Illinois) became the only black member of the Senate. More importantly, the election of a Democratic president, Bill Clinton of Arkansas, offered hope that the setbacks of the Reagan-Bush years would be reversed. Clinton campaigned on policy initiatives, such as health care and job training, that promised benefits to minority communities that had been overlooked during the preceding 12 years of Republican occupancy of the White House. (He also campaigned on welfare reform, a subject that will addressed in more det~~ai~~l and pp. 350–359.) Between his center-left poli~~cy~~ stances and his appointment of 4 African-Americans to his cabinet, President Clinton seemed to be creating an environment conducive to increasing understanding and support from the Congressional Black Caucus.

This relationship, however, was marked by a hard electoral reality. Black voters overwhelmingly (over 80 percent[56]) identified with and supported the Democratic Party, and black legislators overwhelmingly supported President Clinton, because there was nowhere else to go. To be sure, the Democratic Party was more congruent with interests shared by black voters than was the Republican Party. But the Democratic Party could take its black supporters for granted, since those voters lacked alternatives that were more appealing and electorally viable. This electoral reality played itself out in the 1992 Clinton campaign strategy, which attempted to cast the candidate as a centrist "New Democrat." The campaign targeted suburban voters, many of whom had backed Republican presidential candidates during the 1980s, while counting on winning the support of urban minorities. Clinton's electoral success gave minority interests greater access to the White House, but that victory left the president beholden to the more centrist elements within his party.

The tension between the liberal wing of the party and the New ~~Dem~~ocrats manifested itself in relations between the CBC and President ~~Clinto~~n. While the CBC had enough votes to give it the potential to exercise ~~some~~ leverage, its ideological position made it less crucial to the president ~~than the~~ bloc of conservative and moderate Democrats. As in the 1992 elec~~ti~~on knew that CBC members would generally support him; as a ~~result he~~ was freed to attend to his party's right wing, which could more ~~of~~ten to side with congressional Republicans.

Thus, it was unsurprising that some points of friction would emerge between the CBC and Clinton. Within the first few months of the Clinton Administration, for example, the CBC openly expressed frustration and anger over certain revisions the president had made in his original budget proposals, especially those calling for additional cuts in both entitlement programs (e.g., Medicare) and discretionary spending (e.g., programs to create jobs to help alleviate massive unemployment that especially hurt black and minority youth).

The CBC and other black leaders, such as Jesse Jackson, also expressed deep concern over the president's policy toward Haiti. An economically and politically troubled nation, Haiti became a foreign policy issue because its refugees, fleeing military-sponsored violence, tended to land in Florida, where they were hardly given a warm welcome. During his 1992 campaign, Clinton promised to admit Haitian refugees and to discontinue the Bush administration's more restrictive immigration policy. As president, however, Clinton not only decided to follow his predecessor's policy of forcibly returning all "boat people" fleeing Haiti, but then proceeded to defend that policy successfully in the Supreme Court.[57] Pressure from the CBC, as well as from human rights organizations, led President Clinton to pursue a different path that focused on ending military rule and the violence against civilians that precipitated the refugee crisis. In September 1994, the president took several steps toward this end: preparing an invasion; sending a three-man diplomatic mission—featuring former President Jimmy Carter, former Joint Chiefs of Staff Chairman Colin Powell, and Senate Armed Services Committee Chairman Sam Nunn (D-Georgia)—to persuade the military leaders to cede power voluntarily; and sending 20,000 American troops to Haiti to ensure the peaceful restoration of democratically elected Jean-Bertrand Aristide to power.

Another dramatic and visible source of friction between the CBC and President Clinton resulted from the president's decision to withdraw his nomination of Lani Guinier as assistant attorney general for civil rights. Guinier, a black law professor at the University of Pennsylvania, was thought by many to have been superbly and uniquely qualified for the job. Black leaders were especially angered that the president, in withdrawing the nomination, seemed to have succumbed to critics, mostly (but not exclusively) conservative, who charged that Guinier had expressed views in her scholarly writings that were outside "mainstream" American politi[cal] thinking, a charge that Democrats and others had levelled against J[?] Robert Bork in his abortive attempt in 1987 to win Senate confirmati[on] a seat on the Supreme Court. These critics, who subsequently we[re] ported by President Clinton, particularly thought that Guinier's vi[ews] cerning more effective representation of minority interests in ma[ny] legislative forums were beyond the pale of "centrist-mainstrea[m]... whatever the case, the Guinier affair and other friction p[oints] a head in a three-hour meeting of the CBC on June 9, 1993, whose tone was described by one account as "decidedly angry." Indeed, comments made after the meeting by the CBC chair, Representative Kweisi Mfume (D-Maryland), in apparent reference to what was viewed as the president's retreat in his budget proposals, seemed to have captured well the overall strains created by these various friction points between the CBC and the White House. Mfume said that the CBC was not prepared "to accept additional cuts in entitlement programs ... and is something that becomes a point of non-negotiation and imperils efforts to pass this legislation." Mfume said that all 37 black House Democrats, who had supported the president's earlier budget bill, were not ready to give him "blind loyalty" and "be seen and not heard." "We want first-class partnership," said Mfume, who noted that support from the CBC for the final budget bill would surely be needed since the original bill passed the House the month before by only a narrow 219–213 vote.

The 1994 congressional elections, however, illumina.d the sta... ity that the CBC was indeed a "captured" group within the Democratic coalition. And although black legislators suffered few electoral defeats, unlike more moderate white Democratic incumbents, they collectively suffered substantial losses resulting from the Republican Party's takeover of both chambers of Congress. This transfer of control transformed the CBC from a vital swing constituency to a marginalized group within a marginalized congressional minority. President Clinton interpreted his party's overwhelming losses as a sign that he needed to move rightward, in order to recapture the political center. The president did take some stances favorable to the liberal wing of his party. Brandishing the slogan, "Mend it, don't end it," he defended affirmative action against a conservative onslaught, and he held firm in rejecting the Republicans' budget proposals and defending the Brady Bill and other firearm restrictions.[58]

But on the whole, Clinton's agenda paid little attention to the policy needs of minority communities. Perhaps the sharpest example was the welfare bill signed by the president in 1996. During his 1992 campaign, Clinton promised to "end welfare as we know it." He proposed time limits for welfare recipients, but he also proposed job training and other measures designed to move people off the welfare rolls and onto payrolls. Clinton did not push for welfare reform during the first two years of his first term, but the Republican takeover of Congress compelled him to push for welfare reform, lest the GOP unilaterally seize the issue and reap the political benefits stemming from reforming an unpopular system. The final welfare bill, ... the "Personal Responsibility and Work Opportunity Act of 1996," ...ed the more punitive features of the 1992 Clinton proposal while ... the features that would soften the transition for welfare recipi... legislation transformed the Aid to Families with Dependent ...hich had been a federally guaranteed entitlement, into a block

grant program; established time limits for federally funded cash assistance; set stricter requirements for able-bodied, non-elderly recipients of food stamps and cash assistance; and denied means-tested benefits to most legal immigrants who are not U.S. citizens.

CBC members voted overwhelmingly against the bill, and some condemned the legislation as a betrayal of core Democratic principles. But on the whole, public criticism of Clinton was muted. A typical example came at an October 1996 press conference called by Maxine Waters (D-California), who became chair of the Congressional Black Caucus the following year. Waters, joined by such feminist stalwarts as Gloria Steinem, Eleanor Smeal, and Bella Abzug, denounced many features of the welfare bill but maintained support for the president. Said Waters, "We are not going to leave our party because of this bill. The opportunity to correct this bill lies with Bill Clinton and the Democrats."[59] This stance might have reflected two national-level electoral factors: (1) the desire to keep the White House in Democratic hands, and (2) the fear that criticizing the president might lead black voters, lacking any palatable choice at the polls, to stay home on Election Day, thus hampering Democratic efforts to regain control of Congress. An alternative explanation, however, is that CBC members were following their constituents' lead on welfare reform. According to the National Black Election Study, conducted by political scientist Katherine Tate, 64 percent of the 1,121 African Americans surveyed supported a five-year lifetime cap on welfare benefits.[60]

THE CBC IN PERSPECTIVE[61]

Overall, the CBC now seems to have become an institutionalized part of the Washington and national scene. Despite being stripped of its staff and funding by the new Republican majority in late 1994, its role and purpose remain well recognized—to serve as "a more effective catalyst for the economical, educational, and social concerns of Blacks and other underrepresented Americans" by working with other groups to develop and implement "legislative strategies and mandates for minorities."[62] Its annual fund-raising dinners have now blossomed into "Annual Legislative Activities Weekends," the proceeds of which support a full-time staff. And it is this permanent staff that provides "the legislative research, information coordination, and technical support of Caucus activities."[63]

In many ways the CBC operates as an interest group. It certainly exhibits "social solidarity"—the need for people holding similar views "to enjoy the support, fellowship, and solidarity of one another." The Caucus also resembles the expressive interest groups that people join to symbolize and express more effectively their values and opinions with respect to certain causes. The CBC provides an excellent forum (including those provided during the Annual Legislative Weekends) for the expression of opinion. In short, the Caucus as an interest group acts in a sense as a "Washington Lobby" for blacks and the poor, and it has a staff and funds to support these ends.

Just as with other groups, there are factors that affect the cohesion of the CBC. Consider, for example, those factors that tend to plague group unity. For one thing, each member operates from an independent power base (his or her district) and has an independent staff; this promotes independence from the Caucus as a group. In such a situation, the CBC staff becomes of less importance to individual Caucus members who have their own staffs. As a consequence, these independent sources of strength, which accrue from the nature of the office itself, can lead to independence in action that could impair group unity. In addition, in 1991 the once-unanimous Democratic CBC gained its first Republican member, Representative Gary Franks of Connecticut. The idea that black Republicans might see the political world quite differently from black Democrats gains support from the overall voting records of Franks and fellow black Republican J. C. Watts of Oklahoma, as well as from two revealing incidents. One was Franks's vote against the CBC resolution to oppose the nomination of Judge Clarence Thomas to the Supreme Court. The other was Watts's decision not to join the CBC because of the group's general ideological bent.[64]

To be sure, there are strong factors that tend to promote group cohesion. Whether through a formal organization such as the CBC or not, the basic unity and cohesion of black members of Congress in legislative matters would seem likely to persist for some time. The move of the CBC to concentrate (and restrict) its attention to legislative matters appears to be a good strategy. Another overriding factor that promotes a large measure of unity among black legislators is that the similarities in the needs of their constituents invariably lead to similarities in policy positions. This is reflected well in the socioeconomic characteristics that are common to most of the congressional districts from which Caucus members come.[65] Undoubtedly, these common characteristics will serve to promote a large measure of common policy positions among black congressional members.

In addition, we suggest that the *force of blackness* itself stimulates cohesion and identification among blacks in Congress. It remains as true today as it ever was that as long as blacks are disadvantaged as a group, they must work as a group to remove those disadvantages. This might help to explain why the CBC in 1975 refused to approve the application of a white member of Congress [Representative Fortney H. Stark, Jr. (D-California)] for membership in the Caucus. Indeed, in rejecting Stark's application, then-Caucus chair Charles Rangel (D-New York) stated that "the Caucus symbolizes black political development in this country. We feel that maintaining this symbolism," continued Rangel, "is critical at this juncture in our development."[66] Rangel and the CBC reasoned that just as separate caucuses of Democrats and Republicans "have unique interests to protect and project and would not include non-party members in their respective groups, we too have the same needs and concerns." Rangel then drove the point home. "The Black Caucus," he said, "is composed of 17 House Members who share the common social, cultural and political experience of being black in America."[67] This latter point, it seems to us, vividly illuminates that the force of blackness remains a powerful (though not always articulated) influence enhancing black unity.

We may view the CBC from yet another perspective. The change from "protests to politics" reflects a concern to increase black influence (power) in political institutions such as Congress. The formation and continuing activities of the CBC symbolize this concern. A more tangible measure of increasing black political influence, however, is the number of blacks gaining seats in the Congress. Such an increase will depend upon whether or not those congressional districts that have significant black populations[68] will stimulate and put forth strong candidates and strong campaigns.

Black influence in Congress, however, depends upon more than how many blacks happen to be members at any given time. As the dynamics of power in Congress now operate, it is not enough to gain membership in that body; members must be able to remain there for a long time. They need to gain seniority. By doing so, a member can normally become a committee chairman, and such positions provide crucial influence in the congressional power system. Obviously, members wish to gain seniority on the right committee, that is, a committee that is important to the interests of the member's constituents. Of course, if a member does not gain such an assignment initially, there is always the possibility of getting a preferable assignment later. But, as we have also seen, in changing from one committee to another, the member loses whatever seniority he or she had accumulated on the first committee.

The important question that arises here is how to get the right committee assignment in the first place, or how to gain such an assignment later. To a great extent, this depends upon the standing of the particular legislator with congressional leaders and with his or her colleagues. In addition, such standing enhances or retards a member's ability to build coalitions and to gain sufficient support to enact legislation that is important to the legislator and to his/her constituents. To achieve standing, however, members must conform to congressional norms. In general, this means giving proper deference to established procedures and rules and recognizing the importance of bargaining, accommodation, and compromise in the conduct of business. All this, of course, helps members to maintain good personal relations with colleagues and vice versa. In short, "don't push too far too fast," and above all, "don't buck congressional leaders." The leaders, after all, achieved and maintain such positions because they followed the norms. And there are strong built-in temptations and pressures for others to do likewise.

Let us attempt to view this discussion of seniority and standing in terms of black influence in Congress and black politics generally. Consider the situation of black members of Congress. As mentioned earlier, for the most part these representatives come from "safe" districts—"safe" insofar as a black will more likely than not be elected to represent the district. As the district becomes more "safe" in this sense, however, we might find an increasing competition among blacks as to which black can best represent the district. In 1992, for example, Representative Gus Savage of Illinois was defeated in the Democratic primary by another black (and the eventual winner), Mel Reynolds, who has since left Congress and has been replaced by Jesse Jackson, Jr. In general, however, black incumbents seem to follow the incumbency pattern of being highly successful in reelection bids. This continued electoral success, however, could run into trouble. For example, while black representatives may be attempting to meet the needs of their constituents and may indeed have introduced measures and taken other actions toward this end, the fact is that these needs more often than not have not been met and are not being met. Thus, the problems of the district remain. And the incumbent faces the not uncommon campaign charge of having done nothing about the situation. An important difference, of course, is that problems in heavily populated black districts, such as unemployment and poor housing, are highly visible and affect the everyday life of constituents. Under such circumstances, the black incumbent becomes increasingly susceptible to strong campaign challenges. This could pose a serious problem for black incumbents. As one of only a relatively small number of blacks in a collegial institution (House of Representatives) whose majority may not be especially sympathetic to his or her goals, it will be the rare occasion when a black incumbent can show a record of tangible accomplishments in meeting the immediate problems of his or her district.

To appreciate the context in which black officials operate in Congress requires a measure of sophistication (and a prolonged acceptance of the status quo) on the part of black voters that is perhaps unparalleled in American political history. No other group in America has been required to hold to such understanding and with such patient endurance for such a long period of time. Indeed, the problems that blacks face are by definition "controversial" in the context of American politics. Nonetheless, these problems are perceived by many blacks in terms of "non-negotiable demands" that must be met now, not later. But the bargaining, accommodation, and compromise needed to gain widespread support might lead the black congresspersons to temper these demands to get some type of legislation and to show some record of accomplishment. But in doing so, the black legislator will more likely than not have to temper the rhetoric of his or her arguments to avoid friction between the legislator and his or her white colleagues.

This could place severe strains on a black legislator. While perhaps understanding the necessity of compromise on substantive matters in terms of legislative strategy, the black legislator takes certain risks in compromising the rhetoric of his or her argument. Indeed, such rhetoric might prove necessary to satisfy the long-term demands and desires of his or her constituents while simultaneously making present-day substantive compromises more palatable to them. And more important, it might be necessary for political survival, that is, reelection—the one indispensable criterion for gaining influence in Congress. In any event, seniority and standing continue to pose serious and persistent problems not only for black congressmen, but also for black politics generally. Of course it is true, as we discussed earlier in this chapter, that seniority can work to the advantage of blacks and civil rights interests. But as we have also seen, seniority is no longer an automatic guarantee to becoming committee chair. Under these circumstances, standing and good personal relations with colleagues take on added significance. It remains to be seen what the actual costs and benefits of such relations will be to the future of black politicians and black politics generally.

BLACK OFFICIALS WITH MOSTLY WHITE CONSTITUENCIES

Although blacks constitute 11 percent of the nation's voting-age population, less than 2 percent of all elected officials in the nation are black. But this fact should not cause one to ignore the significance of the steady increase in the number of black elected officials in the years following the passage of the Voting Rights Act. In 1995, according to the Joint Center for Political and Economic Studies, there were more than 8,500 black elected officials nationwide, a total over 5 times greater than the number in 1970. Almost half of these officials served at the municipal level, and slightly more than one-fifth served on school boards.[69] Also of interest is the geographical breakdown of these officials. Seventeen states in 1993 had higher percentages of black voting-age residents than the national average of 11 percent, yet in only five states did blacks constitute more than 10 percent of elected officials. All five of these states were southern: Georgia (18.3 percent of elected officials were black), Alabama (16.2), Mississippi (15.2), Louisiana (12.8), and South Carolina (12.2).[70] One could view as progress the fact that the region targeted most directly by the Voting Rights Act of 1965 had more black elected officials (5,492, or 69 percent) than any other.[71]

Despite these signs of progress, blacks have yet to achieve political power commensurate with their numbers. For blacks to reach proportionality in elected office and, more specifically, for blacks to increase their membership in Congress, it seems clear that more whites will have to start voting for black candidates. As recently as 1990, polling data indicated that white voters generally considered blacks less capable of achieving goals, less likely to possess important personal attributes, and less qualified for higher political offices than whites. In addition, a majority of whites surveyed agreed that most whites vote on the basis of race rather than qualifications.[72]

Nonetheless, some black candidates have enjoyed electoral success despite representing majority-white constituencies. For example, Alan

Wheat (D-Missouri) served several terms in the House as a representative of a constituency that was approximately 75 percent white. Republicans Gary Franks of Connecticut and J. C. Watts of Oklahoma each represented overwhelmingly white districts: Franks's district was 4.4 percent black, while Watts's was 7 percent black. More recently, Representatives Cynthia McKinney and Sanford Bishop, both Georgia Democrats, won reelection in 1996 despite redistricting consistent with *Miller* v. *Johnson* that transformed their districts from majority-black to majority-white. That same year, Julia Carson, a Democrat, became the first black candidate to win a House seat from a majority-white district in Indiana.

In addition, a number of black mayors have been elected in predominantly white cities, although the reversion of these mayorships back to whites is also taking place (e.g., New York from David Dinkins to Rudolph Giuliani, and Los Angeles, from Tom Bradley to Richard Riordan). On the statewide level, however, blacks continue to face difficulty. Let us consider these matters in more detail.

Mayor Tom Bradley's gubernatorial campaigns in 1982 and 1986 are especially instructive. Bradley was a well-qualified, noncontroversial politician who had also been able to allay the fears and suspicions that white voters often have about black candidates.[73] However, after leading all of the pre-election polls against his Republican opponent in 1982, Bradley lost the California gubernatorial election to George Deukmejian. Bradley also lost heavily in a 1986 rematch. What went wrong? Analysis of electoral data indicates that racism played a significant role in Bradley's defeat—even taking into account other political factors, such as a high turnout of conservative voters in 1982 to defeat a controversial gun control measure and the Democratic candidacy for the U.S. Senate of the unpopular incumbent Governor Jerry Brown.[74] The influence of racism in the Bradley defeat is somewhat surprising because Bradley did not associate himself primarily with black issues and did not even court the black vote in California during his gubernatorial campaigns.[75] Though the prospects seem bleak for black candidates in white constituencies, a positive example is Douglas Wilder's victory in 1989 as the nation's first elected black governor. Wilder was elected governor of Virginia with 50.15 percent of the vote. In an election marred by negative campaigning, Wilder won approximately 40 percent of the white vote and 95 percent of the black vote. Wilder's opponent, J. Marshall Coleman, attempted to portray Wilder as a liberal. Coleman framed Wilder as soft on crime and untrustworthy. Wilder, who responded with attacks on Coleman, campaigned as a moderate on many issues, including support for the death penalty and right-to-work laws.[76]

Wilder had the most success in attracting white support in Northern Virginia and the Tidewater area, but failed to gain much support in the rest of the state.[77] The white support for Wilder was particularly important since the black population is only 20 percent of Virginia's electorate. Wilder appealed to the white voters in suburban Northern Virginia by claiming that his opponent, who received $3 million in contributions from developers, was the pawn of real-estate developers. In addition, Wilder gained support among the suburban voters in Northern Virginia for his pro-abortion position while his opponent took what was generally viewed as an anti-abortion stance. In the remainder of the state, Wilder did not fare as well as his white Democratic running mate for lieutenant governor, Donald S. Beyer, Jr., who won support in many parts of "Old Virginia," including Richmond and Southside. This suggests that the racial factor may have been more salient in these areas.

Additionally, and as mentioned earlier, blacks such as Alan Wheat (D-Missouri) have also shown it is possible to be elected and reelected to high public office in mostly white constituencies—even when the candidate is sensitive to and supportive of policies of primary importance to black constituents. In fact, some studies indicate that it is a political liability for black candidates to distance themselves from issues important to blacks and other minorities.[78]

Wheat was first elected to Congress from Missouri's Fifth Congressional District as a liberal Democrat in 1982. He was well known for the ability to strike a balance between his core constituency—blacks and white liberals in Kansas City—and other interests, such as the city's business community. He also placed whites along with blacks in key staff posts in his campaign and in Congress in a deliberate effort not to be regarded as solely a black congressman.[79] The strategy worked well for Wheat insofar as it contributed to his string of successful reelection bids from 1984 to 1992. These successes, however, were not followed by success at the statewide level. Wheat resigned his House seat in 1994 in order to run for the Senate seat being vacated by John Danforth. Republican John Ashcroft beat Wheat by a 60–36 percent margin. Interestingly, in Missouri's Fifth District, Wheat's seat went to a white Democrat, Karen McCarthy, who defeated a black Republican, Ron Freeman, by a 57–43 percent margin.

The election of black candidates (such as Wheat) who must appeal to white constituents for support raises questions about the future of black politics. How will the need to appeal to white constituents affect the issue positions and campaigns of black candidates? How might the new coalition politics affect a black official's support from black voters? With respect to the CBC, for example, will the need to articulate issues beyond the special concern of black members of Congress diminish the voice of the CBC as the advocate of black concerns in the legislative process?

Along with Wheat, the four newly elected black members of Congress in 1986 were described as a new generation of black legislators.[80] Four of the five took the seats of white members, and all appealed to white support in their campaigns [Mike Espy (D-Mississippi), Floyd Flake (D-New York), John Lewis (D-Georgia), and Kweisi Mfume (D-Maryland)].[81] It is interesting to note, however, that since 1992, all of the newly elected House members of the Caucus came from congressional districts with black populations exceeding 25 percent. Some of these districts were expressly created to enhance the possibilities of increased minority representation. As the number of congressional districts with sizable (20 percent or more) black populations continues to fluctuate, as black members appeal more and more for white support, and as more conservative blacks are elected, the nature and future of black politics in the legislative process are likely to become increasingly unclear.

CONCLUSION

Let us make several concluding observations with respect to the structure and operations of Congress as a law-making body and as a representative institution, especially as these relate to the problems and opportunities of blacks and other minorities.

1. The structure of elections and representation in the House of Representatives makes it more likely that blacks will have more representation in the House than in the Senate. The concentration of blacks in particular congressional districts makes it more possible for potential black candidates to gain their party's nomination and mount a viable election campaign. Financing a campaign in a single congressional district, for example, is much more within the reach of potential black candidates at this stage of black economic and financial development. On the other hand, governors and U.S. senators are elected on a statewide basis, and chances of blacks getting the necessary resources to launch effective campaigns for their party's nomination for the subsequent general election are much more remote.

2. The structure and operation of the law-making process are such that those who propose new legislation have numerous procedural and political obstacles to overcome before they can achieve their ends. By the same token, those who oppose such new legislation are presented with many opportunities to impede and block its passage. Consider the necessity of gaining subcommittee and committee approval, the agreement of both houses, and the approval of the president (except that a two-thirds vote in both houses could override his veto). Consider, moreover, other factors such as the operation of seniority and the *filibuster*, a procedure whereby senators exercise their right to unlimited debate, thereby delaying Senate business and blocking a vote on a bill. It is, of course, true, as one writer points out, that certain perceived obstacles, such as the filibuster and the seniority system, can also work for liberal ends.[82] But mostly the filibuster has been used to block and impede passage of civil rights legislation. We should note, however, that recent changes in Senate rules now ostensibly make it easier to end filibusters and limit debate.

While the political clout of black members of Congress waned dramatically with the Republican takeover in 1994, these members remained well-positioned to gain sizable influence in the event that Democrats regained control of the House. In the 105th Congress, four black members were ranking Democratic members of their respective House committees: William Clay (Education and the Workforce), John Conyers (Judiciary), Ron Dellums (National Security), and Charles Rangel (Ways and Means).

3. Congress, as a body, is spending more time on legislative oversight functions than in the past. It is true, of course, that such activity might indeed reveal the need for new or corrective legislation. But an overemphasis on oversight activities might well blunt the time and effort needed to develop creative and innovative legislative initiatives necessary to deal effectively with the myriad problems faced by blacks and other minorities. Moreover, rule changes that have limited the importance of seniority and decreased the power of committee chairpersons, when coupled with the breakdown of party discipline, would seem to make it increasingly difficult to enact major social welfare legislation of the type enacted in the mid-1960s. Historically, if one could convince congressional and party leaders and committee chairmen of the need for a particular legislative measure, it was very likely that such legislation would be passed by Congress.

The situation is somewhat different today. Now there seems to be more fragmentation in the leadership in Congress, as well as growing independence among individual members of Congress. This means that a larger group of leaders (e.g., subcommittee chairmen), as well as individual members, have to be won over. Thus, getting legislation through Congress and monitoring its implementation are becoming increasingly difficult and complex tasks, and they require the continuous mobilization and utilization of the kind of resources (money, lobbying, votes) that are generally in short supply among blacks. What one can conclude from this is that, due to both personnel and institutional changes, Congress is less likely to come to grips and deal effectively with the kind of major social-welfare problems (e.g., poverty and unemployment) that impose a disproportionate hardship on blacks and other minorities.

4. There are other effects that some of the changes mentioned in the previous observation can have on blacks. For example, we have focused on the general legislative role of Congress, but there are other particular types of work that occupy the time of members of Congress. These are *pork barrel* and *casework*.[83] Pork barrel is a term that applies to the efforts of senators and representatives to bring federal projects (dams, federal office buildings, urban redevelopment, etc.) to their states and districts. Casework refers to the efforts of members of Congress to answer requests made to them by individuals or groups within their constituencies. Typically, these requests are for information or for enlisting the aid of a senator or representative in dealing with an executive agency. Both pork barrel and casework impart particularistic benefits, which typically accrue to certain individuals or groups within a given constituency. Because pork barrel projects are commonly associated with wasteful spending, fiscal conservatives have long sought to pass the

line-item veto, which would authorize presidents to veto specific spending provisions within legislation, rather than facing a choice between signing the bill and vetoing it in its entirety. Vetoed spending could be reinstated, but a two-thirds majority in each chamber would be required. A line-item veto measure (subsequently involved in litigation) passed the 104th Congress and was signed by President Clinton, who, like his Republican predecessors, favored the measure's enhancement of executive power.

Thus, recent changes in the House of Representatives that have expanded the powers of subcommittees and subcommittee chairpersons can have positive impacts for constituencies represented by blacks in Congress. For example, while black representatives have been only minimally successful in becoming committee chairs, they are beginning to meet with more success in chairing subcommittees. These subcommittee chairs can provide the opportunity for pork barrel and casework activities to deal with problems of at least some of the "people back home." And the fact that many of these activities (e.g., federal office building, urban redevelopment) occur in large urban areas gives black representatives—who primarily come from central city districts—added opportunities and influence to secure such benefits for their constituents. However, these mainly particularistic benefits are far from the sort of comprehensive congressional actions needed to alleviate the broad and multifaceted problems faced by blacks and other minorities.

5. In general, there seems to be a dire need for more black and minority representation in Congress. As mentioned earlier, the number of blacks in Congress is almost invariably related to the size of the black population in a given district. In short, as the black population nears a majority, chances increase for a black representative to be elected. In 1988, for example, studies indicated that of 71 congressional districts having a sizable black population—20 percent or more[84]—only 23 of those districts were represented by blacks. The 1990 round of redistricting did produce a great improvement in black representation that persisted despite the Supreme Court's holdings in *Shaw* v. *Reno* and its progeny, which erected barriers to designing districts to facilitate black representation (see Chapter 5). By 1997, the number of congressional districts with sizable black populations had increased to 74, and almost half (36) of these districts elected black representatives.[85]

More than this, however, we need to know more about the behavior and responsiveness of elected white officials from districts where there are very large and discrete black and minority populations. Conversely, we need to know how black members of Congress deal with the matter of representing white populations in their districts. In general, this raises anew the perennial question of whether or not a particular group can have effective representation in government without actually having a member of (from) that group in government itself. On the affirmative side of this question, Carol Swain has argued that black candidates are capable of winning substantial support from white voters, and that on average, white

Democrats in Congress are as supportive of black interests as black Democrats are.[86] A contrasting view comes from Keith Reeves, who has found that despite undeniable progress in race relations, racial stereotyping still strongly influences how whites perceive blacks, and black candidates more specifically.[87] Given the historical and contemporary context of racial politics and race relations in this country, along with the thorny conceptual issues surrounding political representation more generally, answering this question could prove difficult for any representative, regardless of race or ethnicity. But we suggest that precisely those representatives who are able to overcome such difficulties will do much to improve both race relations and the overall quality of life in this country.

TOPICS FOR DISCUSSION

1. "Due to both personnel and institutional changes, Congress is less likely to come to grips and deal effectively with the kind of major social-welfare problems (e.g., unemployment) that impose a disproportionate hardship on blacks and other minorities." What are these "personnel and institutional changes"? Do you agree with the view presented here?

2. Explain what is meant by the statement that "the structure of elections and representation in the House of Representatives makes it more likely that blacks would have more representatives in the House than in the Senate."

3. What are the advantages and disadvantages of the seniority rule for blacks and for the legislative process in general? Is the seniority system defensible? What alternatives are there to it? Discuss.

4. If a white person in Congress applies for membership in the Congressional Black Caucus (as has happened), should that person be admitted? Why or why not?

SUGGESTED READINGS

Arnold, R. Douglas. *The Logic of Congressional Action.* New Haven, CT: Yale University Press, 1990.

Ceaser, James W. *Upside Down and Inside Out: The 1992 Elections and American Politics.* Lanham, MD: Rowman & Littlefield, 1993.

Clay, William L. *Just Permanent Interests: Black Americans in Congress, 1870–1991.* New York: Amistad Press, 1992.

Coleman, Mary DeLorse. *Legislators, Law, and Public Policy: Political Change in Mississippi and the South.* Westport, CT: Greenwood Press, 1993.

Cox, Gary W., and Mathew D. McCubbins. *Legislative Leviathan: Party Government in the House.* Berkeley, CA: University of California Press, 1993.

Fenno, Richard. *Home Style: House Members in Their Districts.* Boston, MA: Little, Brown, 1978. How members of Congress view their constituencies and the impact of such perceptions on their behavior.

Fiorina, Morris P. *Congress: Keystone of the Washington Establishment,* 2nd ed. New Haven, CT: Yale University Press, 1989. A concise, readable analysis of how Congress works and what congresspersons seek to accomplish.

Fiorina, Morris P., and David W. Rohde, eds. *Home Style and Washington Work: Studies of Congressional Politics.* Ann Arbor, MI: University of Michigan Press, 1989.

Gill, LaVerne McCain. *African American Women in Congress: Forming and Transforming History.* New Brunswick, NJ: Rutgers University Press, 1997.

Hall, Richard L. *Participation in Congress.* New Haven, CT: Yale University Press, 1996.

Jacobson, Gary C. *The Politics of Congressional Elections,* 3rd ed. New York: HarperCollins, 1991.

Kiewiet, D. Roderick. *The Logic of Delegation: Congressional Parties and the Appropriations Process.* Chicago, IL: University of Chicago Press, 1992.

Krehbiel, Keith. *Information and Legislative Organization.* Ann Arbor, MI: University of Michigan Press, 1991.

Lindblom, Charles E., and Edward J. Woodhouse. *The Policy-Making Process,* 3rd ed. Englewood Cliffs, NJ: Prentice Hall, 1993.

Lublin, David. *The Paradox of Representation: Racial Gerrymandering and Minority Interests in Congress.* Princeton, NJ: Princeton University Press, 1997.

Maltzman, Forrest. *Competing Principals: Committees, Parties, and the Organization of Congress.* Ann Arbor, MI: University of Michigan Press, 1997.

Mayhew, David. *Congress—The Electoral Connection.* New Haven, CT: Yale University Press, 1974. Views congressional behavior and activity in the context of members of Congress as "single-minded seekers" of reelection.

———. *Divided We Govern: Party Control, Lawmaking, and Investigations, 1946–1990.* New Haven, CT: Yale University Press, 1990.

McCubbins, Mathew D., and Terry Sullivan, eds. *Congress: Structure and Policy.* New York: Cambridge University Press, 1987.

Peterson, George E., ed. *Big-City Politics, Governance, and Fiscal Constraints.* Washington, DC: Urban Institute Press, 1994.

Peterson, Paul E. *Classifying by Race.* Princeton, NJ: Princeton University Press, 1995.

Polsby, Nelson. *Congress and the Presidency,* 4th ed. Englewood Cliffs, NJ: Prentice Hall, 1986. An examination of the interaction between these two governmental branches.

Reeves, Keith. *Voting Hopes or Fears? White Voters, Black Candidates, and Racial Politics in America.* New York: Oxford University Press, 1997.

Sinclair, Barbara. *Legislators, Leaders, and Lawmaking: The U.S. House of Representatives in the Postreform Era.* Baltimore, MD: Johns Hopkins University Press, 1995.

———. *Unorthodox Lawmaking: New Legislative Processes in the U.S. Congress.* Washington, DC: CQ Press, 1997.

Smith, Steven S. *Committees in Congress,* 2nd ed. Washington, DC: CQ Press, 1990.

Swain, Carol M. *Black Faces, Black Interests: The Representation of African Americans in Congress.* Cambridge, MA: Harvard University Press, 1993.

NOTES

1. Nick Kotz, *Let Them Eat Promises: The Politics of Hunger in America* (Englewood Cliffs, NJ: Prentice Hall, 1969). Reprinted by permission.
2. Gary Orfield, *Congressional Power: Congress and Social Change* (New York: Harcourt Brace Jovanovich, 1975). Reprinted by permission of the publisher.
3. *Reynolds v. Sims,* 377 U.S. 533 (1964).

4. *Ibid.*
5. See *Mahan* v. *Howell*, 410 U.S. 315 (1973); *Brown* v. *Thompson*, 462 U.S. 835 (1983); *Karcher* v. *Daggett*, 462 U.S. 725 (1983); and *Davis* v. *Bandemer*, 106 S. Ct. 2792 (1986).
6. This figure refers to non-Hispanic whites.
7. Jesse Jackson, Jr., replaced Mel Reynolds, who in 1995 was convicted on sexual misconduct and obstruction of justice charges and was sentenced to prison.
8. For an informative overview of these and related factors, see Ronald Smothers, "Black Caucus Gains a New Experience," *New York Times*, November 10, 1992, p. A-10, cols. 1–3.
9. This total does not include the Georgia districts represented by Sanford Bishop and Cynthia McKinney. As a result of *Miller* v. *Johnson*, these districts lost their majority-black status. This total does include District 3 in Florida (Corrine Brown) and District 2 in Louisiana (William Jefferson), each of which, as of 1996, was at risk of losing its majority-black status as a result of judicial holdings.
10. Reed Branson, "Black Opponent Proudly Stumps for GOP, Miss. Contest Gets National Attention," *Commercial Appeal* (Memphis), September 16, 1996, p. 1-A.
11. How much black voting-age population is needed to give black voters equal opportunity to elect candidates of their choice is an unsettled question. Recent scholarship claims that minority-preferred candidates can be elected with black voting-age populations between 40 and 50 percent. See David Ian Lublin, *Gerrymander for Justice? Racial Redistricting and Black and Latino Representation* (1994); and Charles Cameron, David Epstein, and Sharyn O'Halloran, "Do Majority-Minority Districts Maximize Substantive Black Representation in Congress," *American Political Science Review* 90 (1996), pp. 794–812.
12. *Wesberry* v. *Sanders*, 376 U.S. 1 (1964).
13. *1995 Congressional Quarterly Almanac* (Washington, DC: Congressional Quarterly, Inc., 1996), pp. 12–13.
14. Richard F. Fenno, Jr., *Congressmen in Committees* (Boston, MA: Little, Brown, 1973), p. 1.
15. The following account is taken from Richard Cohen, "How to Win—or Lose—Committee Seats," *National Journal* (February 3, 1979), pp. 183–188.
16. *Ibid.*
17. "Origins and Development of Congress," *Congressional Quarterly*, pp. 160–161.
18. Christopher Buchanan, "House: Modest Gains for the Minority," *Congressional Quarterly Weekly Report* 36 (November 11, 1978), p. 3251.
19. *Time*, November 19, 1990.
20. Julie Rovner, "Record Number of Women, Blacks in Congress," *Congressional Quarterly Weekly Report* 46 (November 12, 1988), pp. 3293–3295.
21. Diggs was sentenced to three years in prison, but the sentence was postponed pending appeal. His conviction was upheld in November 1979 by a three-judge panel of the U.S. Circuit Court of Appeals for the District of Columbia, and again in June 1980 by the Supreme Court. Despite being censured by the House in July 1979, Diggs remained in office until May 1980, when he announced his resignation. See the *1980 Congressional Quarterly Almanac* 36 (Washington, DC: Congressional Quarterly, Inc., 1981), p. 525.
22. Nelson Polsby, *Congress and the Presidency*, 3rd ed. (Englewood Cliffs, NJ: Prentice Hall, 1976) Table 3, p. 79.

23. Hanes Walton, Jr., *Black Politics: A Theoretical and Structural Analysis* (Philadelphia, PA: Lippincott, 1972), p. 171.
24. Cf. James Q. Wilson, "The Negro in Politics," *Daedalus* 94 (Fall 1965), p. 961. For more analysis of Powell, see Wilson, "Two Negro Politicians: An Interpretation," *Midwest Journal of Political Science* 4 (November 1960), pp. 360–369.
25. Actually, the House denied Powell his seat in 1967, but the Supreme Court later ruled that he had been unlawfully excluded. *Powell* v. *McCormack*, 395 U.S. 486 (1969).
26. See Robert Salisbury and Kenneth Shepsle, "Congressional Staff Turnover and the Ties-That-Bind," *American Political Science Review* 75 (1981), pp. 381–396.
27. *National Journal*, June 2, 1979, p. 913.
28. See Daniel Rapoport, "The Imperial Congress—Living above the Law," *National Journal*, June 2, 1979, pp. 911, 913.
29. *Ibid.*, p. 912.
30. Kenneth J. Cooper, "Just as Affirmative Action Arrives on Hill, Bills Threaten to Kill It," *Washington Post*, July 19, 1995, p. A-19.
31. *Ibid.*
32. Miles Benson, "Government Lax in Hiring Minorities," *San Francisco Examiner*, December 1, 1991, p. B-10.
33. *Ibid.*
34. For more detail, see Stephen Glass, "The Jungle," *The New Republic*, April 7, 1997, pp. 18–20.
35. *Ibid.*
36. For a review of these methods, see Walter J. Oleszek, *Congressional Procedures and the Policy Process*, 4th ed. (Washington, DC: Congressional Quarterly, Inc., 1996).
37. Alex Poinsett, "The Black Caucus: Five Years Later," *Ebony*, June 1973, pp. 64–73.
38. *Ibid.*
39. Matthew Holden, *Politics of the Black Nation* (New York: Chandler, 1973).
40. See Poinsett, "The Black Caucus," op. cit.
41. See *New York Times*, September 27, 1973, p. 13; September 30, 1973, p. 28; and October 1, 1973, pp. 1, 23.
42. *Ibid.*
43. *Ibid.*
44. The discussion is based on Representative Rangel's account of the meeting in "The President and the Black Caucus," *Focus* 2 (September 1974), pp. 4–5.
45. For an account of the Ford statement on the Boston situation and "forced busing" see *New York Times*, October 13, 1974, Sec. 4, p. 2.
46. See *National Journal*, October 21, 1978, p. 1688.
47. Jacqueline Trescott, "Leland and the War on Hunger," *Washington Post*, September 7, 1983, p. B-1.
48. *Ibid.*
49. "Congressional Black Caucus Rejoices in Growing Strength," *New York Times*, October 6, 1986.
50. Nadine Cohodas, "Black House Members Striving for Influence," *Congressional Quarterly Weekly Report* 43 (April 13, 1985), pp. 675–681.
51. "A Salute to the CBC," *Focus* 16, 9 (September 2, 1988), Joint Center for Policy Studies.

52. "Pessimism Marks Gathering of Black Lawmakers," *New York Times*, October 1, 1984.
53. "Bush's Chance with Blacks," *Focus* 16, 11 and 12 (November–December 1988).
54. *Washington Post*, September 18, 1989.
55. *Washington Post*, May 14, 1989.
56. Byron P. White and Joseph A. Kirby, "New Conservatism May Serve as Call to Action for African Americans," *Chicago Tribune*, August 28, 1996, p. 5.
57. *Sale* v. *Haitian Centers Council*, No. 92-344 (1993).
58. But see *Printz* v. *United States* [138 L. Ed. 2d 914 (1997)], where the Supreme Court declared unconstitutional some parts of the Brady Law.
59. Ruth Conniff, "No More Angry Feminists; Democrat Women Reluctantly Endorse Pres. Bill Clinton," *The Progressive* 60 (October 1996), p. 23.
60. Michael A. Fletcher, "Low-Profile Year 'Extremely Productive' for NAACP, Mfume Says," *Washington Post*, February 16, 1997, p. A-3.
61. For an interesting and perceptive account of the role, organization, and prospects of the CBC, see Marguerite Ross Barnett, "The Congressional Black Caucus and the Institutionalization of Black Politics," *Journal of Afro-American Issues* 5 (Summer 1977), pp. 202–227.
62. Included in Caucus mailing materials announcing the 1979 CBC Annual Legislative Weekend.
63. *Ibid.*
64. Jill Zuckman, "Black Caucus Finds Itself on Sidelines," *Boston Globe*, December 27, 1995, p. 1.
65. For a systematic and easily accessible profile on congressional districts, see Michael Barone, et al., *The Almanac of American Politics* (New York: Dutton, 1996). This volume also includes similar data on U.S. senators.
66. Quotes on the refusal of the Caucus to admit Representative Stark are taken from Congressional Black Caucus press release dated June 19, 1975. Also see "Congress's Black Caucus Rejects White as Member," *Washington Star*, June 19, 1975, p. A-13.
67. *Ibid.*
68. For a detailed look at these districts—those having 30 percent or more black population—see David A. Bositis, *The Congressional Black Caucus in the 103rd Congress* (Washington, DC: Joint Center for Political and Economic Studies, 1993).
69. *Black Elected Officials: A National Roster, 1993* (Washington, DC: Joint Center for Political and Economic Studies Press, 1993), p. xxii.
70. *Ibid.*, p. xxiii. Excluded from this analysis are the District of Columbia and the Virgin Islands.
71. *Ibid.*, p. xl.
72. Linda Williams, "White-Black Perceptions of the Electability of Black Political Candidates," *National Political Science Review* 2 (1990), pp. 45–64.
73. Thomas F. Pettigrew and Denise A. Alston, *Tom Bradley's Campaigns for Governor: The Dilemma of Race and Political Strategies* (Washington, DC: Joint Center for Political Studies, 1988).
74. *Ibid.*
75. *Ibid.*

76. Rhodes Cook, "Wilder Win Marks Differences of Old Dominion and New," *Congressional Quarterly Weekly Report* 47 (November 11, 1989), p. 3101.

77. *Ibid.*, p. 3102.

78. *Ibid.*

79. *St. Louis Post-Dispatch*, July 15, 1984.

80. Richard E. Cohen, "A New Breed for Black Caucus," *National Journal*, September 26, 1987, pp. 2432–2433.

81. Representative Espy was appointed Secretary of Agriculture by President Clinton, and the special election for Espy's House seat was subsequently won by another African American and Democrat, Representative Bennie Thompson (D-Mississippi).

82. Orfield, *Congressional Power: Congress and Social Change*, pp. 38–44.

83. Morris P. Fiorina, *Congress: Keystone of the Washington Establishment* (New Haven, CT: Yale University Press, 1977), pp. 41–49.

84. *Congressional District Fact Book*, 3rd ed. (Washington, DC: Joint Center for Political Studies, 1988), pp. 23–24.

85. See Michael Barone, et al., *The Almanac of American Politics* (New York: Dutton, 1996).

86. Carol M. Swain, *Black Faces, Black Interests: The Representation of African Americans in Congress* (Cambridge, MA: Harvard University Press, 1993), esp. Chapters 1, 9, and 10.

87. Keith Reeves, *Voting Hopes or Fears? White Voters, Black Candidates, and Racial Politics in America* (New York: Oxford University Press, 1997).

Chapter 11

The Presidency and the Policy Process: The "Poverty" of Black Politics

The essence of a President's persuasive task with Congressmen and everybody else, is to induce them to believe that what their own appraisal of their own responsibilities requires them to do is in their interest, not his. Because men may differ in their views on public policy, because differences in outlook stem from differences in duty—duty to one's office, one's constituents, oneself—that task is bound to be more like collective bargaining than like a reasoned argument among philosopher kings.... This is the reason why: persuasion deals in the coin of self-interest with men who have some freedom to reject what they find counterfeit.

—Richard E. Neustadt, *Presidential Power*[1]

The weakness of existing civil rights groups ... was that they came to Washington once a year and talked to the Secretary of Labor or of HEW; the groups pushed for a big law once every three or four years, and forgot about the legislation once it was passed. No one remained to watch when agencies formulated guide-lines or were slow to enforce the laws. Someone was needed in Washington "to run a monitoring operation at the federal level...."

—Robert Borosage, et al., "The New Public Interest Lawyers"[2]

The presidency of the United States is perhaps the most powerful political office in the world. Without question, it is the most powerful and most sought after political office in America. It should come as no surprise that blacks have frequently looked to the incumbent in this office for support of their interests. Since the election of Franklin D. Roosevelt during the depression, African Americans have been a large part of the Democratic party's presidential coalition, that is, the diverse collection of ethnic groups and classes that come together every four years in an effort to elect their candidate to office.

Blacks believed, like others, that their support would produce gains for their causes as it appeared to produce gains for those of others. To some extent this did happen. But, for blacks it did not seem that what was received was commensurate with the effort. Desired corrections of segregation and discrimination did not come quickly. In part, black political strategies failed to adequately consider the nature of the American political system. They did not take into account the fact that the system of politics is also a product of the larger society. It is important for blacks and others who put their hopes in strong presidential action to correct perceived social and political ills to remember that the president is one of a number of political officials who are involved in making and executing presidential decisions. To some, this may seem to be a rather small point; but many Americans fail to appreciate the difficulties involved in presidential decision making. It is for this reason that this chapter was introduced by the excerpt from Neustadt's work.

There are many presidential roles. The president is indeed the chief executive and must take care that the laws be faithfully executed. This, in a sense, casts the president in the role of chief administrator. But the president is also chief legislator. He not only supervises the administration of the laws, but he is also expected to suggest laws that are needed. In addition, as the office has developed in terms of both the formal requirements of Article II of the Constitution and the practices and uses of power by particular occupants, the president performs many other roles. He is commander in chief of the armed forces, chief policy maker, chief of party, and chief of state. When combined, these roles make the president, as many others have suggested, both king and prime minister.[3] Because these roles tend to overlap and reinforce one another, of course, they add to the powerful position of the president in the political system.

BECOMING PRESIDENT

Though powerful, the president is not all-powerful. Power is limited by both the process by which the president is selected and the way in which various roles are carried out. Take the process of selection. "To win the presidency," as one writer put it, "the aspirant must travel a long, hard, treacherous road abounding in bumps and quicksand and divisible into three distinct segments: the pre-convention buildup, the national nominating convention, and the post-convention electoral campaign."[4]

But before one can start this long journey with any viable chance of success, one must possess more than the formal requirements for the presidential office. It is not enough to be a native-born citizen, at least 35 years of age, and to have lived in the country for at least 14 years. Indeed, one must also meet (or have a reasonable chance of meeting) the informal requirements. One must have secured or be able to secure great financial backing. One must be well known, perhaps by having held high office or having rendered distinguished service to the country in some other way.

Nor can one be too controversial; a candidate needs the support of a broad, often diverse, spectrum of people and interests. What is "controversial" could include those things over which a person has control, for example, his stand on major issues. Or it could involve matters over which there is little or no control—religion, race, color, sex. A potential candidate can and may alter stands on issues as the campaign develops. But in terms of ethnic consideration, a candidate has to convince many others that such factors should not stand as barriers to efforts to become president. For example, it was not until 1960 that John F. Kennedy, who had everything going for him (money, organization, charm), was able to overcome the traditional anti-Catholic barrier, and even then just barely. Consequently, one still shudders to guess, despite an increasing number of blacks and women in public office, how long race, sex, and other factors will continue to make particular candidates too controversial.

Generally, the "pre-convention" phase provides a testing ground in which a presidential aspirant can assess his chances. Through presidential primaries, state party conventions, and other campaign forums, one might indeed overcome or gain the necessary informal prerequisites to become a viable candidate for the party's nomination. One can gain publicity and become better known. One might also attract more financial backing, assuming enough money initially to gain additional funds.[5] One might also overcome or temper apprehensions or controversy with respect to one's position on issues, or regarding one's religion, race, or sex. Finally, and very importantly, one might gather the kind of popular support and delegate commitment needed to do battle at the convention stage.

To win the party's nomination at the convention, the candidate must be able to fashion a majority of the delegates. That is, he/she must be willing to form coalitions through negotiating and practicing the art of compromise. One might have to compromise in such areas as the party platform, a credentials fight, the vice-presidential nominee, the national party chairman, and his/her likely position on key issues and appointments if he/she should become president. Managing and overcoming conflict in any of these areas may determine not only who wins the nomination, but also how well the nominee can carry on in the third stage—the post-convention election campaign.

In the post-convention phase, the nominee must try to hold on to the coalition that fashioned the nomination in the convention and must also try to add to it. The nominee needs more campaign workers. He/she needs to appeal to a broader spectrum of voters and will invariably need more money. But gaining new support involves the risk of losing old support. A candidate must constantly assess costs and benefits, advantages and disadvantages. In the end, the candidate who receives a majority of the electoral vote (and almost always a plurality of the popular vote) becomes president. And after becoming president the kind of broad support that put the candidate into office will continue to be necessary to effectively carry out the various roles and responsibilities of office.

ONCE IN OFFICE

In addition to this broad popular support, the president also needs the support of those specifically charged to help fulfill the various roles. The president appoints many people in offices and agencies of the executive branch. The heads of the major departments—for example, State, Defense, Housing and Urban Development (HUD), Health and Human Services—are all appointed by the president. These officials (or secretaries) and several others form the cabinet. Formally, the cabinet members are the president's principal advisers on governmental policies. In making these and other appointments, the president has to remain alert to factors that affect the policies and programs of his administration. For example, will a particular appointment lessen support from an important party leader or an important member of Congress or endanger the support of an important segment of those who voted for him in the presidential election? However, the overwhelming majority of the thousands of employees in the federal government are career civil servants. As such, they are not subject to presidential appointment and their career status also shields these permanent bureaucrats from attempts at blatant manipulation.

The president also relies heavily on the Executive Office of the President. This office, just like the larger departments, consists of presidential appointees and career civil servants. It is divided into various units, such as the White House Office, National Security Council, Office of Management and Budget, and Council of Economic Advisers. While these various units are all directly responsible to the president in helping to carry out many functions, the White House Office is made up of the president's "own people." This allows the president to overcome certain political considerations (such as satisfying different factions of the party) that may dictate whom the president can appoint to administer the more formal governmental structures, such as the various cabinet departments. But in the White House Office the president can appoint aides and assistants of his/her own choosing. And their influence on the president in a given area might be greater than the cabinet member charged with that responsibility. In any event, to carry out the many roles of the office, the president needs the help of these administrators, both in the Executive Office and in the bureaucracies of the large departments. The quality of help received determines how well the president can function.

Clearly, the person who occupies the office of the president has enormous influence in American politics. Through various messages to Congress and to the nation (for example, in the State of the Union address), the president is presented with clear opportunities to set the nation's agenda. He/she can thus propose legislation and through the veto power can dispose of legislation passed by the Congress. Further, the president sets the nation's priorities; budgetary, legislative, and administrative powers give her/him great leverage to make those priorities stick. Also, the many ceremonial functions serve to strengthen the president in exercising formal powers.

The powers at the president's disposal are indeed impressive, and so blacks tend to focus on the person and the office in their struggle for social justice. In part, this concentration can be seen as an attempt to use the symbolism of the presidency to capture broad public attention and support. But to be successful blacks also need the president to support their causes.

Whether or not a president supports the range of issues that are important to African Americans depends on the overall shape of American politics. Just as the issues flow from political circumstances, so too do a president's political attitudes. But there is more to it than that. Presidential views and attitudes on all political issues are also products of the individual incumbent's conception of the presidency.[6] That is to say, a given president may see the office as an instrument for change, utilizing the various powers to vigorously move the country in new directions. That was the view that many observers held of the Kennedy presidency. And it was clearly the conception that Lyndon Johnson had of his proper role in the civil rights struggle of blacks. But not every president will see his responsibilities in such a light.

Presidents may, as was Eisenhower, be less venturesome. Eisenhower's view can be characterized as rather narrowly construing the provision that a president sees to the effective implementation and execution of the laws of the land.

Using the concept of office idea is merely another way of trying to understand what it is that a president believes should be done, fully recognizing that there are numerous constraints on what can be done. Of course, it is also true that "change-agent" presidents need not always do things of which particular groups approve. In general, black interests, for example, were not advanced by the Nixon, Reagan, or Bush administrations. Indeed, blacks have generally fared better under presidents who had an activist and expansive view of their tenures. And because of this African Americans are probably more likely than others in the mass public to approve of a strong president.

The concept of office is not the exclusive creation of the individual. It results from the interaction between the incumbent president (or other officeholder) and the political environment. Messages and cues received are digested and converted into political actions and programs. But this process works both ways, for the president can also influence the views held by those within the political environment, thereby affecting the kinds of messages and cues he will get in return. Thus, Lyndon Johnson's rhetoric in describing a War on Poverty could elicit strong positive responses from the disadvantaged and their supporters that were used to overcome sources of opposition. Similarly, Richard Nixon could marshal broad public support, even among blacks, for a campaign of law and order in the nation's big cities. Obviously, public views are an important part of presidential decision making, but it would be foolhardy for any president to look to the mass public for specific policy guidance. Public opinion, at least as expressed in polling results, is too variable and contradictory. Thus, while Americans want a president to use the powers of office for the well-being of the nation, they also seek to reassure themselves that the use of these powers will not be unrestrained.[7]

From the perspective of black policy interests, public opinion has another flaw. It is simply that the specific concerns of blacks, or any other minority, are amalgamated into generalized policy positions. And as so often happens when there is a particular point that African Americans want to call to the president's attention, it is difficult to discern in the midst of "public" opinion. For a time after the election of President Jimmy Carter, African Americans believed that this problem had been corrected.

Perhaps more clearly than in any previous presidential election, black votes made a difference in the outcome of the 1976 contest between Carter and the incumbent president, Gerald Ford.[8] Initially, blacks were not enthusiastic about the Democratic race, for it produced few candidates attractive to them. But the Republicans could derive little satisfaction from this fact for their man, like the party as a whole, lacked any significant black constituency.

Initially, the Carter candidacy was given little credence by blacks or virtually anyone else. As a one-term governor from Georgia, Jimmy Carter was almost unknown to the public. Moreover, from the point of view of many blacks, his "Deep South" background was a serious disadvantage. To make matters worse, two racial incidents during the campaign only heightened black distrust of the southerner.

The first incident involved Carter's response to a question about housing patterns in the urban North. The candidate responded with a reference to maintaining the "ethnic purity" of neighborhoods. For most blacks this was not a dramatically new statement of white views on residential integration. Nor at first was there much attention paid to the statement. Carter's difficulties came when he was asked to explain what he meant by the phrase. As is so often the case in politics, the candidate's attempts to clarify his position only made matters worse. It was an embarrassment that the media and the other candidates were quick to exploit.

However, Carter weathered the controversy. In this he was aided by a sizable contingent of southern black supporters. At the time, Representative Andrew Young of Atlanta, Georgia, had been Carter's most prominent black supporter. But Young, a member of the Congressional Black Caucus, had no choice but to join with other members of the Caucus in denouncing the "ethnic purity" statement. However, this was more a pro forma gesture than a rejection of Carter.

According to Jules Witcover, the people most troubled by Carter's statement were the white liberals for whom the Deep South candidate's "black support had become a kind of badge of Carter's acceptability (to) white liberal activists."[9] In other words, as long as blacks were not overly concerned with the statement and its subsequent explanations, it was safe for the liberals to support the Carter campaign. And when Carter received the "blessing" of Reverend Martin Luther King, Sr., the father of the slain civil rights hero, the incident was over.

Throughout this affair blacks showed a much more pragmatic attitude toward racial politics. It was also apparent that African Americans were more important to the Carter candidacy than their numbers suggested. Black support, especially that of prominent individuals such as Representative Young and Reverend King, made it easier for him to garner northern white supporters. The Carter campaign was also shielded against some of the usual charges of being anti-black that one hears during presidential races. The explanation of this difference was not solely because of black support. Jimmy Carter helped himself by removing a principal source of racial antagonisms when he defeated his fellow southerner, former Governor George Wallace of Alabama. It was the combination of black support and the elimination of Wallace that contributed significantly to Carter's national acceptance.

The race between the one-term Georgia governor and President Ford was close. And, as we said earlier, the black vote was critical. Almost two-thirds of registered black voters went to the polls in November 1976. Of this number, over 90 percent cast their ballots for Carter. Without this massive black support, the former governor would have lost. Indeed, Carter was the minority choice of all white voters, receiving approximately 48 percent of their votes to Ford's 52 percent.[10]

While we noted in an earlier chapter that the distribution of the black vote is not always a political advantage, it clearly was one for Carter in 1976. Their concentration in states with large blocks of electoral votes made it possible for Jimmy Carter to win while carrying only one state (Texas) west of the Mississippi River. An almost "solid South" and the industrialized Northeast gave Carter the necessary votes in the electoral college.

The nature of the Carter win helps shed some light on one of the little-noticed aspects of black politics. That is to say, while the black political agenda is often viewed as change-oriented, some reforms favored by white liberals, such as abolishing the electoral college, would work to the disadvantage of blacks. The electoral college system of deciding presidential races is a long-standing target of liberals who believe that it undermines the principle of "one-person one-vote." African Americans, who in other instances would agree with this principle, also recognize that in contests like the 1976 campaign between Carter and Ford, their votes had a larger impact than would be the case if the popular vote alone determined the winner. But this inconsistency does not weaken black efforts to gain a greater measure of political power. And in the glow of their contribution to the newly elected Jimmy

Carter, blacks had high expectations of making significant strides toward that objective. Attention was directed to how the new president would repay his supporters. It was generally acknowledged that a cabinet appointment was in the offing. In the end, Carter surprised most observers by appointing two blacks to his cabinet. Patricia Roberts Harris, an attorney and a prominent actor in national Democratic party politics, became the secretary of Housing and Urban Development (HUD), and Representative Andrew Young, who had perhaps been Carter's staunchest black supporter, was named as Ambassador to the United Nations.[11]

In addition, President Carter appointed several blacks to prominent and politically significant subcabinet positions. Eleanor Holmes Norton was appointed to head the Equal Employment Opportunity Commission, Drew S. Days, III, was named assistant attorney general for civil rights, and Clifford Alexander became the secretary of the army.

In some respects, one might have expected blacks to occupy several of these posts because of their importance in policy areas of concern to African Americans. While the "naturalness" of the positions spurs criticism in some quarters, it should be remembered that presidential appointments do take account of various constituency interests. Moreover, in the case of Carter's appointees, it can be argued that he chose blacks for these offices precisely because of the special sensitivities and insights they would bring to their jobs.

President Carter's appointments reflect the power of the black electorate in his 1976 victory and his effort to maintain that support should he choose to run for a second term—a choice he subsequently made. And though black voters remained fiercely loyal to the Democrats—giving Carter more than 80 percent of their votes—the president's bumbling image and increasingly conservative mood helped Ronald Reagan and the Republican party to win the White House. Under Reagan, blacks and minorities came in for very rough times.

Reagan entered the presidency with the stated intention of dismantling and cutting back many social welfare-type programs that in his view accorded the federal government too great a role in the lives of individual Americans and largely at the expense of the legitimate realms of state and local governments. And the president made good on his promise. He repeatedly ignored the traditional bargaining process with other governmental leaders and instead appealed directly to the American people for support.[12] His position was considerably strengthened by the fact that in the 1980 elections the Republicans won a majority in the Senate and gained 33 seats in the House of Representatives.[13] These Republican gains, in addition to a number of sympathetic conservative southern Democrats already in the Congress, provided the kind of legislative support the president needed for really key policy initiatives, reflected vividly in budget cuts and paring down of social programs that were mainly designed to help blacks, minorities, and the poor. This gave a more restrictive role to the federal government in

American politics generally, and resulted in more leeway for state and local governments to fashion policy and practice in a number of policies especially crucial to blacks, including civil rights enforcement. Additionally, President Reagan made special efforts to see that insofar as possible, his overall ideological and policy positions were reflected in the large number of judicial appointments (almost half of all federal judges) he made to our federal courts. For many, Reagan seemed to summarize his administration's attitude towards the interests of African Americans in early 1989 when he accused unnamed civil rights leaders of exaggerating American discrimination towards blacks in order to further their own political careers.

Ironically, it was at this very time that President-elect Bush was attempting to show a less strident opposition to the civil rights legacy. For many, Bush seemed to have at least some credentials as a proponent of the federal government's role in actively pushing for racial equality. At Yale, Bush headed the United Negro College Fund. Furthermore, as a congressman from Texas, Bush was one of the few southern legislators to vote for the 1968 landmark fair housing bill, despite protests from his conservative district in Houston. Yet many African Americans were horrified by what they considered Bush's racially divisive campaign tactics. Campaign manager Lee Atwater's attempt to tie Michael Dukakis to the image of Willie Horton—a black convict who raped a white Maryland woman and stabbed her husband while on furlough from a Massachusetts prison—seemed to prey upon white voters' ugliest fears.

But almost immediately after his landslide election in November 1988, President-elect Bush attempted to reassure blacks that his administration would be sensitive to their needs. Speaking to about 500 members of the American Bicentennial Presidential Inaugural Afro-American Committee, a predominantly black group of Bush supporters, Bush pledged that "bigotry and indifference to disadvantage will find no safe home on our shores, in our public life, in our neighborhoods, or in our home, and that Reverend [Martin Luther] King's dream for his children and for ours will be fulfilled. It will, I promise, be my mission as President of the United States."[14]

Yet Bush's leadership was much less forceful than his rhetoric. Indeed, the major difference between the Bush administration and the Reagan administration's agenda seemed to be one of style rather than substance. Bush seems to have quietly carried on the Reagan administration's agenda, only pausing to avoid the most stigmatizing embarrassments. For instance, in early 1990 the Department of Education announced new policy guidelines that would prevent any school receiving federal funds from earmarking scholarship money exclusively for certain minority groups. Within a week, however, Bush intervened to reverse this policy after the news media pointedly criticized his administration for chipping away at minority opportunities at home, while at the same time sending hundreds of thousands of African Americans to the Persian Gulf in defense of "the national interest." On the other hand, despite his eventual signing of the Civil Rights Act of 1991

President Clinton delivers his 1998 State of the Union speech. (*Greg Gibson/AP/ Wide World Photos*)

(designed to overcome several adverse Supreme Court decisions), Bush's early and repeated opposition to that legislation clearly did not sit well with women, blacks, and minorities. Moreover, and in the final analysis, Bush did little if anything to improve his civil rights record by appointing to the Supreme Court Judge Clarence Thomas, a black arch-conservative, to replace Justice Thurgood Marshall, fondly and accurately referred to in the black community and American politics generally as "Mr. Civil Rights."

In any case, the 1992 election saw President Bush's bid for a second term rebuffed by Democratic candidate Governor William Clinton of Arkansas, whose victory was due in no small measure to the overwhelming support Clinton received from black voters.[15] Clinton's election excited the hopes and expectations of African Americans, and many others, in a manner quite reminiscent of those following the election of the late President John F. Kennedy in 1960. For our purposes here, it is sufficient to say that the general actions of Clinton in his first (1993–1996) administration suggested that blacks and minorities would both have access to and become active participants in running the new Democratic-controlled government and administration. This is evidenced in part by Clinton's appointment of blacks to key posts in his transition team as well as in his cabinet, to which four blacks were appointed. Additionally, Clinton has made good on his promise to use his appointment powers to assemble the kind of representation in the executive branch and in the federal judiciary that is reflective of the richness and diversity of the American population. Nevertheless, Clinton's experience with health care and welfare reform illustrates how a president's ability to push a legislative agenda designed to overcome the serious problems that still disproportionately plague blacks and minorities remains contingent on his commitment to and skill at building coalitions and persuading a skeptical public and Congress to go along.

Indeed, the changing nature and scope of issues facing the black community, as well as the more conservative mood of a Republican-controlled Congress, explain why legislative solutions have not been as central a strategy for blacks as they were prior to the 1990s. Blacks are now demanding presidential action on issues that are less susceptible to legislative initiatives. This does not mean that the issues themselves are new. Indeed, employment and housing are persistent problems for blacks. But neither of these areas offers a president much freedom to act. The difficulty with such issues is that most of the proposed solutions would require a redistribution of wealth and social advantage. Given present conditions, it is highly unlikely that the American political system would support these kinds of changes, because to do so would imply some fundamental changes in the roles of government in society. Presidents, no matter how ambitious or daring, do not usually win elections on pledges to make such changes.

But to overcome severe economic problems that disproportionately affect blacks and similar minorities, it is precisely these types of changes that may be needed—changes that could well modify current patterns of political influence and access. To achieve such changes would seem to call for blacks and others to take a much broader and more active role in politics than they have in the past or have ever taken before. Jesse Jackson's campaigns in 1984 and 1988 for the Democratic presidential nomination suggest that blacks can clearly do just this: Jackson's campaigns—and his relative success—reflect a clear, discernible growth in the sophistication and breadth of policy concerns among blacks. It also reflects the studied attempts on the part of Jackson and others to illuminate and show how the much broader common interests among blacks, poor whites, and others more than overshadow the perceived divisions that may exist among them.

Campaigns like Jackson's and those of others have clearly advanced the political knowledge and awareness of blacks and minorities. But only in marginal terms, at least thus far, has this won for these groups more leverage and clout in presidential politics. This can be seen clearly in the 1992 presidential elections where Clinton overwhelmingly won the black vote without—except in most general terms—promising much in return.

Nonetheless, black advances into the mainstream of presidential politics have given them new vantage points from which to view the workings of the presidency. This can be sobering because it will be seen that a president is not all-powerful. The president cannot govern by fiat because there are other powerful actors who have competing interests. Because the president is a part of a complicated political environment, the ability to initiate major change is limited. But in uncommon circumstances, in which the environment itself is more conducive to fundamental change, the posture of the president can be crucial, even determinative. Such was the case for Roosevelt during the New Deal years, Johnson during the "Civil Rights Revolution," Nixon during the period of "law and order," and Ronald Reagan during his first term when he capitalized on the conservative mood and made severe cutbacks in civil rights and social welfare programs.[16] Similarly, and somewhat ironically, Clinton's ability to use the Presidency to shape public opinion and affect public policy is widely thought to have increased dramatically only after 1994, when conservative Republicans took control of both houses of Congress and Clinton's presidency became the undisputed center of power for the Democratic Party.

In any case, in American politics, broad scale and fundamental changes in national policies may require the kinds of unusual circumstances that aided presidents in the past, and certainly such fundamental changes are needed to deal with the problems faced by blacks. But most policy making takes place under normal, routine circumstances where the president need not be and is not always the most appropriate focal point for policy interests. And it is in this relatively routine area of policy making where African Americans will need to devote more careful attention and resources, for it is this routine, day-to-day policy making that can make a great deal of difference in the quality of life enjoyed (or endured) by most Americans, including blacks and minorities.

In the next section, you will see that we do not give the president as much prominence as he is generally thought to have in the making of public policy. Still, he remains the principal policy maker in the federal government. As we show later, presidential appointees loom much larger and play a much more crucial role than many are willing to acknowledge. The prominence of their roles may reflect individual presidential styles of policy making. For example, a factor illuminated during the 1987 Iran-Contra hearings was President Reagan's management style. Some presidents, such as Reagan, appear quite willing to allow department heads considerable discretion in policy development. Others, however, prefer to retain as much policy discretion as possible within the White House. The discussion that follows illustrates these points, as well as the rich interactive nature of the policy process.

THE POLICY PROCESS: AN OVERVIEW

For our purposes, the policy-making process is divided into four different phases:[17]

1. Agenda setting and initiation
2. Initial outcome: The legislative product

3. Secondary outcome: Administration and impact
4. Response, feedback, and future prospects

Within this framework one finds an interconnected series of actions and interactions involving private and public individuals, groups, and institutions. Also included are the president and his apparatus comprising the institutionalized presidency, members of Congress, the agencies, bureaus, and the political parties as well as the national news media.

We should emphasize that the process under discussion is not limited to a short period of time, say a single congressional term. It can take (and it has) a decade or more before an issue becomes a realistic part of the policy agenda. Sometimes it is even longer before specific policy results. Initiatives may fail but may not be forgotten. Such was the case, for example, with the lengthy struggle for black civil and political equality. This example, and there are others that stimulated less public concern, illustrates one of the most criticized features of the policy process: It is slow to respond to demands. Neither the strong feelings surrounding a group's claims nor their presumed justice weigh quite so heavily in political decision making as one might think. Despite the moral phrasing of the Constitution and the Bill of Rights, appeals to such ideas are of limited use in the political arena if the history of the civil rights struggle is any indication. Minority demands, such as those made by African Americans, mean a sharp break with practices that have matured during the course of American history. Adopting new programs or initiating new ways of dealing with continual problems may pose serious threats to existing social and political arrangements. Thus, policy making can, especially when dealing with questions that affect the scope of political influence, engender dramatic confrontations within and outside government.

Another reason why some things don't get done, or are sometimes done very slowly, stems from congressional "sampling."[18] Since members of Congress cannot attend to every demand made of them, they pick and choose among the issues brought to them for action and decision. Sampling, however, implies the existence of bias; by definition some things are ignored. Constitutionally, both Congress and the president are required to do certain things at fixed times. Congress convenes on a firm date every year (January 3) unless changed by law. And because some legislation expires after a set time, the legislature must act promptly if those laws are to be continued in force. An example of this is the use of the "continuing resolution." This device has financial importance for government agencies whose fiscal year begins on October 1. If Congress has not completed its work on an appropriations bill, the continuing resolution "allows agencies to spend at the rate set for that agency in the previous year ... [O]r if only the House has passed the appropriations bill, at whichever rate is lower, or, if both Senate and House have passed the bill, at whichever of those two rates is lower."[19]

To be sure, Congress can move with more than "deliberate speed" when the circumstances demand swift action. An acute, or crisis, situation presents a must-act condition; other business has to be postponed while elected officials deal with the crisis. A chronic problem of the body politic—for example, structural unemployment for some of the labor force—can be put aside.

We should add that while the president and the "institutionalized presidency," that is, the White House and Executive Office staffs, have a preeminent role in policy making, members of Congress may also, and do, initiate legislation. Thus, the technique of sampling just described must also allow time for the many bills sponsored by the congressional membership. In addition, even though it is not explicitly included under sampling, the particular ideology (that is, the beliefs of committee chairpersons in a policy area) will also influence what and how proposals are considered. This means that a president will try to avoid giving policy proposals to a committee chair who is known to be hostile. However, this searching for a receptive committee chairperson may affect the content of the proposed legislation because the congressional policy system tends to be functionally specific in its organization.

Let us now examine the four policy phases. Although we believe these elements of the policy process are so closely connected that they can be combined, we see a number of patterned relationships.

AGENDA SETTING AND INITIATION

National policy initiation has increasingly become the province of the presidency. Once elected to office, a president stands a good chance to be reelected, though the record since 1960 has been rather rocky. In any event, presidents know that getting their programs through Congress takes time, and those elected to a second term stand a better chance of getting their policies through. A president's first term can be viewed, then, as a time to build a record on which to run for his second four years in office. Therefore, the first four years tend to be oriented toward accomplishing those things that can be done quickly. However, "quickly" is a relative term in the relations between president and Congress. The relationship between initiation and agenda setting focuses upon the expanded role of the executive branch as the initiator of legislation. Through communications such as State of the Union messages, budget messages, and specific program proposals, the president not only initiates policy but also makes an agenda for congressional consideration, debate, and action. What the president wants is made clear, not left to the congressional imagination.

Since the administration of Franklin D. Roosevelt, presidents have also had another means of getting their message to the legislative branch. They have increasingly used the media, especially when there is a potentially strong opposition in Congress. President Clinton seems especially to be taking advantage of major technological advances and different forums and contexts (e.g., electronic and in-person town meetings) in talking directly to the American people. In part, this is an educational technique to inform the public of proposed government actions. But it is also a device to create public support for the president's programs. For example, when former President Nixon wanted to halt court-ordered busing as a means to achieve school integration, he went to the public via television. He told the listening public that lower federal courts

> [h]ave gone too far; in some cases, beyond the requirements laid down by the Supreme Court in ordering massive busing to achieve racial balance.... There are many who believe that a constitutional amendment is the only way to deal with this problem.... But as an answer to the immediate problem ... of stopping more busing now, the constitutional amendment approach has a fatal flaw—it takes too long.... And there's only one effective way to deal with the problem now. That is for Congress to act. That is why I am sending a special message to the Congress tomorrow urging immediate consideration and action.[20]

Likewise, President Reagan was given high marks by the media and others as a great communicator and for taking his proposals—aid for the Nicaraguan Contras, for example—over the heads of Congress directly to the people.

AGENDA SETTING AND ELECTORAL POLITICS

It is, however, realistic to ask where the president's program originates. Certainly technical details are fleshed out by topical experts, both appointive and career officials. But the ideas for presidential programs may also originate in less formalized ways. While somewhat vague and symbolic, campaign promises of a presidential candidate and united parties in mid-term elections may suggest potential agenda items for future legislative and executive attention. Electoral campaigns may show what the candidate thinks about different issues.

Part of the explanation for the absence of clear policy and issue discussion during the campaigns is that getting elected is different from actually doing the job. Quite naturally, a prospective president doesn't want to commit himself too strongly before taking office. In addition, if a candidate does take a firm position on a particular question, as Walter Mondale did on the need to raise taxes in his race against President Reagan in 1984, he or she may find himself giving the opposition an exploitable issue to use against him, which Reagan did. Similarly, President Clinton in the early months of his administration gave Republicans and some Democrats an "exploitable issue" with respect to Clinton's strong pledge during the 1992 campaign to end discrimination against gays and lesbians in the military services.

Perhaps of greater importance, however, is that the campaigns are not designed for a discussion of the issues. Rather, they serve to attract, and make the candidate attractive to, the great middle of American politics. If the presidential hopeful gets too specific, he or she is likely to alienate the middle ground. This is the condition that Senator McGovern unwittingly created in his 1972 campaign with his proposal to pay $1,000 to welfare recipients. On issues like welfare, which have a high degree of ideological content, being specific entails risk. The extent that a campaign tells us anything at all about the kinds of policies we might expect from a candidate if he or she is successful is by way of inference. That is, assuming that the candidate is not a total unknown, his or her past political activity should give some evidence of what he or she will be like as president. Positions that he or she has previously taken on public issues can, if carefully studied, be reasonable indicators of future stances on similar or related issues.[21] This kind of presidential watching, however, requires an investment of time and energy that the general public does not make.

AGENDA SETTING AND INTEREST GROUPS

Certainly, organized interest groups are involved in agenda setting through support of candidates likely to include their needs and wishes on an agenda for action. In American politics it is assumed that patience will at some future time be rewarded by positive government action in desired policy areas. While the denied group waits for these outcomes, it must also attempt to form coalitions with others. Such coalitions may require modification or even subordination of one group's goals in exchange for wider support. Sometimes the goals of the petitioning group can become the umbrella for the larger group. In either case, a broad base of support is often a necessary first step in getting the government to respond favorably to public demands.

Group formation and coalition building has been treated by many scholars as important means by which the interests of politically active publics are placed in the political marketplace.[22] More recently, there have been examples of small-sized interest groups placing their concerns on policy agendas without developing active wide-scale support. Small and less highly structured groups have been able to use the mass media to bring certain situations and viewpoints to public attention. Through use of the media, such groups have activated third-party interests that may be "inconvenienced" by the publicity surrounding the issues in question. These third parties, then, may become concerned enough for their own self-interests to become active in seeking a political solution. The implication is clear that this tactic is more likely to be used by a relatively weak group. Third parties' resources are brought to bear on the agenda-setting process on behalf of a weak organization. Such political action tends to be issue-specific rather than broad and general. Moreover, its use seems to be limited so far to urban political systems rather than national. The restriction appears to result from the ad hoc character of these groups' formation. They are unable to sustain an active membership and effective leadership over time once the original demands are met.[23]

AGENDA SETTING AND DOMESTIC CRISES

Events such as a war and an energy shortage can bring issues to the policy agenda rather quickly. But the natural processes of American policy making, especially on domestic concerns, tend to be characterized by slowness. This was noted by President Nixon in his speech on busing. This incrementalism, as it is frequently called, is closely related to the problem of providing funds for government activities.[24] In addition, we should keep in mind that the two-party system seldom reflects sharp differences on matters of public policy. The basic agreement on political values between Democrats and Republicans reinforces the incremental character of policy making.

When a crisis situation develops, it is difficult for the legislative and executive branches to respond. This is partly because their habitual patterns of response are oriented to regularities or the chronic problems of the political system. The solution to critical problems will generally require an abrupt change in the way the public's business is handled by its officials. However, the nature of that change depends upon political choices made among competing definitions of the problem(s) to be addressed by government action. The timing of crises also contributes to the ways in which they are handled. Most situations defined as crises in political terms are in fact not wholly novel phenomena. That is, one can usually find their antecedents in some one or another chronic problem that has gone unattended. A chronic problem becomes a crisis, in this view, when some part of the public is concerned enough about it to want to act. Moreover, those most directly concerned must also be able to get others to share their concern. The issue, in other words, must have a "ripple effect" among the public.

Naturally, the media has an important part to play in the evolution of a crisis, for they can enhance the "ripple effect." Direct political activity by individuals and groups in bringing the issues to the attention of legislators adds to the role of the media. Nontraditional forms of political behavior—for example, violence or mass protest demonstrations—help foster a sense of crisis, especially if the issue is relatively specific. This specificity implies that possible solutions will be narrow in scope and impact. The tendency then is to define a crisis situation in its narrowest terms consistent with its key issue(s). If this is not possible, the attempt is to find a solution that is politically feasible and satisfactory to the petitioning group but that is, at the same time, not so broad that its scope and impact are likely to have effects within other policy arenas.

AGENDA SETTING AND THE IDEA WHOSE TIME HAS COME

Specific policy proposals may receive little support or interest when first introduced. With the sponsorship of skillful political actors in the legislative and/or executive branch, such proposals gradually gain supporters. Many bills introduced by potential presidential candidates fit into this category;

although such proposals may have little chance of current passage, they can help "build a record," induce interest group support, and perhaps garner media attention. There is a strong relationship between this "idea whose time has come" and the process described in the previous section. Evaluating the civil rights movement in this context clearly yields some rich perspectives on the nature and operation of American politics. For example, the stage for the Model Cities program was created by several articles that appeared in national magazines. These articles emphasized the terrible conditions of the urban poor in the central city. There were pictures of the Watts riots in Los Angeles and other disturbances that occurred in the nation's cities. Consequently, in 1965, a letter and later a conversation between Walter Reuther, president of the United Auto Workers, and President Johnson provided the catalyst to action. They proposed to concentrate federal programs in the center city and give the cities enough money to begin urban renewal programs. As mayor of Detroit, Jerome Cavanaugh, in several conversations with Reuther, had emphasized the need for a massive renewal program based on the existing Model Neighborhood in Detroit. President Johnson found the proposal to his liking. Consequently, the president formed a task force headed by then-Professor Robert G. Wood of the Massachusetts Institute of Technology, later under secretary of the Department of Housing and Urban Development.[25]

The task force was composed of academicians and federal officials who were unfamiliar with the problems confronting urban areas. Wood did possess some expertise in the field of urban renewal. Whether he understood the complicated "human" problems of the urban poor sufficiently to design an adequate program is another question. The task force included only one individual who could really represent the interests of the urban poor, of whom the majority were black. This was Whitney Young, president of the Urban League, an organization not known at the time for aggressively championing black interests. To some extent, it might be argued that these interests were generally represented by the U.S. Conference of Mayors, whose constituencies were increasingly made up of these groups. But, the president and Dr. Wood deliberately selected persons who had not been too strongly committed to or identified with any existing program such as those of the Office of Economic Opportunity (OEO).

What did the task force propose? Why? The task force was strongly encouraged to develop new and innovative programs. In fact, Dr. Wood was given great latitude in terms of the types of proposals that could be submitted. But President Johnson also had some preferences. He instructed Dr. Wood and the task force to construct programs with the following characteristics: (1) Mayors and city councils were to have a principal role; (2) social and physical planning should be coordinated; and (3) racial integration and citizen participation were "desirable goals but would have to be played down in order to facilitate congressional passage."[26]

Initially, the task force had planned to propose that the program be enacted in only six or eight cities. However, they were aware of the congressional process. That is, the members of the task force were aware that congressional approval depended upon whether or not the congressmen's districts would benefit. With these instructions and considerations in mind, the task force set to work.

In January 1966, the task force formally presented its proposal, which contained a number of "innovations." These were clearly fashioned so that they would be accepted by Congress. The most drastic innovation was the concentration of resources in a defined neighborhood in a prescribed number of cities. The proposal also included a number of grant-in-aid programs that were to be coordinated by local officials and the neighborhood. The planning efforts were to be placed in a community development agency that would link the mayor's office to the affected neighborhood. The bulk of the funds would come from existing programs and agencies.[27] This arrangement would supposedly satisfy the demand for participation as well as congressional concerns for official control. Indeed, the task force was very concerned about the proposal's fate in Congress. The "reprogramming" of existing appropriations would also satisfy those members of Congress who did not want to increase federal spending. As we shall see later in this chapter, the task force got a good deal of what it, and the president, wanted in the legislation. And, of course, some congressional modifications were included.

INITIAL OUTCOME: THE LEGISLATIVE PRODUCT

A convenient way to view the legislative phase of the policy process is in terms of coalition building. The sponsor or sponsors of proposals must build coalitions in both houses of Congress, as well as in the relative subcommittees.

Several factors are important to policy coalitions. First, there are the attitudes and actions of the president. Through White House staff and representatives of executive departments, the president lobbies for or against a bill at hearings, with individual legislators, and through the media. Tactics will largely depend on the partisan and ideological makeup of Congress. And naturally, if the bill is an administration bill, the president and his "helpers" will do all they can to help the measure along. Despite the absence of disciplined legislative parties, the president's policy position will usually be a major factor in defining the position of most members of both parties. It is also important to consider whether a president is working to pass or to defeat a bill on its merit, or whether he is trying to gain political advantage for electoral purposes. His tactics will vary accordingly. Compromises may be made in the former situation, but seldom in the latter. Thus, key members of Congress will try to find out the president's feelings on a particular measure before they commit themselves fully one way or the other.

Second, department and agency bureaucrats contribute to coalition construction. In many instances, these institutional representatives have a monopoly on information. How has a program worked? Its administrators have answers that are documented with mountains of supporting data. How will a new program work? Its technical authors can explain the prospects in exquisite detail. In other instances, bureaucrats use longstanding associations with individual legislators to rally support for proposals concerned with their agency. But there is little or no role for the public.

Coalition building in support of or in opposition to proposed legislation is also influenced by a third characteristic, the committee structure of Congress. Because the bulk of congressional work is performed in committee and subcommittee and not on the floor of the House or Senate, these smaller, functionally devised groups can significantly influence the final shape of the legislative product. For example, the policy areas of some committees are more conducive to "log-rolling" or "pork-barrel" tactics than others. That is, the issue being considered may have implications for some tangible interests of the members' constituencies. If the representatives are convinced that those interests will not be adversely affected by the "marked-up" bill, a strong committee coalition is likely when the bill is presented to the full House or Senate for debate and vote. The bill is even likely to attract the support of members whose constituents will not benefit from the bill, since these members count on the support of other coalition members when a bill benefiting their constituents is considered later. If such a committee coalition is bipartisan, strictly partisan voting on the floor is unlikely. This is especially true when the subject matter is not of great interest to many of the legislators.

On the other hand, a committee whose policy areas are subject to ideological conflict—the House Committee on Education and Labor is a good example—is less likely to arrive at a consensual coalition. Therefore, the House or Senate floor becomes the primary arena for coalition building on bills from such committees. Partisan and/or ideological differences are likely to be important factors. These differences will be revealed in the debate that precedes the final vote on the issue.

Similarly, it is important to note that the style of committee operation vis-à-vis House action will often determine whether much, little, or no bargaining and compromising go on at the committee level. When a powerful committee chairperson is determined to bring out a bill that will pass, committee activity is strongly oriented toward coalition formation—even though the subject matter itself may be controversial.

Fourth, legislative parties also affect congressional coalition building. There are many important variables: whether the White House and Congress are controlled by the same party, the relative strength of the majority and minority, the style and influence of party leadership, the amount of cohesiveness in each party, the role and influence of party subgroups such as the Democratic Study Group, and the anticipated closeness of the next election.

A fifth factor can be generally described as constituency influence. However, this does not mean only letters from home. Constituents also include organized groups that serve as important referents—civil rights groups, labor unions, expressive associations, farmer organizations, associations of business and industry, and the like. Such organizations can influence legislators for several reasons. Their members or those they claim to represent may actually be an important segment of electoral constituencies and the organizations may be important to electoral success. Or the groups may simply share the legislator's own ideological leanings, a factor especially important for upwardly mobile representatives and senators. The coalition-building role of such groups typically centers around two tactics: (1) supporting tried-and-true friends and urging them to take more active roles in specific policy battles and (2) shoring up others who might waver in certain instances.

Another important constituency influence is the legislator's perceptions of how the "folks back home" feel about a policy area. It seems likely that what is calculated is not what most voters feel about a particular bill, but what they feel about a given issue area. How this is calculated varies, but certainly communications from major supporters, party leaders, and other key local individuals weigh heavily. Obviously, in many cases the legislator must realize that most of the home folks neither know nor care about the matter at hand!

In any given instance, one or more of these factors will be significant in developing congressional support for a policy proposal. In addition, several studies have indicated that certain policy decisions are more closely tied to presidential influence while others are related to party affiliation or constituency attitudes.[28]

This discussion has revealed the multiplicity of actors and some of their roles in making public policy. Although the general public's direct influence on this process is limited in most cases to letter writing, it is often remarked that their concerns are indirectly articulated through the "interest aggregation" function of the two major political parties. But if some part of the public is perceived or in fact is not influential in the party's decision, even indirect articulation loses much of its meaning. In general, this has been the case with national policy that is relevant to black interests. Thus, the inability of African Americans to exercise significant influence in the policy process on matters that greatly affect them (unemployment, overcoming problems of poverty) reflects the relative weak position of blacks in the political system.

In some respects the lack of influence can be viewed as a by-product of black urbanization. Many problems that affect blacks most severely are related to their urban concentration. Therefore, we could expect that the way in which urban policy is handled would strongly affect African Americans. In general, however, the American "love-hate" relationship with their large cities has been greatly affected by racial problems and conflicts more visible in urban areas. This condition is, of course, intensified by the fact that the potential for urbanization was not considered when Congress was initially organized. Cities, to the extent that they were considered at all by the founders, were the responsibilities of the states, not of the federal government.

Thus, despite the severe dislocations that urban populations suffered during the Great Depression and the obvious implications of the general urbanization of the nation since the 1920s, Congress and the president gave little specific attention to urban affairs. That is, unlike agricultural interests, there was no committee specializing in the affairs of urban communities.[29] Not until the Kennedy administration was an effort made to give urban policy questions an institutionalized status in the policy system. And, Kennedy's attempt to create a Department of Urban Affairs failed in part because some influential southerners in Congress viewed it as having racial/civil rights implications to which they were opposed. The Johnson administration met with greater success. However, that success came at a high price. The creation of the Department of Housing and Urban Development, with America's first black cabinet member as its head, came after several years of violent urban political activity by blacks and extensive damage to some of the nation's largest cities. The passage of the Demonstration Cities Act (hereafter referred to by the more common name of Model Cities) gives us an opportunity to see the policy system in action.

MODEL CITIES: THE POLICY PROCESS IN ACTION

The "Great Society" era's Model Cities initiative offers a good example of the national policy process that we have outlined in the foregoing pages. Although this particular urban initiative is now largely a historical artifact, it remains instructive for those interested in urban policy today. In fact, many contemporary examples of national urban policymaking, including the Bush and Clinton efforts at promoting federally supported "enterprise" or "empowerment" zones in troubled urban areas, closely resembles the Johnson era's Model Cities policy-making effort. The Model Cities program was introduced as three separate bills in the House of Representatives. The bills were referred to the House Committee on Banking and Currency, chaired by Wright Patman (D-Texas). Patman was a staunch supporter of the legislation. And, it is useful to indicate that Patman was also a longtime friend of President Johnson. From the president's point of view it made good political sense to have potentially controversial legislation considered not only by a supporter but also by a friend. That legislation of this type should be handled by the Committee on Banking and Currency may at first appear strange. However, in addition to its jurisdiction over both the general area of banking and currency and the Federal Reserve system, Patman's committee also oversaw matters of housing and home finance and urban redevelopment. Although the president and his task force conceived of the Model Cities program as something new, in terms of committee perceptions it was a variation of the urban renewal legislation with which members were familiar. As such, it was likely that they would not think of the proposed legislation along the lines of novelty that its creators intended.[30]

The Model Cities legislation authorized participating cities the full array of available grants and aid in the fields of housing, urban renewal, transportation, welfare, economic opportunity, and related programs. In addition, the bill provided special grants amounting to 80 percent of the nonfederal cost of the programs included in the demonstration. It also included programs currently being financed under existing federal grant-in-aid programs and those proposed initially as part of the demonstration.

A second bill provided collateral programs for urban development. This was not a major concern in the legislation submitted by the president. The third and final bill authorized federal assistance to finance and equip facilities for group medical and dental practices. It too was a minor segment of the Model Cities program.[31]

The three bills attracted a variety of supporters and opponents. The testimony of the groups' spokesmen indicated their concerns; but it also furnished a basis for evaluating their roles and influence in the final legislative product.

The first individual to testify before the committee was Dr. Robert E. Weaver, later to become secretary of Housing and Urban Development and the first black to hold a cabinet post. He impressed upon the committee members the importance of the legislation in solving the physical, social, and economic problems confronting the nation's central cities. Weaver's comments went directly to the point of community involvement when he discussed the proposed eligibility criteria. Blight alone was insufficient. In addition to urban blight, the applicant would also be required to demonstrate that local officials and residents were able to work constructively together. Weaver stated:

> The areas (must be) willing and able to bring together the public and private bodies whose joint action is necessary to solve their problems—willing to commit fully their energies and resources—willing to undertake actions which will have widespread and profound effects on the physical and social structures of the city.[32]

Unlike the Community Action Programs (CAP) of OEO, which emphasized a dominant role for the "grassroots," the Model Cities programs sought to create a less abrasive relationship between the lay public and elected officials.

Weaver also indicated that federal control would be limited; "this will be a local program."[33] He was attempting to gain the support of legislators and interest groups who had criticized the red tape in the administration of the poverty programs. Weaver continued, "All assistance under the program would be channeled into a demonstration agency established or designated by the local governing body to administer the program."[34] Despite the emphasis placed on local initiative, Weaver also indicated the likely nature of federal involvement. Undoubtedly, Weaver was aware of congressional doubts about urban officials' competence in handling large sums of money. He proposed that a federal coordinator be designated for each approved area; this federal coordinator's function would be to provide liaison and coordination services.

Weaver was followed by spokesmen from the U.S. Conference of Mayors. The support of this body is easy to understand. Cities were in financial trouble and physically deteriorating because the suburban areas were attracting the commercial enterprises, the financially stable families, and other taxable entities. Their livelihoods and the viability of their cities depended upon how well they were able to deal with complex problems. H. J. Addonizio, mayor of Newark, endorsed the legislation on behalf of the U.S. Conference of Mayors.[35] The mayors strongly supported the idea of federal coordinators to provide liaison services in each approved project area. Surprisingly, however, they also urged that coordination be broadened by designating an assistant secretary or an assistant director for participating agencies. Mayor Addonizio was joined by several more colleagues before the committee in support of the proposed legislation. Among these were Mayors John Lindsay of New York City, Richard Daley of Chicago, and Jerome Cavanaugh of Detroit.[36]

Organized labor, of course, had supported the Model Cities proposal from its inception as a result of Reuther's active involvement. Labor also had a self-interest in the program because it would increase the number of jobs available. The legislation called for an enormous amount of construction. Boris Shiskin, secretary of the AFL-CIO housing subcommittee, termed the bills "an important and auspicious step in the right direction."[37] However, he did remind the committee that the anticipated funding level was insufficient to deal adequately with the urban blight and the associated social and economic problems confronting the urban poor.[38]

Additional interest group support came from several groups directly involved in the nation's urban areas. The organizations and their representatives included the executive director of the metropolitan Atlanta region of the National Association of Housing and Redevelopment Officials; the president of the National Association of Home Builders; the president of the National Housing Conference; and the president of the National Farmers Union.[39] Each of these representatives tried to impress upon the committee the importance of the legislation. They argued that the legislation would greatly decrease the misery of the urban areas and their people.

Technical experts also testified in support of the program. Harold Wise, chairman of the national legislative committee of the American Institute of Planners (AIP), strongly endorsed the Model Cities proposals but criticized their presentation as separate bills. He contended that the Demonstration Cities Act (H.R. 12341) and the Urban Development Act (H.R. 12939) could serve the needs of urban areas more adequately if they were consolidated under the same act. Wise felt that the administration was proposing two separate types of programs for two different constituencies—urban areas and growing suburban areas. Another to testify was Morris Ketchum, Jr., president of the American Institute of Architects (AIA), who endorsed the "New Towns Provision." He argued very strongly for specifying high standards for design technology, including cost reduction techniques.

Both the AIP and AIA saw potential gains for members of their respective professions. The architects naturally were interested in the jobs the program might provide. But they also saw Model Cities as an opportunity to introduce new concepts in housing design and construction techniques. The planners meanwhile saw the requirement for comprehensive planning as a vehicle that would put into practice their belief in integrated social and physical planning. And, there was a less obvious dividend for the planners. They were a smaller and less prestigious group than the architects. The possibility of acquiring increased stature and influence through work in Model Cities programs was a consideration.

Although the administration had drawn the legislation in such a way as to gain support from several parts of the political spectrum, there was opposition. Indeed, some legislators believed that their constituents might sustain a loss if the legislation were to pass. For these critics of Model Cities it was essential for Congress to anticipate the "horrible" effects of the legislation. One of these groups was the National Association of Real Estate Boards (NAREB). This association has had a reputation for opposing the liberal viewpoint in housing and urban renewal matters. It had consistently opposed earlier housing acts, and it opposed Model Cities.[40] The realtors argued that the proposal for another federal attempt would further reduce local initiative. In their view the proponents of the legislation should

> stop attempting to spoon feed the Congress and the [American] people in the area of federal assistance to whole communities. We should recognize that a gap in local initiative cannot be bridged by money alone.[41]

With reference to traditional conservative thinking, the NAREB contended that the legislation was an "unwarranted intrusion of Government in the control of the future use of land ... [which] would lead ultimately to the federalization of the nation's communities."[42]

The NAREB opposition was not based entirely upon its fear of federal domination, the unwise use of land, and the cities' lack of initiative to do their jobs. Its position also reflected a belief that its members might lose economically because of the federally sponsored housing. James F. Steiners, spokesman for the Chambers of Commerce of the United States, opposed the measures on similar grounds. He also argued that the proponents of the program were assuming without real proof that the cities did not have adequate resources to solve their own problems. He was harshly critical of the liaison function as well. He foresaw a possibility that the federal coordinator would become a "commissar or czar who would possess vaguely defined powers."[43]

That part of the legislation that provided for federal monies to finance and equip facilities for group medical and dental practice in blighted areas was strongly opposed by the American Medical Association and the American Dental Association. The doctors argued that the proposal was a weapon to put the individual practitioners out of business. Arguments that suggested that the urban poor received poor health and dental care were given only limited attention.

However, opposition to the Model Cities legislation was not that substantial. Nor were the arguments that the realtors and doctors presented persuasive to the committee members. And, in any case, the NAREB position was weakened by the enthusiastic participation of that industry in other federally assisted housing and urban renewal efforts. As for the medical profession, their almost traditional fear of socialized medicine, as well as their expected opposing views, carried little weight. The Committee on Banking and Currency was not studying medical legislation; it was considering problems of urban blight. It was an easy matter for the members of the committee to focus their attention on questions of urban renewal and to downplay the possible implications for socialized health and dental services.[44] The Model Cities bill was accepted by Congress on the president's terms with two exceptions: The federal coordinator was eliminated, and the funding level was reduced.

It is useful, then, to ask one final question about policy making. Who benefits? But merely asking that question implies a larger number of related queries. One would like to know how a particular group or class of beneficiaries benefited from governmental actions. Answers to such questions are difficult to find, as we noted. But there is usually some evidence available from which those who make such inquiries can develop reasonable inferences. The Model Cities program gives us an illustration of this point.

WHO BENEFITED?

Model Cities was expected to relieve the conditions of the urban poor, that is, blacks. It was purported to have been designed to enhance the quality of life within the central cities of metropolitan America. In fact, this was the first national program whose purpose was to deal with the social, economic, and health needs of the urban poor. It was the program that President Johnson viewed as giving meaning to the lives of the urban poor. But what has really been the impact of the Model Cities program on the lives of the urban poor? Has it enhanced the quality of life in the center cities? Or has it worked toward strengthening the local government—that is, the mayor's position as a decision maker?

The studies of the center city areas since the implementation of the Model Cities have produced discouraging findings. They revealed that the urban poor are still living under conditions that were prevalent before the enactment of Model Cities.[45] A study conducted by the National Urban Coalition discovered that the conditions reported in the Kerner Commission Report were still present in the urban areas. The study indicated that the quality of life had not been improved in the cities investigated. In fact, the study revealed that the quality of life had really changed for the worse: (1) Housing is still the national scandal it was then; (2) the rates of crime, unemployment, disease, and heroin addiction are higher; (3) welfare rolls are larger; and (4) relations between minority communities and the police are just as hostile. One change for the better has been the more positive attitude blacks and the urban poor gained of themselves. This is not, however, necessarily connected with Model Cities.[46] Some community activists and planners, however, criticized what they saw as the most detrimental aspects of the program: (1) breaking up ethnic neighborhoods—destroying a sense of community and (2) the forced relocation of the urban poor without adequate provisions for new housing.[47] Similar criticisms were also made of the urban renewal programs that had preceded Model Cities by more than a decade. There was no effective answer to these criticisms.

Some observers have taken the view that the federal government simply cannot correct some of the urban problems that plague American life.[48] And not all those who take this position can be dismissed as conservatives. The politically active among urban blacks have increasingly blamed the government for the failures (real and imagined) of programs like Model Cities. However, passage of a bill by Congress does not end the policy process. Indeed, as we shall see in the following section, the congressional action sets in motion a wide range of activities by other parts of government.

SECONDARY OUTCOME: ADMINISTRATION AND IMPACT

The impact of legislation approved by Congress can be viewed in terms of the following questions:

1. Does the act actually allocate or reallocate resources to certain groups or individuals?
2. If so, who gets what benefits, and who pays what costs?
3. Does the act place regulations on individuals or groups?
4. If so, who is to enforce these regulations? With what sanctions?
5. Does the bill delegate authority to make allocations or regulations? If so, to whom?

Unless a policy is self-executing or the guidelines as to "who gets how much of what" are unusually clear and explicit, there will be some administrative discretion in implementation. To discover the actual impact that a program has on a target population or problem area, several features of administration should be considered.

First, who is given administrative authority? An old-line agency, one that has been upgraded for the task, or a newly created structure? For both the War on Poverty and Model Cities programs, new agencies were developed: the Office of Economic Opportunity (OEO) for the former and a new department, Housing and Urban Development, for the latter.[49] The creation of new agencies may arouse jealousies in the older agencies that heretofore had responsibility in that particular policy area. For OEO and Model Cities, this problem was compounded by the emergence of interagency conflict around President Johnson's desire that federal efforts in the cities be coordinated. This meshing of sometimes competing energies and interests does not just happen; it has to be made to happen. And if the president or someone with his proxy isn't there to see it through, coordination is unlikely to become fact.

Second, if a new administration structure is created, will it be visible and thus vulnerable to political attacks?[50] If so, can such attacks affect the allocation or regulatory function? The staff of a new administration is also important: Recruitment patterns, political ties, past experience in similar policy areas, and possible links to clientele groups must be considered in the selection process.

Third, changes in administrative practices and orientations over time greatly affect the impact of policy. The concept of life cycles of regulatory commissions is one important pattern to be considered. This phenomenon might well apply to structures created to deal with areas such as civil rights, environmental protection, and product safety. Agencies can be and are "captured" by clientele groups, even by those that they are supposed to regulate. In fact, administrator and client can become so closely tied that it is often difficult to distinguish precisely who is making administrative decisions.[51]

Fourth, just as it is possible for an agency to be "captured" by its clientele, so too can a similar "capture" be made by a legislator whose committee works in that particular functional area. The relationships developed between administrators and members of Congress can affect future funding and thus lead to expansion or reduction of program benefits and/or program scope.[52]

Fifth, if administrative structures have discretion in establishing program guidelines, setting standards of eligibility for program participation or approving funding of projects at the state and local levels, what criteria are used for making such decisions? It is quite possible that such discretion can lead to different results from those envisioned by sponsors and supporters of original legislation. Yet many such decisions go unchallenged. This may well be because many congressional coalitions can be built only for statements of general intent and would break down if specific allocations were involved.

Sixth, administrative functions may be diffused through various levels of bureaucratic structures. Until very recently, all the categorical assistance programs were administered in part at the federal level and in part at the local or county level. Such dispersion of administrative discretion created hundreds of welfare "systems." Under such circumstances, the impact of a "national" policy is difficult to discern or measure.

RESPONSE, FEEDBACK, AND FUTURE PROSPECTS

This phase of the policy process theoretically leads back to the beginning of the cycle, assuming first that adoption of a policy has some kind of impact and second that someone notices it. Responses ideally should come from those persons or groups affected by a specific program. However, if those targets are unorganized and without access to political actors or public attention, their pleasure or displeasure with program results may be unnoticed. While young men from low-income families were being drafted in greater proportions and receiving fewer deferments than youths of higher socioeconomic status, there was no available feedback route for complaints about this feature of the Selective Service System.[53] However, when large numbers of middle- and upper-class youths began attacking the draft as part of the Vietnam War protests, this response to an established policy was attended to by both political actors and the national media.

Since few national programs are systematically evaluated in terms of how much change is produced in target populations or whether specific governmental actions actually "solve problems," it seems that much of the content of response is quite subjective in nature. At best, praise or disappointment will often be registered by leaders, real or self-appointed, of target groups. Nevertheless, how leaders with ties to policy actors respond can affect the future of a given policy. Equally important can be the response of persons or groups affected by an unplanned consequence of a program. The reaction to community action registered by local elected officials was important in modifying OEO programs and activities, such as the Green Amendments of 1966 [named for former Representative Edith Green, (D-Oregon)], which gave elected officials a stronger voice in the use of these federal funds. In turn, these modifications were made part of the Model Cities legislation, as we have seen.

Because many programs require the creation of extensive administrative networks, they may also create new constituent and clientele groups with an interest in program maintenance. While part of their feedback may entail suggestions for improvement, it is also safe to predict that their overall response will be positive. Policies that create a significant number of administrative units more or less create support groups with a vested interest in the resulting program's future. Indeed, some have argued that the Model Cities initiative was largely designed to mobilize inner-city black voters on behalf of the Democratic party by bypassing the governors and mayors and funneling federal dollars directly to non-profit organizations and social services agencies in black communities.[54] We should also note the importance of future modifications, increments, or terminations of specific policies to the responses of original sponsors, supporters, and opponents. For example, the subsequent expansion of Model Cities demonstration projects to include a larger number of congressional districts than initially planned certainly helped to assure continued congressional support during the first crucial years of its implementation.[55] By contrast, the ultimately successful efforts of Presidents Nixon and Ford to fold Model Cities into "block grants" that would flow through city hall, rather than directly to community-based agencies, signaled the end of the Model Cities program as initially conceived.

Of course, presidents, legislators, and even "experts," like other mortals, often see what they want to see. They, too, can be seduced by symbolic assurances. However, if association with a certain policy has aided one of these actors politically, it is likely that the actor will wish to continue this association if expansion or modification appears promising. If opponents feel that the program has not produced the dire consequence they predicted, or if their reference groups no longer care very much about the issue, they may accept incremental expansion.

One of the more troublesome situations in the policy process stems from the recognition by participants in the process that they have sponsored and carried through programs that do not appear to be fulfilling their promises. This seems to be the current dilemma of many critics concerning many of our current social programs. It also helps to explain the turn away from "government-led" solutions during the Reagan/Bush years and toward solutions that relied more heavily on the private sector. No initiatives in the 1980s symbolizes this philosophical turn better than the various proposals for "enterprise zones,"[56] which were floated about by both Presidents Reagan and Bush.

Like the Model Cities programs of the 1960s, enterprise zones were conceived as an urban renewal strategy for improving the conditions of inner cities plagued by high levels of unemployment, crime, and economic decay. But unlike Model Cities, which focused on funneling development funds and resources to local services agencies and large-scale capital improvements projects, enterprise zones would operate by offering tax breaks and wage credits to businesses that agreed to locate in blighted areas. This idea banked on the power of private industry to improve the social and economic conditions of the inner-city. But even this modest idea, first proposed by then congressman Jack Kemp in 1980, and later by Presidents Reagan in 1982 and Bush in 1992, did not make much headway in Washington until after Clinton's election. Clinton proposed the addition of modest start-up capital and money for job training to the mix of tax incentives proposed by previous Republican administrations and convinced Congress to approve funds for nine federally funded "empowerment zones" as part of the 1993 budget package.[57] The 13-year lag in enacting what was eventually only a very modest urban aid bill attests to the continuing political weakness of black and other minority group leaders who seek to put urban problems at the top of a national legislative agenda. It also attests to the greater success that such leaders have at furthering their agenda when they can work with a president who, like Clinton, is more sympathetic to their proposals.

While negative responses and feedback are easy to find, new policy approaches to chronic problems are slow to emerge. We recognize also that radical proposals are not likely to be accepted quickly, though they may be at some future time. Perhaps this is simply another indication that there are time lags at all points in the policy process. Or perhaps it substantiates the notion that there is "periodicity" to policy actions, which expands the role of government.[58]

In the meantime, the higher levels of political participation among blacks do imply that the feedback mechanisms of the policy system will contain more politically relevant information from that section of the population. But the pervasive and persistent levels of low educational attainment in most black communities will continue to constrain the effectiveness of African Americans in the policy process, for black legislators, like their white colleagues, need technical and expert information on policy questions. Educational inequalities, which we discussed in an earlier chapter, compounded by the absence of viable alternative resources distributed among black citizens, impose limits upon the ability of black legislators to compete in forming the policy agenda. The inability of blacks to affect the policy process significantly is further evidence of their weakness in the nation's political life. Admittedly, corrective actions to overcome these deficiencies will take time, but the question is how much time.[59]

TOPICS FOR DISCUSSION

1. Do you think that a black candidate can marshal the kinds of resources and support needed to become president? Discuss thoroughly, indicating a familiarity with the various considerations involved in the presidential nominating process and the presidential election.

2. Suppose you were asked by a black interest group to suggest concrete ways to increase black political influence in the policy-making process. What would you suggest? Why?

3. The text states that "black advances into the mainstream of presidential politics have given them new vantage points from which to view the workings of the presidency." Discuss the meaning and implications of this statement for black politics.

SUGGESTED READINGS

Barber, James D. *The Presidential Character*, 4th ed. Englewood Cliffs, NJ: Prentice Hall, 1992. The influence of personality on how the president conducts his office.

Barker, Lucius J. *Our Time Has Come: A Delegate's Diary of Jesse Jackson's 1984 Presidential Campaign*. Urbana, IL: University of Illinois Press, 1988. An interpretative and dynamic personal account of Jackson's campaign as seen by a Jackson delegate.

Barnett, Marguerite R., and James Hefner. *Public Policy for the Black Community: Strategies and Perspectives.* Port Washington, NY: Alfred Publishing, 1976. Analyzes various options through which the black community can attain its policy options in the political system.

Berger, Raoul. *Impeachment: The Constitutional Problems.* Cambridge, MA: Harvard University Press, 1973. An historical and legal analysis of the constitutional provision relating to impeachment.

Blumenthal, Richard. "The Bureaucracy: Antipoverty and the Community Action Program." In *American Political Institutions and Public Policy: Five Contemporary Studies,* ed. Allen P. Sindler. Boston, MA: Little, Brown, 1969. A study of the infighting among agencies over administration of the resources of the Community Action Program.

Brauer, Carl M. *John F. Kennedy and the Second Reconstruction.* New York: Columbia University Press, 1977. Discusses Kennedy's role and attempts to overcome racial barriers in American life.

Braybrooke, David, and Charles Lindblom. *A Strategy of Decision.* New York: The Free Press, 1970. The classic formulation of the idea of incremental decision processes in government.

Cronin, Thomas E. *Inventing the American Presidency.* Lawrence, KS: University of Kansas Press, 1989.

Crouse, Timothy. *The Boys on the Bus.* New York: Random House, 1973. A description of the 1972 presidential campaign and election.

Goldman, Peter, and Tom Mathews. *The Quest for the Presidency: The 1988 Campaign.* New York: Simon & Schuster, 1989. A detailed account of the dynamics of the 1988 presidential race.

Heclo, Hugh. *A Government of Strangers: Executive Politics in Washington.* Washington, DC: The Brookings Institution, 1977. A penetrating study of the relations between political appointees (executives and high-level bureaucrats) and the implications of those relationships for change and continuity in government.

Jones, Charles O. *The Presidency in a Separated System.* Washington, DC: The Brookings Institution, 1994. An account of the nature of governance and the challenges facing the president in a separated system of government.

Kernell, Samuel. *Going Public.* Washington, DC: Congressional Quarterly Press, 1986. A study of the presidential strategy of taking policies directly to the public.

Martin, Roscoe C. *Cities and the Federal System.* New York: Atherton, 1967. An examination of the role of the federal government in the political and policy processes of local governments.

Milkis, Sidney M., and Michael Nelson. *The American Presidency: Origins and Development, 1776–1993,* 2nd ed. Washington, DC: Congressional Quarterly, Inc., 1994. The history of how the presidency was created and how it has developed over time.

Moe, Ronald C., ed. *Congress and the President.* Pacific Palisades, CA: Goodyear Publishing Company, 1971. A collection of readings that focus on various aspects of presidential-congressional relations.

Moynihan, Daniel P. *Maximum Feasible Misunderstanding.* New York: The Free Press,

1969. A description and analysis of the problems plaguing the implementation of public policy decisions during the Johnson years.

National Urban League. *The Urban League Review.* Washington, DC: National Urban League. A semi-annual publication devoted to research and analysis of selected policy areas relevant to black Americans (e.g., housing, unemployment, energy).

Nelson, Michael, ed. *The Presidency and the Political System.* Washington, DC: Congressional Quarterly Press, 1995. A compilation of essays on the relationship between the presidency and the political system.

Neustadt, Richard E. *Presidential Power and the Modern Presidents.* New York: The Free Press, 1991.

Peterson, Mark A. *Legislating Together: The White House and Capitol Hill from Eisenhower to Reagan.* Cambridge: Harvard University Press, 1990.

Phillips, Kevin. *The Politics of Rich and Poor.* New York: Random House, 1990. An analysis of the policies of Republican administrations benefiting the rich and harming the poor.

Pious, Richard M. *The American Presidency.* New York: Basic Books, 1979. Describes the evolution of the American presidency and the various roles that the president must play in the American political system.

Polsby, Nelson, and Aaron Wildavsky. *Presidential Elections,* 6th ed. New York: Charles Scribner's Sons, 1984. A study of the strategies involved in presidential elections with an evaluation of possible reforms.

Pomper, Gerald M., et al. *The Election of 1992.* Chatham, NJ: Chatham House Publishers, 1993. A collection of essays concerning various aspects of the 1992 presidential and congressional elections.

———. *The Election of 1996.* Chatham, NJ: Chatham House Publishers, 1997. A collection of essays concerning various aspects of the 1996 presidential and congressional elections.

Schneier, Edward V., and Bertram Gross. *Legislative Strategy Shaping Public Policy.* New York: St. Martin's Press, 1993. A penetrating empirical-theoretical analysis of congressional policy making.

Sundquist, James. *Politics and Policy.* Washington, DC: The Brookings Institution, 1968. A comparative study of the interplay between congressional and executive politics and policy formulation during the Eisenhower, Kennedy, and Johnson administrations.

Thomas, Norman C., Joseph A. Pika, and Richard A. Watson. *The Politics of the Presidency,* 3rd ed. Washington, DC: Congressional Quarterly, Inc., 1994. A study of how presidents govern, noting changes and developments in the office of the president.

Wildavsky, Aaron B. *The New Politics of the Budgetary Process.* Glenview, IL: Scott, Foresman & Company, 1988. An excellent analysis of budget making and its policy implications.

NOTES

1. Richard E. Neustadt, *Presidential Power* (New York: The Free Press, 1990), p. 35. Copyright 1990 by The Free Press. Reprinted by permission.
2. Robert Borosage, et al., "The New Public Interest Lawyers," *Yale Law Journal* 79,

p. 1081. Reprinted by permission of the Yale Law Journal Company and Fred B. Rothman & Company.

3. James W. Davis, Jr., *An Introduction to Public Administration* (New York: The Free Press, 1974), p. 21. Of course, literature on the presidency is voluminous. See the Suggested Readings section for this chapter.

4. Louis W. Koenig, *The Chief Executive*, 3rd ed. (New York: Harcourt Brace Jovanovich, Inc., 1975), p. 35.

5. Candidates, of course, might qualify for funds under the Federal Elections Campaign Act of 1974.

6. In recent years, a growing number of political scientists have used the tools of psychology and psychiatry to explain presidential behavior. While interesting and suggestive of substantial insights, this literature causes considerable controversy. For the students (and others) who are interested in this area, we recommend Alan C. Elms, *Personality in Politics* (New York: Harcourt Brace Jovanovich, Inc., 1976) as a useful starting place. Elms's work also contains a lengthy bibliography for those who might wish to pursue the issues in greater depth.

7. Emmett John Hughes, *The Living Presidency* (New York: Penguin, 1974), pp. 69–74.

8. On the impact of black votes, see *The Black Vote: Election '76* (Washington, DC: Joint Center for Political Studies, August 1977). More general discussions of the 1976 campaign can be found in Gerald Pomper, *The Election of 1976: Reports and Interpretations* (New York: David McKay, 1977); and Jules Witcover, *Marathon: The Pursuit of the Presidency 1972–1976* (New York: Viking, 1977). Witcover's book is especially useful for its treatment of the campaigns for election by the two major parties. For more information on the black vote, see the Suggested Readings section for this chapter.

9. *Ibid.*, p. 306.

10. Pomper, *The Election of 1976*, pp. 60–61.

11. However, some critics noted that filling only two cabinet positions with blacks was hardly a sufficient return for their efforts on Carter's behalf. In 1979 Harris was transferred from HUD to HEW, and Ambassador Young resigned his position. For more on Young's resignation, see Chapter 9.

12. See Samuel Kernell, *Going Public* (Washington, DC: Congressional Quarterly Press, 1986), esp. pp. 115–117.

13. Congressional Quarterly, *CQ Guide to Current American Government* (Washington, DC: Congressional Quarterly Press, 1981), p. 14.

14. Maureen Dowd, "Bush Says the Dream of Dr. King Will Be a Vision for His Tenure," *New York Times*, January 17, 1989, p. 1.

15. For an overall detailed analysis of the 1992 presidential elections, along with commentary on the congressional elections, see Gerald Pomper, et al., *The Election of 1992: Reports and Interpretations* (Chatham, NJ: The Chatham House Publishers, 1993).

16. There are a number of recent works available on the presidency. We suggest that an interested student should begin with Richard E. Neustadt, *Presidential Power*. One collection providing a broad sampling of literature is Michael Nelson, ed., *The Presidency and the Political System* (Washington, DC: Congressional Quarterly Press, 1995.

17. These phases represent a combination of ten functional activities of policy making presented in Charles O. Jones, *An Introduction to the Study of Public Policy* (Belmont, CA: Duxbury Press, 1970).

18. Polsby, *Congress and the Presidency*, pp. 4–6.

19. Richard F. Fenno, *The Power of the Purse: Appropriations Politics in Congress* (Boston, MA: Little, Brown, 1966), p. 421.

20. Quoted in George A. Davis and O. Fred Donaldson, *Blacks in the United States: A Geographic Perspective* (Boston, MA: Houghton Mifflin, 1975), pp. 157–158.

21. See, for example, James David Barber, *The Presidential Character: Predicting Performance in the White House* (Englewood Cliffs, NJ: Prentice Hall, Inc., 1992). A somewhat more accessible discussion of some of the points made here is contained in Nelson Polsby's "Our Quadrennial Drama," in his work *Presidential Promises: Essays and Commentary on American Politics* (New York: Oxford University Press, 1974), pp. 165–171.

22. See, for example, David B. Truman, *The Governmental Process* (New York: Alfred A. Knopf, 1951); Robert H. Salisbury, *Interest Group Politics in America* (New York: Harper & Row, 1970); Earl B. Latham, *The Group Basis of Politics* (Ithaca, NY: Cornell University Press, 1952); and Robert A. Dahl, *A Preface to a Theory of Democracy* (Chicago, IL: University of Chicago Press, 1956).

23. See Michael Lipsky, "Protest as a Political Resource," *APSR* 62, 4 (December 1968), pp. 1144–1158.

24. Charles E. Lindblom discusses this feature of policy making in his essay, "The Science of Muddling Through," *Public Administration Review* 19 (Spring 1959), pp. 79–88. Additional details on incrementalism can be found in Aaron B. Wildavsky, *The New Politics of the Budgetary Process*, 3rd ed. (Glenview, IL: Scott, Foresman & Company, 1988).

25. Judson L. James, "Federalism and the Model Cities Experiment," *Publius* (Spring 1972).

26. *Ibid.*, p. 72.

27. *Ibid.*, p. 73.

28. See Aage Clausen, *How Congressmen Decide: A Policy Focus* (New York: St. Martin's Press, 1978); and John Kingdon, *Congressmen's Voting Decisions*, 3rd ed. (New York: Harper & Row, 1989).

29. For more on this failure, see Frederic N. Cleaveland, "Congress and Urban Problems," *Journal of Politics* 28, 2 (May 1966), pp. 289–307; see also the study by Roscoe C. Martin, *Cities and the Federal System* (New York: Atherton, 1967).

30. See Aaron Wildavsky, "The Analysis of Issue Contexts in the Study of Decision Making," *Journal of Politics* 24 (1962), pp. 717–732, for a perceptive discussion of the influence of issue contexts and settings on the formation of public policy.

31. U.S. Congress, House Committee on Banking and Currency, *Congressional Quarterly* 9 (1966), p. 463.

32. *Ibid.*, p. 493.

33. *Ibid.*, p. 494.

34. *Ibid.*, p. 495.

35. Addonizio was later defeated in his bid for reelection by Kenneth Gibson, the first black mayor to emerge in the wake of the mid-1960s urban violence. In

1987, Gibson was defeated by Sharpe James, a black candidate. For a useful discussion of lobbying by mayors and other government officials, see Donald H. Haider, *When Governments Come to Washington: Governors, Mayors, and Intergovernmental Lobbying* (New York: Free Press, 1974).

36. U.S. Congress, House Committee on Banking and Currency, *Congressional Quarterly* 10 (1966), p. 563.
37. *Ibid.*
38. *Ibid.*, p. 564.
39. *Ibid.*
40. *Ibid.*
41. *Ibid.*, p. 605.
42. *Ibid.*
43. *Ibid.*
44. It should be stated, however, that similar arguments by the medical profession were successfully used in opposing earlier efforts to develop a national health care plan. Data from Survey Research Center election surveys for 1956–1971 suggest that public support for such a plan was at a consistently high level over this 15-year period. Cf. Richard E. Dawson, *Public Opinion and Contemporary Disarray* (New York: Harper & Row, 1974). More recent evidence of the medical profession's effectiveness can be found in an examination of the defeat of President Carter's "hospital cost containment" proposals of 1979.
45. See National Survey of Housing Abandonment, conducted by Center for Community Change, National Urban League, April 1971; George J. Washnis, "An Overview of the Program's Progress," *Model Cities Service Center Bulletin* 2, 9 (June 1971); and National Urban Coalition, "State of the Cities," 1972.
46. "State of the Cities."
47. *Ibid.*, p. 9.
48. See, for example, Edward Banfield, *The Unheavenly City* (Boston, MA: Little, Brown, 1971). A different perspective on many of these issues can be found in the Advisory Commission on Intergovernmental Relations report, *City Financial Emergencies, The Intergovernmental Dimension* (Washington, DC: Government Printing Office, 1973).
49. Actually, the Department of Housing and Urban Development was simply given this function. It had been created in the administration of former President John F. Kennedy. Model Cities was its first "new" activity.
50. Matthew Holden has suggested that political attacks may not all be of a partisan type. Interagency rivalries may also lead to conflicts that he calls "imperialism"; see his essay, "Imperialism in Bureaucracy," *APSR* 60 (December 1966), pp. 943–951.
51. See Francis E. Rourke, *Bureaucracy, Politics, and Public Policy* (Boston, MA: Little, Brown, 1969), pp. 11–24; and Grant McConnell, *Private Power and American Democracy* (New York: Albert A. Knopf, 1966). See also Philip Selznick, *TVA and the Grass Roots* (New York: Harper & Row, 1966). For those who think that pressure politics is engaged in only by big corporations, a look at the actions of professional social service organizations should prove instructive. See, for example, Gilbert Steiner, *The Children's Cause* (Washington, DC: The Brookings Institution, 1976).

52. For a discussion of this phenomenon, see Wildavsky, *The New Politics.*
53. See James W. Davis and Kenneth M. Dolbeare, *Little Groups of Neighbors: The Selective Service System* (Chicago, IL: Markham Publishing Company, 1968).
54. See, for example, Dennis R. Judd and Todd Swanstrom, *City Politics: Private Power and Public Policy* (New York: HarperCollins, 1994), pp. 170–173, and authorities cited therein.
55. *Ibid.,* p. 173. Judd and Swanstrom note that initial proposals included as few as five demonstration programs. By the time the enabling legislation was passed, it included 75 programs in the first year and that number was doubled in the second funding cycle of the new initiative.
56. For a historical account and general argument of the enterprise zone idea, see Stuart M. Butler, *Enterprise Zones: Greenlining the Inner Cities* (New York: Universe Books, 1981).
57. For a brief critical assessment of the politics surrounding enterprise zones legislation see Judd and Swanstrom, *City Politics, supra,* pp. 301–303. Congress approved the first funds for "empowerment zones" as part of the Economic Empowerment Act of 1993. President Clinton established the Community Enterprise Board by executive order on September 9, 1993. The board was headed by Vice President Gore and was charged with the duty of selecting the first federally approved empowerment zones.
58. See James Sundquist, *Politics and Policy* (Washington, DC: The Brookings Institution, 1968). For a detailed examination of the problems involved in presidential-agency relationships and program management techniques, see Richard Rose, *Managing Presidential Objectives* (New York: The Free Press, 1976).
59. One study specifically addresses these weaknesses of blacks; see Harold L. Wolman and Norman C. Thomas, "Black Interests, Black Groups, and Black Influence in the Federal Policy Process: The Cases of Housing and Education," *Journal of Politics* 32 (1970), pp. 875–897.

Chapter 12

The Authors Speak Out

AFFIRMATIVE ACTION: WHAT IS THE QUESTION?

MACK H. JONES

At this point in American history, the most widely discussed question in the area of race and public policy is: Should individuals be given special consideration in seeking access to jobs, educational institutions, and other coveted societal positions because of their race? That was the question debated by the U.S. Supreme Court in the landmark affirmative action cases of *Richmond* v. *Croson* (1989), *Miller* v. *Johnson* (1995), and by the Circuit Court in *Hopwood* v. *Texas* (1996), and that was how the issue was defined in the California referendum on Proposition 209. The issue was framed in a similar fashion in 1997, when the Michigan legislature called for an investigation of its flagship university for discriminating against "better qualified" whites while admitting "lesser qualified" black students. To ask whether one should be given special consideration merely because of race is to guarantee that the answer will be no. No intelligent proponent of democracy would argue that special consideration should be given to any individual or group merely because of their race. But in the context of the struggle for racial justice in America, that is not the appropriate question to raise now, nor has it ever been the question. The pertinent question is: Should special consideration be given to individuals who belong to a group that was singled out for unequal treatment by the Constitution of the United States and by statutory law at all levels of American government—national, state, and local—and whose unequal treatment was sanctioned by social custom and reinforced by the use of terror and economic intimidation and who, as a result of that government mandated and culturally sanctioned oppression, lag behind white Americans on practically every indicator of socioeconomic well-being? The question is: Should members of that oppressed group receive special consideration until such time that the gap between them and the dominant group on these indicators of well-being is eliminated? That is the question that history and ordinary logic would lead us to raise. And if that were the question posed for the public policy debate, the dialogue would certainly be different. But that is not how the question is phrased, because the ordinary rules of logic are rarely, if ever, followed in the discussion of race and public policy in America. Questions about race are almost always raised in such a way as to deny the reality and severity of racial oppression as a fundamental force in American life and culture. To understand the contemporary debate about affirmative action and other so-called race-specific remedies, it is necessary to understand how this came to be. To do so we must go back to the very founding of the country.

On matters involving relations between European and other peoples of the world, the United States was founded on a fundamental contradiction. The Declaration of Independence, and the Constitution that was adopted subsequently to bring about the new state envisaged in the Declaration, spoke of the rights of man as the major pillar of human society. Yet the framers of these documents were slave holders in a slave holding society that owed its very existence as an economically viable state to the then ongoing genocide of the native inhabitants and to the unrequited labor of millions of enslaved Africans. As a slave holding, multi-ethnic, and multiracial society founded on the principle of white supremacy, America evolved a uniquely racist culture that made qualitative distinctions not only among the different socially constructed racial groups but also among the various ethnic communities within the different racial groups. Europeans were placed at the apex of the racial hierarchy, followed by Asians, Native Americans, and Africans, in that order. Within the European group, Aryan-featured Europeans received top billing, with their more swarthy, central and southern European compatriots occupying the lower rungs. The hierarchy among the ethnic groups in the Asian and African communities (i.e., Chinese versus Koreans, West Indians versus North American born blacks, etc.), was more fluid depending upon white interests at any given historical moment.

The idea of white supremacy and its corollary, the notion of black inferiority, provided the ideological justification for this pernicious rank ordering of humanity. It created and sustained ideologies that justified the most inhumane treatment of people of color. At the same time, the basic documents of the country that proclaimed belief in the equality of all humanity were cleverly written to disguise the racists principles imbedded in them. For example, those who drafted the Declaration of Independence managed to call for the creation of a new political system dedicated to the proposition that all men were created equal and had the inalienable right to life, liberty, and property—while at the same time enslaving millions of African people and holding countless thousands of their white compatriots as indentured servants.

Following their successful war of independence, these self-proclaimed democrats drafted a constitution that retained the legitimacy of slavery, forbade the new government from legislating on the matter for at least 20 years, and obligated the National government to use its powers to return those who managed to escape enslavement to their erstwhile slave masters. The framers put all of this in the Constitution without ever mentioning the words slavery, African people, or anything else that would indicate the real nature of the society they had built and were trying to maintain.

Hence, since its inception, the United States has been a thoroughgoing racist society, but one in deep denial and one in which everything is done to maintain white supremacy and domination at home and abroad while denying that racism and racial oppression are major elements of American political culture and practice. Indeed, the principle documents of American history raise self-deception to the level of an art form. One of the results of this charade in self-deception has been the development of a culture in which the normal rules of logic are often suspended when the subject is race and racial oppression. Concepts and conceptual frameworks are developed to facilitate public policy discussions of the reality of racial oppression while at the same time denying that it exists. I have in mind concepts such as minorities, the disadvantaged, inner cities, individuals at risk, multiculturalism, and diversity, to name just a few.

The development of such concepts and their use in generating propositions about the nature of American life and the place of black folk in it defy the rules ordinarily used in developing empirically useful concepts and making logical inferences about experience. Instead, we get discussions that are more non-logical or illogical than logical. At the same time, however, those of us who are grounded in the American conceptualization of such matters are conditioned to accept this illogical discussion of race as if it makes sense. This spastic dance of self-deception is joined by practically every segment of American life, without regard to race, class, gender, creed, or color. Indeed, an interplanetary visitor from Mars who observed America at work and play and saw the great racial divide manifested in these activities and then listened to the public discussion about it would certainly find it incredulous.

There is, however, a transcendental logic to this illogical dance. The transcendental logic is that it serves to maintain and reinforce the system of white supremacy and black subordination while, to borrow a term from a different but related area of inquiry, leaving space for plausible denial by those who have a need to do so.

Nowhere is this more apparent than in contemporary discussions of race and public policy, particularly discussions about affirmative action and other so-called race-specific remedies. When the question is stated as "should individuals be given special consideration because of race," it camouflages the historical reality and the systemic character of black oppression. And even more perniciously, by asserting that the pertinent category is race rather than oppression and that the question is should special consideration be given because of race, it equates the lived experiences of the various racial groups as theoretically and historically coordinate and prepares the public to accept the argument that what is done or not done for one should be done or not done for all others.

But the theoretical, historical, and empirically useful category that gives rise to affirmative action as an intervention strategy is oppression, and not race or minority status. Special consideration is being sought for members of a group that occupies a subordinate position in society, not because of their race or their minority status, but because of an empirically demonstrable, specific pattern of historical and contemporary oppression. This concept of oppression, as inferred in the opening paragraph of this essay, can be easily and scientifically operationalized. No other group falls into this category. To be sure, other groups have suffered oppression in America, but none was the subject of slavery and constitutionally mandated oppression and none suffered through centuries of violence and terror. The matter of terror and violence is especially important because, more than anything else, it is this that prevented blacks from accumulating wealth during the early days of primitive accumulation in the republic; as Oliver and Shapiro have demonstrated, this lack of wealth is perhaps the major factor that guarantees the continued subordination of black Americans.

To reinforce this point, many have forgotten and perhaps even more never knew that for almost a full century, lynching was used as a primary tactic to maintain black subordination. The practice was so widespread that, beginning in 1881, Tuskegee University began issuing annual reports on the lynching of black Americans. It was not until 1952, 71 years later, that it reported no lynchings had been brought to its attention. (*World Almanac*, 88). It was through violence and terror that the southern planter class reimposed its dominance on the emancipated black nation and sowed the seeds for the enduring "race problem." However, the ideology was so strong that Congress repeatedly refused to make lynching a federal crime.

Rather than acknowledge the reality of oppression and use it as the triggering mechanism for remedial legislation, policy makers prefer to use terms such as "minority" and "diversity" to justify affirmative action initiatives. Taken together, such terms paint a rather benign and self-serving portrait of the problem while reinforcing the image of the United States as a racially and ethnically diverse society in which some groups are overwhelmed because of their smaller numbers and, as a result, are underrepresented in various societal institutions. To compensate for this and because they believe that there is some special virtue in diversity, this portrait implies, dominant whites develop programs to increase the number of minorities in these institutions. Affirmative action becomes an act of majority benevolence rather than one of reparation to atone for past and continuing crimes against humanity.

But if we put the question of affirmative action and other so-called race-specific remedies in proper historical context, we begin with a quite different set of questions, and a decidedly different and more useful discussion unfolds. We begin by asking how and why did blacks get so far behind white Americans on practically all indicators of socioeconomic well-being. The answer, of course, is to be found in slavery and the century of state-mandated and culturally sanctioned oppression that followed emancipation. The angry white males and their sympathizers would prefer not to hear this. For them, slavery and its aftermath were merely an accident of history that has no connection to contemporary problems and should be forgotten. To insist on the salience of slavery as an important causal factor in the current unequal position of blacks is decried as whining victimization.

However, while we may will that slavery and its aftermath be forgotten, their social and systemic consequences have proven to be more stubborn. How else can we explain that none of the pressing societal problems of the current age—deteriorating inner cities, public welfare, the urban underclass, inadequate public schools, crime, poverty, structural unemployment, drugs, and the militia movement, to name a few—can be understood apart from the issue of race and racism in society?

At the time of emancipation, as even the most unenlightened cannot deny, blacks lagged behind whites on all measures of socioeconomic well-being; after Sherman's aborted experiment in the sea islands, nothing was done to promote socioeconomic equality. Instead, states passed laws requiring segregation and discrimination, and the national government, through its own policies, reinforced the discrimination and oppression mandated by the states. This was true in education, in government service, in corporations and labor unions, in sports, in the church, and in the military. These oppressive policies were culturally sanctioned and enforced by terror and violence. As a result, from the beginning of their freedom blacks had higher unemployment rates, a higher incidence of poverty, lower educational attainment, higher infant mortality rates, lower incomes, and lower life expectancy (see U.S. Bureau of the Census, *The Social and Economic Status of the Black Population in the United States, 1790–1978*). The gap between blacks and whites that existed following emancipation never went away. An elementary rule of causal analysis says that the cause must exist prior to the effect. Since the gap dates back to emancipation, more recent contemporary effects cannot be its cause.

When the civil rights movement erupted in the 1960s, these inequalities that initially developed during slavery and its aftermath still characterized black life. In spite of remedial laws and court decisions, the gap between black and white well-being remained substantial. It was the realization that changing laws would not necessarily change the material conditions that led to the push for what came to be known as affirmative action.

Affirmative action as an intervention strategy to reduce the gap between blacks and whites grew out of a particular understanding of the nature of the American political economy—an understanding that viewed the economy as analogous to a big gun that fires a shot and at the same time recoils. Out of one end it produces advantages, such as employment, good jobs, wealth, advanced education and training, comfortable housing, enviable health care, safe neighborhoods, and a host of other desirable outcomes. Simultaneously, out of the other end comes the debilities—unemployment, poverty-level jobs, substandard education, poor and limited health care, and a litany of other undesirable outcomes. The important thing to understand here is that both the advantages and debilities, the good things and the bad, are all routine outcomes of the American political economy. Low-paying jobs are not created by the people who hold them. Both high- and low-paying jobs are systemic creations. The relative mix of high-paying and low-paying jobs at any given historical moment is a function of the dynamics of politico-economic processes. We see this in the current reduction of the number of high-paying industrial jobs and the concomitant rise in the volume of lesser-paying service sector positions. And we see it when increases in unemployment follow decisions of the federal reserve system to raise interests rates to temper inflation.

The compelling question in this regard is: What forces determine who will get the advantages routinely produced by the system and who must settle for the debilities? How will the disadvantages be allocated? American political thought says that individual initiative determines who gets ahead, but experiential reality is much more complex. As even the casual observer knows, individual initiative is exercised within a framework structured by major systemic forces. Thus, the critical questions are: What forces structure the environment within which individuals strive? and How does this structure impact the allocation of advantages and debilities?

The law is one major force. For a long time in America, the law guaranteed that whites would get more than their fair share of the advantages and, correspondingly, that blacks would get more than their fair share of the debilities. Laws limiting black access were put in place to regulate the lives of free blacks during the slave epoch and were carried over and elaborated upon following emancipation. For example, when the law denied blacks the right to enter the only state school that offered degrees in, say, engineering, medicine, or law, it ensured that whites would get more than their fair share of the advantages and, conversely, that blacks would get more than their fair share of the debilities. Even when blacks managed to obtain such training in spite of the law, other social forces operated to ensure their subordination. The advantages for whites were cumulative and transgenerational, as the sons and daughters of the graduates of such professional programs accumulated wealth that guaranteed that their children would start with even greater advantages over the sons and daughters of blacks whose opportunities had been constrained by the law. The systemic impact of such laws was recognized by the Supreme Court in *Sweat* v. *Painter* (1950).

But it was not only the law that guaranteed this inequality. The social, financial, cultural, educational, and economic systems functioned interdependently to ensure that whites, particularly white men, got more of the advantages and less than their fair share of the debilities. We should keep in mind that in the decades immediately following emancipation, the preponderance of blacks lived in the southern states where they constituted substantial proportions of the population, in some areas approaching majority status. This meant that in the then-racist, patriarchal, class-based society, white men of means had to compete only with themselves for the most coveted societal positions. Perhaps that should be designated as the first era of affirmative action. Under current conditions, the competition is much keener, and perhaps, hence white men's anger.

Oliver and Shapiro captured the systemic character of deprivation when they asserted the following:

> ... Our examination ... shows that unequal background and social conditions result in unequal resources. Whether it be a matter of education, occupation, family status, or other characteristics positively correlated with income, wealth, blacks are most likely to come out on the short end of the stick....
>
> We argue, furthermore, that the racialization of the welfare state and institutional discrimination are fundamental reasons for the persistent wealth-disparities we observed. Government policies that have paved the way for whites to amass wealth have simultaneously discriminated against blacks in their quest for economic security. From the era of slavery on through the failure of the freedman to gain land and the Jim Crow laws that restricted black entrepreneurs, opportunity for asset accumulation rewarded whites and penalized blacks. (1997, p. 174)

To return to the argument of systemic deprivation and to demonstrate how the various systems working interdependently reproduced and continue to produce racial inequalities, we might reflect on the plight of the child of a low income black family living in inner city America and compare it with that of a white child in suburbia. To make the comparison we might ask how the financial system and the labor market impact their respective chances for living in a safe and commodious neighborhood. How do the political and educational systems determine the quality of elementary and secondary schools each will attend, and, in turn, how do these systems influence their respective scores on college admission tests; on devices used for screening applicants for professional schools, such as law and medicine; and on their financial ability to matriculate at such an institution? *To raise these questions is to dramatize the extent to which individual initiative is constrained by systemic forces that predict group outcomes.*

Here, the phrase *group outcomes* is important because opponents of affirmative action are quick to point out that countless black individuals from such neighborhoods have succeeded and that their success is evidence that individual initiative rather than systemic conditions determines outcomes. However, the question, or at least the one that interests me, is not about individual success but about why there is such a wide gap in well-being between *blacks and whites as groups* and how the gap can be reduced. The argument being advanced here is that sustained intervention in the various systems reinforced by supportive changes in other societal institutions would change the systems themselves and eventually produce different group outcomes. Greater numbers of blacks would receive the advantages and fewer would get the debilities. Eventually, more blacks would occupy pivotal positions in these systems and, in turn, the systems would begin to produce different and more equitable outcomes.

Systems, of course, are resistant to change and can easily co-op limited and short-term interventions, but they can be transformed through concerted action. The hiring of a few black loan officers, for example, would not necessarily change lending policies, but the presence of significant numbers of black bank directors and bank officers committed to policy changes could, over a long period of time, change how the system works. Indeed, the changing racial complexion of American institutions of higher education is evidence of the impact that sustained intervention may have and the deliberately deceptive debate over so-called political correctness and the present anti-affirmative action hysteria dramatize the resistance that it may generate.

Let me close this essay by commenting on the arguments of some of the critics of affirmative action and other so-called race specific remedies. A popular argument among some whites is the lament that while affirmative action may have been necessary early on, it is no longer the case since racial discrimination is a thing of the past (Cohen, 1996). It is interesting to note that those making this argument vehemently opposed efforts to end state-mandated segregation and discrimination in the 1950s. In response to the Supreme Court ruling *Brown* v. *Board of Education* (1954), these opponents argued that segregation (and by inference, racism) was a valuable and enduring aspect of American culture and that cultures could not be transformed by legislative, judicial, or other political acts. Cultures, they argued further, could be transformed only through gradual, self-initiated change. Political actions, they continued, would only heighten tensions between the races and make things worse.

However, a few decades later, after fighting tooth and nail against all efforts to overturn the racist order, these erstwhile proponents of state-mandated segregation declared that racism had indeed ended and that the question of race and oppression should no longer be a public concern. The inequities and inequalities that were carried over from the era of state-mandated discrimination are declared to be functions of individual and/or group failures. Indeed, some go as far as to argue that affirmative action and other so-called race-specific remedies are the cause of current inequalities. As alluded to above, such assertions contravene the elementary principles of causal inference.

There are other criticisms, particularly those coming from conservative black intellectuals, that merit consideration. Some argue that affirmative action only benefits the black middle class and, as such, its social divisiveness outweighs whatever benefits it may bring (Loury, 1984). Two responses to that criticism come quickly to mind. The first is that the validity of the claim has not been established. It is true that affirmative action and set-aside programs do not target low-income jobs, but no intervention strategy was necessary to give blacks access to low-paying, dead-end jobs. The important question is: Who are the people moving into the middle-income positions and university spaces made available through affirmative action? I am unaware of any systematic studies designed to answer such questions. I do know, however, scores of persons from poor families, myself included, who have achieved middle-class status with the assistance of such efforts.

The other response to the claim that affirmative action benefits the black middle class disproportionately is that the United States is a class-based society and that in such societies all public policies are biased in favor of the more well-to-do. All of the other government intervention programs favor those who are better off. This is true of the farm programs, the various housing/mortgage programs, programs offering assistance to businesses, and programs focusing on international trade, to name only a few. Even programs established expressly to assist poor individuals invariably do more for privileged classes than they do for the poor. So even if it is true that affirmative action has a class bias, that is no different from any other government-sponsored intervention program. Thus, the criticism is more of an indictment of America as a class-based society than an indictment of affirmative action as an intervention strategy.

The class issue, however, is central to any enlightened discussion of the controversy over affirmative action and other so-called race-specific remedies, and it should be confronted head-on. To the extent that these programs benefit middle-income blacks, working-class whites with lesser incomes and material privileges may justifiably feel aggrieved. After all, they are being taxed in one way or another to assist those whose material conditions may already be greater than their own. But that is true for all of the government intervention programs mentioned. The fact that the class bias of affirmative action and other race specific remedies are recognized and opposed while the similar bias of other intervention programs are cheerfully indulged cries out for explanation. Those who oppose affirmative action because of its class bias, especially black intellectuals, should broaden their opposition to include all class privileges. In doing so they would fulfill the role of enlightened dissenters called for by Martin Luther King, Jr.

On the other hand, underlying the argument for affirmative action and set-aside programs (though rarely clearly stated) was the commitment, however tepid, to create a class structure within the black community that mirrored that of the broader American society. That was the focus of the various government and privately sponsored black capitalism schemes, including efforts to have franchises for capital intensive operations, such as automobile dealerships and television stations, awarded to prosperous blacks and to award multimillion-dollar contracts to black construction firms. If properly structured, the debate over the class bias of affirmative action and set-asides could be used to educate all Americans about the systemic implications of the class character of American society and make white working class people more conscious of their own self interest.

Another anti-affirmative action argument advanced within the black community is the assertion that it is detrimental to black self-esteem, because affirmative hires do not command the respect of their white colleagues (Carter, 1991). In response to this assertion, at the risk of sounding flippant, one could argue that the lack of white approbation may be a small price to pay for group advancement. I know of scores of black men and women who hold advanced degrees from prestigious universities, earn a comfortable living, and are in positions to advance the cause of racial justice as a result of the boost provided by affirmative action. Indeed some of these critics would not have had access to the very forums from which they launch their criticisms were it not for affirmative action. This is especially true for the growing number of conservative black commentators in both the print and electronic media. They are hired and promoted because they are black (Jones, 1997). Yet their self esteem seems intact.

On the matter of affirmative action and self esteem, whites held negative stereotypical attitudes toward blacks long before affirmative action. Indeed it is instructive to remember that even an intellectual giant such as Dr. W. E. B. DuBois, who earned a Ph.D. at Harvard in the 1890s in the very shadow of slavery, never had the respect of his white peers. He was offered no positions commensurate with his training and talents. To further clarify the issue of self esteem and inter-community approbation, it is worth noting that historically when whites achieved enviable status without having to compete with blacks, it did not cost them any self esteem or loss of public approbation. Babe Ruth, the baseball hero, for example, was not ashamed of his home run record, even though he did it without having to compete against Satchel Paige, the fabled black pitcher of his era. Nor has it tarnished his image among contemporary whites. Instead, we know that Hank Aaron was censored by some for daring to challenge Ruth's record.

Finally, there are those who argue that affirmative action is unnecessary because many blacks have excelled without it and that their performance is sufficient evidence that any individual, no matter their color or previous condition of servitude, can do so if they put their mind to it. Suffice it to say that during slavery some enslaved Africans were so industrious that they were able to not only buy their freedom and that of other loved ones but became wealthy freepersons whose material conditions outstripped that of many of their white neighbors (Berlin, 1974). However, individual successes, no matter how spectacular, do not change the reality of group oppression. Within every group the law of random distribution ensures that there will be high and low achievers. The problem addressed by affirmative action is the negatively skewed distribution within the oppressed community. Affirmative action and other so-called race-specific remedies are intervention strategies designed to correct that maldistribution.

Affirmative action, the critics should understand, is really a weak remedy designed to address an intractable problem, a problem that can be adequately resolved only through comprehensive reparations. However, as long as American culture remains in denial about the crimes for which reparations are due, affirmative action may be all that we can get. The struggle should be to expand it rather than end it.

References

Berlin, Ira. *Slaves without Masters: The Free Negro in the Antebellum South*. New York: The New Press, 1974.

Carter, Stephen. *Reflections of an Affirmative Action Baby*. New York: Basic Books, 1991.

Cohen, Carl. *Naked Racial Preference: The Case against Affirmative Action*. Madison, WI: Madison Books, 1996.

Jones, Mack H. "The Political Thought of the New Black Conservatives: Analysis, Explanation, and Interpretation." In *American Political Issues*, ed. Franklin Jones and Michael Adams. Dubuque, IA: Kendall/Hunt, 1987.

Loury, Glenn. "A New American Dilemma." *The New Republic* 184 (December 31, 1984).

Oliver, Melvin, and Thomas Shapiro. *Black Wealth/White Wealth: A New Perspective on Racial Inequality*. New York: Routledge, 1997.

U.S. Bureau of the Census. *The Social and Economic Status of the Black Population in the United States: An Historical Overview, 1790–1979*. Washington, DC: Government Printing Office, 1979.

World Almanac. *Words That Set Us Free*. New York: Pharos Books, 1992.

WELFARE REFORM: SCRAPPING THE SYSTEM AND OUR IDEALS

KATHERINE TATE

We want to "end welfare as we know it." But we do not want to replace it with welfare as we do not want to know it. We do not want to codify a policy of national child abandonment.

   —Marian Wright Edelman, Children's Defense Fund[1]

If it were 14 weeks after the election, [Bill Clinton would] say no.

   —Senator Daniel Patrick Moynihan[2]

In his 1992 bid for the presidency, Bill Clinton pledged to "end welfare as we know it." Few candidates, it seems, ever actually fulfill their campaign promises once in office. Yet President Clinton did. Just months before the conclusion of his successful re-election bid, he signed a welfare reform bill that received near unanimous support from Republicans, but divided the Democrats. The essential feature of the new welfare law is that it provides a lifetime maximum of five years of welfare benefits for poor families. While conservative Republicans had agitated for years to abolish the federal welfare system, the surprise is that a Democratic president did just that. In ending the federal government's 60-year guaranteed protection of poor families, Clinton's new welfare reform law goes much farther than President Reagan's eight-year assault on the welfare system. Whereas Reagan's cutbacks in welfare spending punctured large holes in the federal safety net for more poor families to fall through, Clinton's welfare law once and for all abolished it.

Where do blacks stand on this? Here is another surprise. Although most blacks are divided in their opinion about the new reform law, most, nevertheless, side with Bill Clinton. Not only was Clinton's vote among black Americans in 1996 exceptionally strong but the 1996 National Black Election Study survey reveals that 60 percent of blacks favor the new welfare law that guarantees only five years of lifetime support to families in poverty. Why do most blacks favor welfare reform? The short answer is that political optimism and naivete about the political process have blinded liberals and blacks to the hard consequences that this welfare reform law will have for children born in poverty. Moreover, President Clinton's own political ambitions have overshadowed basic liberal moral imperatives. These two factors, and a political context where black leadership is moribund, account for this devastating step backward for America.

Surprise, Surprise: The Liberal Reformers Are Betrayed

That Clinton would sign a law that ended poor families' entitlement to food and a minimum living stipend was no surprise; he had, after all, campaigned to "end" welfare in 1992. Liberals, nonetheless, were taken by surprise in the end on a number of fronts. First, liberals assumed that the welfare reform bill was part of a package deal that would include broad new social policies. One new social program was universal health care. In contrast to citizens in every other industrialized democracy, Americans lack a government-sponsored health care system. The poor, however, did have health care as part of welfare. While the benefits of public welfare are meager, it still provided medical protection for welfare recipients, something that poor working families did without. Most jobs don't provide benefits such as health insurance that match welfare. Thus, welfare advocates argued that health care reform was essential if poor families were to make a successful transition from welfare to work.

Moreover, entry-level, minimum wage jobs don't provide a "living wage," that is, one that could sustain the needs of single-headed households. Thus, staying on welfare makes the most economic sense for single women with children when a working salary can't be stretched to meet basic needs, including housing and health care, and still cover new transportation and child care expenses. Health insurance, higher wages, and child care support would all have to be in place to make working more economically feasible for families on welfare. Finally, the federal government would help states go after fathers for child support. Thus, welfare reform would include federal aid for state-assisted child care, medical care, tax credits for the poor, and child support enforcement.

Clinton helped maintain the illusion that welfare reform was a package deal that would include new health care legislation by immediately, and with great fanfare, introducing a bill to create a national health care insurance program. For a number of political reasons, including that it smacked of, and in fact was, "big government," his health care initiative died. Still, the Clinton administration managed to raise the minimum wage and increase the earned-income tax credit. The earned-income tax credit (EITC) was another policy that would help welfare reform work. EITC gave working families whose incomes approached the poverty line cash back in the form of tax refunds. EITC is not a big deal; in reality, the refunds are relatively small. In 1990, for example, the average EITC refund check was $910. The increase in the minimum wage was a far bigger deal for the working poor than EITC. Little did one anticipate that states stuck now with the federal mandate of moving people from welfare to work would consider exempting the new welfare workers from minimum wage law, however.

Liberals fell sway to a second illusion—that they alone would be the architects of welfare reform. At the beginning of Clinton's first term, there was no reason to suppose otherwise. The Democrats were in control of Congress, and Clinton had appointed to Health and Human Services a number of noted liberal welfare policy experts. Prominent among them was David T. Ellwood, a Harvard public policy professor. He would resign from the Clinton administration, burned by the experience. Reeling from the sudden and dramatic drop in his approval ratings during the first year of his administration, Clinton would increasingly turn to conservatives for political advice. Liberals, like Ellwood, would find less and less support for their policy ideas. No longer would welfare reform be a "package deal," and a harsher version would serve as the centerpiece of Clinton's re-election campaign. Ellwood, in a *New York Times* interview, would admit to his own naïveté about the political process.[3]

That Clinton's own political interests would critically influence the welfare reform process was one unanticipated turn of events; another was the Republican party's takeover of the House of Representatives in 1994. In 1992, basking under the glow of a Democratic presidential victory, virtually no one but the most fanatical Republican would have imagined that the House would in two short years have a Republican majority. Democrats, after all, had controlled the House for more than 40 years. Moreover, the

Republicans elected in the 1994 GOP landslide were exceptionally conservative, hostile toward any government spending program. The idea that a welfare reform bill acceptable to the House Republicans would include a nest of new social programs, including federally subsidized day care centers for the working poor, was ludicrous. With Republicans now controlling Congress, only the most rash kind of Democrat would have continued the course toward welfare reform after 1994.

Clinton, nevertheless, engaged in this reckless kind of negotiation with the Republicans because of his own desire to strengthen his re-election bid. Twice earlier Clinton had vetoed welfare reform bills that were considered too draconian because they imposed the five-year limit without providing much financial support to states to help welfare recipients find jobs. Because the Republicans had suffered politically from their hard-line positions that resulted in the shut-down of the federal government, Clinton advisors convinced him of the electoral benefits of appearing "flexible" and "moderate." His signature on a welfare reform bill would attest to his flexibility and moderation.

While his strategy of political centrism worked amazingly well (his approval ratings shot up while those of the Republicans, including the Republican House leader, Newt Gingrich, plummeted), Clinton did not need to sign the bill in order to win the election. At the time of the welfare bill negotiations, Clinton was enjoying a huge lead over Bob Dole. The political benefits of being able to claim that he had fulfilled a chief campaign promise to reform welfare were minimal and inconsequential and came at too dear of a price. His desire to appear moderate resulted in a welfare reform bill that basically has undone the government's effort to protect America's poor. The liberal architects whom he had recruited to reform welfare resigned in droves out of protest against Clinton's support for this bill.

The third welfare reform bill that cleared Congress was not much different from the first two. It turns over the responsibility for welfare to the 50 states; it limits individuals to five years of support over their lifetime and requires half of the state's welfare recipients to be working or training for a job by 2002. Furthermore, food stamps aid was cut. Clinton had originally sought to increase federal spending on welfare programs by $9.3 billion. The welfare bill Clinton signed cut $56 billion from federal welfare funds. Moreover, legal immigrants who have worked less than ten years in the country were barred from Medicaid. Single, jobless adults would only be able to collect food stamps for three months each year, over a three-year period.

Surprise, Surprise: Few Protest

It is unfair to use the slain Dr. King as the yardstick from which to evaluate today's black leaders. Still one can't help but imagine that Dr. King would not have been silent on the subject of welfare reform. One lone black voice attacked welfare reform early on, and that voice, Marian Wright Edelman, was representing children. The excuses for the silence by black political organizations are many.

First, the big civil rights organizations that remain had deteriorated to a point where their own survival was at stake. The NAACP was reeling from the revelation that its president had used the organization's funds to keep a former female employee from filing a sexual harassment lawsuit against him. Black civil rights organizations also suffer from, not only a financial crisis, but a political one as well. As the controversy over the nomination of Clarence Thomas to fill Thurgood Marshall's place on the Supreme Court had illustrated, black organizations were not ready to speak with a united front on new, emerging topics. Gender may very well be another factor. The heads of the big civil rights organizations, with a brief exception, have been men who certainly don't identify with the plight of welfare-dependent mothers. Moreover, class may be another reason. The big civil rights groups don't reflect well the interests of the black poor because they are not members. Besides, although welfare is closely linked with the public's attitudes toward blacks, the welfare reform debate was carefully presented by those involved as a "non-racial" issue. Civil rights organizations kept out of the debate.

Meanwhile, while all black Democrats, with the exception of Sanford Bishop of Georgia, and the lone black member of the Senate, Carol Moseley-Braun, voted against the welfare bill, they had not spoken out against welfare reform. One reason for this is that the CBC had also been hit organizationally. Once the Republicans won control of the House, the CBC found itself de-funded. Black members of Congress were also mindful that this was an election year. Not only did they not want to endanger the re-election of President Clinton, their dependence on the power of the White House had increased sharply. Black House legislators were also running for re-election themselves, and they found that blacks were divided, with most in favor of welfare reform. Thus, they voted with their conscience but kept quiet.

Jesse Jackson would also oppose the bill, but lined up with all the other Democratic leaders to support Bill Clinton's re-election bid. As discussed in Chapter 8, Jackson's address at the party's national convention was strikingly unlike his previous addresses. Jackson's speech did not highlight the shortcomings of the Clinton administration or of the party's representation of blacks; it was a stump speech to re-elect Bill Clinton, pure and simple. The reasons for Jackson's support, as well as that from other black Democrats, are straightforward enough. Basically, black Democrats needed Bill Clinton more than he needed them. Republican control of Congress, in fact, increased their dependence on the goodwill of the president. Thus, given his 15 percentage-point lead over Bob Dole, whatever blacks thought of the new welfare act, Clinton was going to be re-elected.

Surprise, Surprise: Public Opinion Shows That Blacks Are Divided

More than Clinton's self-serving political calculations, Republican control of Congress, and the weak response of black political leaders, it was black public opinion that registered the biggest surprise in the welfare reform debate. In the 1996 National Black Election Study (NBES), 1,216 black respondents were asked several questions about welfare reform. Early surveys conducted in 1993 found that the vast majority of blacks, like whites, approved of reforming the welfare system. Eighty-one percent of blacks and 83 percent of whites felt that the "current welfare system discourages poor people from finding work." Most blacks, 73 percent as opposed to 90 percent of whites, favored imposing work requirements on welfare recipients, as well.[1] In the 1996 NBES, 66 percent of blacks favored putting a five-year lifetime limit on how long someone can receive welfare benefits. Respondents were also asked if they believe that a woman on welfare who has another child should be denied an increase in her welfare check. This policy is called a family cap. Forty-eight percent of blacks favored a family cap, while 46 percent thought that a woman should not be denied extra money for having additional children while on welfare. Moreover, blacks' support for welfare reform corresponds with a slackening in support for increasing welfare benefits for families. In the 1984 NBES, 49 percent of respondents favored increasing federal spending on food stamps; in the 1996 NBES, only 21 percent hold this opinion today. Why are blacks disenchanted with the welfare system, and why are they less supportive of federal aid for poor families?

Welfare mothers have long served as easy scapegoats, and this has been the case even in the black community. While blacks had emphatically rejected the anti-welfare language of Ronald Reagan during the 1980s that included the stereotypical black "welfare queen" who owned furs and drove Cadillacs, many in the 1990s found persuasive the more subtle attack on black welfare mothers as irresponsible, who, instead of striving to provide for their children were actually damning them to a lifetime of crime and welfare dependency. For decades now, black social problems, such as gang violence, the drug epidemic, and teenage unwed pregnancy, have been placed on the heads of black women. Scholars have certainly validated such claims. Assigning blame for inner-city problems to poor, unmarried mothers and not to the dearth of jobs and failing public schools is sexist as well as unfair. Fathers and their abandonment of their children to poverty and welfare were not made part of the debate over welfare. Consider the public reaction to a bill that would force fathers, and not simply the mothers taking care of the children, into workfare. Would the overwhelmingly male Congress even take up such a bill? Moreover, no one took note of the fact that the typical jobs reserved for women pay substantially less than those generally held by equally qualified men. Even so, concentrating solely on black women or on black men obscures the link between them, their children, and the rest of America—the link of racism, living in high-unemployment communities, racial segregation, and failing public institutions such as schools.

Blacks also found convincing the argument, made originally by conservatives but picked up by "new" Democrats like Clinton, that "welfare is flawed." In the national debate over the causes of poverty, liberals not only were relatively drowned out by loud, conservative voices, but they had conceded a major point: that the current welfare system was bad. David Ellwood, the chief policy expert, accepted the premise that the welfare system was inoperable and should be scrapped. Welfare, liberals as well as conservatives now argued, eroded the will to work. The positive aspects of welfare, that for 60 years it kept families together and from starvation, were overshadowed by the claims that welfare needed reform. Studies established that less than 20 percent of the welfare population remained on welfare for more than five years. The charge that the much-maligned Great Society programs from the Johnson administration created poverty and dependency is flatly wrong. Once these programs took effect, poverty rates dropped from 17 percent in 1965 to 11 percent in 1973.

Daniel Patrick Moynihan's negative portrayal of black female-headed households in *Negro Family: The Case for National Action* did much to ripen the conditions for the manner in which welfare was reformed.[5] However, Senator Moynihan ironically (and perhaps out of his own sense of complicity) has expressed the most public outrage for the new law. His point is that the current system, for all its flaws, protected the nation's most vulnerable: our children. Children obviously bear no responsibility for the miserable condition they may find themselves in. Whether children are psychologically better off having working mothers as opposed to those who stay home is a debatable issue. But a percentage of mothers on welfare don't work for a number of reasons, including mental illness and drug addiction. Incapable of working, some may simply abandon their children. Many more single mothers on welfare lack the skills and education for jobs that pay a living wage, but the Act failed to provide adequate support for job training. Earning a high-school diploma or college degree under the new law will not exempt poor parents from the five-year limit.

Many blacks and liberals want to believe that the new welfare reform law will help, not hurt, poor families. They believe the misleading hype that it will eliminate welfare dependency, restore the will to work, and make mothers more responsible, instead of the truth that after five years, many families will be cut loose and sink more deeply into poverty.

States: Not Will, But Can They Protect the Poor?

Right now, state welfare rolls are shrinking, some by as much as 30 percent, which many are wrongly and jubilantly attributing to the impact of the new welfare law. The strong economy and low unemployment mostly have reduced state welfare caseloads. The fact is that the law has not yet taken effect. Families have not hit the time limit yet and have not yet been forced off the rolls. We won't know the real impact of the act until the country's economy slows down, which is inevitable. Nevertheless, there is public support for the new welfare law because of the rosy state of affairs and the positive news stories about state efforts to enact new programs to assist welfare families. In the midst of this era of good feeling, optimistic souls are claiming that the states can do a better job than the federal government in assisting the poor.

States now bear the responsibility of protecting our children from hunger and homelessness. While many wonder if states will, in fact, protect the poor, the overlooked question is, can they? There are a number of reasons why states should not be given the responsibility of welfare protection. First, their response to the challenge of protecting poor children will vary significantly. Some governors and state legislatures will spend the necessary money to help welfare recipients find jobs that can support families. Others will not and will simply abandon to poverty those families that hit the five-year time limit. State generosity to the poor will depend upon the economic resources of the states. The poorest states, those also burdened with the highest welfare caseloads, simply can't afford to provide poor families with the type of assistance necessary to make a successful transition to work. Secondly, welfare policy will suffer from the vagaries of politics. Politicians will fight over welfare expenditures, as they cut into an ever-larger share of state expenditures. States will craft wildly different policies because not only will they have different political philosophies about welfare, but political control by the parties may change every two and four years. The power of states to control welfare, along with economic factors, will likely result in a tangled mess of programs and policies that will be difficult for poor families to follow. Moreover, states will be under tremendous pressure to reduce welfare benefits because of inter-state competition.[6] No state by virtue of having generous welfare programs that work will want to become a "welfare magnet."

Finally, states, even those with high per capita incomes, lack the federal government's vast financial resources. Nearly every state, in contrast to the federal government, is constitutionally required to balance its budget. Given the current strong economy, with additional revenues flowing to the states, many have initiated generous and innovative but costly programs to assist welfare recipients. But in an economic slump, states will be forced to cut back or even eliminate those programs. Or they can turn to the federal government for additional aid.

Turning the responsibility of welfare over to the states will subject the poor to weaker, more complicated programs that will likely cause widespread confusion and humiliation. And the new victims in all this are our children.

Why Welfare Reform Will Hurt Children

As Marian Wright Edelman wrote, while everyone wanted to reform welfare, no one wanted to scrap the welfare system only to replace it with one that is far worse. Even Clinton acknowledged before signing the welfare reform bill that it was inadequate, and he pledged to undo some of its worst features in his next term in office. He recently did that, restoring medical assistance to legal aliens who had previously received it and some of the billions of dollars of the federal aid to the states that the act cut from welfare programs. The centerpiece of the new budget bill he signed is its provision of new medical assistance to poor children. Children no longer eligible for welfare will have the possibility of medical treatment through this new program.

While the new medical program for children and the restoration of some of the aid cut from welfare are welcome corrections to the new and disgraceful welfare reform law, they cannot undo the worst of the act—its five-year lifetime limit. The conservative framers of the welfare bill argue that the five-year limit was a necessary "tough love" component that will ultimately benefit children. But let's expose this lie and be clear about who is actually going to benefit from the welfare reform act. Through its sizable reduction in the cost of the federal welfare program, and in passing off the future financial responsibility of the nation's welfare burden to the states, members of Congress and the President can pass the savings to the affluent in the form of tax cuts. And in 1997, they did just that.

It was during the Great Depression that Americans came to accept the collective responsibility for the poor and elderly. Clinton's welfare reform laid waste to a large part of that ideal. We are left only with Social Security and Medicare, our most costly welfare programs. They survive only because of the wide misperception that they are funded by the savings of the working Americans and are not entitlement programs like Aid to Families with Dependent Children, or what we know as "welfare." Meanwhile, while poverty among the elderly has declined dramatically since the 1960s, the poverty rate for children now surpasses that of the elderly. The Census Bureau estimates that 20 percent of those under the age of 18 live below the poverty line, as opposed to 10.5 percent of those over the age of 65 in 1995. The new welfare policy will push even more children into poverty. The tragedy is how many lives must be adversely and irreversibly affected before the majority of Americans come to realize our current welfare system should be scrapped and that we start anew? A new welfare plan must include the core ideal of a federally backed safety net for poor children.

Notes

1. Marian Wright Edelman, "Say No to This Welfare 'Reform,'" *Washington Post*, November 3, 1995, p. A-23.
2. Quoted in *U.S. News & World Report*, August 12, 1996.
3. Jason DeParle, "The Ellwoods: Mugged by Reality," *The New York Times Magazine*, December 8, 1996, p. 64.
4. Karlyn H. Bowman and Everett Carll Ladd, "Reforming Welfare," *The Public Perspective* 4, 6 (September/October), Roper Center for Public Opinion Research, 1993.
5. See Lee Rainwater and William L. Yancey, *The Moynihan Report and the Politics of Controversy* (Cambridge, MA: MIT Press, 1967) for a copy of this report.
6. Paul E. Peterson and Mark C. Rom, *Welfare Magnets* (Washington, DC: The Brookings Institution, 1990).

REALITY CHECKS FOR THE NATIONAL CONVERSATION ON RACE: THE PRESIDENT'S CALL AND A WRITER'S RESPONSE

LUCIUS J. BARKER

Even though he gave an obviously well-crafted speech, history and experience have led me to treat President Clinton's call for a National Conversation on Race with a cautious (wistful) optimism tempered by an unvarnished (objective) realism. But as one deeply attached to both hope and reality, I feel impelled to join the "conversation" and offer a few reminders (reality checks), which, if heeded, could spur both *conversation* and *action*.

The President's Call

In his June 14, 1997, speech to graduates of the University of California-San Diego, President Clinton formally laid out the overall context for his call for a national conversation on race. The President began by summarizing the "achievements" we have made as well as the "challenges" that are still "out there." Then President Clinton zeroed in on the continuing problem of "America's racial divide." Said the President:

> "But I believe the greatest challenge we face ... is also our greatest opportunity. Of all the questions of discrimination and prejudice that still exist in our society, the most perplexing one is the oldest, and in some ways the newest, the problem of race.
>
> Can we fulfill the promise of America by embracing all our citizens of all races, not just at a university where people have the benefit of enlightened teachers and the time to think and grow and get to know each other, but in the daily life of every American community? In short, can we become one America in the 21st century?
>
> Within the next three years here in California, no single race or ethnic group will make up a majority of the state's population. Already five of our largest school districts draw students from over 100 different racial and ethnic groups. At this campus, 12 Nobel Prize winners have taught or studied [who are] from nine different countries. A half-century from

now, when your own grandchildren are in college, there will be no majority race in America.

Now we know what we will *look* like. But what will we *be* like? Can we be one America, respecting, even celebrating, our differences, but embracing even more what we have in common? Can we define what it means to be an American, not just in terms of the hyphens showing our ethnic origins, but in terms of our primary allegiance to the values America stands for and values we live by?

Our hearts long to answer yes, but our history reminds us that it will be hard. The ideals that bind us together are as old as our nation, but so are the forces that pull us apart.... Though minorities have more opportunities than ever today, we still see evidence of bigotry from the desecration of houses of worship ... to demeaning talk in corporate suits.

But those who say we cannot transform the problem of prejudice into the promise of unity forget how far we have come, and I cannot believe they have ever seen a crowd like you. When I look at you, it is almost impossible for me to even remember my own life. I grew up in the high drama of the cold war in the patriotic South. Black and white southerners alike wore our nation's uniform in defense of freedom against communism, and they fought and died together from Korea to Vietnam. But back home, I went to segregated schools, swam in segregated public pools, sat in all-white sections at the movies, and traveled through small towns in my state that still marked restrooms and water fountains 'White' and 'Colored.'

As you have shown us today [however], our diversity will enrich our lives ... [and deepen] our understanding of human nature and human differences, making our communities more exciting, more enjoyable, more meaningful.

That is why I have come here today, to ask the American people to join me in a great national effort to perfect the promise of America for this new time as we seek to build our more perfect union. Now, when there is more cause for hope than fear, when we are not driven to it by some emergency or social cataclysm, now is the time we should learn together, talk together, and act together to build one America.

Let me say that I know that for many white Americans, this conversation may seem to exclude them or threaten them. That must not be so. I believe white Americans have just as much to gain from an America where we finally take responsibility for all our children, so that they at last can be judged, as Martin Luther King hoped, not by the color of their skin but by the content of their character.

What is it that we must do?... First, we must continue to expand opportunity. Full participation in our strong and growing economy is the best antidote to envy, despair, and racism. We must press forward to move millions more from poverty and welfare to work, to bring the spark of enterprise to our inner cities, to redouble our efforts to reach those rural communities prosperity has passed by. And most important of all, we simply must give our young people the finest education in the world.

In our efforts to extend economic and educational opportunity to all our citizens, we must consider the role of affirmative action. I know affirmative action has not been perfect in America. That's why, two years ago, we began an effort to fix the things that are wrong with it. But when used in the right way, it has worked....

Let me say, I know that the people of California voted to repeal affirmative action without any ill motive. The vast majority of them simply did it with a conviction that discrimination and isolation are no longer barriers to achievement. But consider the results. Minority enrollments in law school and other graduate programs are plummeting for the first time in decades. Soon the same will likely happen in undergraduate education.

We must not resegregate higher education or leave it to the private universities to do the public's work. At the very time when we need to do a better job of living and learning together, we should not stop trying to equalize economic opportunity....

What do I really hope we will achieve as a country?

... We have torn down the barriers in our laws. Now we must break down the barriers in our lives, our minds, and our hearts. More than 30 years ago, at the high tide of the civil rights movement, the Kerner Commission said we were becoming two Americas, one white, one black, separate and unequal. Today we face a different choice. Will we become not two, but many Americas, separate, unequal and isolated? Or will we draw strength from all our people and our ancient faith in equality and human dignity, to become the world's first truly multiracial democracy? That is the unfinished work of our times, to lift the burden of race and redeem the promise of America.

A Writer's Response

Given its continuing significance in American life, the President's speech and the work of his National Advisory Board might well stir wide conversation on America's racial divide. But history shows that to deal effectively with the matter of race requires much more. Above all, it requires extraordinary leadership from the President himself. It requires similar leadership from both the public and private sector, which again only the President himself is in a position to generate. And it might require even more.

To begin with, the massive efforts needed to overcome the pervasive problem of race requires *real* consultations with *real* leaders who are committed to work toward this end. These must perforce include leaders from government and the public sector (e.g., the presidency, congress, states, and cities). It must also include leaders from the non-government and private sector (e.g., the business and corporate world; the education and information industry; labor and agriculture; science, engineering, and technology; law, medicine, and the professions; and religious, civic, and community groups).

This, of course, does not minimize or denigrate at all the absolute need for the kind of citizen participation and consultation so properly envisaged by the President and so important for effective constitutional-democratic government. For in the end, active citizen participation and consent constitute the indispensable foundation upon which democracies are built and survive.

To be sure, what is suggested here calls for a massive mobilization of leadership and resources. Indeed, history demonstrates vividly that it is just this kind of mobilization that is clearly needed to deal effectively with massive socio-political problems, such as race.

But, as the President suggested, the task will be difficult. Obstacles and impediments abound. For one thing, blacks and whites see the world quite differently, as evidenced dramatically by black/white reactions to the trial and verdict in the criminal case against O. J. Simpson. Indeed, major black/white differences over race discrimination doggedly persist and do not seem amenable to effective remediation. The underlying problem, often overlooked, is that the tragic history of slavery and racial segregation, followed by continued discrimination against African Americans, has fostered and perpetuated an environment in which such discrimination against others has also been practiced and tolerated. Thus, to deal effectively with America's continuous and seemingly intractable problem of race would perforce do much to overcome an environment that perpetuates discrimination against other groups as well (e.g., women and Latinos).

Another troubling concern, experienced firsthand by this writer and many other African Americans, is that *stereotyping* on the basis of *race and color*, and not *class and social status*, continues to be the primary yardstick by which most African-Americans are perceived and treated. Once known, however, class and social standing might well make for differences in treatment. That they might not, however, has been cogently captured by Professor Keith Reeves, in recounting an "episode involving General Colin Powell—four-star general, national security adviser, former chairman of the Joint Chiefs of Staff, mastermind of Operation Desert Storm, [and] possible presidential contender...."[1] Reeves describes this episode as follows:

> "Frank Carlucci, national security adviser in the Reagan administration, sent Powell to speak with North Carolina senator Jesse Helms about a policy matter. Some time later, Senator Helms relayed to Carlucci that 'he'd listened to that *black general* (emphasis Reeves) you sent up here.' Powell tells us, 'See, now Jesse just don't know any other way to see folks. As cordial as Jesse and I are now ... if you think Jesse can ever see me as anything other than a black general ... [t]hen we'd have arrived. But we ain't arrived.'"

The Powell episode demonstrates convincingly that, no matter contrary data, etc., *race and color* remain the triggering mechanisms to stereotyping that stirs racial bias and prejudice.

Another disturbing problem concerns the increasingly hostile climate toward dealing forthrightly with race discrimination. Very directly, the reality is that since about 1970, actions emanating from our political and judicial leadership have provided support and stirred anew negative or mixed attitudes of whites toward black Americans generally. Most troubling, President Clinton's "mainstream" politics seems to impel him to find compromise with conservative Republicans on major issues of vital importance to blacks (e.g., welfare reform and balanced budget legislation). When combined, these trends clearly signal that African-Americans are in for uncertain, even rough times, from *both* major parties.

Nor are African-American interests likely to find strong representation in the federal judiciary. Indeed, the strength of Reagan-Bush appointments in our federal courts is exemplified vividly in the U.S. Supreme Court by the nature and tone of decisions, such as those relating to affirmative action and congressional redistricting. Given present circumstances, however, the President and other leaders must somehow work to overcome this climate problem that they themselves have helped to create.

It is in this hostile climate, where black civil rights groups are needed most, that we find them virtually at their weakest. While some reenergizing is clearly taking place, the resources available to these groups in 1998 are simply insufficient to protect, much less promote, their vital interests. Of course, in addition to the hostile political-social climate, part of the difficulties may be attributed to internal problems plaguing civil rights groups—lack of funds, poor administration and management, and dwindling memberships. And such plight in turn might be attributed to the hostile climate.

Conversely, this climate and the relative weakness of traditional civil rights groups might well strengthen the hand of a group such as the Nation of Islam (Black Muslims). Many of their tenets (e.g., self-sufficiency) as well as their charismatic leader, Minister Louis Farrakhan, hold strong appeal in the black community, particularly among the young. As a result, when traditional civil rights groups were perhaps at their weakest (in 1995–1996), it was left to Farrakhan and the Nation of Islam, through the Million Man March, to dramatically bring to the fore serious problems affecting the black community, including those being perpetuated by anti-civil rights interests.[2] To be sure, the Black Muslims are not the typical civil rights group, having tenets that are somewhat at odds with more traditional civil rights groups (NAACP and Urban League) and the white establishment generally. But it may be suggested that the vitality and strong appeal of the Black Muslims, as well as the obvious decline of more traditional civil rights groups, may both be attributed in large measure to the increasingly hostile climate that exists. In any case, the strength and appeal of the Black Muslims in the black community suggest clearly that it too must be included in our national conversation on race.

In general, this hostile climate is fed by currents of opinion emanating from various leaders and institutions in the public and private sector. Some of these currents suggest, for example, that successful efforts to overcome racial segregation and discrimination *in law* have resulted in our now having a *color-blind* society *in practice*. Hence, regardless of race, color, ethnicity, or sex, individuals who have the initiative, determination, and drive can make it on their own and actually live the American dream.

But such currents of opinion—especially those relating to a "color-blind society,"—clearly defy *everyday reality*. Nonetheless, in symbolic and perhaps substantive terms as well, these currents hold strong appeal to many whites and some blacks as well. While some of these persons know or at least ought to know better, it is clear that many Americans really want to believe the very best about their country. In doing so, we become too tolerant of the intolerable and too oblivious to reality.

Given these circumstances, it is altogether clear that President Clinton and other leaders must purposefully work to overcome this difficult climate that they themselves helped to bring about. To be sure, the President has laid out for himself and all of us perhaps the most laudable as well as the most difficult challenge that continues to face this nation, and indeed the entire world. But the President himself must take the lead in this effort in both word and deed. He must demonstrate clearly his commitment and willingness to meet this challenge by using the full authority and prestige of his office. He must, for example, make full use of the White House "bully pulpit"—through his Saturday morning radio talks or through "fireside chats," town meetings, or other creative means. He must be willing to push relevant legislation, as well as issue relevant and appropriate executive orders on his *own* authority. In this regard, he must use his office to convene and harness the ideas and support of relevant others, such as business-corporate leaders, who have found affirmative action strategies helpful to their businesses.

Further, he must ascertain, insofar as possible, that those whom he appoints to various positions in our government—including federal judges—are fully committed to meeting this challenge. Such judicial appointments are clearly justified given the unique role of courts and judges to interpret and articulate the very constitutional-democratic norms and values that give the highest authority to the President's challenge itself. The reality is that the appointment of such judges is clearly needed to counteract many Reagan-Bush judges whose appointments and resulting decisions have impeded rather than advanced the challenge the President articulated and now must work to meet. And the President should let it be known in advance that he is mindful of the probable resistance such appointments are likely to encounter from a conservative, Republican-controlled Senate. Thus, the President must let it be known that his is a reinvigorated presidency that will no longer back away from controversial nominees and is willing to use the full array of powers and resources available to win confirmation of such judicial appointments.

But more than presidential leadership (and resources) might be needed to overcome the racial divide that continues to plague our politics and society. Indeed, the nature of American politics suggests that "broad scale and fundamental changes in national policies may require the kinds of unusual circumstances (e.g., social movements, crises situations) that aided presidents in the past, and [might again be needed to foster the kind of] fundamental changes ... needed to deal with the problems faced by blacks [and minorities]." The President and other leaders must straightforwardly state that the challenge posed by this issue involves not only constitutional-legal problems, but a *moral* problem as well. Though himself initially reluctant to push civil rights legislation, it was perhaps President John F. Kennedy who best captured the essentially "moral crisis" we face in regard to the continuing problem of race. On June 11, 1963, in response to wanton acts of violence against blacks and their supporters, Kennedy bluntly told the nation:

On June 13, 1997, John Hope Franklin and President Clinton hold a meeting for "One America in the 21st Century: The President's Initiative on Race." (*Ruth Fremson/AP/Wide World Photos*)

Law alone cannot make [persons] see right. We are confronted primarily with a moral issue. It is as old as the Scriptures and is as clear as the American Constitution. The heart of the question is whether all Americans are to be afforded equal rights and opportunities, whether we are going to treat our fellow Americans as we want to be treated.... We face, therefore, a moral crisis as a country and as a people. It cannot be met by repressive police action. It cannot be left to increased demonstrations in the streets. It cannot be quieted by token moves or talk. It is time to act in the Congress, in your state and local legislative body and, above all, in all of our daily lives.... Those who do nothing are inviting shame as well as violence. Those who act boldly are recognizing right as well as reality."

Viewed in this context, the President's speech is no less than a call for full realization of the American dream. To make this dream a reality for *all* persons, however, requires extraordinary leadership from the President and other leaders in both the public and private sector, who, supported by people of good will, are fully committed to make an extraordinary form of government—democracy—work.

Notes

1. Keith Reeves, *Voting Hopes or Fears: White Voters, Black Candidates, and Racial Politics in America* (New York: Oxford University Press, 1997), p. 110.
2. The Million Woman March, which took place in Philadelphia on October 25, 1997, was organized not by the Nation of Islam, but by local community activists lacking ties to national organizations. Several speakers at the event, however, were affiliated with the Nation of Islam, while none of the more mainstream civil rights organizations—e.g., NAACP, Urban League—were represented in this program.

Index